Princess of the Hither Isles

Princess of the Hither Isles

A Black Suffragist's Story from the Jim Crow South

Adele Logan Alexander

Yale
UNIVERSITY PRESS
New Haven & London

Published with assistance from the foundation established in memory of
Philip Hamilton McMillan of the Class of 1894, Yale College.

Yale University Press books may be purchased in quantity for educational, business, or
promotional use. For information, please e-mail sales.press@yale.edu (U.S. office) or
sales@yaleup.co.uk (U.K. office).

"Race," copyright © 2001 by Elizabeth Alexander, reprinted from *Antebellum Dream Book,*
with the permission of Graywolf Press, Minneapolis, Minnesota, www.graywolfpress.org.

Set in Monotype Bulmer type by Integrated Publishing Solutions.
Printed in the United States of America.

Library of Congress Control Number: 2019935203
ISBN 978-0-300-24260-7 (hardcover : alk. paper)

A catalogue record for this book is available from the British Library.

This paper meets the requirements of ANSI/NISO Z39.48-1992 (Permanence of Paper).

10 9 8 7 6 5 4 3 2 1

For those who preceded, accompanied, and sustained me,
who are wiser, braver, and kinder than I, and whom I've
most admired and loved

Contents

Princess of the Hither Isles

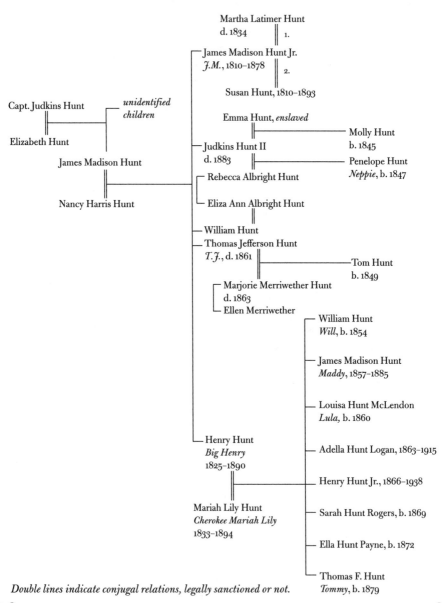

The Hunt Family

Martha Latimer Hunt
d. 1834 ‖ 1.

James Madison Hunt Jr.
J.M., 1810–1878 ‖ 2.

Susan Hunt, 1810–1893

Capt. Judkins Hunt

unidentified children

Elizabeth Hunt

James Madison Hunt

Nancy Harris Hunt

Emma Hunt, *enslaved*

Molly Hunt
b. 1845

Judkins Hunt II
d. 1883

Penelope Hunt
Neppie, b. 1847

Rebecca Albright Hunt

Eliza Ann Albright Hunt

William Hunt

Thomas Jefferson Hunt
T.J., d. 1861

Tom Hunt
b. 1849

Marjorie Merriwether Hunt
d. 1863

Ellen Merriwether

William Hunt
Will, b. 1854

James Madison Hunt
Maddy, 1857–1885

Louisa Hunt McLendon
Lula, b. 1860

Adella Hunt Logan, 1863–1915

Henry Hunt
Big Henry
1825–1890

Henry Hunt Jr., 1866–1938

Mariah Lily Hunt
Cherokee Mariah Lily
1833–1894

Sarah Hunt Rogers, b. 1869

Ella Hunt Payne, b. 1872

Thomas F. Hunt
Tommy, b. 1879

Double lines indicate conjugal relations, legally sanctioned or not.

The Hunt and Sayre Families

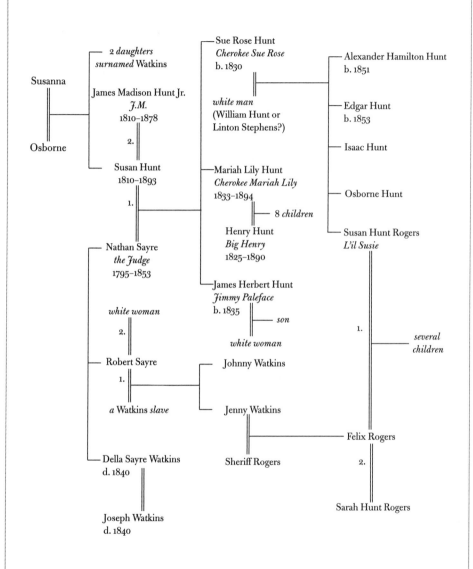

Susanna

Osborne

2 *daughters*
surnamed Watkins

James Madison Hunt Jr.
J.M.
1810–1878

2.

Susan Hunt
1810–1893

1.

Nathan Sayre
the Judge
1795–1853

white woman

2.

Robert Sayre

1.

a Watkins *slave*

Della Sayre Watkins
d. 1840

Joseph Watkins
d. 1840

Sue Rose Hunt
Cherokee Sue Rose
b. 1830

white man
(William Hunt or
Linton Stephens?)

Mariah Lily Hunt
Cherokee Mariah Lily
1833–1894

8 *children*

Henry Hunt
Big Henry
1825–1890

James Herbert Hunt
Jimmy Paleface
b. 1835

son

white woman

Johnny Watkins

Jenny Watkins

Sheriff Rogers

Alexander Hamilton Hunt
b. 1851

Edgar Hunt
b. 1853

Isaac Hunt

Osborne Hunt

Susan Hunt Rogers
L'il Susie

1.

several
children

Felix Rogers

2.

Sarah Hunt Rogers

The Hunt, Logan, and Alexander Families

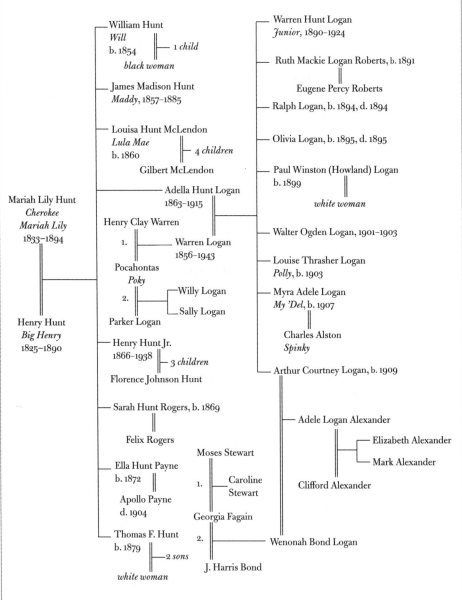

William Hunt
Will
b. 1854 — 1 *child*
black woman

James Madison Hunt
Maddy, 1857–1885

Louisa Hunt McLendon
Lula Mae
b. 1860 — 4 *children*
Gilbert McLendon

Adella Hunt Logan
1863–1915

Mariah Lily Hunt
Cherokee
Mariah Lily
1833–1894

Henry Clay Warren
1. — Warren Logan
1856–1943
Pocahontas
Poky
2. — Willy Logan
— Sally Logan
Parker Logan

Henry Hunt
Big Henry
1825–1890

Henry Hunt Jr.
1866–1938 — 3 *children*
Florence Johnson Hunt

Sarah Hunt Rogers, b. 1869
Felix Rogers

Ella Hunt Payne
b. 1872
Apollo Payne
d. 1904

Thomas F. Hunt
b. 1879 — 2 *sons*
white woman

Moses Stewart
1. — Caroline
Stewart
Georgia Fagain
2.
J. Harris Bond

Warren Hunt Logan
Junior, 1890–1924

Ruth Mackie Logan Roberts, b. 1891
Eugene Percy Roberts

Ralph Logan, b. 1894, d. 1894

Olivia Logan, b. 1895, d. 1895

Paul Winston (Howland) Logan
b. 1899
white woman

Walter Ogden Logan, 1901–1903

Louise Thrasher Logan
Polly, b. 1903

Myra Adele Logan
My 'Del, b. 1907
Charles Alston
Spinky

Arthur Courtney Logan, b. 1909

Adele Logan Alexander
— Elizabeth Alexander
— Mark Alexander
Clifford Alexander

Wenonah Bond Logan

Legacies

IN 1983, *MS*. MAGAZINE PUBLISHED AN article I'd submitted about "finding" my paternal grandmother, who was a pioneer in the woman suffrage movement. The editors said this: "Adele Logan Alexander is working on a book-length biography of Adella Hunt Logan." Since then, I've written many other things, taught history, acquired a headful of gray (I like to think silver) hair and a glorious rainbow of grandchildren. But I continued pursuing that intriguing political activist, that little-known, outspoken "black" woman who looked white, for whom I was named.

I learned about Adella and more about our country's grievous war during which she was born and the next half century in the southern United States. I explored relationships among her kin, as well as theirs with both obscure and renowned figures of that era. Among them, my relatives talked about the fellow they admired, respected, and often saw in New York City but called "Dr. Dubious"; another, the brilliant scientist whom they warmly referred to as "Uncle 'Fess" Carver; and the family's Alabama neighbors, "the Great Man," Booker T. Washington, and his obdurate spouse. There was a long-gone President Roosevelt too, not the Democrat who in my childhood I thought always had and always would hold that omnipotent position but an earlier one, a Republican, whom my grandfather Warren Logan seemed to have known rather well. Ultimately, I also realized that my grandmother Adella Hunt Logan's legacy as she worked to acquire the vote for women was her way of trying to give them a voice, of empowering them.

And looming over their lives was Jim Crow, the ugly nemesis whom they scorned, defied, and struggled to outsmart.

My father and aunts often reminisced about Tuskegee, a fabled place sometimes called the "Hither Isles," which they both loved and loathed, and about Atlanta University, where most of them had attended school. And before those venues, I learned, there was Sparta, Georgia.

I slogged through versions of Adella's story that were conventional history and other fictionalized ones but ultimately determined that this should be neither a traditional biography nor a novel. Rather, it's an intricate memoir about an era, places, and mostly a woman to whom I'm irrevocably bound. Here I've tried to reveal and reconstruct Adella from a plethora of archival and published materials but more through what my family and others boldly trumpeted, whispered, or surreptitiously confessed. To do that, I've unraveled many snarled threads, spun them out again to weave into a comprehensible whole the often perplexing documentation that I accumulated. I've speculated about how and why results that I know for certain might have come about and tried to understand and interpret the incredible accounts that I heard and believed over the years but can't incontrovertibly prove.

Some of Adella's stories were inspiring; others were almost too painful to retell.

As I position my grandmother in her world, I'm reminded of phrases we hear and voice today: "Black Lives Matter," "Equal pay for equal work," "My body, my choice," "Votes for all," and "#MeToo." The times, words, and players change; the issues and their urgency do not.

I grew up in a family whose members proudly considered and spoke of themselves as "Negroes." They healed, taught, and counseled "Our People," identified with and staunchly defended "the race," never boasted of their Native American or white "blood," but were mostly blue-, green-, or hazel-eyed and paler skinned, narrower featured, and straighter haired than many of my Jewish friends at school and my diverse, upper-Manhattan neighborhood's Italian American cobblers and greengrocers. And those relatives who looked "white" all had darker-skinned spouses. It didn't seem unusual to me. That's just how my world was populated.

I also heard about my father's "mystery uncle" Thomas Hunt (he roared with laughter about having an "Uncle Tom"), who'd "disappeared" in California, where he saw his even whiter-looking but black-identified sister Sarah "by appointment only." And once a year, my own uncle Paul came from "way out west" to visit us. Even as a child, I sensed that his siblings loved, disdained, and mistrusted him in roughly equal parts. Living in the Big Apple, I surely knew no one else whose uncle was a forester and lived in Oregon: a faraway, mythical realm.

In past generations, I learned, there had been other legendary relatives: someone called Judge Sayre; his "wife," Susan Hunt (one of my great-great-grandmothers); and their daughter, known as "Cherokee Mariah"— her name pronounced with a long *i* and spelled with an *h*.

During my earliest years, a pale and frail old man whom my father and his sisters called "Dad" came north every December. Only once, however, did he bring along his wife, about whom my aunts hissed, "She's not your grandmother! Georgia is." I already knew that Georgia Stewart Bond, who often lived with us, was my mother's mother and my beloved Nana. But that other woman, that unwelcome visitor, they confided, was the wicked witch who'd long ago exiled my then eight-year-old father from his Alabama home.

Georgia Bond's older daughter, my maternal aunt Caroline Bond Day, had written an awesome tome, which was our family's secular Bible. Titled *A Study of Some Negro-White Families in the United States,* it began as her Harvard-Radcliffe master's thesis in anthropology. It's filled with photographs, among many others, of various Sayres, Hunts, Logans, and Bonds. Arcane designations, "1/4 N, 3/4 W," "1/8 N, 1/8 I, 3/4 W," even "4/4 W," appear below them. Interracial hybridity, Carrie had demonstrated in the 1920s, wasn't something that suddenly would make its disquieting appearance in the late twentieth century. Rather, it was and is a phenomenon bred deep in the American bone, sometimes accompanied by dire warnings from fearful or angry white folks about the threat of "mongrelization." Recent scientific advances and knowledge about DNA have complicated but also confirmed this old-but-new phenomenon. We need to better understand the similarities with and differences between the children of our recent, post–*Loving v. Virginia* generations and the myriad pre-*Loving* offspring, born as a result of sometimes (fortunately) true loving or (unforgivably) rape or comparable coercion. In "the old days," they and others like them didn't call themselves "mixed," "black," or "African American" but "Negroes." A few of them, however, "passed" and dwelt uneasily in the white world, where the menacing gargoyles of exposure, shame, and expulsion always lurked.

Several summers when I was young, I was taken to visit my aunt Carrie in North Carolina. Only years later did I learn that my capable, tan-skinned mother circumvented the indignities, discomfort, and perils of segregated train travel, and our antagonist Jim Crow, by purchasing in advance our round-trip tickets for a first-class Pullman roomette, not in the South (impossible!) but rather in New York City's open-to-all urban cathedral: Pennsylvania Station.

I had no siblings or close cousins, so as everyone's only child, usually there were no contemporaries for me to play and talk with at family gatherings. The adults thus had little choice but to include me in their conversations (if they didn't, I listened and participated anyway), as they drank champagne or scotch on the rocks, smoked Chesterfields, and flat-out adored me but also impressed on me "our responsibilities." My aunts played carols, classics, and jazz on their baby grands, cooked in a garrulous flock, ate caviar, lox, sukiyaki, or juicy slabs of watermelon, collards, "trotters," pig tails, and "everything but the squeal." They served up tasty morsels of gossip and wisdom and adages such as "learning will empower you," "know the law and use the law," "always carry a hatpin," and "a pretty face can be a colored girl's curse."

They rarely mentioned her name, but Adella Hunt Logan hovered over everything. Her haunting oil portrait first hung on one aunt's wall, then another's, then my parents', then (and still) my own. Her children found it painful to talk about her, but for years, I didn't know why. And even now, I can't quite remember how, when, or from whom I learned that she'd left them.

This search for my elusive forebear leads me to think more about intergenerational bonds. One of the most significant ties I explored was that between Adella and her own grandmother Susan Hunt. The links between me and Adella, whom I never had the privilege of knowing, and with my maternal grandmother, Georgia Bond (who'd been Adella's friend and fellow suffragist years before their children, Arthur and Wenonah, who'd ultimately become my parents, were born), are vital to this memoir. Those old relationships also seem to connect me to my grandchildren. This story is for them and, someday, for their eagerly awaited progeny too.

Ultimately, the question wasn't whether I'd tell Adella's story—I *had* to tell it—but when and how. Finally, it became clear that the narrative should begin with Susan.

The People Who Can Fly

IN BOTH THE GOOD AND THE BAD OLD days in the all-too-real but also legendary Old South, Adella's grandmother Susan told her many stories. As she shared them, she'd often say this: "You can't know where you're going, my precious, until you know where you came from."

From her memory books, Susan Hunt had pulled out tales that she'd first heard way back when and where. Many of them even were true—at least in part. True as the most solemn oath, possible, improbable, fantastical, or even a start-to-finish, flat-out lie, this was Adella's favorite.

"Once upon a time, Our People lived in the Home Place," Susan often had begun. "In those bygone years, they had awesome powers, and some of them knew magic. They also could fly, because they had mighty wings. They'd clamber onto a gate, pause there for a minute, then rise on the soft winds and soar across the savanna with streams of feathers trailing behind them. For many centuries, the Evil Ones stole Our People away, and they sometimes abandoned their wings because they couldn't bring them across the Big Water in the tight-packed slave ships. Still hoping to conquer the skies, a few of the captives leapt overboard and drowned in the ocean.

"One day, in the dark and dismal morass known as the Hither Isles, Sir, which was the name that Our People gave the overseer, bullwhipped one of the Daughters because her baby wouldn't stop crying. Blood flowed down her back and legs and soaked the ground. The earth around her turned sour, and nothing grew there anymore. The girl felt so wounded and weary that she wept: 'I want to go back to the Home Place, Old Woman, but I don't know how.'

"The Old Woman, however, challenged the Daughter's doubts and fears. She told her, 'You're wrong about that, my precious, because you always can go home. You pretty much could do it yourself already, but I'll teach you everything else you need to know.'

"She prepared a feast for the journey and whispered her secrets into the Daughter's ear. Soon the girl's shoulders itched, and she started feeling the power of what began growing there. She drew the baby tight against her bosom, picked up the knapsack of delicious food, climbed onto a wooden gate, and lifted one foot in the air as the magic and the music surged inside her. Then she raised the other one, stretched, flexed, and flapped her new wings and began floating up and away. Her little one stopped weeping, and they soared off together as if they were gulls, eagles, or angels. Father Sun warmed them each day, and Moon Woman never waned. She glowed like a huge silver dollar to guide them through the darkest nights and keep them safe from the Raven Mocker, hounds, lynch mobs, despoilers, and the other Evil Ones, like Sir, who lurked nearby. As the Old Woman watched, the Daughter with wings and the baby she held close to her body vanished, and no one knew where, when, or even whether they'd alight again.

"After Our People had suffered the most but survived the worst, others of them listened, and sometimes they too heard the whispered secrets. Then, like the winged Daughter, they'd climb onto a gate to rise up on the breezes until they formed a huge flock silhouetted against the sky. They glided over the fields, hills, and bayous, borne aloft by the warm winds, singing about the Home Place, freedom, and Jubilee. Some of them sang about how they were members of one beloved family who were crossing the Big Water together. The Great Bear roared his blessings; honey bees buzzed songs of salvation; pigs squealed, cows mooed, chickens clucked, and geese honked. Br'er Rabbit jumped for joy in his briar patch, while on the riverbank even mean Br'er 'Gator grinned, as Sir, the overseer, shook his fist. He gnashed his teeth, spat, cursed, hollered, pointed his rifle into the air, and fired at the flyers. Boom, boom! trying to shoot them down.

"But the Old Woman only laughed. At first, her laughter tinkled like tiny Christmas bells or a mountain brook, then it grew louder and exploded into the rolling thunder of a mighty cyclone or monsoon. She beamed her golden sun rays all around, shook her gorgeous headful of moon-silver curls, and said, 'You can't shoot us down, Sir. Don't you know who we are? We're the Bird Clan. We're the People Who Can Fly.' Then she too rose up and flew away."

Adella's grandmother shared that legend with her, then it became hers and her children's too. But there was much more to Susan Hunt than just a single story could reveal.

Susan's Stories

AS SUCH SAGAS USUALLY DO, OR PROBABLY should, Adella Hunt Logan's began long before she was born. She devoured her forebears' myriad truths and legends, especially those proffered by her black-Cherokee-white grandmother who taught her to fly. Adella adored Susan Hunt and considered her both the best storyteller and the finest person who ever walked the earth.

Adella's uncle James Madison (J. M.) Hunt Jr., however, enhanced the family narrative. He was one of her Anglo relatives who'd claimed the name long before they imposed it on their chattel and the other people of color whom they deemed their inferiors. J. M.'s grandparents were Capt. Judkins Hunt and his wife, Elizabeth, who'd lived in Virginia, where he'd fought for the English colonies' independence. They were the first of their "paleskin" tribe who migrated to the Deep South. In 1787, as the nation's fractious white male founders were hammering out their Constitution, the Hunts began an arduous trek southwestward in a convoy of twenty-nine: twelve free white people and seventeen enslaved black ones whom their otherwise enlightened and rightfully acclaimed new document singled out and depreciated as "three-fifths persons."

With the people they held in bondage performing the most onerous labor, the white Hunts cleared vast expanses of Georgia's fertile frontier land near a creek called Shoulderbone. When they arrived, their acreage still was part of Washington County, but a few years later, the state lopped off its northern half and designated the new entity Hancock. Sparta—its name extolling the white settlers' self-proclaimed mettle—has been Hancock's county seat right from the start.

Adella's white forebears built a sturdy home from oak logs, sixteen inches in diameter. They and their enslaved minions mud-daubed, mossed-in, and pine-tarred the chinks, barricaded the roof, enclosed the whole enclave with a stockade fence, and named it Fortitude to reflect their resistance to the indigenous people whom they considered and called "marauding savages."

With a single exception, however, Capt. Judkins and Elizabeth Hunt's children continued westward. Only James Madison Hunt remained in Hancock County, where he married Miss Nancy Harris. James Madison Jr. (J. M.), was the oldest of Nancy Harris Hunt's five sons. Over the next fifteen years, she bore Judkins (named for his paternal grandfather), Thomas Jefferson (T. J.), then William, and last but hardly least, because he grew to be the tallest of all at nearly six and a half feet, Big Henry. Years later, he'd become Adella's "Daddy-longlegs."

Her grandmother Susan also shared stories about Adella's maternal grandfather, Nathan Sayre, a lawyer from New Jersey who was short in height but a towering intellect. She learned more when she received a two-foot-long pine crate, a foot wide and equally deep, trisected by a pair of wooden dividers and packed with attorney Sayre's leather-bound journals that had 1818 through 1852 stamped in gold on their spines. Forty years after he died, Adella began plowing through his diaries, which began with this entry: *1818 Jan 10. Head'd west to Hancock C'nty. Our group includes my Bro Robert, Sis Della, her husb'nd Joseph Watkins & their 15 negroes.*

Those journals also introduced Adella to some of Nathan Sayre's associates, among them the contentious Presbyterian Rev. Carlisle Pollock (C. P.) Beman who was known to preach that the Declaration of Independence excoriated tyranny and included soaring language that compared an enchained colonial status to the "peculiar institution."

Rev. Beman also maintained that "the Cherokees have progressed more than any of the other civilized tribes." Most white Georgians feared or loathed the Native people, but some of them became custodians to a few of the children who were left behind as the older "redskins" were forced west after the conquering Anglo newcomers imposed on them a series of abysmally one-sided treaties. Perhaps, the reverend argued, a few of their "abandoned" youngsters might be further "civilized" and molded into reliable servants. To that end, he'd baptize and bestow on them names such as Cherokee Sue Rose and Cherokee Mariah Lily. Adella Hunt heard those monikers often in her childhood, because the former was her aunt and the latter her mother.

C. P. Beman also dared to suggest "a Christian duty and benefit in educating the slaves" (at least minimally so), though that stance placed him in opposition to state law and local opinion, since most white southerners maintained that teaching people of color to read and write was the first dangerous misstep down a slippery slope toward anarchy. One Georgia statute even specified that as punishment and to set an example for others, a black writer's forefinger might be cut off.

Susan shared this story: "I don't remember my daddy, Adella, but I know that his name was Osborne, which means the Great Bear. His white owner-and-father held Osborne's black mother as a slave, but as the boy became a man, he no longer accepted being anyone's property. They tied him down to keep him at the plantation, yet sometimes he escaped and ran away to a nearby settlement called Cherokee Corners, where he met and fell in love with an 'Injun' named Susanna. Within a few years, Susanna bore Osborne's three daughters, and I was the youngest."

"Whenever Osborne disappeared," Susan continued, "his master hired a posse to drag his son back. When those men heard that Susanna had given birth again, they leashed their hounds, loaded their rifles, mounted up, and rode after him. And they were right, because he'd sneaked off to meet me, their new baby. That night my father and mother awoke to panting and snorts and heard whispered curses as the slave catchers and their dogs surrounded her cabin. The men battered down Susanna's door and fired at Osborne, but he slipped off and disappeared into the darkness. When the posse took off after him, your great-grandmother lit a kerosene lamp, saw a red streak on my chest, and realized that a shotgun pellet had hit me just below my left shoulder. She howled so plaintively at Moon Woman that flights of starlings dropped right out of the sky.

"Osborne wasn't ever found, so Susanna still hoped that he'd survived, since she hadn't seen the Raven Mocker, sheathed in scales or fur, with green sparks trailing him like a comet's tail. It takes strong magic, my precious, to keep the Raven—that's the Cherokees' omen of death—from stealing a dying man's heart. Osborne's footprints faded, but he lived forever when he climbed into the night sky and became the Great Bear."

Susanna never again saw her beloved in the flesh, and she wouldn't let anyone excise the lead pellet from her baby girl's chest. Decades later, Susan bared her bosom and told her granddaughter, "Touch it, child." The gristly little silver-blue scar tingled under Adella's forefinger.

But unlike the vast majority of the South's myriad people of color, Susanna wasn't enslaved. Nor were her daughters or their children after them. This entry in Nathan Sayre's diary helped Adella better understand that distinctive circumstance:

> *1819. Sep 1. We br'ght this squaw Susanna & her 2 old'r d'ght'rs to work for us, tho Susan, the young'st, will stay w. the Hunts. The girls' fath'r was a slave, but Susanna is ½ Ch'rokee & ½ white so her childr'n are free, since Geo. laws spec'fy th't ev'ry child's condit'n derives from its moth'r. It's a concept call'd partus sequitur ventrem ("birth follows the belly") & turns upside down a central concept of English common law—th't the fath'r sets a child's status. Thus, whoev'r impregnates a slave, the mast'r keeps own'rship of her progeny. Our statutes specify th't folks w. any "black blood" at all are negroes, appear'nce notw'thst'nding.*

For several years, Susan's mother and two sisters worked in the home of the Watkinses, Nathan Sayre's sister, Della, and her husband, Joseph, and assumed their surname. On one occasion, they even entered the Georgia state lottery and won a hundred virgin acres. But Susan, who'd been the neighboring white Hunts' house servant for as long as she could remember and used their name, had different ideas about who she was and what she wanted. Whenever she felt restless, Susan saddled one of the Hunts' horses and galloped off. She'd ride around, learning more things like those that her mother first had taught her about "Injun" lore and healing and about Moon Woman, Father Sun, and their maternal tribe, called the Bird Clan.

Over time, the white Hunts' oldest boy, James Madison Hunt Jr., called J. M., and Susan became best friends, and they talked, laughed and wrestled, fished, hunted, and smoked together. When J. M.'s youngest brother, Henry, was born, they hugged, kissed, and tickled the baby, pretending that he was their own. They both were sixteen at the time and recently had started coupling in the Hunts' barn. That's when J. M. began calling her his Black-Eyed Susan.

The widowed Nancy Hunt wanted her oldest son to wed and have children as soon as possible, but since Susan was "colored," marrying her didn't seem to be an option. Nancy knew that Susan and J. M. loved each other and wanted to stay together, yet when he turned twenty, as a practical woman, she negotiated the terms of a dowry with a white couple named Latimer.

When J. M. informed Susan about the pending contract for Marjorie Latimer, his bride-to-be, Susan later told her granddaughter, "I pounded his chest, howled like a cat in heat, then saddled a horse, lashed a rifle to the pommel, stuck a Bowie knife in my belt, and rode off again."

Marjorie's father owned and operated a haberdashery in Sparta. He and his wife wanted their girl married into a respected family, one that might be a bit cash poor but owned thousands of acres where they held hundreds of people in slavery. So early in 1828, the Latimers handed over their daughter to J. M. Hunt with the prearranged dowry. Nancy Hunt gave her son's bride her own favorite house servant, a girl named Tilly, and Rev. Beman married the young couple.

"After that, I rode around in the woods for a month, all by myself," Susan told Adella, "but finally stopped my sniveling and returned to the Hunts and the only home I knew." As her cuts and bruises healed, folks in Hancock County saw that Susan had metamorphosed from a gangly girl into a tall, golden-skinned young woman with a glorious mane of unruly black hair.

Nathan Sayre observed those events from his own perspective and wrote,

1828. Oct 12. Susan, the young'st of our col'd-Indian-white fam'ly, runs away th'n returns at will & acts all sull'n since

JMHunt married. The Hunts don't know what to do with her!
But we c'ld use her help here, 'cause Susan's moth'r & old'r
sist'rs are leaving us aft'r winning those acres in the land
lott'ry. So we'll give Susan a try. & a fine-looking animal she is!
I don't like the idea of bedding down someone I <u>own</u>, as my bro
Robert does, but since S is <u>free</u>, this c'ld be diff'r'nt.

Nathan Sayre's reference to Susan as *"a fine-looking animal"* and his comments about whom he'd like to *"bed down"* took Adella aback, but she plowed on. His career flourished as he served on the staffs of several of Georgia's governors; he was elected seven times as Hancock County's representative to the legislature and then to the state senate. His granddaughter's main interest, however, lay in his private life, as this diary entry partially revealed:

1829. Jan 4. Susan runs our household v'ry well. She's tall'r
& strong'r than I am, so I dar'd not d'mand (or ev'n ask for)
anything intimate, but last n'ght, she knock'd at my bedr'm
door. Want'd to know if she was disturbing me & I said "no."
Th'n she cross'd to the bed, lift'd my n'ght shirt & her chemise
& mount'd me! Wh'n we'd complet'd the primal act she ask'd,
"Was th't o-keh, sir?" I was br'thless but said, "Yes, indeed, just
fine." More to come, I hope.

That spring he wrote,

Susan visits my bedr'm oft'n now. I enjoy her attent'ns, so
sometimes I ask, "Wh't c'n I do for you?" Last w'k she said:
"W'ld you teach me to talk like Miz Della, sir?" Susan mostly
learn'd fr'm the Hunts who speak well enuf, but hardly like my
sist'r Della's copious vocabulary, perf'ct grammar & syntax. I
told her "Yes." Said I'd give her reading & writing lessons too,
tho it'd defy Geo. law to do so. She answer'd, "I don't want th't,
sir, but I do want to know about <u>ev'rything</u> th't's in y'r b'ks, so

why don't you read 'em to me?" Thoro'ly surpris'd, but th't's
wh't I'm doing now: reading (& more!) to her almost every night.

The second row of his crated diaries opened with this announce-
ment:

1830. Jan 26. Susan c'ld d'liv'r any time now! I'm hoping for
a boy—don't we all? Yest'rday, I want'd her to brew me a pot
of my fav'rite Indian tea & she ask'd, "Is th't 'Injun' like my
Cherokees?" I explain'd th't the Indians who grow the tea I like
live on the oth'r side of the w'rld. "So if we're diff'rent people
from diff'rent places," she said, "I'll keep calling my people
Injuns, not In-dee-ans, if th't's alr'ght w. you, sir." Fac'd w.
her faultl'ss logic, I agreed.

Susan Hunt, however, didn't give birth to a boy but to a girl, whom
she and Nathan Sayre called Sue Rose.

A year later, Susan's mother and sisters decided to sell the acreage
they'd won in the land lottery and buy homes in nearby Milledgeville, the
state capital. To do that, however, someone had to act as their surrogate,
because the state of Georgia treated all people of color as minors or chattel.
"Free" or not, in the eyes of the law, anyone who wasn't certifiably white
was closely akin to a slave and thus wasn't legally considered an adult. On
their own, they couldn't enter into any legal contracts, such as purchasing
or selling property or even marrying. But attorney Sayre could, would, and
did so for them. "Know the law and use the law," he often said.

By then, Susan had a solid grip on Nathan Sayre's heart, and as a man
set in his ways, he felt well satisfied with his life and chose not to marry a
white woman. In 1833, he also designed and oversaw the construction of a
grand new mansion built in the Greek Revival style. It had a paneled library,
marble fireplaces, silver hinges and escutcheons on each door, carved mold-
ings and crystal chandeliers throughout. Its foundation was Georgia granite
with brick above. Thick walls moderated heat and cold, and the ground
level included a wine cellar, pantry, kitchen, and dining room. Two half

flights of stairs accessed a deep front piazza that featured four tall Doric columns, a small tympanum, a pediment, and a parapet all around the roof. But Nathan Sayre's *"stroke of genius"* was the *"secr't inn'r house"* he laid out for his "wife," Susan, and their child. He wrote,

> *At the right rear, I includ'd a suite for them. Main r'ms h've*
> *12-ft. ceilings, but in S's 3-story apartm'nt, they're only 8-ft,*
> *thus for the el'vat'ns: 2X12-ft.=24-ft. or 3X8-ft.=24-ft. My*
> *bedr'm's side door leads directly to hers, so she'll sleep just a few*
> *steps fr'm me! I hear that T. Jefferson did the same thing for*
> *"Dusky Sally Hemings" in his private quart'rs at Monticello.*
> *A friend gave me a lovely rend'ring of my home which shows the*
> *windows of S's private suite.*

Susan told Adella about that home. "Your grandfather wanted to call it 'Elm Drive,' but I said, 'I'm sorry sir. This house deserves better!' I planted pomegranate bushes because my 'Injuns' used the blossoms, peel, pulp and seeds, and he told me that the 'other Indians' believed they brought the occupants healthy children. So I suggested 'Pomegranate Hall' and he agreed."

At a ceremony shortly after they moved in, Rev. Beman recited a Christian prayer. Susan followed him and sanctified her new home with an old Cherokee one: "May the Great Spirit bless all of those who enter here and may a rainbow circle 'round your shoulder."

Susan already had one baby with a second expected soon, but J. M. Hunt's wife, Marjorie, remained childless. She also had no patience for Tilly, the sweet-tempered girl whom her mother-in-law had given her. But as Tilly had been trained, each morning she'd tote a breakfast tray to the annex where the young couple slept. She curled Marjorie Latimer Hunt's limp hair, buffed her nails, lotioned her hands and feet, and swatted away the 'skeeters during her afternoon nap. Once, when Tilly singed a gown she was pressing, J. M.'s wife snatched the hot iron and held it against the girl's forearm. Tilly ran off howling, but Marjorie insisted that she had to punish "my slave," and taunted Nancy Hunt: "You wouldn't take that sassy picka-

Pomegranate Hall. (Rendering courtesy of Georgia-based artist Sterling Everett.)

ninny's side over your only daughter-in-law's, would you?" The triangular scar on Tilly's wrist never faded.

Dr. Edmond D. Albright, the county's leading physician, often went out to Fortitude to minister to Marjorie. He poked, probed and leeched her, then told Nancy Hunt, "Miz Marjorie likely will conceive pretty soon, but she could use some exercise, and more beef and potatoes." He also began training Susan as his "granny," as everyone in the Old South called midwives.

Marjorie Latimer Hunt was both childless and disagreeable. But her in-laws still wanted her to be happy, so as a fourth anniversary present, J. M. gave her a mare called Daisy. He selected several cowhides that his slaves fashioned into a double-pommeled lady's sidesaddle. They also made her a pair of calfskin boots and a crop from a willow cane encased in a sheath braided from nine pigskin strips that ended in nine thongs, each tied off in a pebbly knot. Marjorie's father brought her a blue velvet jacket and matching plumed hat from his haberdashery.

On the anniversary morning, Tilly dressed her mistress in the new regalia. J. M. planted one of his wife's boots in the stirrup and anchored the other between the pommels. She gathered the reins in her right hand, held the switch in her left, and began slowly circling the turnaround. But Daisy didn't step out briskly enough for her ornery jockey's taste, so Marjorie flogged her. The nine-tailed switch must have felt as if nine angry horseflies had stung Daisy, because she snorted and shied just enough to send Marjorie tumbling off, but one of her boot heels became trapped under the saddle's belly cinch. The gentle horse ambled along with her hatless rider hanging upside down, emitting shrill pig squeals as her ruffled petticoats flapped over her head.

J. M. ran over and extricated his wife. She'd suffered no physical injury, but seeing her mistress looking like a gigantic, upturned mushroom cap made Tilly giggle. Marjorie heard that laughter, and once freed of her entanglements, right side up and fully mobile, she stormed across the yard, raised her horse crop, and slashed the girl. Before J. M. could restrain her, she'd rained down a dozen harsh strokes and hissed, "You ruined my anniversary, you dingy bitch."

The assault sliced off a pink nubbin of Tilly's lower lip and half an eyelid. For weeks thereafter, Marjorie kept ranting about how she "had to teach that sassy Tilly a lesson." And she did. The girl lost much of her eyesight, purple welts crisscrossed her sweet caramel face, she couldn't close her mouth or speak clearly anymore, and she soon began failing in body and mind.

An ensuing entry in Nathan Sayre's journal came on the heels of that tragedy at Fortitude and documented the event that ultimately determined Adella's existence.

1833. May 27. 2nd d'ght'r born & we nam'd her Mariah Lily. She looks diff'r'nt fr'm Sue Rose, w. pal'r skin, dark'r eyes & hair (S calls it "Injun hair"), but anoth'r pretty one! They don't carry my name 'cause they're not my prop'rty, but it's okeh with me that they're all Hunts.

And that summer, a fortuitous development ensured Nathan Sayre's financial success. He and his brother, Robert, buggied over to Athens to attend James Camak's first meeting that would incorporate the Georgia Railroad and Banking Company. Dr. Camak, a professor at the state college, aspired to stitch together all of Georgia with an interlocking grid of rail lines. *Th't sh'ld bring our state real progress and profits for us inv'stors,* attorney Sayre wrote. *I'll get wealthy, while most of these backw'rd Sothrons continue inv'sting in the obsolete institut'n of slav'ry.*

At Fortitude, however, Nancy Hunt had to care for her daughter-in-law too, since Tilly's replacement wouldn't go into Marjorie's bedroom anymore because she'd curse and smear her with feces. Marjorie's cheeks were sallow, eyes rheumy and hollow with muddy smudges under them. Every week more ash-blond hairs became tangled in her brush, and her urine smelled like molasses. She ate very little and rarely, and when she did, the food streamed right through her.

"For Marjorie's distress, I gave the Hunts unaker. That's the medicinal kaolin clay my 'Injuns' use that I'd dig from the hills near the old burial mounds," Susan told her granddaughter. "But nothing helped, and soon after J. M. and Marjorie's fifth wedding anniversary, she died."

When Nancy Hunt's favorite slave, Tilly, passed away later that year, the family feared that Nancy might die too. They knew she'd never be happy at her old home anymore, so Judkins, her second son, decided to take her away. Just north of Shoulderbone Creek, his slaves built him a plantation house that he called Nancy's Fancy. His mother always knew it was her special place.

The next few years passed with few complications for the Hunts, while Nathan Sayre's legal career flourished, and two girls and then a boy occupied them at Pomegranate Hall. In 1835, he delighted in his only son's birth but was peeved that Susan named him James (called Jimmy), for J. M. Hunt, who'd been her first love. He, however, was the only child who had his father's light eyes. That, Nathan Sayre reported, was when Susan told him, *No more babies now!*

When Rev. Beman came by Pomegranate Hall to bless the infant, attorney Sayre congratulated him too. He'd keep his church in Hancock County but also had been appointed as principal at the new Presbyterian Oglethorpe College for boys over in the next county.

Nathan Sayre's devotion to Susan and their children and their ambiguous places in his life and in their unique home was a secret that most Spartans knew but few spoke openly about. And soon after Jimmy was born, attorney Sayre penned this entry about his older children:

> *1839. Feb 20. I negotiat'd an arrangem'nt to get my d'ght'rs educated at the Sparta Female Acad. & a lot of my $$$ pass'd hands! Geo. statutes prohib't teaching <u>any</u> col'd folks to read & write, but teaching them <u>music</u> is o-keh. (Know the law & use the law!) Chaz du Bose's* [Nathan Sayre's new law clerk] *wife Kate, who's join'd the faculty, will see th't they get some basic academics too & it's bett'r than sending them to the nuns who instruct a few col'd girls in N. Orleans & Quebec. I'd nev'r ship them off like th't, since Geo. law's clear: <u>any f.p.c.'s</u>* [free people of color] *who <u>leave our state can't ev'r r'turn</u>. Not to mention how I mistrust the Papists!*

Within a few years, Nathan Sayre's daughters, Sue Rose and Mariah Lily Hunt, became the academy's best harpist and pianist and excelled in school recitals, and Kate du Bose tutored them too. Mrs. du Bose had benefited from a rigorous education in the North and passed on that learning when she taught Sparta's well-to-do lasses, attorney Sayre's two little girls among them.

Sad stories also punctuated the diary. Nathan's sister, Della, died at

fifty-two, only a week after her husband, Joseph Watkins. The Sayre brothers had to deal with the people whom the Watkinses had held as slaves, so
Robert kept those in whom he maintained a "special interest" (his bedmate
and their children, Johnny and Jenny Watkins), and Nathan brought a few
others to Pomegranate Hall as his servants. Susan oversaw their work and
managed the whole estate.

As Nathan Sayre was mourning Della's death, he acquired an unusual book: Alexander Walker's *Intermarriage; or, The Mode in Which &
the Causes Why Beauty, Health & Intellect Result from Certain Unions, &
Deformity, Disease & Insanity from Others.* Walker's scientific findings impressed attorney Sayre, and he quoted them in his diary: *"Int'rmixture of
the races improves the int'llectual powers as much as bodily proport'ns, tho
such findings are at odds w. Southern'rs' views ab't mulattoes."* Dr. Walker
insisted that they weren't "skunks" or "mules," as many white folks claimed,
but might be *"a smart'r & strong'r new 'mix'd race.'"*

Susan's refusal to register herself and their children as free people of
color as specified by law, however, distressed Nathan Sayre. In 1840, he was
appointed as overseer of the federal census for Hancock County. As such,
he pledged to accurately tally up the entire local population but ruefully
admitted,

> *I've been dishon'st ab't my own fam'ly. Geo. law r'quires all
> f.p.c.s to regist'r at the c'nty c'rth'ses, but Susan refuses. For
> that "offense," she & our childr'n c'ld be jail'd or sold into
> slav'ry, ev'n if I vouch for them. So und'r my sup'rvision, this
> decennial compilat'n won't list them at all. It frankly both
> worries & embarrasses me!*

An ensuing entry said this:

> *My boy Jimmy just lost his 1st milk teeth & his l'ft eye's iris
> turn'd copp'r color'd, tho the r'ght one's still gray like mine. Rev.
> Beman talks ab't Jimmy attending Oglethorpe College one day,
> tho I know he'd have to "become white" to go there.*

The third row of his journals began with the volume for 1842, in which Nathan Sayre announced that he'd earned a seat on the state Superior Court. Looking back on his legislative career, he wrote,

> I've had a few achievem'nts, but done nothing to upset the status quo, except supporting legislat'n "to exon'rate certain free persons of color fr'm form'r penalties & forfeitures." That propos'l (tho it didn't pass) w'ld've forgiv'n col'd people such as Susan who have no free pap'rs & <u>will not register</u> w. the county clerk. She was furious when I back'd anoth'r bill to r'move <u>all</u> of her "Injuns" fr'm Geo. & rail'd at me: "White men stole the Injuns' lands & the Afric'ns' bodies!"

His new position also resolved the matter of what to call Nathan Sayre. There would be no more "Senator" or "Massa" but also no "Daddy" at Pomegranate Hall. Thereafter, he was "the Judge" to Susan, to their children, and to virtually everyone who knew him. Then this:

> 1843. Sep 12. Baptisms last Sunday for both of our girls. CPBeman sprinkl'd 'em, so they're now JC's [Jesus Christ's] own Ch'rokee Mariah Lily & Ch'rokee Sue Rose—my Snow White & Rose Red. But their moth'r (my stubb'rn Susan!) refuses to accept Jesus as her savior.

Susan Hunt remained a pagan, but her grounds became a garden of Eden. Mariah told Adella, "Your grandmother raised all sorts of fruits and vegetables. She'd tell us, 'never waste anything,' as she composted, mulched, and used every last bit of rind, stem and core. The neighbors' children often sneaked over to play backgammon and chess with us (we always won). Their parents couldn't keep them away, but they also called us 'the Judge's mongrel bastards.'"

The late 1840s brought major changes for the white Hunts. At a double wedding, Judkins and William Hunt married Dr. Albright's nieces, Rebecca and Eliza Ann. Judkins took Rebecca Albright to live at Nancy's

Fancy, and William also stayed in Hancock County with his new wife, Eliza Ann. Then their brother Thomas Jefferson Hunt, who they'd thought would be a bachelor forever, went up to Boston one Christmas and returned a month later with a Yankee bride.

Susan told her granddaughter about her midwifery too: "In '46, I went over to Nancy's Fancy to help Emma, who was your uncle Judkins's much too young undercook, give birth. A few months later, I did the same for Hancock's richest planter David Dickson's favorite slave, Julia, and also assisted T. J. Hunt's wife and lots of other white women in the county."

Then in 1850, Robert and Nathan Sayre planned a journey. The Judge had wanted Susan to join them, but Georgia's laws stipulated that any free people of color who left the state or the country never could return, except as slaves, and he wouldn't risk losing her. Shortly before he departed, he put his affairs in order, and Charles du Bose helped him draw up a will—just in case.

The Sayre brothers took a train to New York, where they boarded an ocean steamer bound to Liverpool. From London, the Judge wrote,

> *1850. Jul 10. Visit'd England's Royal Small Arms Fact'ry &
> purchas'd a custom-made rifle for my boy. It'll have a silv'r
> nameplate engrav'd "James Herbert Hunt" on a walnut stock.
> But conflicts abound! Geo. laws say <u>no</u> col'd people c'n own
> guns, tho our US Constitut'n suggests <u>ev'ryone</u> c'n. In Paris, I'll
> buy a harp for Sue Rose, th'n on to Ger. to cruise the Rhine &
> ord'r a Steinweg piano for Mariah. Fin'st instruments in the
> world! C'llecting gold coins wherev'r we go, Belgian carp'ts, lace
> in France, brocades in Italy.*

Nathan Sayre returned home in September bearing a few small *cadeaux* for his family, among them a ten-franc French coin for Susan that he had pierced and threaded onto a fine gold chain. Other gifts, including the rifle and treasured musical instruments, arrived later.

Mariah also told Adella how her brother, Jimmy, first "became white" when Judge Sayre donated to Oglethorpe and enrolled him there. "For a while, your uncle got a good education in its preparatory program, until a teacher expelled him for punching out a classmate who'd cussed the 'lazy niggers' and 'dirty redskins' one too many times for our Jimmy's liking." Even the Judge's counsel and financial generosity didn't persuade Rev. Beman to overrule that dismissal.

"In '51, your daddy Henry started courting me," Mariah went on, "then your aunt Sue Rose gave birth to her first son, Alexander Hamilton Hunt. We had our suspicions, but she never told us who his father was. And that same December, the Judge deeded my sister a plot of land and gave her the money she needed to build a cottage, though she usually seemed to have enough support from that unnamed but well-to-do someone to buy nice things for herself and her baby."

"But the Judge didn't want that sort of life for me," Adella's mother shook her head. "He wanted me properly married, like a white lady, so when your father asked him for my hand, your grandfather figured out how to make that happen. He gave me several acres near Sue Rose's, and your daddy oversaw a crew of the Hunts' slaves, and they built our new home— where you'd be born a decade later. When it was finished, a team of draymen toted over my Steinweg piano and lots of rugs, furniture, crystal, and china from Pomegranate Hall to get it ready for me."

Nathan Sayre wrote in his diary about what else he arranged for his princess bride:

> 1852. Oct 26. Took a sack of coins & an old dent'd sterling tea service to Otis Childs, Mill'dgeville's silv'rsmith. Ask'd him to craft a set of tableware for Mariah. He'll melt down my silv'r & c'nfigure it into a patt'rn he calls "Fiddlehead"—real pretty, & I want'd a d'sign th't reflect'd her musical talents. A new Daguerrean studio shares th't b'ldg, so I contract'd w. Joseph Miller, the propriet'r, to make images of the brid'l party at our upcoming celebrat'n. Also ask'd if I c'ld h've a b'k mail'd to him. It's Mrs. Stowe's new abolit'nist tome: Uncle Tom's Cabin. I do <u>not</u> want it deliv'r'd to the courthouse, my law offices, or Pom. Hall.

Finally, Adella reached the last entry in those old journals:

*1852. Dec 31. Xmas, th'n M's wedding! Henry Hunt's a tanner
and cobbler who owns farml'nd & 30 slaves. I'm sure he'll care
for my girl, but I'm irk'd b'cause Rev. Beman says he can't
marry 'em, & <u>technic'lly</u> he may be r'ght. Geo.'s laws call M
col'd, tho to see her you wouldn't know it. She & Henry H c'ld
go anywh're they're not known to wed, but can't <u>officially</u> marry
in our state. They, or anyone who <u>p'rforms</u> such a service, c'n be
flogg'd, fin'd, or ev'n imprison'd!*

Despite those harsh stipulations, Nathan Sayre would not be deterred.
He continued:

*But I want'd it <u>all legal</u>. So as a judge, I p'rform'd the cer'mony
myself here at Pom. Hall's library: "Und'r the author'ty vest'd
in me by the state of Geo." etc, etc. Susan button'd our Mariah
into an Alençon lace gown & she carried my fam'ly Bible. In
addit'n to my bro. & a few of the white Hunts, Doc Albright &
the du Boses join'd us. David Dickson, Hancock C'nty's "prince
of plant'rs," br'ght his fav'rite slave Julia & their daught'r
Amanda, whom Susan had deliv'r'd, as well as a gen'rous
gift. The Daguerreotypist Joseph Miller buggied ov'r fr'm
Mill'dgeville lad'n down w. his equipm'nt, & the table silv'r
I'd order'd too. He also br'ght my new H. B. Stowe nov'l. In a
few w'ks he'll deliv'r finish'd images of the newlyw'ds, Nancy
Hunt, Sue Rose, Jimmy & me—tho not my Susan who look'd
<u>gorgeous</u> in ruby satin th't I b'ght her in Italy. But she goes all
"Injun" on us at the worst of times, & said: "Oh, no! Th't eye
will steal my soul." Mr. Miller, howev'r, took a sheet of bl'ck
pap'r & pair of scissors, cut out a silhouette of her & mount'd
it on a white pasteb'rd. Th'n she grinn'd, "Th't's not me, Mr.
Miller, b'cause it's only bl'ck & white, no red." So he cut a
snipp't of ribbon fr'm her bodice, glued it at the neck of his*

cut-out & said: "There's y'r red, Miz Susan. Now it's you
fer sure!"

The judge also reported some family conflict that day:

After our comp'ny left, I had a spat w. Sue Rose who says she's
expecting ag'n, but won't name the scoundr'l. I suspect one of
the Hunt bros (Wm!), or my colleague, Judge Linton Stephens. I
call'd her a Jezebel & she fir'd back: "You rais'd me to be a lady,
but Geo. has no place for col'd ladies. I'll nev'r be any white
wom'n's cook or maid. I can't make a living teaching girls to
play the harp & who'll marry me? So I use this body God gave
me & white m'n want." I'm irk'd, yet maybe she's r'ght! I'm also
exhaust'd as 1853 arrives. But Mariah's married now, & I've
put 4 l'ge pouches fill'd w. gold coins into my safe (1 for Susan &
1 for each child) & gave M the combinat'n. Now I'm at peace.

That was Nathan Sayre's final diary entry. But the large wooden case
was segmented into three rows, each with exactly space enough for a dozen
volumes, and where the thirty-sixth should have been was a paper-wrapped
parcel mailed from a major Philadelphia publishing house. Four decades
later, Adella unwrapped it for the first time and found the copy of Harriet
Beecher Stowe's novel, *Uncle Tom's Cabin,* that Judge Sayre had ordered.
Milledgeville's daguerreotypist must have taken the notorious book to
Pomegranate Hall on the day of the wedding, but the Judge clearly never
had a chance to read it, or even to open the package.

His fatigue never let up after that, and a week later, he suffered a massive seizure that left him paralyzed. "I feared the end was near, and knew
that the Raven Mocker wanted to steal the Judge's sharp brain and kind
heart," Susan told her granddaughter, "so each night I slept with my hand
pressed against his shoulder and put plates of cornbread next to Pomegranate Hall's outer doors to stave off the greedy bird. If you hear a raven caw,
Adella, death's always nearby."

Judge Sayre died six weeks after officiating at Mariah's wedding.

Adella couldn't forget the date because her grandmother often reminded her that she was born exactly ten years later.

In accordance with Cherokee tradition, Susan Hunt cut off her long hair and put the French coin on its gold chain into a miniature jewel case. Most of the region's wealthy citizens and civic leaders attended Judge Sayre's funeral. The few people whom the Sayres held as slaves, as well as Susan, her children, their aunts, cousins, and others for whom the Judge had provided reliable legal assistance, stood in the balcony of Rev. Beman's church, then out by the cemetery's rough, lichened walls. Their black silk umbrellas, Susan told her granddaughter, "looked like a whole 'Injun' village." Robert Sayre ordered a marble obelisk and had it installed in Sparta's town cemetery. It bore only these words:

IN MEMORY OF NATHAN SAYRE
BORN NEWARK, N.J. JULY 22, 1795
DIED SPARTA, GEO. FEBRUARY 3, 1853
AN HONEST MAN

Two weeks later, attorney du Bose filed Nathan Sayre's will at probate. He left most of his estate, including Pomegranate Hall, to his brother, Robert. No mention was made of Susan or their children, but Mariah already had retrieved and distributed the four large, coin-filled leather purses that he'd secured for them in his safe. After the will's main provisions had been carried out, Robert Sayre and Charles du Bose organized an auction of the Judge's belongings. That event would be held early in April, at dusk, by candlelight at the Hancock County courthouse.

People came from all over, to buy or just to gawk. Surprisingly, in a region where the majority read little other than the Bible, the Judge's books were the primary attractions. He'd had no fields and owned few acres or slaves, but in his library, lauded as "the finest in the state," he'd overseen an uncommon domain built on ideas, words, and valuable shares of railroad stock.

On the appointed evening, an auctioneer described each lot, intoned his litany, and sixty-seven times he cried, "Going, going, SOLD!" Men such as the Hunt and Stephens brothers (the latter were prominent bibliophiles), Dr. Albright, and Rev. Beman purchased their mementos. After everything had been scavenged, Susan and her son toted away several loads of the Judge's belongings that no one had bought—including the hefty wooden crate that held his journals.

Mariah Hunt also shared this story with Adella. For some time, her uncle Robert Sayre had been calling on a conniving spinster who'd focused her eyes on Pomegranate Hall and took advantage of his grief. Yielding to her stratagems, Robert married her, but soon his new wife groused, "I won't have that nigger squaw running my house!" Robert thus reluctantly explained to his brother's "widow" Susan, "the Judge arranged for you to return to Fortitude, where J. M. Hunt will care for you and your boy." Squeezed between her son, Jimmy, and J. M. Hunt in his laden-down Conestoga wagon, Susan Hunt left her home of twenty years. "Just wait," she'd hollered so loudly that almost everyone in town heard her, "I *will* come back here one day!"

"But pretty soon," Mariah continued with a wink, "Robert's bride stormed off, because, she squawked, 'my husband prefers sharing a bed with his nigger wench and the company of their colored bastards.' Those 'bastards,' Adella, are our cousins Johnny and Jenny Watkins."

Susan and her son, Jimmy, settled in at Fortitude with J. M. Hunt. Cotton remained their money crop, but they also bred stock and raised grains and vegetables. And after she'd been there for a decent interval, J. M. asked and she agreed to be his Black-Eyed Susan once again.

J. M.'s brother Henry ran the county's largest tannery and lived with his wife, Mariah, on what folks in Sparta called Hunts' Hill, since she, her sister, and other kin owned property there. Mariah and Henry soon had two boys, whom they named William (Will) and James Madison (Maddy) Hunt for their white uncles, and then, just as the big war started, a girl: Louisa Mae.

As the Judge had urged, Mariah and her mother sometimes visited attorney Charles du Bose to hear about what was going on elsewhere in the country that might bear on their lives. In April of 1857, he'd dropped them a note asking that they stop by his law office—as they did.

"In the case of this fella named Dred Scott," Mr. Du Bose began, "the highest court in the land has ruled that colored people, both slaves and free folks like you and Mr. Scott who have any black ancestors, can't ever be citizens of this country or any of its states." "The justices found negroes to be 'inferior beings,' more akin to property than to people, who are 'unfit to associate with the white race,'" he shook his head. "So all of them, you Hunts and your descendants included, the decision says, 'have no rights that the white man is bound to respect.'"

But Susan, Sue Rose, and Mariah didn't let such obstacles deter them and continued to "associate with the white race" in many ways. When Sue Rose bore her first child, whom she'd named Alexander, some folks speculated that his father was William Hunt and gossiped, "Them Hunt men can't keep it buttoned up 'round those creamy-skinned gals." Others reckoned it was Linton Stephens (he too "had an eye for the yaller wenches"), one of Judge Sayre's colleagues on the bench. Judge Stephens's brother, Alexander Hamilton Stephens, was Hancock County's longtime congressman. In either case, it was definitely a white man with money to spare.

"Over the next few years, my sister gave birth to Edgar, Isaac, and Osborne—named for our enslaved grandfather. When Sue Rose told me she was expecting again, I teased that she'd name her fifth son Ulysses," Mariah laughed, "but it was a girl, so we called them 'A, E, I, O and Li'l Susie,' or 'the children of strangers,' because my sister never said who their daddy was."

Shortly before Christmas of 1859, Susan and Mariah Hunt answered another summons from Charles du Bose, who asked, "Have you heard about John Brown, that cockeyed white abolitionist?" They had indeed, since everyone in Sparta seemed to be ranting about "Ole Man Brown an' his Bible-thumpin', nigger lovin' Pottawatomie Rifles from Bleedin' Kansas."

"Two months back," Mr. du Bose went on, "he and his gang of black and white rascals raided the federal arsenal at Harpers Ferry, Virginia, planning to steal lots of arms and munitions, thinking that slaves everywhere would rise up to support them. But they didn't, and the U.S. Army captured, killed, or jailed most of his crew. John Brown himself was tried, convicted, and hanged a few weeks ago, still calling himself 'a martyr for our nation's sins.' I'm telling you this, 'cause a couple of his free colored boys escaped, and people here are hoppin' mad about it. I'm afraid some of them will take out their anger on decent folks like you. Our newspapers are speculating that the South's going to secede pretty soon. Maybe even go to war with the North."

Pursuant to John Brown's raid, Adella's father and her uncle J. M. learned that a pack of hoodlums planned to "git" Hancock County's "free niggers," so they rounded up those on Hunts' Hill as well as Johnny and Jenny Watkins, who lived at Pomegranate Hall with their father, Robert Sayre, and took all of them out to Fortitude. They brought a cow and several laying hens into the dogtrot, shuttered the old house's windows, bolted the doors, and barricaded the tall gates. The men clambered onto the roof, where the first white Hunts in Georgia had erected bulwarks to fend off attacks by the "heathen savages"—which, in fact, never came. Jimmy Hunt armed himself with his English rifle, and he and the others took turns standing vigil twenty-four hours a day.

They heard cursing and shouting, and torches flickered off in the woods. J. M.'s dogs howled like wolves, then suddenly stopped. His pigs squealed louder than ever, and just after midnight that Christmas, Mariah recalled, one of the cows bellowed "like Gabriel's trumpet."

"Finally," she went on, "Uncle Robert and Mr. du Bose came by to tell us that they'd cabled the governor over in Milledgeville, to tell him that a mob of rowdies had surrounded us at Fortitude. He threatened to send his militia to Hancock County to arrest the bullies, because our supporters who'd reported the siege were respected white men. That ended the standoff. Four of J. M.'s hounds had been poisoned, lots of his pigs had been disemboweled, and one of his cows that'd just calved lay in a puddle of mud and blood." Susan added, "We wanted to move on, but the white folks' craziness kept flaring up all around. Then the next fall the country chose Mr. Lincoln as president. And, I'm sorry to say, things here in Georgia got even worse after that."

Adella's grandmother also told her how she'd often stop by Sparta's cemetery: "J. M. had my heart again, but the Judge still kept my head screwed on straight. So I'd visit him there. I was afraid that if those bone-headed southerners who hated Honest Abe Lincoln split up the country, they might split up our family too, and I didn't want that to happen. Your father and his brothers claimed to own about three hundred Negroes, but I hoped they still believed in the *United* States that their grandpa Capt. Judkins Hunt had fought so hard to bring about. Back then, when my son (your uncle Jimmy) was young and cocksure, he could get pretty hotheaded too, so I worried that, like Ole John Brown, he might try something righteous but foolhardy. Most of us colored people, enslaved and free alike, came down on the Yanks' side, because we heard that if they had their way, they'd end slavery everywhere—but we had no say in it whatever."

"I had only one question for your grandfather Sayre that December and asked him right out: 'Judge, you used to say, know the law and use the law. So tell me, Your Honor, can all of your precious laws keep these angry, pathetic white fellas, who just want to hold onto their slaves and their women, from unmaking our country?' No, my precious, he didn't answer me in so many words, but I knew exactly what he was thinking—even from beyond the grave."

THREE

The Hunts' War

ADELLA WAS BORN TWO YEARS AFTER THE great war began, but many Georgians told her stories about it. Later, she also met scores of Yankees who shared their reflections on how it restored the Union and ended bondage, the nation's original sin. But the conflict didn't dominate those northerners' every thought, every day, as it did for most southerners. The ugly behemoth came close enough to smell its sour sweat and putrid breath: stomping along roads, bridges, and rails, gobbling up anything in its path, burning plantations, crops, and towns. Countless white men marched or rode away, often to be maimed, to die, or never to return. But the wounded region survived, and in Georgia alone, the venal ownership of half a million people would end at last.

In February 1861, bolstered by cries of "slavery forever," "Deo vindice!" and "states' rights," Georgia seceded from the Union. Pitched battles played out between those who argued that the government mustn't compromise those rights, at least not the right to own their fellow human beings, and dissenters, including Congressman Alexander Stephens (President Lincoln's old friend and colleague) and his brother Linton. At first, as self-appointed interpreters of constitutional law, the Stephenses stood among those who declared the Union inviolable. But by midwinter they reversed course and embraced secession. One major challenge for the region's privileged minority was how to maintain the allegiance of the indigent majority: how to convince those white near paupers that their brash new Confederacy would assure the continued empowerment of all such men, no matter how destitute they might be. As long as the Anglos maintained dominion over their human property, the "darkies" constituted an immutable mudsill that filled the entire bottommost rungs of the South's economic, political, and social ladders.

For several months following President Lincoln's election, like the Stephens brothers, most of Adella's white relatives agreed that Georgia should remain with the Union. But though they lived, ate, and slept with their women of color in defiance of state laws, even her father and uncle J. M. soon succumbed to Georgia's shifting majority pressure. Only her uncle Thomas Jefferson Hunt continued touting the country's indivisibility. Susan and Mariah believed that T. J. was the only sensible one of them, because he insisted that the North, with its rail networks, shipyards, munitions factories, and infinitely more men-at-arms, would handily thrash the South.

But prominent Georgians such as Alexander and Linton Stephens and lesser-known ones like four of the five Hunt brothers read the definitive writing on the wall, and soon they wholly supported secession and the Confederate States of America's precipitous formation. Alexander Hamilton Stephens became the Confederacy's first and only vice president, positioned Hancock and its surrounding counties at its heart, and celebrated slavery as the South's deepest taproot.

"The cornerstone of our Confederacy, rests upon the great truth that the negro is not equal to the white man," he notoriously pontificated. "Slavery, his subordination to the superior race, is his natural and normal condition, and is based upon that undeniable moral and physical truth."

Most people of color disagreed but couldn't do so openly, while with few exceptions, white folks "didn't give a rat's ass" what any of the "darkies" thought and considered them lazy, childish, and fatuous—but devious and potentially dangerous too. Linton Stephens echoed his older brother's racist credo, began recruiting troops, and soon commanded his own company.

Adella's mother and grandmother, who'd loved Thomas Jefferson Hunt and his wife, told her their story. T. J. had been a thirty-five-year-old bachelor when, shortly before Christmas of '47, he'd visited Massachusetts, where he introduced himself to a beguiling skater named Martha Merriwether, whom he'd watched spinning figure-eights on the Boston Common's frozen Frog Pond. Only a month after meeting, with Martha's sister,

Ellen, as the bridesmaid, they married at the old Episcopal church where the Merriwether family had worshiped for a century. Following a reception at his in-laws' Back Bay mansion, T. J. spirited his Yankee bride back to Georgia.

Two years later, Martha almost died while giving birth to her only child, Young Tom, but as a skilled midwife, Susan Hunt saved her life. Martha adored her husband and son but missed her parents and sister, ice-skating, and Boston itself. She thought that both servants and potatoes should be Irish, wanted cod and baked beans, not limas, yams, catfish, and fried everything, and refused to eat grits or "slimy okra." Once the fighting began, Martha worried that her husband never would recover from his bitter clashes with the secessionists. Then suddenly, he died.

"I think my T. J. died from a broken heart," his widow wept as she announced her intent to drape his coffin with Old Glory: the thirty-four-star, red-white-and-blue American flag that Confederates derided as "the candy stripe." Mariah told her daughter that she, her mother and sister, and T. J.'s slaves went to his funeral, but their white kin refused to attend. Martha's son, Young Tom, sniveled that she'd shamed him, so he left home and went to live with his uncle William.

Shortly after T. J. Hunt's burial, Martha summoned all of her enslaved men, women, and children to the yard behind the big house and announced, "My husband wanted to free you, and so do I"—though Georgia's laws pretty much forbade such acts. "I'll keep a few of you here as my servants, not slaves, and you still can work our land." They rushed to kiss "Miz Marthie's" hands, which made her Yankee skin crawl, and rejoiced: "We's free, praise Jesus, we's free!"

But they scarcely could read, write, or compute and suspected that the white folks were stealing them blind. No one would hire them or buy their eggs, syrup, and pies. Their children went hungry and sickened, mules were lamed, tools filched or broken, wells and dogs poisoned, and shacks torched. They had no travel papers, as Georgia law required for all people of color, so the "patty rollers" (low-class white men whose "night work" gave them intoxicating whiffs of power) threatened them whenever they tried to drive their rickety wagons around the county.

Within a few months, Martha Hunt's "darkies" began pleading to work for her again—as her slaves. At least as "property," they'd probably survive. Martha's "harebrained" attempt to challenge the white folks' iron-clad intent to maintain the "peculiar institution" had swiftly failed.

Unlike most Americans who considered the Confederate attack on Fort Sumter the event that triggered hostilities in the War of Northern Aggression, as southerners were exhorted to call it, many Georgians instead dated its onset to a shocking incident that occurred much closer to home. If John Brown at Harpers Ferry, Virginia, gave the Union its martyr, Laura Jane Albright inadvertently assumed the fiery mantle of the Confederacy's Maid of Orleans. Penelope (called Miss Neppie) Albright Hunt, one of Laura Jane's cousins and Adella's too, shared that story.

"With everything heating up and the issue of secession properly settled by the spring of '61," Neppie Hunt began, "we *true* southerners wanted to celebrate our new status."

The residents of White Plains, a village just beyond Hancock County's northeast boundary, began planning a gala event that called for battle songs, oratory, food, libations and revelry, and a bouquet of fair maidens who'd symbolize the purity of white womanhood for whose honor many southern gentlemen vowed they'd fight to the death.

Fourteen-year-old Laura Jane's faux-Grecian toga was stitched from white cotton voile and bound, sashed, and hemmed with red and blue sateen ribbons—the colors of both the American and most Confederate flags. Several black seamstresses made it to drape from her shoulders to her feet. She'd hold the Stars and Bars in her right hand and, in her left, "the torch of freedom." Enthroned on burlap-wrapped bales that signified King Cotton's reign, eleven girls would surround her, each representing a Confederate state. Musicians, preachers, and politicians, including Governor Joe Brown and Alexander Hamilton Stephens, "our great Confederacy's great vice president," Neppie Hunt proudly told Adella, "had rehearsed their roles for weeks."

Adella's white kin were struggling to move beyond what they called "the humiliation that befell us due to T. J.'s treachery and that disgraceful Yankee funeral," followed by his widow's "shameful plan to let the Hunts' darkies go free." So their "servants" began preparing a lavish picnic, and on the designated morning, they loaded food and drink, crystal, china, linens, and folding seats onto mule-drawn wagons (called Georgia chariots) to accompany the white family members who piled into a small armada of carriages that set off from Judkins Hunt's plantation.

As they arrived at the fairgrounds, everyone felt magic in the air. The "darkies" had rigged a velour curtain across the makeshift stage, and ferns, crape myrtle, and wisteria cascaded over it. "The candles that illuminated the proscenium winked and flickered," Neppie Hunt recalled, "and the audience gasped when the taper-lit platform revealed the patriotic tableau."

But those gasps became shrieks, because as the curtain opened, it tipped over a footlight candle. The candle grazed the hem of Laura Jane's toga, which encircled her ankles so that she'd resemble a marble Nike—but it also immobilized her. She toppled over and rolled across the platform like a blazing Yule log. Before any saviors could provide smothering blankets or buckets of water, the flames incinerated her gown. The Stars and Bars that she carried caught fire, as did her halo of blond ringlets. Critically burned, heavily sedated, slathered with lard, and swathed in yards of carbolic-acid-soaked gauze, Laura Jane lay in agony for five days in her uncle Dr. E. D. Albright's infirmary. "When she died, it seemed almost a relief and a blessing," Neppie wept.

" 'Vengeance is mine,' saith the Lord!" Rev. Beman thundered the following Sunday from his pulpit. No rational person could blame the Yanks, yet they did. The owners of the slaves who'd sewn Laura Jane's gown had them whipped and sold one of them down to Mississippi, because, they raged, she too bore a measure of guilt, as did the "worthless darkies" who'd strung up the curtain that upended the incendiary candle. Perhaps it was "an act of nigger arson."

As for the white Hunt men, only Adella's father, Henry, still in his thirties, was young enough to be conscripted. A gubernatorial mandate "requested" him to enlist, as he did, while his surviving older brothers carried out their civic duties by maintaining cotton production as well as discipline on the home front through the county's newly organized Vigilance Militia.

Until Henry Hunt was called to duty, he continued working at his tannery, crafting boots, holsters, and livery trappings, but before 1861 ended he was activated as a cavalry sergeant. As was common in the chaotic Confederacy, that company quickly disbanded, so he rode off as a lieutenant with another unit. He and several others, including Chaplain Atticus Haygood, a young Methodist Episcopal minister who lived near Sparta, transferred into Linton Stephens's Hancock Grays. Col. Stephens, an old friend of the Hunts, soon promoted Henry to captain.

Henry Hunt went off to Virginia with the Grays, but six months later he was granted another leave to head home and resume his cobbling for a while. He thus missed his unit's deadliest encounter at Bull Run. It also became apparent that he'd spent intimate time with his wife on Hunts' Hill, because when he departed, Mariah was expecting their fourth child.

He was back again in Virginia when his second daughter was born on February 3, 1863, a month after President Abraham Lincoln (whom few whites in Hancock County acknowledged at all since they considered themselves citizens, not of the United States, but of Georgia and the Confederacy alone) issued his "notorious" Emancipation Proclamation.

Georgia's slaveholders feared that if "our darkies" learned about it, they'd demand their freedom, then might rise in rebellion. "But why," they asked, "are they so ungrateful, when people like us rescued them from Africa's jungles, filled with disease, cannibals, and wild beasts? We fed them well enough and introduced them to Jesus and our blessed southern civilization."

Adella's birth date also was exactly ten years after her grandmother's first "husband," Nathan Sayre, had died, and Susan thus saw it as an omen of momentous things to come. She and Mariah named the baby for the late Della Sayre Watkins, the Judge's sister, as they insisted he would've wished, and when Capt. Henry Hunt returned home yet again, he followed a tradition that he'd started with his first daughter and gave his wife a second sparkling diamond.

A month after Adella's birth, T. J. Hunt's widow buggied up to Hunts' Hill to meet her sister-in-law's infant. "Martha had become a wraith," Mariah told her daughter. "Her hair was matted, she reeked, wailed about her husband's death and how her son had left her, and swore that the

Albright-Hunt sisters were trying to murder her—which may have been true.
A week later, the servants found her dangling like a bunch of rags from the
rafters in the barn. I was the only one who even bothered to write Martha's
family up in Boston to tell them she'd died."

The drama that unfolded in October 1863, however, shocked many
Georgians. It played out several miles south of Sparta in a part of Hancock
County where David Dickson, the state's wealthiest cotton baron, was letting some of his fields lie fallow. Among the participants were Mariah's
brother, Jimmy Hunt, called "Jimmy Pale Face"; their cousin Johnny Watkins, who was the son of Robert Sayre and his favorite slave; a bondman
named Abel McGee; another known as Slow Joe Cain; and a dozen or so
more. Each Saturday evening, the conspirators walked or rode their owners'
"borrowed" mules or horses and sneaked down to the deserted Dickson
property.

Jimmy Hunt was free, and his cousin Johnny Watkins was enslaved in
name only; so they could move about more easily than the rest. They eaves-
dropped on what the white folks were saying, called the others together
every weekend for a month, and tried to figure out how they might head off
southeast to join the Union troops that occupied Georgia's Sea Islands or
west to meet up with those they'd heard controlled the lower Mississippi
River. But they didn't know in what direction or how far either of those
destinations might be, since most of them couldn't read a map, or anything
else, and hadn't even been as far as the state capital over in the next county.

Years later, Adella's uncle Jimmy wrote her this:

> *We'd been fooling around with some of the cracker gals & joked
> about how we'd like to have the same kind of fun with Hancock
> County's "ladies" that the white gents often did with our own
> mothers & sisters. And like those Yanks that we admired so
> much, we were soldiers of the Lord, out to free the slaves.*

They'd stand at attention holding a few real firearms (Jimmy Hunt
carried the English rifle that his father had given him), hoes, rakes, or
broomsticks over their shoulders and salute their "captains." They'd cho-
sen Jimmy and his cousin as officers, because they were light complexioned,

were more or less free, could read and write, were audacious and facile with words. The darker-skinned slaves thought that Jimmy and Johnny must be smarter than the rest of them. Jimmy's letter continued,

> *On Oct. 15, there was a full moon, & back at school I'd learned about how that mid-month time, called the Ides, provided a chance for serious disorder. Everything started out fine that night & we were so caught up in our drill routine that we didn't notice anything amiss until we spied the patrols—armed white fellas that the hounds were dragging behind them. We heard a loud "Halt!" & saw about 30 men pointing rifles at us.*

The sheriff bellowed, "Drop down on your faces!" Most of the conspirators obeyed, but Jimmy and Johnny lit off into the woods. Then they heard a loud report, glanced back, and saw Abel McGee's head explode like a pumpkin. Half of the men were hogtied and loaded into mule carts, while the others were roped together into a coffle and had to slog barefoot all the way to Sparta.

Their captors foresaw a problem en route to the county jail, because it had only one cell designated for "darky" felons. Before the war, most punishment of the bondmen had taken place right on the plantations, and even the scurviest white lawbreakers would protest if a deputy tried to confine them in a lockup that recently had housed a "nigger." The posse thus roped their prisoners together in the town square and chained them to rings bolted to the iron hitching posts.

Jimmy heard that Slow Joe Cain had gone out drinking and boasted that their little crew had big plans afoot. He'd later write his niece Adella this:

> *Someone tipped off a militiaman who collared Slow Joe, pressed a pistol to his head & swore he'd shoot if Joe didn't spill the beans. Of course, he told them when & where we'd be meeting, "confessed" that we wanted to kill lots of white fellas, diddle their women, torch Sparta, then skedaddle off to join the Union army.*

Jimmy Hunt led Johnny through the woods to Mariah's house because he knew her husband was off fighting the Yanks. He was sure that the next morning local militiamen would pound on each door and search every house on Hunts' Hill. That, whites in Sparta grumbled, was where "them uppity, trouble-making free niggers lived."

Shortly after midnight, Jimmy tapped on his sister's window. She awakened and gasped, but he pressed a finger to his lips. He'd been shot in his left arm and Johnny in his right thigh, and they both had deep gashes, stings, and snake bites that needed attention. Susan Hunt was the county's best healer and the only one they'd trust. They had to reach her as soon as possible.

Mariah bound their wounds, told them to catch forty winks in the barn and, at sunrise, to hitch up the mules. "Then," Mariah told Adella, "I bored several air holes under the wagon seat, lit a kerosene lamp, got out my pen, inkwell, and paper, and sat at the kitchen table to compose the most important document of my life. When the message itself satisfied me, I squared off and emboldened my usual handwriting to make it look like a man's. This is what I wrote:

> I, J. M. Hunt Hancock County taxpayer, voter & Vigilance
> Militia officer request free passage thru all checkpoints for
> Mariah Hunt & her 4 tikes. Their father, my brother Capt.
> H. A. Hunt, is off serving with Col. Stephens company & left
> them in my charge. They are headed from Hunts Hill to
> Fortitude, my spread near Mt. Zion. My housekeeper Susan is
> Mariahs mother & an old herb woman. Capt. Hunts children
> has been exposed to the pox & needs her tending right now.
>   Signed: Militia Maj. J. M. Hunt, 15th day of Oct. yr. of
> Our Lord 1863. Sparta, Geo. C.S.A.

Mariah Hunt folded the note into her skirt pocket and saved it for the rest of her life.

At dawn, Mariah awakened her older son, Will, and told him to take their chamber pot, empty the night soil into one of the dried gourds Susan

Hunt had given them, then plug it up tight, while she dressed her second boy, Maddy, and her daughter Lula Mae. Then she diapered Adella in three thick layers of muslin. She handed Maddy a hatpin, and Will carried the heavy stoppered gourd. He also secured Adella in a canvas sling tied Cherokee style (as his grandmother had showed him) across his chest. Mariah gathered up the reins and guided her Georgia chariot into the roadway. The fugitives were stuffed as tight as ticks under the wagon's hinged seat, atop which Mariah and her children sat four abreast.

As they started down Hunts' Hill, the sentry at the first checkpoint waved them on as soon as he read the chilling word "pox." Then Mariah crossed the courthouse square, where she saw a group of black men sprawled on the ground, chained to the hitching posts, and manacled to each other. They lay in puddles of puke, feces, and blood, were cradling their heads in their hands, and hadn't been bandaged, fed, or given any water since their capture. The white armed guards barely glanced at the dark-haired, dark-eyed woman and her children who passed by.

The sentry on the far side of Sparta presented no problem either, but when Mariah encountered a third one on her journey's final leg, he ordered her over to the roadside. His cohorts stood by, leaning on their muskets, scratching their privates, and spitting brown threads of tobacco. "I thought they were the Spinks brothers," Mariah told her daughter, "nasty white trash from the south county that we always thought had led the pre-war Christmas siege at Fortitude."

Ike, the scurvy trio's leader, drawled, "We's lookin' fo' some excaped niggahs whu' tried tuh burn down Sparta, murduh us gennamins, an' have dare way wif ahr whi' ladies, so we gotta stop ever' wagon dat come by heah an' check ever'tin' in 'em."

Mariah reined in the mules, silently mouthed "Sing!" to her children, and embarked on her narrative about "the pox"—although Susan previously had inoculated everyone in the family. She felt her hidden cargo shift and heard a groan, but Will, Maddy, and Lula Mae already had started loudly singing, "Amazin' Grace, how sweet the sound, that sav'd a wretch like me."

Ike Spinks glowered and barked, "Show me yer pass!" So she handed over the document supposedly composed by J. M. Hunt. At first, Ike pretended to read it because he didn't want to lose face by letting on that he couldn't. "But my mules could read better than he did," Mariah laughed. "Then he mumbled, 'My eyes is gone a li'l blurry, so why don' yuh read it tuh me?'" She did, but Ike still wasn't satisfied and didn't know if he ought to say "ma'am," so he called her nothing. If she was colored—though she didn't look it or show him the expected deference—he didn't want to give her any respect, but if she was a white lady, he'd best not insult her.

So he just grumbled, "Y'all gotta step down now so's we kin look up inside yer wagon."

Mariah turned around slowly to dismount, which was Will and Maddy's next cue. Will emptied the gourd filled with night soil between the layers of Adella's diaper and handed her over to Mariah, while Maddy, seeing his mother raise three fingers behind her back, pulled the hatpin from his pocket, bit his lip, and jabbed his baby sister three times in her milk-white thigh. Adella shrieked, and her face turned beet red as the foul odor of excrement wafted over the patrols. "Always carry a hatpin!" remained one of the Hunt women's most pragmatic maxims.

Mariah Hunt was certain that even if the threat of pox didn't deter them, this would, so as sweet as pie she said, "If you'd hold my baby for a minute, I'll climb down and . . ." Young men (pretty much all men, Mariah believed) hated nothing as much as a putrid, screeching infant, and Adella smelled worse and bawled louder than any baby the Spinkses had ever encountered.

So as his brothers guffawed, Ike snorted, "Pee-yew, whudda stink!" and waved them on, muttering, "Aw right, nevuh min'! 'Spose nuttin's up in yer wagon whu' shudden be dare. Be on yer way." Mariah picked up the reins and clucked to her mules. Her tormenters didn't notice the rust-colored drips that trailed behind the wagon as they rolled westward down the red-clay road.

Early that day a post rider had stopped at Fortitude and told J. M. Hunt about the previous night's "darkies revolt," so he'd hitched up his buggy and driven into Sparta. He was suspicious and ready, if need be, to take charge of Susan's twenty-seven-year-old "boy" Jimmy Hunt—whom she'd named for him. J. M. thus was long gone when Mariah and her children arrived.

A neighbor also informed Susan that she'd heard that Hancock's sitting trial judge wanted J. M. Hunt to serve on the jury that would try "them villainous niggers" for their part in what newspapers around Georgia began calling "The Great Darky Conspiracy in Sparta."

As word of the aborted uprising spread around that morning, Judge Sayre's brother, Robert, wondered if his own son, Johnny Watkins, might be in the thick of it, so he'd gone over to the courthouse square too but found that Johnny wasn't among those who'd been hauled in. Robert Sayre and J. M. ran into each other there and decided to head out to Fortitude together.

Susan Hunt efficiently doctored Johnny and Jimmy, and Adella's wound from the hatpin stabbing wasn't serious; so Susan told her daughter, "Take the little ones home, but stick to the old logging roads, because J. M.'s probably on his way back and I don't know what he might do if you ran into him." By late afternoon, Mariah had transported her children to Hunts' Hill again.

Susan's patients were dozing in Fortitude's hayloft when J. M. Hunt stormed in. He spotted the fugitives right away, and Robert Sayre helped him drag them from their roost. They stripped them naked, jerked their hands above their heads, and lashed them to an iron chain screwed into an overhead beam. J. M. pulled down his bullwhip from a wall peg and uncoiled it.

Then J. M.—usually a gentle soul who'd almost never beaten either his slaves or his animals—began brutally whipping the young men as he cussed and sobbed, "You black ingrates. (*Thwack!*) This is how you repay us when we treat you decent, let you live like white men (*Thwack!*), teach you to read and write, and let you own land, guns, and horses. (*Thwack!*) But remember this: you're still just a coupla goddamn nigger bastards. (*Thwack!*) 'Specially you, Jimmy Hunt, you mongrel devil. You tarnished my good name too. (*Thwack!*)"

As J. M. bellowed out his vicious litany, his mules brayed and tried to kick through their stalls. The air grew even fouler when the cousins' bowels erupted and emptied. Blood coursed down their backs, splattered Robert Sayre, J. M., and Susan, and pooled like glue under their feet.

"Don't you want to get in some licks on your boy?" J. M. panted, holding out the bloody strap. But Robert already had regurgitated his last meal as he'd watched J. M. lay on more than fifty cruel strokes, heard the whip's whistle, snap, and splat, Jimmy and Johnny's howls, and smelled their sour piss and feces. They frightened him far less than did J. M.'s savagery.

Finally, Robert protested, "I understand your anger, J. M., but you have to quit this right now, 'cause we both know you don't want to kill these scoundrels." Dripping with their gore, excrement, and his own sweat, J. M. flung down the whip and stormed over to the main house.

Robert and Susan untied the young men. She covered their nakedness, then said, "Take one of our horses, Mr. Robert, and head back to Pomegranate Hall. I'll deal with the mess here."

Susan didn't rest at all after sending Robert home. "The posse's bullets only had passed through my guys' flesh," she told Adella, "and hit no bones or vital organs, but their skin was sliced up with those raw slave stripes that looked like the burning bush spread across their backs. I gave them feverwort and pennyroyal for the pain and poisons, and valerian mixed with willow bark shavings that I'd steeped in some of J. M.'s home brew so they could get a little sleep."

She lit a lantern, took a spade, went out to Fortitude's graveyard, and dug for an hour until she'd unearthed two skulls. Susan asked all of the ancestors' forgiveness, because she couldn't tell if they belonged to the white Hunts or the people they claimed to own. Then she yoked a pair of oxen to J. M.'s Conestoga wagon, roped a cow to the back, lashed a cage of hens on one side, stowed her medicines and fishing gear beneath the front seat, and stuck a Bowie knife in her belt. Under the tarpaulin she stashed an iron spider, coffee pot and skillet, hardtack, oats, dried fruit, bacon, corn, and yams for her passengers, herself, and the animals. Susan loaded Jimmy's rifle and her own, made travel bunks for her patients, tucked her blankets over them, and set out before J. M. even arose the next morning. She was transporting her cargo westward to the Union lines.

"I made myself out to be a crazy Cherokee (which I was), going to join my tribe in the Oklahoma Territory (which I probably wasn't), because lots of the Injuns out there were fighting with or for the Secesh," Susan continued. "Johnny Watkins wasn't all that dark, but he did look colored; so I lied and claimed I owned him, since some of the Cherokees—yes, my own people—kept Negro slaves back then. If a patrol stopped me, I'd say I'd whipped Johnny because he was lazy, mouthy, and kept running away. I hid my son, Jimmy, who looked white, under the canvas tarp until we got out of Georgia, where the militias were trying to track us down and telegraphing around descriptions of the 'darky desperadoes' who'd escaped. I lashed the skulls I'd dug up to the front staves, so my message came through loud and clear: they'd been scalped," she laughed. "I'd done it before, and I'd do it again if someone made me angry enough."

"One nosy patrol," she continued, "asked how I expected to cross the Mississippi since the Yanks controlled that whole stretch of river, but I told him, 'I'll find me a friendly ferry captain, sonny,' and bragged (really, I lied) that I planned to join our Georgia-born-and-bred 'Stand Fast' Watie, the South's only Cherokee colonel, out in the Oklahoma Territory." The "nigger hatin'" Col. Stanhope Watie was leading the South's First Indian Brigade of the Army of the Trans-Mississippi. The Rebels soon promoted him to general, and later he became the last Confederate officer anywhere to lay down his sword—three whole months after Appomattox.

Southerners still used the Native names for many of their settlements and waterways, and Susan Hunt passed over the crude plank bridges that spanned the Ocmulgee, Tallapoosa, Tombigbee, and Pelahatchee Rivers and skirted remote towns called Chehaw, Tuskegee, and more.

"I don't know how long it took me to cross western Georgia, Alabama, and Mississippi," Susan went on, "but after Moon Woman twice cycled down to a sliver, I asked directions from some crackers who looked too dimwitted to know what was going on, and they said, 'Yes'm, yer gittin' near tuh Vicksburg.' By the time I reached the big river, my guys were well healed."

The young men bid Susan farewell and volunteered to fight for the Union. Johnny Watkins enlisted in a Louisiana regiment composed of *créoles de couleurs libres,* while her son, Jimmy, joined the Yankees' Army of the

Tennessee as a white man. His enlistment form also noted an anomaly. It read "age: 27 / ht. 6′ 1″ / wt. 160," but under "color of eyes" the examiner printed, "right: gray / left: brown." That phenomenon was quite common in the Hunt family.

"Injuns and colored folks call it 'the evil eye,'" Adella's grandmother frowned as she retold the old legend, "because it's supposed to signify that a while back a white fella had raped one of our colored women. When some people see it, they make a fist with their thumb stuck up between the first two fingers, hop three times on their left foot, then spit in the dirt to ward off the curse. I don't believe in most omens and didn't care what Jimmy claimed to be, because I'd saved my young men. And I knew that they'd help the Yanks win the war and free the slaves."

Susan sat in her wagon staring out at the muddy river and thought about crossing it to join the "Injuns" in the Oklahoma Territory, although she'd heard that like Col. Watie, those western Cherokees supported "the Secesh" too. Her staples nearly were gone, but she hadn't broken an axle or lost a cotter pin. Her hens were laying, so she didn't have to toss them into a stew pot, and she still could net fish. So she yoked up her oxen again and turned back east.

The insurrectionists' trial in Sparta had both started and ended quickly, and J. M. Hunt did indeed serve as a juror. He and the other men held that the uprising had occurred because "them bad boys" had been allowed to move about freely, "almost like citizens." Abel McGee was killed in the raid itself, another conspirator died during the trial from "a hard cough and the bloody flux," and three more were sentenced to be "hanged by the neck until dead, dead, dead."

County officials returned the rest of them to their owners for punishment. Slow Joe Cain, who'd tipped off the authorities (one of Sparta's wags joked, "Cain rose up an' slew his brother Abel!"), was deemed "a good example for the darkies"; so the judge pardoned him, while white Georgians remained on the lookout for "them notorious free niggers what excaped." Mariah told her daughter that after the trial she'd seen three black men's severed heads impaled on spikes at the nearby crossroads, awaiting the buzzards. That gruesome display warned slaves and other people of color who passed by to avoid any future waywardness—or face the consequences.

Susan had been gone for four months when near dusk on a cold February day, J. M. Hunt trudged home from fox hunting and saw someone pumping water from his icy well. At first, he thought it was a vagabond or military deserter, because the tall "stranger" was filthy and rail thin, and he'd begun to doubt (although Mariah never did) that Susan ever would return. The silence that divided them dragged on as Susan Hunt remained at Fortitude, but not in J. M.'s bedroom.

Late that summer, General William Tecumseh Sherman's Union forces swarmed from Tennessee into Georgia. The Confederate ranks were thinning fast. Food was in short supply, and brawls, wildfire strikes, and desertions abounded. Governor Joe Brown released a horde of vicious white inmates from the state penitentiary to buttress the depleted regulars and pressed black men into service as body servants and to perform the most arduous maintenance.

In early November 1864, Sherman's bluecoats besieged and burned Atlanta, then began slogging southeast toward the Atlantic, following rutted dirt roads and stream beds, wrenching out railroad tracks, torching houses, fields, and ginneries, gobbling up everything they laid their hands on. Georgia's capital, Milledgeville, was the next major plum for the Yankees to pluck.

Those troops marched into Milledgeville the last week in the month. (President Lincoln recently had designated that Thursday as a national day of thanksgiving.) Dark-skinned women greeted them with tears and hymns of gratitude; but in the Yanks' eyes, Georgia's poor whites seemed little better off than the blacks, and they guffawed about the "moral turnip-tude" of the "cracker gals" who "spread they legs" to swap what little they had to offer for whisky or snuff.

After leaving the capital city in shambles, the bluecoats headed east through Hancock. A few rode mules or slouched atop caissons and supply wagons, but more trudged along on foot. White Georgians tried to put the fear of God into the black youngsters by warning, "Them Yanks is devils with horns, cloven hoofs and fork-id tails. They'll slice you pickaninnies' greasy black ears right off, fry 'em in a skillet, then gobble 'em up like breakfast bacon." But many of the weary northerners who limped through Georgia seemed little more than children themselves.

The following spring the decimated South surrendered, and whatever Rebel soldiers who could do so began slogging home. "When your daddy came back to us two months after Appomattox," Adella's mother told her, "he was bitter, half starved, and almost white haired."

He returned to find a gabby, dark-eyed, dark-haired toddler and custom ordered for her—directly from France—an Old Paris porcelain cocoa cup rimmed with gold leaf. Glazed on one side in ornate letters encircled by a laurel wreath, also in gold, was her name: Adella Hunt.

Both Adella's mother and her cousin Neppie shared their memories of the Hunts' post-war shindig. On a hot July Saturday in '65, the white clan, almost two hundred of the people they'd enslaved, and a variety of the county's few, formerly free people of color gathered at Nancy's Fancy, Judkins and Rebecca Hunt's plantation.

Sherman's men had raided many of Hancock's homes and farms, but since the Hunts mostly lived in the north county, they'd missed the worst of it; so they butchered, bought, or borrowed all they needed to pull together a major collation. Mouthwatering aromas filled the air as oxen and whole hogs turned, sizzled, and browned on long iron spits throughout the night before, and the Stars and Bars and Bonnie Blue flags fluttered atop poles set out around the yard.

"The servants arranged linen-covered tables under the elms and tupelos, fanned away the 'skeeters, and toted over extra pillows if the white folks demanded more comfort," Mariah said. "My sister-in-law Rebecca snapped out orders to the women in her kitchen. They fried everything they could, churned ice cream, and baked Robert E. Lee lemon cakes next to Nancy's Fancy's first and second cooks, Emma Hunt and her daughter—that's our cousin Molly." "Both of those pretty ladies," Mariah winked, "huddled up extra close to your Uncle Judkins."

The former slaves rang the same plantation bell that used to summon them to work each morning, then for grub, and again at bedtime. The white people dined first, served from silver platters offered by the servants, then the field workers ate yams, chitlins, and cracklins heaped on johnnycakes and watermelon laid out on the old wooden trenchers. The musicians strummed their banjos, clapped, and jigged (as expected), and the buglers tooted as Judkins Hunt played his fiddle with them and strutted around his plantation domain crowing like a king-sized rooster.

"It seemed as if half of Hancock was related, and most of us went out to Judkins's place for that post-war jamboree," Mariah recalled. In addition to the older children, Adella's parents took her to the picnic. She was just two and a half years old but always claimed to remember the epic event. Susan alone flatly refused to attend, although after the South's surrender, J. M. finally apologized and promised, "I'll always take care of you and your children, darlin'." Then she returned to the big bedroom and once again became J. M.'s Black-Eyed Susan.

Several ministers preached the Gospel, praised the Lord, and thanked Him for their deliverance. Rev. C. P. Beman spoke to and for the Presbyterians, while Rev. Lucius Holsey came over from his humble new Ebenezer Church on the far side of Sparta. He mounted a platform that the former slaves had hammered together amid the black, brown, tan, and white Hunts and exhorted his impromptu congregants, "Yea, we marched through a long dark valley, facing down the Four Horsemen of pestilence, war, famine, and death. But thanks to our faith in Thee, oh Lord, we've come through it unbowed and better for all our travails. Amen, amen."

As the son of a white planter and a woman whom he'd claimed as property, the reverend contended that "the way that 'malgamation's been brought about in Georgia is enough to make the savages in the jungles of Africa blush with shame!" Such statements made Sparta's whites uncomfortable, but they lauded him anyway as a "worthy darky" when he echoed their beliefs by preaching that "slavery was a blessing in disguise to me and many others, because it made our race what we never could have been in our native land." An undying faith in Jesus, "my Lord and savior" (Rev. Holsey raised his right hand), and donating a few pennies to his church each week while leading hardworking, sin-free lives were the best answers to their ongoing travails.

The whole clan wept that steamy afternoon for the three hundred white Hancock County men who'd been among the myriad bodies shoveled into the gaping furnace of war, though far more Confederate soldiers died from cholera, measles, and the bloody flux than from any bluecoats' bullets or swords. The old geezers debated "our very own" Vice President Alexander Stephens's role in negotiating the peace—as well as his pending trial and imprisonment.

The white attendees shared their relief that Judkins Hunt's "brave brother 'Big Henry'" and most of the local men who'd fought with the Rebs had returned alive but often suffering mightily, many with black eye patches and empty sleeves, hobbling on crutches, or itching and twitching for opium. And a few of them still complained about how Adella's uncle "Jimmy Pale Face" and "that treacherous Watkins boy"—their fathers "white gentlemen" and their mothers "mongrel wenches"—had been "ringleaders in that nigger plot to ravage us all."

Hancock County, Georgia's white folks remained surly and mistrustful, and many suspected, but none knew for sure, that the "notorious pair" had slipped away thanks to their ties to "them uppish free colored Hunts." That weekend and for years to come, they ranted about how "that black-hearted redskin Granny Susan prob'ly conjured up the whole nasty bidness."

The Hunts, Albrights, Sayres, Watkinses, Holseys, Bemans, and more offered yet another prayer for Rebecca Albright Hunt's martyred niece Laura Jane, the South's first woman (and a virgin too) "to die for our noble cause," as the curtain fell on their War of Northern Aggression—though, of course, it really never ended at all.

F O U R

School Days

WERE IT NOT FOR THE STORIES TOLD by others, Adella would have recalled little about the war, but she knew it had cost millions of lives, divided families, generated epic losses of property, prestige, and power that had benefited the Old South's elite—and also that a crazed secessionist had assassinated the president who'd ultimately insisted that slavery must not divide the nation. Government-sanctioned bondage had been stifled, the country was nominally whole again, and those Hunts who considered themselves "colored" hoped that they and others like them who, as they often were told, "lacked the blessings of whiteness," finally would be treated as equals.

The Hunt plantations had been among King Cotton's sturdiest anchors, as were thousands of similar endeavors, and continued to provide whites in that family with most of their declining income. And the cotton still had to be sowed, chopped, picked, ginned, and baled, food raised, animals tended, buildings erected, property maintained and cleaned, meals prepared and served, clothes sewn and laundered, children reared, but all of that work was now done by nonslave labor.

Before and during the war, even Adella's father, the least affluent Hunt brother, had held thirty people as chattel. White Georgians' certitude that one person could own another, much as they owned livestock, houses, and acreage, had made Mariah's blood boil, but she had no say about who labored in Henry Hunt's fields or tannery. She oversaw her home, had four children, with more to come, and a husband who tried to shield her from the white folks who called their marriage "an abomination." To ease her life and labors, a laundress, a cook, and a yard-and-stable man who'd once worked at Pomegranate Hall performed much of the more arduous domestic work, while Mariah tried as best she could to oversee "the help's" financial and personal affairs.

Mariah Hunt had grown up in that mansion built and serviced by the dark-skinned people whom the whites in her family had held in perpetual bondage, but thanks to her father, Judge Nathan Sayre, she and her siblings had enjoyed privileges that exceeded those of virtually any other children of color in Georgia and many white ones too. After the war, state laws no longer specified that educating them was a crime, although their small portion of "black blood" still determined their legal and social standing. Eager to make the best of their limited opportunities, Adella's mother and grandmother Susan made it clear to her: "Learning will empower you."

Even as slavery stumbled into the past, the county's white folks continued dragging their feet and for three years provided no formal education for the thousands of black children there, while state lawmakers decreed, "the white and negro races shall not be taught together in our schools." Then in mid-1868, a white Yankee named R. W. Gladding arrived in Hancock as an agent of the federal Freedmen's Bureau, which had been charged with the mission of facilitating the South's Reconstruction. Soon he began teaching in a tumbledown stable that he'd mucked out, patched up, and furbished, and he called his humble facility the Sparta Institute for Negroes.

In his first year, Mr. Gladding enrolled seventy students ranging in age from five, like Adella, to sixty, and in appearance from those who resembled their African ancestors to the small minority such as the "look-jes'-like-white" Hunts. He kept his school open eight hours a day, twenty-five days a month, including some Sundays, when the adults crowded in after church to fill his benches, wrestle with their ABCs, and learn a little basic arithmetic so that they might equip themselves to hold their own with the white landholders for whom they tenant farmed or sharecropped, Sparta's predatory merchants, and the well-to-do matrons in the homes where they still cleaned and laundered, prepared and served meals, and nursed, soothed, or scolded the children.

The Freedmen's Bureau soon opened two more schools in Hancock, although given the thousands of black children in the county, relatively few could attend. Of those who did, many arrived barefoot and in rags, covered with rashes, sores, and scabs. And unlike the handful who lived in modest comfort on Hunts' Hill, most of Adella's new classmates couldn't bathe or clean their teeth, because their hovels had no plumbing, running water, wells, or latrines. They had to squat in the fields or creeks and share their homes with poultry, swine, and vermin, received virtually no medical care, and often ate worse than their parents had during their interminable enslavement.

Then late one night about a year after Mr. Gladding arrived in Sparta, the clatter of retreating hoof beats and a pungent, waxy odor intruded on his sleep. He awoke to crackles, surges of heat, and garish flickers cast by the angry flames that were engulfing a cotton-wrapped, kerosene-soaked ten-foot wooden cross that had been set ablaze between his bungalow and the schoolhouse as a warning to him "an' any othuh meddlin' damn-Yankee Republicans, scalawags, an' carpetbaggers wut's givin' ar darkies dang'rous notions." He, his students, and their families somehow extinguished the threatening bonfire with few injuries and little loss of property.

The Ku Klux Klan, which instigated the attack, first had raised its head in neighboring Tennessee soon after the war ended, then surged outward like a plague of locusts. A majority of the South's half-million hate-spewing Klansmen were ignorant white people who resorted to such barbarism because they feared that "our niggers" no longer would be confined to society's bottommost ranks, "where they belonged." Many other overtly estimable, comfortably situated, collaborating white supremacists, however, financed those efforts and avidly spurred on the night riders, whom they often accompanied with menacing chants of "White men rule!"

One day soon thereafter, Mr. Gladding sloshed down the road in a rainstorm holding an umbrella for the elderly black woman who cooked and cleaned for him, but several lowlifes interpreted that civil gesture as a heinous breach of racial protocols. The next morning, a posse of hooded Klansmen blasted shotgun fire into the Sparta Institute. Adella's fellow students shrieked and bolted through the door as the blackguards snatched up their teacher, trussed him like a porker they were readying to spit-roast, and dragged him to the fishpond in the courthouse square, where they dunked his head under the murky water until he retched and gasped for air. As soon as Georgia was readmitted to the Union, R. W. Gladding packed up and fled, and the despised (by white southerners) Freedmen's Bureau shut down its "nigger schools" for good.

Adella's earliest formal education had taken place amid such enmity, but then, like all youngsters of her designated race in Sparta, she no longer had any school to attend. Her mother, however, knew from her own rare antebellum tutelage how critical a first-rate teacher could be, so she badgered her husband until he agreed to seek a solution in his brother Judkins's household.

Judkins's younger daughter, Penelope Albright Hunt, a twenty-three-year-old spinster who was known by everyone in Hancock as Miss Neppie, already had been teaching girls in the county for six years. Mariah hardly knew and never liked Neppie Hunt, yet had to agree with the majority of local folks who insisted that she was "smart as a whip and a dandy schoolmarm."

Yielding to his wife's insistence, one autumn afternoon, Adella's father finished working at his tannery, scrubbed his reeking body clean, re-dressed himself, and hoisted his daughter into their Georgia chariot. They set off from Hunts' Hill for Nancy's Fancy, the sprawling plantation where Judkins Hunt and his family lived—although Judkins's wife, Rebecca, always disdained her brother-in-law's support of his "colored wife and their houseful of tykes." She called them "Henry's mongrel curs." "Those folks think too much of themselves and refuse to accept their proper place," Rebecca Albright Hunt sneered. In that instance, she was absolutely right.

Henry coaxed his mule into Nancy's Fancy's turnaround and tethered him to his brother's grinning, cast-iron black jockey hitching post—Judkins loved everything to do with horses. "Big Henry" clambered down from the wagon and knocked. When a servant answered, he asked to speak with his niece. Summoned by her father, Neppie cracked open the door and squinted out.

"I see you hiding in there," Henry smiled, then pointed to his wagon. "Well, this here's my daughter, Adella. She's your cousin, and she's the one who pesters us with all these gosh-durned questions we're hard-pressed to answer. Mariah and I try to explain the Secesh, war, politics, and such to her, but she always wants to know more. Keeps asking us 'why?' There's no school in Hancock for her now, so please, won't you teach her some of your book learning?'"

He'd scarcely finished that entreaty when Neppie turned on her heel and slammed the door. Adella, however, was relieved, since several of her former schoolmates whom her Uncle Judkins previously had held as his slaves called Neppie Hunt "the nastiest bitch in Georgia."

One afternoon each week for the next month, "Big Henry" reassumed his stance on his brother's verandah and repeated, "It's only this one, my second girl, that I'm asking you to teach, Neppie dear. She's sharp as a tack. I promise she'll work real hard and she's your own blood too," although his niece grew increasingly agitated as he carried on about their "common blood."

Judkins Hunt didn't openly criticize his younger brother's living arrangement, though he didn't understand it either, since Henry actually had married Mariah. But his own cook, Molly Hunt, who was just a year older than Neppie, had been born and still lived right there at Nancy's Fancy. Everyone knew that she was Judkins's "outside child" by his former slave Emma.

Even in his late fifties, Molly and Neppie's father continued his prodigal ways: gambling on horse races and cockfights, shooting craps, playing high-stakes poker as he drifted into debt. Judkins smoked cigars, guzzled rye whiskey, and often reeled out of Sparta's Old Eagle Tavern stinking like a pig sty after wild bacchanalias during which he fiddled away and joined in bawdy songfests. Then most Saturday nights, he hightailed it up to Emma Hunt's cottage on The Hill.

On yet another afternoon when Neppie returned home after her usual teaching day, she minced over to the front door, where her uncle Henry once again had rapped to announce himself. But this time she opened it, pressed her clenched fists onto her fleshy hips, glared, "harrumphed," and said, "I don't suppose you'll ever give up on all this folderol, will you, Uncle Henry?"

Henry shook his head, "No, my dear niece, I promise you, I'll not give up."

So Neppie pursed her thin lips and sighed, "Well then, bring her 'round to the kitchen."

Dressed in her best cambric frock and a striped pinafore, Adella stood by the rear door, untied and removed her poke bonnet, and stared down at the buckled shoes her father had made.

First, Neppie asked if she could read, and Adella mumbled, "Yes, ma'am."

Neppie snapped her fingers: "Look here and *e-nun-ci-ate* when you answer me, girl."

So Adella redirected her eyes upward and carefully repeated, "Yes, ma'am."

Her grandmother often said, "Stand up straight and look them right in the eye."

"I hear your mamma plays the piano real well. Is that right?" Neppie demanded.

White folks in Hancock County snickered into their sleeves when that subject arose, but few knew how or why Adella's mother and aunt had studied at Sparta's Female Academy long before the war. Its rosters never listed them or specified that they were "free colored girls" or even confirmed that they'd taken music lessons there with the headmaster's understanding that his school would benefit from the counsel and largesse of their affluent father, Nathan Sayre.

"The Steinweg piano that Judge Sayre bought for Mamma in Germany sits in our parlor. She and her sister play it and Aunt Sue Rose's French harp almost every day," Adella explained.

"And do you play an instrument?" Neppie persisted.

"I play the piano, but just a little."

"Your father says you ask too many questions for a child. Is that true?" she continued.

"I do ask lots of questions," Adella blundered on, "and my Granny Susan says it's . . ."

"Don't ever mention that heathen conjure woman. Do you hear me?" Neppie interrupted.

Adella glumly replied, "Yes, ma'am, I hear you."

Thus, the eight-year-old embarked on her education "of a private nature."

After her lessons finished, Adella would leave by way of Nancy's Fancy's rear door and head back to Hunts' Hill around twilight when she was bone tired and hungry as a bear.

"What did she teach you today?" Adella's mother often prodded as her daughter slurped hot cocoa from the precious Old Paris porcelain cup that was decorated with her name in gold.

Sometimes, Adella fibbed a little and said, "Miss Neppie didn't teach me very much."

"Is Nancy's Fancy pretty inside?" Mariah pressed on.

"Yes, it's beautiful," Adella sighed, although for some time she actually saw only the back porch and the kitchen where she and her white cousin-tutor toiled away with pens, ink, and composition tablets, chalk on a slate board, and books strewn across the oak table. Neppie also insisted that Adella always buckle up her shoes and wear stockings, because she must never let a man see her bare feet, and urged her to keep a bonnet on whenever she went outside. "Or," she warned, "carry a parasol to keep your skin pretty and fair by shading it from the sun."

At Judkins's insistence, their cook, Molly, still slept in a cramped room next to the pantry and prepared the white folks' meals. Rebecca Hunt had dismissed Molly's mother, Emma, soon after the war, but when Neppie appropriated her half sister's culinary domain as a classroom, Molly scowled, cut her eyes, rattled her iron skillets to the back of the stove, and strode out of "her" kitchen. She was offended that Adella, her own "light-skinned-but-still-colored" cousin, would be invited to Nancy's Fancy as Neppie's student, almost a guest, while she remained one of the family's servants. Adella really didn't know what to say to her cousin Molly.

A year after Adella began those lessons, Neppie ushered her into the parlor and directed her to sit at the grand piano. She couldn't read music at all and knew only a few compositions by heart. But soon Neppie introduced Adella to her own favorite Old South songs with their "doo-dah, doo-dah" refrains about the "jolly, banjo-strummin' slaves" and others such as "Bonnie Blue Flag" and "Dixieland," which, she said, "always heartened our valiant troops."

"Did you know that my uncle 'Big Henry'—that's your daddy, of course—and a bunch of my brave Albright cousins fought for the Confederacy to save us from Lincoln's Raiders and keep us free like God and the Founding Fathers intended?" Neppie asked.

"So I've heard, Miss Neppie," Adella said—but wondered whose freedom she meant.

She also listened to Neppie's accounts of the War for Independence and learned that their mutual Hunt great-grandfather had been an officer with the Patriots in Virginia. Neppie further told Adella that she admired "the 'civilized' Indians, because I'm partly descended, on my mother's side—the Albrights—from the princess Pocahontas and her English savior, John Rolfe."

Miss Neppie insisted, "Back in the old days the Hunts treated our darkies well. They tried not to separate the pickaninnies from their mammas, never let them go hungry, rarely used the whip, and taught them to love our Jesus." "But since the war," she ranted on, "the nigrahs have become malingering pig thieves. They put on airs, and now they're reverting to a condition of savagery like they once knew over in Africa." Adella, however, knew no such black savages.

Then Neppie Hunt looked skyward and intoned, "Georgia's was the word and theirs the will to die." That was her doleful signature phrase, but Adella didn't yet fathom its meaning.

Neppie taught Adella on the afternoons when she walked in smiling but also when she arrived biting her lip not to cry, as she did the day after she'd learned that a white thug had cudgeled Ida Watkins, one of her favorite little cousins. With Mariah Hunt's assistance, Ida's father had written Eli Barnes, their new black Reconstruction state representative, *My girl Idas head was beet into jelly & her arm cut down to the bone.* But everyone in Hancock County knew that, as Mr. Watkins further wrote Representative Barnes, *Thare will be nothing dun.*

And Adella learned more from her tutor than just the old Rebel songs. Neppie made her execute scales and fingering exercises and pulled out sheet music to teach her classical etudes. She rapped her knuckles or switched her slender calves with a willow cane if her fingers didn't dance nimbly enough and assigned a daily hour of practice at home. Within a couple of years, Adella's uncle Judkins came in when she and Neppie sat side by side and played increasingly ambitious duets with increasing proficiency. Judkins applauded, "Bravo, girls!" unlatched his instrument case, pulled out and tuned up his fiddle, and rosined his bow to accompany them.

Adella's cousin Neppie sometimes sent her home with books that her father had purchased at the auction of Judge Sayre's estate—Mariah was so happy to see them again. Neppie also spent ample time teaching about "our great American legacy, including the Constitution," which she called "the noblest of all documents, though flawed by recent amendments." Together they read history, poetry, Andersen's fairy tales, Jane Austen's novels, and more. Adella hardly faulted Neppie for excluding Harriet Beecher Stowe's *Uncle Tom's Cabin,* which was reviled throughout the white South. She also didn't know Phillis Wheatley's poetry and certainly hadn't read the words of a giant such as Frederick Douglass. Adella herself only learned years later about those epic writings by those whom, despite her family's mixed racial ancestry, her own misleading appearance, and her rather privileged life, she always considered her own people.

Neppie also shared legends about the Greek gods, with their flying horses and three-headed monsters, but especially their pantheon of heroines. She informed her younger cousin that "Athena was the goddess of wisdom" and asked, "Why did my namesake, Penelope, weave and then unravel her funeral shroud?" Neppie, who'd attended the Sparta Female Academy and thus had a better education than her parents, uncles, or most other people in the county, introduced Adella to William Shakespeare's plays, then she demanded, "Could Portia have been a real lawyer?" and "Why would Queen Cleopatra press that deadly asp to her breast?"

"Don't ever sass me, girl," Neppie wagged her finger as she warned, "and listen carefully to what I say. If I'm in error, respectfully challenge my flawed reasoning. Always hear out others, but think for yourself. Learning should be your true religion and lifelong adventure."

To sharpen Adella's wits Neppie introduced her to palindromes, such as "Madam, I'm Adam" and "Live not on evil," and other word games too. "Quickly now," she'd snap, "give me five anagrams for 'stop.'" Soon, Adella nimbly answered, "opts, post, pots, spot, tops."

Her brain was awhirl as she arrived at Nancy's Fancy one afternoon, confronted her tutor, and said, "Here's my own anagram, Miss Neppie: Adella Hunt. Without 'Athena' I'd be 'dull.'"

Neppie hesitated for a moment, then a smile creased her moony face. "That's right, Adella Hunt, you are indeed 'Athena' and never one bit 'dull.'" She made daunting demands but also lauded her private student's accomplishments and sometimes called her "my Athena."

Stuffed like sausage meat into whale-boned bodices, Neppie mostly taught Adella from her books, while Susan, wearing calicoes and loose denims, shared her own never-written-down stories that she'd heard from the black people and the Cherokees. Her granddaughter believed that Susan Hunt was the wisest person in the world, though she'd had no formal education at all.

"I could teach you to read and write, Granny," Adella offered soon after she turned nine.

Susan smiled and said, "No thank you, my precious, but the Judge and his sister, Della, used to read to me. Maybe now you'll do the same. Would you like that?"

Indeed, Adella would like that, and that's exactly what she did.

When Susan introduced her to lore about "my mother's Cherokee tribe," the Bird Clan, and shared stories about "Our People" who'd grown wings on their shoulders, risen, and soared off on the tropic winds to escape their bondage, Adella dreamed that she too could fly.

Susan Hunt knew nothing of Neppie's Greek gods but all about the Cherokees' Raven Mocker and Moon Woman, who circled the heavens and made herself as round as a pumpkin or slim as a blade of grass. She told Adella about mean Br'er 'Gator and sassy Br'er Rabbit, who jumped into the briar patch, and sometimes evoked her "Injun" kin who'd been forced to trek westward for years—starving and half frozen, their tongues swelling and skulls shrinking.

In a small, velvet-lined image case she placed next to the Sayre family Bible, Adella's mother kept the daguerreotype taken at her wedding, of her silver-eyed, silver-haired father.

"I believe your grandpa looked a lot like Jesus, my Lord and savior," Mariah sighed.

Adella shared that story with her grandmother, who laughed until she cried. When Susan wiped her eyes, Adella said, "Mamma prays for you, Granny, but she's afraid you're going to burn in hell because you weren't baptized. I know that Rev. Beman sprinkled Mamma when she was a little girl, but last Sunday our own Rev. Holsey dunked her all the way under in his pond, so now she'll find life everlasting in the loving arms of Jesus, who died on the cross for our sins."

Shaking her head, Susan assured Adella, "I don't want to live forever in Jesus's arms, my precious, and I promise you, no white man ever died for my sins, your mother's, or yours either."

Together they burrowed through the ancient burial mounds near the Hunts' graveyard by Shoulderbone Creek. From an arm's length underground Adella helped Susan scoop out cupsful of the soothing, medicinal white kaolin clay that the Cherokees called "unaker."

Her grandmother also taught her how to track wild game, and Adella shot a stag with her uncle J. M.'s carbine, which kicked back and almost fractured her shoulder. They split open its belly, extracted the entrails to burn as a sacrifice, sawed off the crown of antlers, and wall-mounted it as a rifle rack at Fortitude. Susan and her granddaughter stripped the pelt, butchered the carcass, tossed the bones and innards to the dogs, salted, smoked, and preserved the flesh.

"Now you've got it right," Susan hugged her and applauded. "Never waste anything!"

Adella helped her clean, shave, and knead the hides until they became as soft as velvet. Susan sliced one deerskin into twelve pieces, stitched six each together with horsehairs, sewed and inserted scarlet silk linings, and gave Adella those moccasins that fit like gloves on her feet.

She only wore them in the house and pulled on Susan's boots when she was learning to ride "like a Cherokee": straddling the pony, at first tumbling off more than she stayed on. When Adella scraped her elbows, her grandmother pressed cobwebs on the abrasions and rubbed away her aches with cool witch hazel. The girl also frequented her uncle's stables, barns, orchards, gardens, and fields. J. M. never let her sow, chop, or bag cotton alongside his black 'croppers, with their ragged clothes, scarred hands, and rheumy eyes, who rarely spoke in his presence, but he'd kneel down, grasp her shoulders, and say, "Remember this, Adella: you're a *real* Hunt!"

The local plants and soils supplied Susan with treatments for every known sickness of body, spirit, or mind. She and her favorite granddaughter picked fruits and vegetables and made pickles and all sorts of preserves. Adella printed the date and contents in ink on the paper labels that she pasted onto the containers, then lined them up alphabetically on Susan's pantry shelves.

Susan taught Adella about the region's hills, valleys, flora, and fauna, while Neppie continued as her "classroom" teacher. With a few notable exceptions such as the Sparta Female Academy, rural Georgia's schools for its white youngsters were fair at best, and Adella was certainly Hancock County's only nonwhite girl who was getting a first-rate education.

When Adella was twelve, an ad hoc committee composed of the local "'spectable colored folks" went, hats in hand, to persuade the county's "quality whites" that their youngsters needed a school again. With such a facility, the elders pleaded, they could improve their deportment, learn to be better cooks, house servants, and farmhands, even become teachers, preachers, or undertakers for their own. They persuaded those white men to help them launch an endeavor that would serve their community and named it the W. H. Bass Academy to honor the county's superintendent of education, who granted them use of a small plot of his land for the new facility.

Adella didn't leave Neppie's tutelage, but she also began attending the new Bass Academy, as did her precocious ten-year-old brother, named Henry for their father. And Susan Hunt, scolding her daughter about "too many babies for too many years," went up to Hunts' Hill to assist Mariah through labor and childbirth. Three younger children, Sarah, Ella, and finally Tommy, completed Mariah and "Big Henry's" family, and they too ultimately attended Bass.

Adella's older siblings, born before the war, had received no classroom schooling, though she could tell how smart they were. Maddy was sickly, but Will knew everything about fishing, hunting, and farming and could build or repair anything at all, while Lula gardened, baked, quilted, embroidered, told amazing stories, and read the Bible every day. But lacking any formal instruction, they never conquered the daunting conventions of English spelling and grammar.

As her uncle J. M. grew increasingly frail, Adella saw less of him and her grandmother but continued the lessons with her cousin Neppie Hunt. They were more challenging than most of what Bass Academy's "Professor" Richard Carter taught her. But he was certainly a good teacher, who'd recently graduated from Atlanta University, a new normal school and college dedicated to educating a very few, very fortunate students of color.

To help motivate his pupils, Mr. Carter invited friends such as his college buddy, the captivating Rev. Edgar Penney, to visit the Sparta school. He'd hold a copper coin between his thumb and forefinger, smile, wink at the youngsters who fell under his spell, and ask, "Do you want a little magic in your lives, boys and girls? If so, here's a *penny* for your thoughts."

They'd giggle and flap their hands in the air, trying to win his attention and his coin, then ooh and aah as it "magically" vanished, only to be extricated seconds later in a swirl of fingers from a lucky student's ear, mouth, sleeve, or pocket, as he slyly whispered, "Prestidigitation!"

Three years after the school bearing his name opened, Superintendent W. H. Bass examined two separate factions of the county's young people, and that summer, Sparta's weekly newspaper reported that "three white aspirants, Miss Bea Ella Ralston, Mr. Calvin Beman, and Mr. Judah Albright," and six "col'd" ones, including Adella (but not, of course, "Miss") Hunt, had been found qualified to teach. The following spring, she embarked on her first classroom teaching assignment: assisting Richard Carter at Bass Academy.

Adella knew she was his favorite, and he believed she'd benefit from further education; so he sent her name to William Jonathan Northen, an affluent and influential Hancock County planter. Eli Barnes, Sparta's black former representative who'd tried to help Adella's injured cousin Ida Watkins, recently had been accused, arrested, charged, and convicted of a trivial offense, and after Mr. Barnes was summarily removed from office, W. J. Northen succeeded him. Adella's teacher praised her in a note to Mr. Northen as "highly qualified to be appointed to attend Atlanta University."

Under a new statute's provisions, every Georgia county was entitled to have one full-tuition scholarship student matriculate each year at that school, although most of the state's white male legislators refused to nominate anyone at all to fill those slots.

Adella's future education also easily might've been sidetracked by the feud that began tearing her family apart when it became known that J. M. Hunt was preparing a will. At first, it was only rumored that J. M. planned to exclude his white relatives entirely and leave all of his assets to Susan Hunt and her descendants, but when Rebecca Albright Hunt heard that, she called her brother-in-law "stone-cold crazy." Also, she raged, "no mulatto bastards such as these ever have inherited an entire estate anywhere in our sovereign state of Georgia." True enough!

In his final months, J. M. deeded Susan a plot of land on Hunts' Hill, as the document of transfer specified: "in consideration of the services she rendered to me as my nurse." But soon thereafter, Susan told Adella, "your uncle shriveled up into a husk. His mind drifted away like curls of smoke, then one night he just forgot how to breathe."

At that juncture, Rebecca Albright Hunt threw down the gauntlet. She engaged legal counsel in the person of her nephew Thomas Jefferson Hunt Jr. (called Young Tom), one of central Georgia's up-and-coming lawyers, and they prepared to contest J. M.'s will.

Attorney Hunt assured his aunt Rebecca that "questions pursuant to J. M.'s testament and the inheritance should give the court no problems." But recalling Judge Sayre's admonition to "know the law and use the law" and in response to the white Hunts' challenge, Susan Hunt and her daughters retained the Judge's old law clerk and friend, attorney Charles du Bose.

Since J. M. recently had passed away, Adella worried that her grandmother might have to fend for herself at Fortitude. But Susan assured her that "J. M.'s people," the sharecroppers and tenant farmers who still worked the Hunt lands, "will see to my needs if I can't do for myself."

"And don't forget," Susan added, "you're the favorite daughter of a favorite daughter, the Judge's predestined grandchild—born exactly ten years after he died. Your grandfather Sayre would've insisted that you go off to that new college, because common sense and grit combined with book learning will always see you through. One day your good looks may fade, but for now I have to tell you, a pretty face can be a colored girl's curse. Be smart, not vain, my precious," she smiled, "and make sure that none of those randy fellas in Atlanta get you in the family way."

Adella blushed, shook her head, and promised not to let that happen.

Then Susan pulled out of a tiny jewel box and looped around her granddaughter's neck a delicate chain with a small, shiny disc threaded on it. It was a ten-franc gold coin, dated 1850. "This gift is from me to you, but before me, it came from the Judge himself, straight from Paris, France. And someday," Susan added to Adella's astonishment, "you might even get to read law like he did. Wouldn't that be quite something?" It would indeed.

Exhorted by his resolute daughter Neppie, Adella's uncle Judkins provided another endorsement of her quest for higher education. Representative W. H. Northen also knew that Adella had the solid backing of Sparta's "upright colored men" such as Rev. Lucius Holsey and her teacher Richard Carter, although few of them were able to cast ballots anymore as Reconstruction's very limited and fleeting liberalism ebbed and harsh (certainly for the South's black residents) Redemption took hold. Adella, however, recently had learned that her cousin and longtime tutor, Neppie Hunt, was denied the franchise too.

W. H. Northen then gave Adella's white father a note for her to hand-deliver to Atlanta University's Yankee president, Edmund Asa Ware. "Upon the certification of my constituents and her teacher," Mr. Northen had written, "I commend Adella Hunt to your instruction & free tuition." That endorsement formally confirmed her college admission and scholarship.

Trains, Rains, Pedagogy, and Savagery

ON A SEPTEMBER SUNDAY IN '79, ADELLA headed off to embark on the next chapter in her life. She and Amanda Dickson, another local woman, were driven to Sparta's depot, whence they'd depart for Atlanta University—though calling it a university at that time was, perhaps, an overstated presumption. It was, however, one of the region's most ambitious new institutes, normal schools, and colleges that provided solid academic training beyond the elementary level to a very limited number of "colored" southerners.

Amanda was the only child of David Dickson, Georgia's wealthiest cotton mogul, and a woman whom he'd previously enslaved. A decade earlier, Mr. Dickson had arranged his daughter's "marriage" to one of his white cousins, but she'd recently ditched that ne'er-do-well and returned with her sons to the Dickson plantation. David Dickson always wanted to give Amanda every possible advantage, so he sent her off to college at the age of thirty-one.

The steely monster carried them across iron-arched bridges, past cotton fields bare and spiky after the picking, by white-columned mansions and wretched 'croppers' shacks on its way to Atlanta, previously known as Terminus, because it was situated at the convergence of several rail lines. During the war, Sherman's troops and torches had ravaged the city, but the state capital relocated there in 1869, both because of its convenient rail access and also because a number of Milledgeville's white hoteliers, restaurateurs, and other public purveyors had flatly refused to service Reconstruction Georgia's unwelcome handful of black and tan representatives.

But the ladies from Sparta had little time to rest and quickly plunged into their new routine. Adella was somewhat peeved, because although her prior education outstripped that so far achieved by most of her new classmates, she learned that women could enroll only in the two-year normal program geared to preparing teachers, not the four-year "gentlemen's course." She yearned to tackle that more demanding curriculum and believed that teaching was her talent and mission, yet she also wanted to maintain the option of pursuing other professions. Some northerners of her sex, including a handful of her race, recently had embarked on rigorous training in medicine and law; but she feared those choices wouldn't be open to her with only a teaching degree, so she petitioned President Ware for admission to his full college program. Any challenges to authority were routinely tamped down, however, and he rejected her plea; so she accepted her fate and soldiered on, remaining optimistic about what she *could* accomplish at this fine institution.

The young ladies who enrolled in the "upper normal" program studied educational disciplines, literature, mathematics, Latin, French, history, civics, and sciences. They practice taught at an on-campus elementary school and also had to take classes in cookery, sewing, and nursing. When Georgia's education department's all-white, all-male Board of Visitors examined them on their expertise in the kitchen, one enthused, "I've never tasted better rolls, pies, cakes, and cookies, all baked by the girls themselves." Adella took pride in her culinary capabilities but bristled at the assumption that she was destined for and primarily suited to domestic pursuits.

"Simple gingham or wool dresses are the approved apparel for the girls," the school catalogue stipulated, adding that "satins, velvets, and costly jewelry are indicative neither of good taste nor good sense." Adella nonetheless always tucked the French gold coin on a chain that her grandmother had given her into her cotton shirtwaist. But in addition to the designated lace-up or buckled footwear (Adella's had been made in her father's cobblery), whenever possible, she slipped into the silk-lined deerskin moccasins that Susan Hunt had crafted for her.

The school's academic rigors and daunting parietal rules, however, thwarted Amanda Dickson. Her doting father already had paid to have a wood-burning fireplace installed in her private dormitory room, because, she'd complained, "the coal stove makes me terribly ill." But Amanda, who truly missed her sons, abandoned her formal education after less than a year and returned to Sparta. In the meantime, Adella made new friends, especially the spirited and very pretty Cora Calhoun, who often invited Adella to visit her family's gracious nearby home.

The autumn Adella arrived, Atlanta University had fewer than seventy pupils in its upper normal and baccalaureate programs combined. Among them were several fellows from the University of South Carolina, because during Reconstruction, when a majority of the state's voters were men of color, its public college had taught the races together. But resurgent white politicians had wrested control from the majority-black male electorate and barred the youngsters from further higher education there, so several of them transferred to the Atlanta school.

President Ware, who'd welcomed those out-of-state students, had graduated from Yale College less than twenty years before and adopted his alma mater's educational model for the new institution in Georgia. His faculty included Lucy Case, an inspiring English teacher; Horace Bumstead, who taught the sciences; and Rev. Cyrus Francis, who also was minister of the new, nearby First Congregational Church of Christ. Rev. Francis oversaw the school library, where, one Board of Visitors member scoffed, "the young Sambos can delve into the wisdom of the ages and learn about their cannibal sires in the African jungles. Yet whom are they indebted to for their civilization? The disparaged white slaveholder." Several religious and secular trusts and foundations and a number of northern donors helped fund Atlanta University, and the state legislature also grudgingly provided a little financial support. The school had been launched only a decade before Adella arrived, and to whatever extent President Ware and his all-white, all-Yankee faculty could do so, its student body incorporated all classes, colors, and religions.

The words "amalgamation" and "miscegenation," however, generated shudders among white southerners who were loath to acknowledge that the statutes prohibiting any "licentious interracial relations" often were violated, as were those that banned "mingling of the races in our classrooms."

But the school's administrators tried to circumvent those laws' racially separatist intent by insisting that the latter directive applied only to Georgia's public schools. "As a chartered institution," E. A. Ware insisted, "ours should remain exempt from such provisions."

Theirs also was the Deep South's only such "university" where the white faculty didn't maintain dining facilities separate from those of its "colored" student body. For every meal, eight youngsters sat around each oak table, where a professor presided. The school cook, whom everyone called Sergeant, was its sole black employee, since the students performed most of the serving, cleaning, and maintenance chores themselves to help defray the costs of their education.

Rev. Cyrus Francis taught history and government and also oversaw the spiritual lives of members of their community. Both the rigid Presbyterianism of Adella's white family and the "colored" Christian Methodist Episcopalians' seemingly blind assent that her mother and older sister embraced dissatisfied Adella, but she liked the Congregationalist ethos, which stressed morality and civic responsibility. Rev. Francis thus agreed to baptize her, and she joined his church.

Many white Atlantans ridiculed First Congregational as "Congo One" because of its majority-black parishioners. A number of Adella's classmates considered it far too priggish but still called it "Big Church." In addition to those at their school, Cora Calhoun's family and others like the photographer Thomas Askew also became members. Some such light-skinned Georgians had been "privileged" house slaves or were white men's out-of-wedlock offspring with women of color. They sometimes deemed themselves superior to the darker-skinned "field niggers," but shown the way by her mother and grandmother, Adella rejected such presumptions.

Georgia's governor, who'd previously argued that "negroes are an inferior race and we were right to have held them as slaves," had imposed rigorous examinations "to prove that we'd been right." Later, however, he recanted, admitting, "I was wrong and have been converted. These exercises dispelled my prior assumption that members of the African race are incapable of achieving any high degree of mental culture." But he was mortified when he had to concede that the scholarship at Atlanta University surpassed that which his Board of Visitors encountered at the state's all-white, all-male college. They compared the spotless facilities, rectitude, and intellectual rigor at the Atlanta school to the vandalism and obscenities scribbled on dormitory walls that confronted them in Athens and exhorted the latter's administrators to "limit your future classes to fewer respectful and industrious scholars instead of enrolling so many idlers."

When Adella Hunt practice taught, a few of her pupils were faculty children, who studied in the same classrooms as the darker-complexioned students. One evaluator carped, "Some fair-complected colored youngsters I saw there made me think that the school is racially mixed." He observed a few attendees (such as Adella) "who could pass for white anywhere" and advised that "those unfortunate girls should be designated 'Caucasian' and taken someplace like the West's mining camps, where the men aren't squeamish, wives are much in demand, and their identity with the children of Ham can be extinguished." The threat of western exile horrified Adella, and it rankled her that others might measure her worth solely as a marital appendage and further assumed that she wanted to "extinguish" her Negro identity. Her pale skin and support from white kin gave her a leg up, but "hard work and character, never color," her grandmother and mother insisted, took precedence. Such students were hardly alone at Atlanta University, however, and one white Visitor noted with surprise, "I observed a thick-lipped, sooty-skinned blackamoor that translated Latin, chopped logic and recited rhetoric with remarkable facility."

Whatever the students' physical characteristics, they were just a fortunate handful. Between the few northern "white" colleges that admitted a few of the race and the South's few and new "colored schools" that offered any curricula in higher education, scarcely two hundred all told had earned any such degrees. Their numbers didn't approach what later would be designated a Negro "Talented Tenth," a one-hundredth or, at first, even a privileged one-thousandth.

Adella's whole family came to Atlanta for her 1881 graduation. Her father wasn't doing well financially because cotton production had become less profitable since the war, and orders at his cobblery were dwindling as former customers began buying cheaper footwear that was being mass produced in northern factories. But in addition to taking a button-bursting pride in his favorite daughter's rare accomplishment, Henry Hunt wanted to attend because his old army comrade Chaplain Atticus Haygood would give Atlanta University's commencement address.

"Big Church," the ceremony's venue, filled to overflowing that morning with more than seven hundred alumni, faculty, students, and their families. Unlike such occasions at most of the South's public facilities (a recent ordinance had segregated Atlanta's streetcars, with black people shunted to the rear), where strict racial separation was becoming the rule, President Ware designated and reserved no discrete sections of the nave as preferred seating for whites.

Among the institution's financial supporters who came that day were a couple named Leo and Patience Bullock, who also sponsored an elementary school in Albany, Georgia. Adella Hunt had agreed to teach for them, having been exhorted to do so by her professor Lucy Case, who'd taught in that town prior to relocating to Atlanta. The Bullocks wanted to meet her, and before the ceremonies began, Mrs. Case introduced them. Patience Bullock smiled warmly, while Leo assured Adella how much he valued his lady teachers and anticipated her arrival in Albany.

Each of the top five graduates would present brief formal talks. As soon as Cora Calhoun finished, Adella, knowing she came next alphabetically, walked forward, braced her elbows and knees against the lectern, and began: "I speak today about our country's natives and also of the Africans who were cruelly kidnapped from lands far away. Both groups have benefited from Christianity's blessings, but whites exploited them and caused Indian and slave women alike epic despair. They suffered heinous depredations at the hands of powerful men who brought the words of Our Lord to this land and made it wealthy. But at what cost? They ousted the Indians from their ancestral homes and oppressed the Negroes whom they'd stolen and enslaved."

"Missionaries nurtured the heathens and carried healing, education, and Our Father's messages to the masses," she went on. "Our colored women nurse, nourish, and train the young, even as some white soldiers of light and love teach, protect, fortify, and pry them from the arms of temptation in the forms of tobacco, the demon rum, and other things too depraved to mention. We must help these mothers as we march forward together, knowing that only through our women's strength will the darker races rise to take their rightful places in our country."

After the student essays had been delivered, Rev. Francis asked the congregants to open their hymnals, and they chorused, "Rock of Ages, cleft for me, let me hide myself in thee."

As the organ chords faded, President Ware introduced his featured speaker, Rev. Atticus Haygood, the president of Emory College, a small Baptist school for white gentlemen in Oxford, Georgia, between Sparta and Atlanta. Adella had caught glimpses of its campus when she traveled that route by train, but she'd also heard about the reverend from her father's war stories. He was making quite a name for himself with his new book, *Our Brother in Black,* and he'd cull his talk from the chapter that dealt with the freedmen's education.

Rev. Haygood began, "We must maintain separate schools for the negroes. White parents will not allow their children to share desks with colored ones, and they don't want to sit next to white youngsters anyway. But racial separation disturbs only a few fanatics."

Atticus Haygood had been raised on the ownership side of a slaveholding household, and he ranted on about "the hardships our people endured": "We lost a billion in slaves, more in the support of our brave troops, and untold amounts through the destruction of property by Lincoln's Raiders." Perceiving some white attendees' sympathies, he added, "Our negroes were set free pursuant to Union demands, so the Yankees bear a burden for educating these primitive people."

As to the school's honorees, he added, "Much of the work of training the darker race must now be done by the negroes themselves, and most of today's graduates, I understand, plan to teach. Soon there may be a few colored lawyers, doctors, and certainly more preachers. There's no reason why some of the boys here shouldn't help their people in those ways."

Another hymn followed, then E. A. Ware distributed eighteen diplomas with the same number of small silk American flags to all of his college and upper normal graduates.

The commencement was bittersweet for Adella. She loved her alma mater and deemed education to be the one, true religion, but also, perhaps in some part due to her prodding, President Ware announced that he'd soon open his four-year "gentlemen's program" to ladies. The Wares' central mission was preparing them to teach their own at every level, and as a major step forward, the following September, the school hired one of Adella's fellow graduates as the first of their race on its faculty. Reflecting Rev. Haygood's predictions about the men's possible future achievements, another classmate earned a law degree and built a successful legal practice in Boston, while a third would become the city of Denver's chief medical examiner.

After the ceremony, Thomas Askew photographed the graduating class on the church steps. They, their families, faculty, and guests, including the Hunts, attended the Wares' garden party and headed back to Sparta that evening. Adella, however, stayed only long enough to see friends and relatives and repack her belongings. After that, she returned to Atlanta to visit Cora Calhoun, then trolleyed over to the city's south-side station to embark on her new venture.

She watched northern Georgia's pines and red clay dwindle away as the train rattled south into the Black Belt, so designated both for its dark soil and for its residents' often very dark skins. Albany, however, was atypical in at least one way, since a decade before the war, a contingent of Austro-Hungarian Jews had settled there. They reestablished their traditional religious lives even as they started new businesses and made their livelihoods on the black people's backs. In that respect, they followed the example set by the local white Christians, most of whom almost equally loathed the "foreign interlopers," with their alien accents, beliefs, and practices.

The Flint River, beside which Adella's train proceeded, rose from underground springs near Atlanta. Its tracks paralleled the waterway, which snaked south, joining the Chattahoochee on its way to the Gulf. As the train approached her destination, it screeched to a halt on a trestle high above the river. Noting her curiosity, a conductor asked, "Is you new to Awl-*benny,* missy?" He told her that a self-taught slave engineer, whose structures helped to extend (slightly) the Confederacy's ill-fated life, had designed the bridge they were crossing. Peering down, she spied a tangle of dark riverine creatures silhouetted against the sandy bottom. They looked like prehistoric reptiles lurking on the mud banks and churning through the shallows.

The uniformed trainman had been rudely ogling her all along, then he smirked: "Them's 'gators, missy, and likes tender meat best, so they'll smile and eat you right up if you acts naughty." Adella had been warned that such saurian monsters sometimes attacked house pets and even recalled hearing one of Hancock's vicious "crackers" call black babies "'gator bait." She further wondered if the presumptuous conductor suspected her racial "secret," because it seemed unlikely that he'd otherwise laud any black man's accomplishments or assume such a tone with a white lady. Or perhaps he too was "passing." But as the locomotive creaked into the depot, he scurried off to assist other passengers—only white ones—so she never knew.

Residences, white Protestant churches (the ones that Dougherty's black folks attended were located beyond the town limits), and the unlikely synagogue occupied the central quadrant, which also included banks, apothecaries, grocers, professional offices, and houses of ill repute, whose workers and clientele were as much divided along racial lines as almost everything else.

Some of the outlying near-palaces that dated from King Cotton's heyday had been abandoned or crumbled into ruin, but Leo Bullock had persuaded county officials to supply him with a gang of black convicts who'd work under Albany's white glaziers, carpenters, masons, and stone cutters to build him a mansion that replicated those antebellum estates. The locals warned that he was situating it too near the Flint, yet he paid no heed, positioned his home on a gentle embankment that took advantage of the fine views and cooling zephyrs, and named it Flintlock.

More than for such private ventures, Dougherty's incarcerated labor force carried out various public projects. Black men and boys were chained together during grueling workdays, fed a little slop, then confined at night in a fortified stockade, where securing and disciplining the prisoners provided coveted employment for some of the region's most scabrous white men.

After meeting Adella at the depot and loading her luggage into his wagon, her senior teacher W. C. Green (also an Atlanta University alumnus) followed the corduroy road's jarring route through the swamps south of town. He told her that Dougherty's black folks outnumbered whites by a ratio of five to one yet wielded no power as a result of that numerical dominance since they had little or no money, property, or education and rarely could vote. On their way to the cluster of ramshackle cabins known as "the Ark" where Adella would board, Mr. Green warned her about some perils she might face. "In their isolated estates, Miss Hunt, a couple of Dougherty's former slaveholders recently shot and killed several of our people," he cautioned, adding, "Those overlords rarely heed any laws but their own." (But Adella already knew that.)

Soon their journey brought them to the school. It was a two-room, whitewashed plank house with unglazed windows and a corroded tin roof. Adella's shabby interior domain featured several rows of splintered benches for the children. A crude teacher's desk faced them, a sooty potbelly stove squatted in one corner, and a cracked blackboard was propped up in another.

"The girl who's been helping me out was one of Mrs. Case's best former students here, but her education hardly compares to ours up in Atlanta," the slightly older teacher boasted.

Soon their apprentice arrived. She was a shy seventeen-year-old named Essie Dwyer, and Mr. Green had arranged for Adella Hunt to board with her parents, Emmaline and Sam.

W. C. Green also shared with Adella what he knew about the Winstons and Bullocks.

"Patience Winston Bullock's family provides most of our school's financial support," he began, "because her father's a successful merchant up in Troy, New York. In the old days, the Winstons were abolitionists, and in recent years they've been trying to help the freedmen. Their only children were twin girls named Prudence and Patience."

"Early in the Civil War," Mr. Green continued, "Prudence Winston married Leo Bullock—who I unfortunately suspect bought his way out of the draft—but a couple of years later, his wife died in childbirth, leaving him with a son named Ethan. Mr. Leo had no independent income, so he had to stay in his father-in-law's good graces, and to do that, he agreed to wed the spinster Miss Patience. At the senior Winstons' behest, the boy remained with his grandparents in Troy when the younger couple relocated down here. With added funds from some of our Jews, Mr. Winston refinanced Albany's bankrupt Dixie Cotton and Corn Company. It's become Leo Bullock's local financial base, and it's also our county's largest commercial enterprise."

Allocating a portion of the profits to help train Dougherty's black youngsters was central to the mission that the elder Winstons mandated for their son-in-law, who quickly settled into his role as a new southern merchant. Leo Bullock stocked everything the locals needed, and when he'd finished attending to the demands of his white customers, he might ask a dark-skinned sharecropper who'd trudged in through the back door, "What do you want now, Sambo?"

Well, "Sambo" Dwyer wanted Leo Bullock to "furnish" him. That meant advancing him what he needed to sow, raise, and harvest his cotton. The "furnisher" executed liens on such men's meager assets in return for supplying them with tools, seed, and rations. If a 'cropper fell ill, Mr. Bullock might pay the doctor and the blacksmith too if a mule needed to be shod or a wagon shored up. And if Mr. Dwyer brought in a successful crop, he wasn't encouraged to save but rather was exhorted to spend more—and his rent would be raised. But if the crop was poor and he fell into arrears, his mule and plow could be confiscated. Dougherty's whites insisted that letting black people purchase land or giving them access to decent credit would result in failure or, worse, would encourage the Negroes' "inborn criminality." Thus, the majority remained mired in a debilitating and irreversible serfdom, not far removed from their parents' former bondage, while Leo Bullock controlled access to all of the nearby ginneries, as well as the services of the cotton brokers and shippers. He'd always get his pound of flesh in cash, in labor, or in kind.

Once the cotton was picked, Leo sold it, deducted charges for his own services, and paid the white landowners. Usually, nothing was left for the 'cropper, whose debts, escalating with high, compounded interest, carried over to the next year. In the region's single-crop economy, cotton itself was the prevailing currency, and those who cultivated it inevitably fell into arrears.

The Bullocks financed Dougherty's only school for its thousands of black children too, so like Essie Dwyer and Adella Hunt, W. C. Green really worked for Leo Bullock. Leo also "furnished" his older brother, who was one of many sharecroppers who'd fallen into his debt.

About a year after Adella began teaching there, Mr. Bullock stopped by the school one day. "My wife's been feeling poorly," he said, "so I want you to come out to Flintlock, play the piano, and read to her twice a week. I'll pay you an extra ten dollars a month." Patience Bullock had seemed congenial when they'd met at Adella's graduation, so she agreed to his demand.

The following Tuesday afternoon, the Bullocks' liveried coachman, Prince, pulled up at the schoolhouse in a stylish carriage to fetch her. When they reached Flintlock, her driver-escort took her around to the rear door at the insistence of Leo Bullock, who explained, "This isn't my choice, Adella, but I have to modify my Yankee habits to accommodate Georgia's customs. What would my neighbors think, say, or do if I let a girl like you come in the front way?"

Grasping her elbow, he steered her into the music room, where his wife awaited.

Patience Bullock greeted Adella warmly and asked her to read aloud a chapter from *Jane Eyre*. Then they discussed the motifs, characters, and plotlines at some length. Following that, Adella agreed to play a medley of classical etudes on the Bullocks' spinet.

Patience Bullock (née Winston) had graduated from a seminary in Troy that was founded by and named for Emma Willard and, Mrs. Bullock told Adella, "was also attended by Elizabeth Cady, who's now Mrs. Stanton. She and my parents worked together as abolitionists, and now she's collaborating with Miss Susan B. Anthony, trying to get the vote for women." Adella hadn't previously heard those names and knew next to nothing about such efforts.

Adella Hunt and Patty Winston Bullock soon became friends, and within a few months the older woman felt comfortable enough to ask, "Can you help me to understand why you call yourself a Negro? You look as white as I do."

"All of my father's people are white, but I take pride in and especially identify with my mother's Negro and Cherokee ancestors. I'd never deny the heritage of those who did the most to nurture me," Adella explained, adding, "and Georgia's laws also define me as such."

Mrs. Bullock accepted that explanation, though it didn't satisfy her, then in a minor act of defiance she insisted that Miss Hunt use the front door, recognizing the import of that gesture.

But Adella's students consumed most of her time and energy. Except for the rare Bibles, which few of their parents could read, their homes had no books whatever. And their physical afflictions, malnutrition, and lassitude made teaching them a challenge, even when they had the opportunity to attend school, since their folks often kept them out because they needed help with the 'cropping. Adella also showed them her silk American flag but warned, "We mustn't fly it outside here in Georgia." The youngsters' lack of self-esteem, however, most concerned her.

One day her favorite student, a sparkly-eyed, dark-skinned girl, asked, "I knows that Miz Chase, our old teacher, was white, but is you white too, Miz Hunt?" Adella insisted that they call her by her surname so they'd understand that people of color deserved such respect as much as Caucasians.

"Remember to say, '*Are* you white?'" she gently corrected, but added, "and no, I'm not. I'm a Negro as you are but look somewhat different because I have Indian and white relatives as well as black ones. We should honor and love everything we are, my precious."

But Adella's heart nearly broke when her pupil added, "I want to look like you, so I'm gonna cover myself in flour or get boilt like we does the hominy, then maybe I'll turn fair and white too." The yearning to become white saddened Adella. How could she reach these children in whom racial bigotry often already had instilled a hatred of their own features and skin color?

She also worried about Essie Dwyer, who'd felt slightly indisposed for several months.

As for her employer, Leo Bullock, Dougherty County's people of color recognized his venality, so they began spreading lurid (but true) stories about him. In May 1883, for instance, his college-bound son, Ethan, came south for a visit. Leo wanted to arrange a treat for the lad, so he slyly winked, "I'll get you a clean, obliging colored wench to bed down with anytime, son."

Shocked by his father's proposal, Ethan recoiled, never before having known of such predatory rituals. So backtracking in hopes of providing a comparably "manly" activity, Leo proposed a bird shoot instead. He'd include several cronies, to whom he confessed his paternal gaffe. One pal assured him, "I'd like me a wench even if Ethan don't, and I'd really fancy me a Hunt after the hunt. Your tasty, biscuit-colored schoolmarm would do me just fine."

Adella heard later that Leo Bullock and his friend had roared with laughter at the "joke."

Dougherty was a paradise of wildfowl, so on the appointed morning the men loaded their guns and mounted up, preparing to track down and shoot doves, woodcocks, and quail all day. One black youth bugled and helped the hunters reload, while another served as the bagger who toted the increasingly heavy burlap sacks into which he tossed the dead birds. Li'l Caleb, the bagger, had been granted that honor because his father, Big Caleb, was Mr. Bullock's butler.

The white men had been drinking, riding, and shooting for several hours when Li'l Caleb scuttled off again to collect the bloody prey, but this time, an inebriated huntsman fired wildly and winged the bagger instead of a quail. Ethan rushed over to assist, rigged up a tourniquet to try and stanch the child's bleeding, secured him on his horse, and hastily returned to Flintlock.

Three hours later Leo Bullock sat alone in his sanctuary cleaning his fowling piece. He called in his butler and sighed, "I'm sorry, Caleb, we tried hard, but couldn't save your boy."

At first Big Caleb just gaped, but when he grasped the full, horrific meaning of Mr. Bullock's statement, he collapsed into the arms of his employer, who later told the sheriff, "When he fell forward, my gun just went and fired off on me." "No way I could help shooting that nigrah. Then he bled out right here." Leo Bullock pointed downward. Dougherty County's authorities designated the first death a "hunting accident" and the second "self-defense."

Big Caleb's blood soaked into Leo Bullock's parquet floor. His lack-eys scrubbed it three times with bleach, linseed oil, and sand but couldn't remove the ugly stain. That made Leo even angrier at the two deceased Calebs and also at his son, Ethan, whom he heartlessly pilloried as a "sissy Yankee pantywaist." The mortified young man cut short his visit and en-trained for the North, while Leo gave Big Caleb's widow five dollars in compensation for her double loss.

When Adella heard about those tragedies, she drove the Dwyers' wagon over to Flintlock to console Patty Winston Bullock, who clutched her arm and whispered, "I may have to leave Georgia very soon. Won't you join me? If we went north to Troy together, I'd pay you a good wage to be my companion. You're so pretty and well spoken that I'm sure you'd soon meet and marry a fine Harvard or Yale gentleman. No one even would need to know that you're colored."

Shocked yet also briefly tempted by the offer, Adella hesitated but said she couldn't leave, citing her students, work, and family. Then Patty gasped, "I'm so sorry if I offended you."

"Don't worry, we'll always be friends," the younger woman reassured her, and she continued reading and playing the piano at Flintlock twice a week for another month.

Then one afternoon, Adella arrived to find Eli Bullock alone. He steered her into his study, where guns and hunt trophies adorned the walls, much as they had at Fortitude, the old Hunt family home in Georgia. He draped an arm across her shoulders and murmured, "Two days ago my wife's physician insisted that she leave right away for treatment at Dr. Kel-logg's Sanitarium in Battle Creek, Michigan. I'm afraid she'll be gone for quite a while, but you must stay, Adella. I want you to play the piano and read to me as you did for her."

Leo Bullock totally controlled the school's finances, and thus he was, in fact, her employer. Adella had been raised to respect her elders too, so she remained courteous but soon claimed that she had a blinding headache. Then she hastened back outside, and Prince drove her home.

She'd already been thinking about her future, however, and given the day's unexpected events, she composed a letter to Atlanta University's pres-ident, Edmund Asa Ware, saying,

*I hesitated to write but feel that I must. To remind you, I
have been teaching for almost two years at the colored mission
school in Albany, with W. C. Green, but under the Bullocks'
aegis. Mr. Green cannot help me because his brother is deeply
in debt to Mr. Bullock, who often threatens him with incarcer-
ation. I also fear that, although she's unable to speak up, our
young assistant here has had her honor compromised—I suspect
(but cannot be certain) by the same man.*

*Just today, I learned that Mrs. Bullock left Georgia due to
her poor health but I think also exacerbated by marital strife.
Then her husband almost demanded that I play the piano or
read to him as I'd done for her for the past year. Feigning
illness, I left.*

*I have, however, received a recent inquiry from Miss
Olivia Davidson, who learned of my pedagogical work in
Sparta, in Atlanta, and here. You may have heard her name
because she is helping Prof. Booker T. Washington launch his
institute in rural Alabama. I wouldn't have bothered you
without serious reflection but would be grateful for any guidance you might offer.*

Four days later Adella received a telegram from him urging, COME
HOME NOW TO TEACH WITH US IN ATLANTA, but she already
had in hand the employment proposal from Olivia Davidson. Miss Davidson herself had graduated from Virginia's Hampton Institute, and their
fledgling school in Tuskegee had only six instructors, all from Hampton;
but Adella Hunt's pedagogical training and experience, she informed her
recruit, could be critical to their mission, expansion, and success. Olivia
Davidson offered her a teaching position starting in September.

But Leo Bullock became increasingly demanding and often dispatched
his coachman, Prince, to fetch Adella from the schoolhouse. She put him
off through May, when the rains never ceased, but as June arrived, a somewhat drier day dawned. W. C. Green pleaded, "Please come out to Flintlock with me this afternoon, Miss Hunt. If you don't, the boss will fire me
for sure, then he'll send my brother off to the chain gang."

So she relented. Uttering not another word, her fellow teacher drove her to the mansion as storm clouds rolled in and the showers resumed. As they pulled up, Adella sternly shook her finger and scolded. "Do not leave, Mr. Green. Wait for me right here at the stable with Prince!"

W. C. Green silently nodded as Prince unfurled a large, black umbrella and escorted her to the back of the house. He also apologized: "I'm real sorry, Miz Adella, but since Miz Patty she be gone now, Mr. Bullock he say I gotta bring you 'round to his kitchen door again."

Leo Bullock had dismissed his house servants. He ushered Adella into his den, where she admired the glass-paned doors and vitrine cabinets that housed his rifles, pistols, and shotguns—including, of course, a vintage flintlock. The sight and musty scent of his leather-bound books enraptured her. The stench that shrouded the man, however, made it obvious that he'd been smoking cigars and guzzling spirits for some time, and he refilled his snifter from a heavy crystal decanter. "I'll get one for you," he mumbled, "or if you don't like brandy or whiskey, have some Madeira, my-dear-a!" He almost choked with laughter at his own pathetic pun.

"I don't drink alcoholic spirits of any sort" (which wasn't altogether true), Adella frowned, "but I'll fix myself some tea in the kitchen." She stepped out of the salon as he too exited his splendid quarters. When he returned, she was sipping a steamy cup of Orange Pekoe.

He drained his glass, poured yet another shot, and jostled her across the room.

"Your wife liked me to play Chopin's chamber pieces for her," Adella suggested.

Rejecting that proposal, he growled, "But I prefer minstrel songs, the bawdier the better."

She shook her head and said she knew none—also untrue—but then she countered, "I was reading *Sense and Sensibility* with Miss Patty and can continue with that if you'd like."

Jane Austen didn't suit him, but he smirked: "How 'bout a different English novel? John Cleland's *Fanny Hill*'s my favorite, and I've got an illustrated first edition here in my bookshelf."

Adella was unfamiliar with *Fanny Hill*, but Leo Bullock extricated a heavy volume with its title and the author's name inscribed in gold leaf on the embossed, burgundy leather cover. He heaved it onto his desktop, then opened it to show her full-page, full-color engravings of amply endowed, stark-naked men and women entwined in poses unlike anything she'd ever seen.

"I want you to see what you're missing, like in these etchings." Mr. Bullock slurred his words. Then, without forewarning, he unhooked his britches, which dropped to his ankles.

He wore no undergarments, and Adella cringed as she glimpsed his puny, venous member peeking from its bristly roots. He slapped her cheek, twisted her neck to lace his fingers through her hair, and dragged it down in a dark curtain. As he wrenched her right arm behind her back, she felt a shooting pain in that shoulder. He tore her shirtwaist, pinched her breast, and hissed, "Don't you know you're made for my pleasure, you creamy slut, like your ma and grandma were made for their white gennamin? Just 'cause you're good looking and almost white, don't go thinking you're better'n any other colored gal. Don' fight me, you vixen. I'm gonna horn into your slit, pop your cherry, and make you squeal like a pig 'fore I let you loose today." Adella recalled her grandmother Susan's warning: "a pretty face can be a colored girl's curse."

She jerked away, knocking over her cup and saucer, his decanter and snifter. They all shattered on the floor. Her tea scalded him, and she thrust her bony elbow into his soft belly. He toppled over and caught himself on his palms, which gushed blood. Adella raised her skirt and sprinted down the hall. Leo Bullock staggered to his feet and lurched after her, but he was so intoxicated that he again tripped over his sagging trousers, crashed on his face, then rolled over onto his back, groaning, clutching his bloody nose, and snoring loudly. She paused, inhaled, and barely resisted the temptation to crush his vulnerable windpipe under the heel of her shoe.

W. C. Green had promised to wait for her, but when she ran outside, Prince said, "Sorry, Miz Hunt, but Mr. Bullock made him skedaddle a while ago." Then he asked, "Is you o-keh?"

Adella claimed that she was, but he knew his employer well. "I can't drive you tonight," he whispered, but he offered her the horse he saddled, adding, "Just send him back here."

Her skirt ripped as Prince hoisted her up. They took off, and she spurred the mount into a gallop. Her chest heaved, her teeth rattled like nails in a barrel, her hair and clothes were sopping wet and clung to her skin, chilling her to the core. She hadn't ridden in two years, so her inner thighs chafed raw and her uninjured arm trembled as she struggled to contain the beast.

They plunged through the storm for half an hour, and when Adella reached the Dwyers' home at the enclave, more aptly than ever during that deluge called "the Ark," she dismounted, smacked Leo Bullock's horse on its haunch, and he bolted away in the direction of Flintlock.

The couple with whom she boarded asked no questions but gently dried her off and, at her insistence, burned every last stitch of the drenched, torn, and contaminated clothing she'd been wearing. Then they settled her into bed, where she lay shivering and wide awake next to their pretty daughter. No one mentioned Essie's "delicate state," but Adella gently touched the girl's distended belly and guessed she'd be giving birth within a couple of months.

The tempest raged through the night; the Flint rose and silt oozed through the Dwyers' floorboards. The flood inched toward Flintlock too, isolating it on a peninsula, which then became an island. The locals had warned Leo Bullock not to build so close to the river, but he'd wanted (and had) a stately mansion with the finest vistas in southwestern Georgia. Cottonmouth moccasins, six feet long and as sinewy as a smithy's arm, slithered out of the turbulent river and festooned the live oaks' shaggy boughs. Lured by the scent of blood, a monstrous 'gator agitated by the rising tide lumbered up the grassy embankment. Wielding his armored tail like a scythe, the beast whacked through Flintlock's glass-paned portals and lurched into the conservatory.

The morning after Adella had galloped away, Prince sloshed in and tripped over his employer, who lay sprawled on the buckling parquet, clutching a pistol. Leeches had clamped onto his jowls, blanching them as white as the fireplaces' marble façades, and Br'er 'Gator, who'd gnawed his leg and mauled his exposed genitals, grunted off as Prince arrived. The sheriff found bullet holes in the floor, china and glass shards around Leo, and cuts and scald blisters on his hands but couldn't determine if he'd shot himself, if "some nigrah" did it, if he died from blood loss, snake-bite venom, or both. The deputies toted off the mutilated corpse as the water deepened; the house creaked and swayed, then slowly crumpled inward. Books, papers, Patty Winston Bullock's spinet, Leo's crystal decanters, his hunt trophies, and more bobbed off downstream.

Adella didn't wait to find out what happened after her hasty departure and never shared her story with anyone. She knew that either she'd be blamed herself or the incident wouldn't be taken seriously or believed. Then she crammed her belongings into two valises, paid the Dwyers room and board for an extra month in thanks for their help and compassion, but had no opportunity to bid Prince, her students, or W. C. Green farewell. She also seethed at his cowardice in leaving her behind at Flintlock.

Sam Dwyer drove her to Albany's rail depot, where at the adjacent telegraph office she dictated a cable for Olivia Davidson in Tuskegee, Alabama: SITUATION IN ALBANY CHANGED. I ACCEPT OFFER OF TEACHING POSITION. ARRIVE CHEHAW 8:30 TONIGHT. WILL TAKE WAGONETTE TO TOWN. She sent another to her family in Sparta: HEADED TO TUSKEGEE. MORE NEWS SOON. I LOVE YOU ALL.

Her kindhearted landlord loaded her luggage onto the westbound Selma & Meridian train, from which she'd transfer seventy miles later to the Western Alabama system.

As to the Wares' proposal that she join their faculty, Adella was flattered and tempted, and thanked them for the honor, but declined the offer. At that point, she'd have been their only Negro instructor, since they'd eased out her classmate who'd been teaching with them for two years. She loved her alma mater and remained devoted to her mentors there but thought that she might contribute more in a pioneering milieu. She'd heard ominous reports that shortly after the Civil War, Klansmen had torched Tuskegee's three black churches as well as its only school for the former slaves, but she also remembered her grandmother's story about how she'd driven by that town as she'd spirited off her fugitive son, Jimmy, to join the Union army back in '63.

Olivia Davidson, Booker T. Washington's partner at the school, had recruited Adella and promised that she could develop and oversee the institute's entire pedagogical curriculum. It also was the only establishment where (she then believed) women carried equal weight with men, and those of her race controlled the entire operation. She was weary and wary, but she was on her way to a terra incognita, which was at or even beyond the end of the world she then knew.

SIX

The Hither Isles

ADELLA'S TRAINS WERE DELAYED AT every juncture, so it was nearing midnight on June 5, 1883, when she completed her exodus from Albany, spending the journey's last leg on what she later learned that south-central Alabama's African Americans called the Ku Klux local: a narrow-gauge wagonette that rattled five miles south from the Chehaw junction to the town of Tuskegee.

Rainless thunder growled from afar, and the stygian environs felt clammy—teeming, she imagined, with fanged and taloned monsters. Was that a snarling bobcat or only a house tabby? Aladdin's screeching roc or merely a rooster impatient for the dawn? Inhaling the damp, fecal miasma and in pain of all sorts, she sat anxiously on her valises by a rickety platform near (she hoped) her intended destination. An hour later, a mule-drawn farm cart rattled to a halt, and a tall, moon-pale phantom toting a kerosene lantern vaulted down and strode toward her through the murk.

The question "Are you Miss Hunt?" pierced the dark. Adella confirmed that she was.

"First," the wagon driver scolded, "you've kept us up very late. Second, I read your cable since Miss Davidson's off in the North. Third, I'm Logan, the school's bookkeeper, and we have no money to pay you 'til September, when you were told to arrive, and fourth," he paused, "no one can see to your needs, because Mrs. Washington's expecting her baby any-time now. We sent a student to fetch the doctor from town, but he hasn't come yet."

It was an inauspicious beginning. And surprising too, since she hadn't known that Booker T. Washington was married, much less about to become a father. Adella also had suspected that he and Olivia Davidson had set their eyes on each other, although the latter's letters never really implied such a thing. But soon she learned that Mr. Washington's wife was the former Miss Fannie Smith, who'd hailed from his original hometown and then followed him to Hampton Institute. They'd been longtime sweethearts and had married the previous summer.

But Adella hadn't traveled so far to be thwarted, so she blurted out the first words that came to mind which might give evidence of her indispensability: "I know something of nursing and midwifery, Logan, so perhaps I can assist Mrs. Washington until the doctor arrives." Logan (she didn't know at first if it was his surname or a given one) looked doubtful but couldn't reasonably dismiss her offer, so he heaved her luggage into his vehicle and drove a mile out to the principal's abode: a shabby converted barn that the small faculty shared.

A resonant voice responded to Logan's knock and summoned them in. Adella observed that Logan was taller and also better looking, she thought, than the midsized fellow with cocoa-brown skin and luminous gray eyes who was clasping a young woman's clenched fist. She lay on a rumpled, soggy bed, and though barely conscious, she was writhing in pain.

"This is Miss Hunt," Logan whispered. "She has nursing experience and thinks she can help Fannie." The man nodded, moved aside, and gave Adella access to his suffering wife.

She acknowledged his tacit approval, approached her chance patient, and said, "I'm Adella Hunt, Mrs. Washington. Do you think I might assist you?"

The woman groaned her consent, so Adella embarked on her mission. She felt Fannie Smith Washington's brow (feverish), took her pulse (fluttering like a hummingbird's wings), sponged her off, folded a damp rag between her teeth for her to suck and bite down on, placed a kettle on the stove, and directed Logan to make coffee and bring her some lard and fresh linens. Pursuant to Adella's explicit instructions, the father-to-be rolled his wife onto her side so he and Logan could change the sodden sheets, then as Adella's grandmother had shown her, she massaged Fannie's lower back and taut belly with softened lard each time the contractions gripped her.

She worried too, fearing what more she might need to do if the physician didn't come soon. It had to be a white man, since Logan, clearly someone who spoke precisely, had specified "doctor," and no woman or person of color was licensed to practice medicine in Alabama. Finally, they heard buggy wheels crunch on the gravel, and Logan ushered in a rather disheveled fellow. Adella detailed Mrs. Washington's condition and said, "Why don't you take off your jacket, roll up your sleeves, wash your hands and face, and have a cup of hot coffee, Doctor?"

Her presumption clearly startled the man, yet he did as she directed without protest. By midmorning the practitioner made his manipulations, eased out the baby, tied off the umbilicus, and placed into the crook of Adella's uninjured left arm a wrinkled, purple-faced girl. She swaddled the slippery infant and turned to hand her over to the new father, at which point Mr. Washington's eyes rolled up in their sockets, he swayed, then he keeled over in a dead faint.

Logan fanned his face and helped him to his feet. Booker T. Washington quickly recovered his consciousness and composure, paid the doctor, and thanked Adella. Then he asked her, "What do you think of the name Portia, Miss Hunt?"

"It's a fine name for your baby, Mr. Washington, because it suggests a woman of wisdom, generosity, and beauty," she answered, then added, "The quality of mercy is not strain'd. It droppeth as the gentle rain from heaven upon the place beneath," quoting the fictional Portia's most memorable soliloquy. Thus, they acknowledged their mutual love of Shakespeare.

Though still suffering from Leo Bullock's thwarted assault, for the next fortnight Adella slept on a cot next to Fannie Smith Washington. Since she'd proved her worth, Logan arranged that she share the loft with the school's other single lady teacher and informed her that his Christian name was Warren. But she continued calling him Logan as he'd introduced himself.

The Tuskegee Normal School and Industrial Institute had opened a couple of years before, and over the summer Logan showed her around its hundred acres situated two miles west of the town of Tuskegee—the seat of Alabama's Macon County. By September, the institute had ten African

American faculty members and 135 students ranging in age from fifteen to forty.

Booker T. Washington, his instructors, and a cadre of local youths had repaired and refitted several old farm buildings, and the newcomers initiated some modest agricultural endeavors. Through trial and error, they learned to make bricks, which became a mainstay of the school's nascent building program and a dependable source of income. The nearest significant edifice was an antebellum mansion called Gray Columns that quite resembled Nathan Sayre's Pomegranate Hall. That big house, a short distance down the main road, dominated a shabby plantation owned by the aristocratic but land-poor Varner family, who'd given their old brick kiln to the institute.

During her first summer there, Adella helped however she could and prepared her fall syllabi as her body and spirits healed. That's when she started her diary too, scribbling into it not only current events but the dark, irreverent, or other musings that she'd speak aloud to no one.

Just as classes started that fall, Adella's sister Lula Mae in Sparta wrote her to report a shocking death in their family, and she also heard from W. C. Green, her former co-teacher in Albany, who apologized for abandoning her at Flintlock. He told her about Leo Bullock's demise, his home's devastation, and Essie Dwyer's fatal parturition. Her baby survived, but without medical attention, Essie had hemorrhaged and died. Adella sent a condolence note for the elder Dwyers through Mr. Green, instructing him to deliver and read it for them, composed another to Patience Winston Bullock, and mailed it off in care of her parents in Troy, New York.

As Warren Logan's hard shell began to crack, he asked the school's new teacher to join him on his "morning constitutional: exactly fifty minutes, starting at six a.m. sharp."

At twenty-five, Logan was still lanky but sported a handsome mustache, and as they walked, Adella assessed his light eyes, brown curls, and ivory skin. He looked not unlike the men in her family, so she asked if his biological father was white. Her bluntness took Logan aback, but he confirmed her suspicions and added that he thought he knew the man's identity but had been told to think of him only as his and his mother's former owner. Understandably so, because the man in question was Rev. John Paul Smith, a pious, revered Presbyterian minister.

"Rev. Smith was serving the Lord in Charlottesville, Virginia," Logan began, "when his first wife and their baby died in childbirth. That town's Watson family owned my mother Pocahontas, whom everyone called Poky. Her father, whom she never knew, was white, but she had Indian and colored forebears too. Mary Watson, who'd soon marry Rev. Smith, had told her slave Poky that she was descended from the Indian princess of the same name who'd welcomed the British at Jamestown, and before they baptized and married off the earlier Pocahontas to one of their own, she'd borne the child of a Powhatan chief. The Watsons insisted that the Princess Pocahontas's firstborn daughter had been my mother's ancestor—hence she also was mine. I can't prove the story's verity, Miss Hunt, but my mother's tall and copper skinned. As a child, the local Powhatans had shunned her, though her Indian heritage seems obvious to me."

Adella wondered why Logan embraced the demeaning soubriquet Poky, which seemed to reinforce such wretched racial and sexual stereotypes. She didn't say that, however, but gently teased him: "We might be distantly related, though generations back and pursuant to several marriages, not blood, because my cousin and former teacher told me that her maternal kin also were descended from Pocahontas, but through her second husband, the Englishman John Rolfe."

Her anecdote seemed to puzzle Logan, but he continued: "In 1858, my mother had a son. Yes, that was me. No one ever explained why Poky insisted on naming me Warren or said who my 'real' father was; but I was conceived shortly before the widowed Rev. Smith remarried, and my presence seemed to make him feel extremely ill at ease. He and his bride, Mary Watson, however, colluded on what I've always considered to be a far-fetched yarn about 'a University of Virginia student from a prominent Kentucky family' who'd put Poky in the family way."

"Having no choice in the matter," Warren Logan wryly added, "when I was two years old, my mother and I moved to North Carolina with Rev. Smith, his second wife, and their baby boy. Once down there, the reverend took over Greensboro's First Presbyterian Church."

"Poky and I slept in one of the slave cabins out back, and soon I began working every day at the rectory, so I spent my waking hours in the same home as Paul J—the reverend and Mary Smith's son, who's a year younger than I am," Logan added. "Folks in Greensboro didn't dare say that he and I were blood kin but often joked that we looked like 'two peas in a pod.'"

Starting when he was five, Mary Watson Smith gave Warren the chance to learn to read, write, and cipher alongside her own child: "so long as I'd first finished polishing the silver and furniture, sweeping the floors, waiting on the table, and fanning away the flies," he told Adella.

"After the war, my mother took up with a carpenter named Parker Logan and had his children: Willy and Sally. When the laws changed and let Negroes marry, they did, and I took Logan as my surname, since Rev. Smith insisted I not use his. That's when we relocated to the shabby neighborhood that folks in Greensboro called Darkwater," Adella's new friend added.

"I developed a strong singing voice, and learned hymns, oratorios, and chorales in Rev. Smith's church. Every Sunday, my mother and I listened to him preach from up in the balcony; but in 1871, all of us colored folks left First Presbyterian to form our own church, and our new preacher opened Greensboro's first school for Negroes. I was one of its original students, and in a couple of years I began teaching there too. That's where I started hearing the old slave sorrow songs; but I still performed my classical solos at First Presbyterian, and the reverend's white congregants still whispered about my 'close kinship' with their pastor." Warren Logan saved the pittance he earned from teaching until 1874, when he headed off to Virginia's Hampton Institute.

The institute stretched across a low-lying peninsula where Chesapeake Bay gapes toward the Atlantic, and as soon as Logan arrived, he was assigned to the Senior Cottage, which originally had been a barracks erected during the Civil War to house white Union soldiers. It became the school's first residential hall, and a slightly older student who already lived there befriended Logan. He'd taken for himself the imposing name Booker Taliaferro Washington.

Logan spent much of his next three years leading Hampton's singing quartet, which toured the Northeast raising funds for their school. "The

New Englanders who attended our concerts praised the 'tall young white man,'" Logan chuckled. "Yes indeed, that was me! I managed our schedule, arranged and conducted the music, and tallied up whatever money we took in. Our Yankee audiences never wanted us to perform any classical compositions or popular new songs, but they'd weep and wail and open their wallets extra wide if we ended our concerts with 'Swing Low, Sweet Chariot.' So we pretty much stuck to 'dem good ole cullud speerichuls.'"

"At Hampton, I helped the less prepared students under the supervision of my favorite teacher, Miss Mary Mackie, a white woman who'd come south from Vassar College to teach the freedmen," he told Adella. "I'd impress on my schoolmates the importance of cleaning their bodies and using their own toothbrushes. For those who'd started in the worst circumstances, even sleeping on cots with bed linens, wearing night shirts, and eating at a table with forks and napkins was altogether new. 'Civilization and order' had (and have) to be our watchwords."

"My stepdaddy, Parker Logan, took good care of my mother and their children," Logan went on. "He and I were cordial, but we never grew close. Hampton's General Samuel Armstrong, however, was already Booker T.'s 'Great White Father,' and soon he became almost my father too. During the war, he'd commanded a unit of the U.S. Colored Troops, stayed on with the Freedmen's Bureau, and then opened his own school. He insisted that we colored boys abstain from all political activities until, he told us, we'd been 'civilized' with rigorous training that would purge what he called our 'strong tendencies toward sensuality and sloth.'"

"When the Civil Rights Act became law a year after I arrived," Logan continued, "the general warned that we mustn't try to access facilities designated for white Virginians only. He grounded our regimen on his stint in the army, so we began every day with military drills."

Warren Logan integrated those practices into his current morning constitutionals, as he and Booker T. Washington replicated much of Hampton's regimen at Tuskegee. Bells rang out on their campus almost every half hour from 5:30 a.m. (rising) to 9:30 p.m. (lights out), much, Adella mused, like those that had regimented the enslaved workers on her uncle Judkins's plantation.

General Armstrong taught his students practical skills, but he didn't expose them to much of an academic education such as that from which Adella had benefited at Atlanta University. But as with her alma mater, Hampton's primary goal was preparing teachers for the freedmen.

Mr. Logan also told Miss Hunt that he'd titled his commencement talk about his musical fund-raising endeavors "In the North with the Hampton Singers." In light of that experience-based essay, Adella decided not to share details of her own valedictory speech about the endemic abuse of black and Native women. She suspected that he'd consider it an intemperate screed.

After a summer in Greensboro, Logan returned to Hampton Institute, where he worked for a year as a bookkeeper. When he'd completed that internship, he went to teach in St. Mary's County, Maryland, on the upper Chesapeake Bay. "I boarded in a 'cropper's house and taught nearly a hundred colored children in a back room of the white folks' Episcopal church," he told Adella. "It was good experience, though after four years it became mighty tiresome, but that's when I got the letter from Booker T. that changed my life." Logan heeded the call to join him and Olivia Davidson in south-central Alabama, arriving only ten months after they opened the new school.

Adella liked Mr. Washington, Logan, and others at Tuskegee but missed her family and old friends. And a few months later, she received a response from Patience Winston Bullock, who began,

> *Thank you for your letter of condolence following my husband's death. I only failed to respond before now because so much has transpired since then. But first, should you need exemplary health care, my stay at Dr. John Kellogg's Sanitarium was thoroughly restorative.*

Patty then segued into her letter's substance: *I expect you realized before you left that your assistant teacher, Essie Dwyer, was "in the family way" and also may have heard that she passed away in childbirth.* She then revealed an ugly secret that Adella already had suspected:

After my husband died, Essie admitted to her parents that
he was responsible for her condition. He'd forced her to have
sexual intercourse (there, I've finally written those forbidden
words!) with him to keep her father, who was heavily in my late
husband's debt, from being imprisoned.

When my health allowed, I returned south to salvage what
I could from Flintlock's ruins. I also went to see the Dwyers, who
were caring for their granddaughter. They named her Della for
you. She resembles Mr. Bullock (tho prettier!) and looks as white
as you do. Loving children but being childless myself, I told them
I would like to bring her north with me. The Dwyers have few
assets, and my sincerity and what I offered in material ways
persuaded them, so they agreed.

You might disapprove, but I am rearing her as the white
girl she appears to be. My nephew Ethan (who is Della's half-
brother, but I won't tell her that) and I will give her affection
and see that she gets a good education, I hope one day at Emma
Willard's academy, right here in Troy. I also gave her my
parents' surname: Winston. "Bullock" should play no role
in her life! I enclose a carte de visite photo.

I salvaged many books from Flintlock's library that I will
send you—with a contribution.

Adella admired the photograph of her namesake Della but vowed
never to say anything to her friend (or anyone else) about her own abhorrent final encounter with Patty's deceased spouse.

That winter, however, a pall fell over Tuskegee Institute when Fannie
Smith Washington was paralyzed after falling from a farm wagon. She died a
few weeks later, leaving behind her grieving widower and their baby, Portia.

Olivia Davidson had been away for much of Adella's first years at the
school, raising funds, mostly from northern women, and trying to restore her
health. When she returned after Fannie's death, she and Adella realized how
similar they were in their passions for teaching and literature. Olivia reim-
mersed herself in her mission as she toiled past the point of exhaustion.

Olivia was the school's lady principal, but Warren Logan served as its mathematics teacher and accountant. Soon he assumed the added duties of treasurer and vice principal, was appointed to the board of trustees, acted in Booker T. Washington's stead during the principal's absences, and became liaison to, among others, Rev. Atticus Haygood, who'd given Adella's commencement address and, before that, had served with her father in the Confederate army.

Like most white southerners, Rev. Haygood was a segregationist, though unlike the more noxious of his caste, he thought that the former slaves might be trained in a variety of fields, as long as those efforts didn't prompt them to consider themselves white men's equals. For several years, the reverend had served as an Atlanta University trustee, but he expressed his disapproval when he visited those almost color-blind facilities where its Yankee leaders gradually assembled an integrated faculty. He'd recently resigned both that post (the Georgia legislature concurrently withdrew its financial support from that progressive institution) and the presidency of the all-white Emory College to become chief agent with the Slater Fund for the Education of the Freedmen, the country's largest foundation that helped to support the South's struggling new schools for African Americans. In 1885, Atticus Haygood bestowed an initial Slater Fund grant on the young Alabama institute, while both B. T. Washington and Warren Logan promised that Atlanta University's "elitist philosophies and social engineering never will come to pass at our school."

Mr. Washington exhorted his faculty to read Rev. Haygood's *Our Brother in Black,* as well as Frederick Douglass's memoirs, while Adella collected whatever she could that was written by, for, or about people of African ancestry. She knew that white folks sometimes appropriated and mocked their black culture but nonetheless enjoyed Joel Chandler Harris's recently published *Uncle Remus Tales,* since he'd been reared in a county adjoining Hancock and his stories quite resembled her grandmother's. She especially, however, sought out works that bore relevance for their women, such as the enslaved Phillis Wheatley's Revolutionary-era poetry, William Wells Brown's novel *Clotel: The President's Daughter,* Frances Ellen Watkins Harper's diverse oeuvre, and even *Adela, the Octoroon,* a maudlin novel

by a white man named H. L. Hosmer. Her nascent book assemblage gradually expanded, and in addition to teaching, Adella Hunt became Tuskegee
Institute's first librarian and informed Logan that she needed some basic
amenities to house her expanding inventory. The school's few buildings
had many competing demands on their limited space, but he heeded that
request by allocating her a ten-by-twelve-foot curtained alcove that their
student carpenters lined on three sides with oak book shelves. That makeshift library was essentially an annex to Warren Logan's office.

Booker T. Washington was away on one of his frequent solicitation
trips in the North when Logan opened a cable from the Slater Fund. Its
agent, Rev. Atticus Haygood, was touring the South to assess the distribu-
tion of his foundation's bounty. Because he proposed to see their school only
three days later, there was no time to reschedule his travels to accommodate
Mr. Washington's absence, so Logan arranged and hosted the reverend's
first visit to their campus.

At least a hundred students marched past their guest, lined up in
military formation, and displayed their livestock, farm produce, and crafts.
Several teachers answered Rev. Haygood's questions, then Logan escorted
him back to his own office. Adella remained silent and invisible behind the
curtain in her adjacent book nook and wasn't about to barge in and introduce herself as "Captain Henry Hunt's daughter," but she heard the ensuing conversation as clear as a bell.

"I'm sorry that Principal Washington had to miss your visit, sir, but
hope we've been able to show you everything of interest," Logan began, then
added, "Might I escort you to our new indoor lavatory or offer you a cool
beverage or a light repast before you catch your train?"

"No, nothing more, Logan, and I'm pleased with what I've seen
today," the reverend replied. "You and Booker T. are working in line with
my directives about the sort of education your boys and girls should have.
In the past, my fund has assisted Atlanta University," he continued, "but I'm
ending that support very soon, since its Yankee president keeps trying to fill
his young darkies' woolly heads with foolish notions about equality and
teaching them Plato and Locke, rather than training them to make bricks,
raise crops, and breed livestock as you do here."

"Though maybe I should've seen it coming," he further mused. "President Ware's white faculty and his colored students eat at the same tables, and when I delivered the graduation address there four years ago, he reserved no separate and preferred seating for his white guests. One sassy urchin who spoke that day even tried to blame us white men for all of the hardships that've befallen colored women from time immemorial! Can you imagine such insolence?"

The reverend plunged on: "Your girls can be more treacherous than your boys, you know. As the race advances, there may be opportunities for a few lawyers, doctors, and ministers in your own communities, but women must be kept out of our courthouses, operating rooms, pulpits, and voting booths. Such activities are contrary to God's divine plan, are beyond women's capacities, and conflict with their temperament, physiology, and domestic mission. Don't you agree?"

Logan may have nodded, but he said nothing aloud as Adella listened to that diatribe from her adjacent hideaway. She hadn't mentioned her graduation talk to Logan, so he didn't know that Rev. Haygood had been castigating the "sassy urchin" Miss Hunt for her "insolence."

"Helping these youngsters make something of their lives is too critical for us to make mistakes," he continued, "and I know that you and Booker T. tolerate no nonsense here."

"You're right, sir. We allow none of that," Logan quietly responded.

"Since that's the case," Atticus Haygood concluded (Adella heard the chair legs scrape the floor), "I assure you, the Slater Fund will continue its beneficence toward Tuskegee."

Logan opened his office door, shut it firmly behind them, and double-clicked the lock.

But more pertinent to their leader personally, Adella had been prescient about Miss Davidson's and Mr. Washington's mutual affection. The principal and Olivia married just over a year after Fannie Smith Washington died, and despite Olivia's fragile health, within a few months she confided to Adella that she was expecting. But her pregnancy was touch-and-go from the start, so Cornelius Dorsette, a Hampton schoolmate and friend of Mr. Washington and Logan who'd recently become Alabama's first licensed African American physician, came over from Montgomery to assess her condition.

He knew she wouldn't be adequately cared for in the Jim Crow South, so he referred her to a Boston hospital, where a few months later she bore a son.

Because of Olivia Washington's precarious new maternity, Adella assumed much of her work during her absence and after she returned. Booker T. Washington temporarily conferred on her the title lady principal, in addition to those of librarian and teacher of English and pedagogy. But her salary, while highest of the female teachers, remained much less than those of the male faculty who had inferior educations, had fewer responsibilities, and, she believed, weren't as capable as she was. Adella protested that disparity to both Logan and Mr. Washington, but to no avail.

She also brought to fruition Olivia Davidson Washington's plan to start a "teaching laboratory" at the model school they called the Children's House. But to Adella's dismay, in line with most white southerners' beliefs about the sorts of skills that her people ought to develop and pursue, the institute began training increasing numbers in its agricultural and industrial divisions and fewer in academics. "Normal School" soon would be slashed from its official name.

Adella nonetheless remained committed to her pedagogical efforts. Sam Courtney, one of Booker T. Washington's Hampton protégés, shuttled between his winter job as a field agent for Tuskegee and his medical studies at Harvard University and helped her arrange the teaching colloquia that she conducted throughout the South. In June '87 Logan joined her and Sam at a seminar in Hampton, Virginia, where they also attended the graduation of Logan's half brother, Willy.

But after the ceremonies concluded, Willy informed his older sibling that their mother's "Negro consumption" had worsened. So as Adella and Sam entrained for the journey back to Alabama, Warren and Willy Logan set off together for Greensboro, North Carolina.

They found Poky without medical care, gasping for breath, and coughing up blood at her squalid bungalow in Darkwater. In a long letter, Logan informed Adella what transpired there.

He began,

> *I am sad yet relieved. Infinitely sad because my mother*
> *passed away last night yet relieved since her departure from this*

vale of sorrows finally ended her suffering. Shortly before she died, she unburdened herself at last and shared with me the circumstances that led to my conception and birth: memories of the events that she and the people who'd owned her, the Watsons and then the Smiths, had kept under wraps for 30 years.

He'd already told Adella that the Watson family had been his mother's original owners. But like many other white Virginians, they'd found themselves with too many slaves and too little income, so in 1857, they'd hired out Poky to a widow named Mrs. Ives, who provided room and board for some of the (all-male, all-white) students at "Mr. Jefferson's school."

Logan's letter continued,

My mother told me that they were foul-mouthed and often drunk, and while intoxicated, one of them assaulted her. He knocked her to the floor, kicked her, robbed her of her innocence, then exhorted his fellow boarders to do the same, hollering, "Let's all have some sport with this nigger-squaw!" Four others did as he urged, chanting "poke-a-poke-a-Pocahontas" as they violated her.

One youth alone held back. Poky was bloody and bruised, but he helped her to a seat in his bedroom. Then they made a pact, which my mother said provided her with a measure of protection. He told Poky that if she'd come to his bed whenever he summoned her, he'd keep the other brutes from ravishing her again. And he kept his word. She promised not to tell anyone they were lying together, but that's what they did most nights for the rest of the semester. She described him as tall, with gray eyes and sandy hair. He told her to call him "Mr. Warren," but at the time, she knew no more than that about who he was or whence he came.

Within a few months, the letter added, the inevitable came to pass.

Poky found that she was with child. When she told her owners, Mr. Watson (Mary Watson's father) went over to Mrs.

*Ives's house and demanded the names of the students who
boarded with her, which the landlady reluctantly shared. He
read the list to my mother, who identified her five assailants
and the one chap who'd treated her half decently: Henry Clay
Warren. "Mr. Warren," she learned, was closely related to the
man known as "The Great Pacificator"—the late Kentucky
senator and presidential aspirant: Henry Clay.*

*Mr. Watson asked the university's chancellors to oust the
malefactors, but to no avail. They said, "Boys will be boys, and
we'd have no students left here if we expelled everyone who'd
just bedded down a colored wench." That ended it, though the
Watsons did learn that Henry Clay Warren, shamed by his
exposure, promptly left the school and headed home to Kentucky.*

*I was born several months later. Poky told her owners that
she wanted me to carry the name Warren, so Rev. Smith, who
I'm now convinced was <u>not</u> the man who impregnated my
mother, baptized me as such. When he and Mary Watson married soon thereafter, her parents gave them Poky and me as part
of the bride's dowry. No one was to mention the ugly events at
the boardinghouse, and 'til my mother told me 2 days ago, she,
at least, never did.*

That gave credence to the story Logan had been told about his paternity. He now knew, as Mary Watson Smith and her husband always had asserted, that the fellow in question had attended the University of Virginia,
and he was indeed "a member of a prominent Kentucky family."

He signed himself *(Henry Clay) Warren Logan.*

Logan's account of his mother's rapes and sexual exploitation horrified Adella. She understood his curiosity about his "real" father but also
was outraged (though not surprised) that, as a baby, Logan had been given,
like money, acreage, or livestock, as a wedding dowry.

He returned to Tuskegee still grieving but eager to welcome something new into his life, and a month later, he wrote Adella's father asking his
permission to court her. They seemed well suited to each other, so Warren
Logan proposed marriage and Adella Hunt accepted.

It was nontraditional, but Adella entrusted him with the diamond that her father had given her mother to celebrate her birth. That made it seem less a bridal purchase price and more a badge of commitment and respect. Logan had the Hunt family jewel set into an impressive engagement ring that his fiancée showed off to everyone she knew, especially her college friend Cora Calhoun, when Adella attended Cora's marriage to Edwin Horne. She'd use the Calhoun-Horne wedding as the prototype for her own nuptials, which she began planning a year in advance.

And Adella Hunt also embarked on a solo adventure. She'd aspired to complete the four-year college degree denied her by Atlanta University, so in the previous and then the next summer, she took on the equivalence of a year's study in a couple of months at the Chautauqua Literary and Scientific Institute in western New York State, where renowned white professors introduced her to the work of Darwin, Galton, Agassiz, and Lamarck on the subjects of heredity, evolution, and more. Yet she found herself dissatisfied both by those scholars who argued that "nature" alone predetermined the human condition and by their rivals who insisted that given the "right" or "wrong" environment and training (nurture), anyone could be molded to greatness or might as easily descend into moral, mental, and physical dissolution. Seven years after earning her upper normal division diploma from Atlanta University, and following two summers of intensive study, the Chautauqua granted Adella its certification for the bachelor of arts degree.

And her wedding approached. She'd written Rev. Cyrus Francis (who'd become Atlanta University's president following E. A. Ware's premature death) about her plans and asked him to officiate at the ceremony. He agreed, and they scheduled the nuptials for late December 1888, when both Atlanta University's and Tuskegee Institute's faculties enjoyed a post-Christmas holiday break.

But no one at the institute or in the town of Tuskegee, Adella believed, was skilled enough or could obtain the elegant fabric she wanted for her wedding gown, so she engaged the services of a Negro dressmaker in Atlanta, then took the train back and forth for several fittings. Feeling on one hand that she should share the travails that others of her race endured, sometimes she opted to sit in the "colored car," but whenever she did so, an agitated conductor would insist that she was in the wrong place and must return to the "ladies carriage." Thus, she abandoned her egalitarian efforts and reverted to the subversive practice of "traveling while white."

The modiste fashioned her dress from patterned ivory satin and fitted its snug belt, wrist-length sleeves, and chin-high collar. She'd wear no veil, but lace medallions cascaded across the bosom and dozens of narrow tucks overlaid a deep yoke. Horizontal pleats enhanced the skirt's swagger, and significantly for her sense of independence, she paid for it with her own earnings.

When Adella shared her plans, Atlanta University's former president E. A. Ware's widow insisted that she sleep at her home the night preceding the ceremony. The following morning, she helped Adella dress, rouged her pale cheeks, and swept her long hair into an elegant topknot. She'd carry the Sayre family Bible that her mother had held when she'd wed at Pomegranate Hall thirty-five years before, and her father would escort her down the aisle. Big Henry was relieved that, at almost twenty-six, his favorite daughter "finally" was marrying.

Her mother had insisted that she ask their white relatives, but they didn't respond to the invitations, although many from Hunts' Hill attended, as did several of her former professors and leaders of neighboring Clark and Morehouse Colleges. Nearby Spelman Seminary's principal and its black Canadian physician, Dr. Sophia Bethene Jones, came too. In contrast to Tuskegee's all-Negro faculty, and with the exception of Dr. Jones, those school leaders all were northern white men. Patty Winston couldn't make it from upstate New York, nor could Cora Calhoun Horne join them, because Adella's wedding coincided to the day with that of her only sister, Lena.

Except for Logan's half siblings, however, he had no family. His stepfather and his mother had died, his former owners didn't come, and his "real" father, Henry Clay Warren, of course, was out of the question. The Slater Fund's Atticus Haygood attended, and as Confederate veterans often did, he and Capt. Henry Hunt reminisced a quarter century after their stint together during the "War of Northern Aggression." Atlanta University's officials and Rev. Haygood greeted each other stiffly, and fortunately, he failed to recognize Adella as the "sassy urchin" who'd presented the "offensive"

Adella Hunt in her wedding dress, December 1888. (Collection of the author and
the Herndon Home, Atlanta; original photograph by Thomas Askew; reproduction photograph by Mark Gulezian.)

essay when he'd delivered her graduation address in 1881. Neither Olivia
Washington, who was in the final month of a second perilous pregnancy, nor
her husband, who was away wooing donors, however, could join them.

Thomas Askew (Atlanta University's official photographer and a parishioner at First Congregational) took Adella's picture in his nearby studio, then she went over to the church itself, where Rev. Cyrus Francis officiated. On the year's final Saturday, holly festooned the candlelit altar and oak pews. Family, friends, and poinsettias surrounded them as Warren Logan slipped onto Adella Hunt's ring finger a narrow platinum band inscribed *W.L. to A.H. Dec. 27 '88.* As an avid anagramist, she wondered if with Logan added to her original name, she'd become "Dull *Anglo* Athena." Still Athena, perhaps, but hopefully neither "dull" nor "Anglo."

Atlanta University's president and Mrs. Francis hosted the reception, which was catered by Sergeant, the school's longtime cook. Though teetotalers themselves, the Francises treated the younger couple to a case of champagne, as the celebrants sang, laughed, and waltzed late into the evening.

Following a sleepless night, Adella, her new husband, and several relatives and friends left Atlanta after attending Rev. Francis's Sunday-morning service. Their party that headed southwest toward Tuskegee included Dr. Samuel Courtney, Adella's sister Sarah, brother Henry Jr., and Florence Johnson, his fiancée. Traveling in the first-class carriage, as their tickets entitled them, they were a few miles past the Georgia-Alabama state line when their train pulled into the Opelika station, where passengers could detrain to purchase refreshments. Sergeant had prepared and packed them a tasty picnic lunch, but they also wanted some cool beverages.

As Sam Courtney later told the story, "We were a party of well-dressed, light-skinned Negroes headed home after a wedding. But many white southerners think it's a crime for any members of our 'inferior' race to ride in the same cars as those of their 'superior' one, and when we pulled up in Opelika, several gun-totin' crackers began taunting us."

"One of them," Sam went on, "yelled, 'There's a bunch o' fair-skinned coons what's tryin' to 'pass' up in first class!' 'We can't allow that. Put 'em off!' a cohort hollered back, as four hooligans menaced us. 'Don't you know better than to ride in the white folks' car?' they shouted. 'Rather than let you colored boys back on, we'll fill you with lead right here and now.'"

Although Logan, Sam, and Adella's brother Henry never knew her sordid chapter of the story, in their absence, several of those vulgarians ogled her, emitted grunts and whistles, and began rhythmically stroking their crotches. One leered, beckoned, made a *V* from two fingers, then thrust his tongue in and out between them. As usual, she held her hatpin in readiness, but fortunately she didn't have to use it since the bullying louts soon tired of their hateful "game."

The gentlemen in their party returned and advised the ladies they'd be safe only if, as the white thugs demanded, they relocated to a different car. Thus, they endured the next leg of their ruined journey in the cavern of stale smoke and liquor fumes that was the overcrowded Jim Crow carriage. When the train stopped again, Logan complained to the station master, who suggested that they hire a private rail car for the ensuing stretch, then growled, "But y'all hafta pay a twenty-dollar surcharge." Adella started to protest when her husband hissed, "Hush, Mrs. Logan!" At that point, they gave up on the railroad altogether and engaged a stagecoach. Its driver reloaded their luggage and transported them the final thirty miles to Tuskegee Institute.

They were frightened and angry but unhurt, which was a blessing, since more than seventy of their race had been lynched in Alabama during the five years Adella had lived there, usually for "offenses" no worse than theirs.

She'd also heard about the recent ordeal of Ida Belle Wells, a spunky young brown-skinned teacher who'd been traversing neighboring Tennessee in a reserved seat on a first-class "ladies carriage" when a conductor ordered her to yield her place to a white woman. When she refused, he tried to drag her off, but she resisted, braced her feet against a seat back, and clamped her teeth onto his hand. Bellowing in pain, he booted her out the door onto the gravel roadbed. She was deeply insulted and slightly injured and took her complaints to court. First, she received a positive legal judgment, but the railroad company appealed, bought off her lawyer, and finally won its case. Those were challenging times for the South's people of African ancestry, even ones such as Adella Hunt Logan who knew, relatively speaking, how fortunate they were.

Cautiously selecting his words, Booker T. Washington rose to their defense when he wrote to Alabama's leading newspaper: "If railroad officials do not want us to ride in their first-class cars occupied by white passengers, let them give us separate ones just as good and exclusive and there will be no complaint. We can be as separate as the fingers of the hand and have no desire to mix. If they will not give us first-class accommodations let them sell us tickets at reduced rates. There are many colored people with whom one does not care to ride, but let the assortment be made on the ground of dress and behavior."

Therein lay a critical difference between Adella's views and those of Mr. Washington, Logan, and "moderate" white southerners such as Atticus Haygood. They thought that what the United States Supreme Court soon would cast in stone as "separate but equal" was the most pragmatic, indeed the only, way to deal with those issues. Yet given most white people's hostility toward "the race," Adella was convinced that separate facilities never would be equal.

Adella called her new home in Tuskegee "The Rookery," because crows, blackbirds, and ravens raucously vied for their turf and cohabited under the eaves. In a gesture of defiance and over her husband's protests, she displayed in their front window the small, silk American flag from her Atlanta University graduation. It was the first time that Old Glory had "flown" in Macon County since before the Civil War. Most everyone at the institute nonetheless felt honor bound by Mr. Washington's repeated decrees that they distance themselves "from all political matters and the discussion of any questions that might generate conflict between the races."

Adella also was deeply concerned about Olivia Davidson Washington's recent physical decline, and only a month after that, Dr. Cornelius Dorsette came from Montgomery to deliver her second son. But just three nights later, a blaze that started in a fireplace flue flamed out of control at the Washingtons' residence, only forty yards from the Logans'. Cradling her babies in her arms, with Portia wailing behind them, Olivia stumbled barefoot through the hoarfrost at three a.m. Beset by paroxysms of coughing, she pounded on Adella's door. Blood flowed between her legs and formed icy, raspberry-sherbet footprints wherever she trod.

Booker T. Washington was fund-raising in the North at the time, so Dr. Dorsette, who'd been sleeping on the Logans' sofa, cabled a respected Boston medical facility and arranged for Olivia's relocation. Her husband joined her there and sat numbly at the bedside for six weeks. But afflicted as she was by laryngeal tuberculosis, with her suffering palliated only by escalating doses of opiates, she died. Olivia's death left the widower and their entire campus bereft.

A few months later, though still mourning, Booker T. Washington decided that, at least figuratively, he had to get back into the saddle. He thus attended the commencement exercises at Nashville, Tennessee's Fisk University (he was one of that school's trustees), where an attractive graduate named Margaret Murray finagled an introduction to the recently widowed visitor. Admiring both Miss Murray's obvious intelligence and ample curves, but without, Adella feared, any thoughtful evaluation, Booker T. Washington promptly hired her as an English teacher.

As soon as Margaret Murray arrived at their campus, she began positioning herself as her sponsor's right hand. She succeeded Olivia Davidson Washington in academic, official, and, after what Adella considered an unfittingly brief period, more personal respects too.

And Adella's father, Henry Hunt, also died that December, almost a year to the day after he'd walked her down the aisle. He'd been a slave owner but also had married—with the white Hunts' consent, Judge Sayre had performed Henry and Mariah's service, "according to law"—and lived for thirty-seven years with the woman of color who'd borne and reared their eight children. Before his body even had cooled, however, Adella's cousin Neppie commandeered control over her war-veteran uncle's interment and had him buried in Sparta's "white" cemetery.

With "Big Henry" gone and few educational opportunities remaining for people of color in Hancock County, Georgia, Adella persuaded her mother to let her youngest son, ten-year-old Thomas Francis Hunt, come to live with her and attend school at Tuskegee. Adella also noticed that the iris of "Little Tommy's" green right eye had turned hazel, as had her uncle Jimmy's. That usually rare aberration appeared surprisingly often in the Hunt family, so she researched the phenomenon in an anatomy textbook and learned that it was called *heterochromia iridum*.

Adella had been unprepared for Logan's almost unceasing lust (which she sometimes shared), but she hoped to defer pregnancy for a while by

Mrs. Warren Logan

This image of "Mrs. Warren Logan" was taken around the time of Adella's marriage but appeared in 1902, in D. W. Culp's *Twentieth Century Negro Literature.* One hundred African American leaders, writers, and thinkers provided essays for the book. The borders around the contributors' images depict slavery's harsh legacies, contrasted with symbols of progress, enlightenment, and education and familiar Americana. (The New York Public Library Schomburg Center for Research in Black Culture, Manuscripts, Archives and Rare Books Division.)

drinking the dogbane and wild carrot tisane that her grandmother concocted. Two years after marrying, however, she gave birth to Warren Hunt
Logan, with her grandmother in attendance. He wasn't Susan's first great-
grandchild, but he immediately became her favorite, since Adella bestowed
the Hunt name on him. And the new mother was grateful that he seemed
healthy, in contrast to her recently married cousins' baby, who was blind
and deaf, with six toes on one foot. Given her recent readings on genetics,
Adella feared that "inbreeding" between those close biological relatives
might have been responsible for their daughter's infirmities.

Then a year later, their school hired its first physician-in-residence.
Adella was pleased that Booker T. Washington found a woman to fill the
position, despite widespread misogynist presumptions like Atticus Haygood's, Miss Murray's outspoken opposition, and the students' reluctance
to believe that Halle Tanner Dillon, that "little colored lady," could be a
"real" doctor.

Halle Dillon had been a young widowed mother when she'd attended
the Philadelphia Women's Medical College, and her brother was a classical
painter who'd emigrated to France when he found that he couldn't live
safely in the United States with his white wife. Their father was the African
Methodist Episcopal Bishop Benjamin Tanner, and he accompanied his
daughter to Tuskegee, where he lectured for a year at the institute's new
Bible school, which was headed by Adella's old teacher Richard Carter's
classmate and friend Rev. Edgar Penney.

In Montgomery, Dr. Cornelius Dorsette tutored Halle Dillon to prepare her for the state medical examination, and when she passed with dis-
tinction, she became Alabama's first licensed female physician. The vast
majority of southerners (male and female, white and black), however, considered medicine an unfitting, even a scandalous, profession for any woman.

Dr. Dillon assumed responsibility for the well-being of 350 students,
thirty faculty members, and their families, as well as many others of Macon
County's black people. She compounded medications, managed a small
drug dispensary, and initiated a limited curriculum for training nurses. The
doctor was hardworking and capable, and Adella supported her mission
but found her uncompromising in her rigid adherence to modern method-

ologies and pharmaceuticals, as she flatly rejected the merits of any and all folk traditions, treatments, or practitioners.

Adella's grandmother, however, still sent her small cardboard boxes filled with kaolin clay, which she mixed with applesauce. That always settled her stomach, but Dr. Dillon scoffed that "only ignorant country Negroes eat dirt," while several colleagues smirked that "Mrs. Logan does that to make her children white," though Adella had little question that only her own and her husband's forebears' combined genetic legacies determined such characteristics.

And soon, Mr. Washington confided to his friends that Rev. Penney would marry him and Margaret Murray just a few weeks later. "Dear Lord," Adella fumed, "a third wife for a 'black widower' who's barely in his thirties. Miss Murray admits that she dislikes 'the little folks' too, and in an unguarded moment she even told me, 'I dread being thrown in with his daughter Portia for a lifetime.' And what's their big rush anyway?" Adella provoked her husband.

Despite Logan's avowal that Margaret Murray "will make our principal's life more complete and better ordered" and his assertion that Booker T. Washington definitely wanted more children, Adella refused to attend the nuptials. As expected, her spouse scolded, "First, that's rude, Mother. Booker T., Miss Murray, and I would deem your absence almost insulting. Second, Portia's and the Washington boys' well-being always will be assured, and third, you shouldn't cast aspersions on Miss Murray's virtue by questioning their early wedding date."

But vanity more than pique, frankly, kept Adella away, and she officially attributed her absence to her advanced pregnancy. And belying her suspicions, she had to admit that the third Mrs. Washington gave no indication whatever of having been pregnant prior to her marriage.

Only a month later, Adella yielded to Dr. Dillon's obstetrical expertise, and Ruth Mackie Logan made her squalling debut. She could hardly object when her husband insisted on naming his daughter to honor both Tuskegee's white board chairman, the railroad magnate William Baldwin's wife, Ruth, and Mary Mackie, his favorite teacher at Hampton Institute.

In the year after Ruth's birth, Adella took on some revised assignments. She assessed the academic faculty, tried to reinvigorate the school's waning academic curriculum, and introduced, organized, and coached its coeducational debate team. But with two babies and little household help, she couldn't resume a full-time teaching schedule, so to supplement her domestic agenda, she embarked on a mission of self-enlightenment on issues pertaining to women's citizenship.

Patty Winston, who no longer used her married name (Bullock) at all, had begun sending Adella what she called "feminist literature," including Charlotte Perkins Gilman's controversial new novella *The Yellow Wallpaper* and the first two volumes of Elizabeth Cady Stanton and Susan B. Anthony's *History of Woman Suffrage*. Adella thus was especially pleased when she learned that Frederick Douglass, whom many people called the "King of the Freedmen" but who also boldly championed women's rights, would visit their school. What she knew about his resonant demands for black men's suffrage ("with no apron strings attached") during the late-1860s debates leading to the ratification of the Fifteenth Amendment inspired her. He'd also raged, however, about how "our mothers, wives, and daughters are beaten, assaulted and hung from lampposts, not because they are women, but because they are colored."

Booker T. Washington informed his colleagues that Mr. Douglass had agreed to deliver their 1892 graduation address, but Adella felt sure that his wife wouldn't join him in that part of the country, where interracial unions were forbidden by law and often brutally penalized in practice. Many white southern savages were primed to assault *any* man of color who appeared to have *any* intimate relationship with *any* Caucasian woman such as the second Mrs. Douglass.

The Washingtons held a reception to honor their distinguished visitor, at which Adella shared with him how much she admired him and his friends and colleagues Sojourner Truth and Susan B. Anthony, then persuaded him to sign his three memoirs for the school library and a photo for her. She'd hang that striking image in her home and several years later heard her son tell an inquisitive friend, "Mamma says his words are thunder, so I think he must be God."

Cradling Adella's small hand in his huge one and admiringly beaming down on her, Mr. Douglass said, "Thank you for your compliments, Mrs. Logan. And I deeply respect those of you who toil so nobly here in the vineyards of these hither isles."

Before dawn the next day, hundreds of black Alabamians began flocking to the school. They ranged from small tykes to grizzled old-timers who'd driven wagons or trudged through the night. The ceremony itself and Booker T. Washington drew some of them, but Frederick Douglass, who in later years Adella would remind Junior and Ruth (whom she took with her to the historic event) that they'd met in person, attracted far more. He'd taught himself to read and write in the face of daunting odds, recruited African American troops to fight for their freedom, served his government at home and abroad, and touted racial equality and women's rights. He was their lion in winter who'd resisted, escaped from, and evangelized against human bondage but also had opposed Abraham Lincoln's proposals to repatriate his people to Africa. They too were Americans, he'd insisted, and belonged in the United States as much as did any white men.

Mr. Douglass was a bit hoarse and palsied, but despite his seventy-five years, he stood arrow straight on the flag-draped platform as he imparted his wisdom for the ages. Revisiting his familiar speech, "The Self-Made Man," he first addressed Tuskegee Institute's white guests as he eloquently urged, "If a Negro cannot stand, let him fall. Give him a fair chance, then leave him alone, but make sure that you do give him that fair opportunity." "Without exertion," he continued to and for the graduates, "there will be no acquisition; without labor, no knowledge; without friction, no polish; and without conflict, no final victory." "Work with your hands, my young people, and they'll grow strong," he roared. "The same is true when you work with your mind. And remember this: right is of no sex; truth is of no color!" For years that powerful maxim had graced the masthead of his renowned abolitionist journal: *The North Star*.

He also addressed what many whites called "the negro problem." "But there is no such problem," he insisted. "The true problem is whether the American people have honesty enough, honor enough, and patriotism enough to live up to their own Constitution." He further declared himself impressed by the changes he perceived from what he'd learned during the years of his enslavement, as well as everything he'd heard about Alabama's past racial horrors.

Adella thought he saw himself as passing the torch of leadership to a younger generation, especially to their principal. Frederick Douglass, with his *My Bondage and My Freedom,* and Booker T. Washington, who spoke of his own journey "up from slavery," seemed much alike. They agreed that the strongest would survive and thrive, but offered scant compassion or solace for those whom race, sex, poverty, illiteracy, violence, and injustices impeded. Mr. Douglass no longer was the virile stallion she'd envisioned from years past, but with his noble brow, piercing eyes, and huge, frizzly pewter mane, he was the most spellbinding person she'd ever encountered.

But Adella was pregnant again and, despite her intermittent academic duties, running an efficient household, satisfying her husband's varied demands, and rearing two little ones; her original home and birth family never seemed far away. The previous decade's most joyous benchmark on Hunts' Hill had been her sister Lula Mae's marriage to a dependable stonemason named Gilbert McLendon, followed by their uncle Judkins's death. To make sense of much that ensued, Adella often revisited that past era in Sparta, Georgia.

SEVEN

Vanished

A FEW MONTHS AFTER ADELLA HUNT arrived at Tuskegee, Alabama, she received an urgent letter from her recently married sister Lula Mae Hunt McLendon:

> *dere sis*   *Sparta. Sept. 1883*
>
> *uncle Judkin jest dide. he past away at Miz Emmas hows lass saterdy nite but doc Albrite lide & tole miz Rebbeca & cuzzen Neppy it happin sumplace else. Rebbeca wone have no funerial but Jesus love awl his chilrens even siners like Judkin. he shud have a deecent christean bureal!!!*
> *God bless and love frum me my husban Gilbert & the others heer on Hunts hill. Lula Mae*

Because she'd had no formal education, Lula Mae's spelling and punctuation could be capricious, but her account of Judkins's death proved accurate. Adella acknowledged that loss to both of his daughters: her cousin Neppie Hunt, the child of her Uncle Judkins's wife, Rebecca, and another cousin, Molly Hunt, the child of his former slave Emma. She didn't know if Molly could read, but someone in the family surely would interpret Adella's condolence letter for her.

And Judkins Hunt's demise might have been anticipated. Despite sound advice from his physician (E. D. Albright, his wife Rebecca's uncle) that he cut back on his gorging, drinking, and smoking, Judkins had kept on doing just as he pleased. He'd become too obese to ride horseback anymore but continued his weekly visits to Hunts' Hill to see his "other wife," Emma.

His relationship with Emma had a long and volatile history. She'd been one of the Hunts' slaves, as were her parents, but early in 1845, she turned thirteen and blossomed, seemingly overnight, from a wiry "picka-ninny" into what Judkins called "a fine young filly."

The day's early chores took Emma to the dairy barn, where she milked the cows and churned the butter. Judkins often followed, hid in a dark stall, and watched her cool the milk in the ice house, pour it into a churn, and begin cranking. She'd lick the paddle to learn how it was clotting, skim off some buttermilk, and take a sip. Just after she did that one morning, Jud-kins charged in, said nothing, but snatched her up from the stool. She thrashed in vain as he coiled his arm around her waist and dumped her face down on a pile of hay. Her chin slammed on a plank, and a front tooth cracked. Emma was sinewy, but at twice her size, Judkins easily flipped her over, tore off her knickers, yanked down his britches, plunged in, and had his way with her. When he'd taken his pleasure, he jerked her up, flicked a cow patty from her shift, pressed a penny in her palm, and warned, "Anyone asks, just say you slipped and fell. You hear me, gal?"

She nodded in mute agreement. Then he picked up the ivory-handled revolver that had slipped from his holster, swatted her rump, and scolded, "Stop your sniveling now and get on with salting Miss Nancy's butter. We both got work to do."

When she saw his pistol, Emma had feared that Judkins might shoot her. Her heart hammered, her stomach heaved, and she puked up sour bile. But she did have work to do, so she straightened her clothes, wiped herself off, and trudged back to the big house. Her mamma asked how that tooth got chipped and why her lip was puffy, but Emma said only, "I slipped and fell," as Judkins had ordered. Enslaved women usually obeyed such com-mands and survived by adhering to a practiced code of silence. Emma told no one what had taken place. Who'd believe her story, take her word over that of a white man, or even care that she'd been assaulted?

Several months later, the Hunts' cook, who'd seen her master ogling Emma, was pretty sure what had happened and warned, "Your belly'll get big as a melon 'til your button pop out. And when that baby start coming, you're gonna feel some real ugly pains." She speculated that it was Judkins who'd put her daughter in that condition but asked no more. Either of them might be whipped, sent to live in the quarters and toil in the fields, or sold away from loved ones. If they slept in a slave shack, of course, they wouldn't be on call for the white folks, seven days and seven nights a week, every week of every month of every year, but they'd also no longer receive the big house's limited benefits: receiving cast-off clothing, tastier food (though it was only table scraps), doing slightly less physically grueling work, maybe even learning to read and cipher a little. Their lives could be worse than they presently were in Nancy's Fancy's kitchen.

When Emma's time came due, her mamma marched up to Judkins's mother and said, "You gotta send for Granny Susan to come help out my gal." And Nancy Hunt did just that.

Susan Hunt was too young to be a real "granny" back then, but that's what southerners called midwives. Enslaved and free, black, brown, tan, and white women sought Susan's help in delivering their babies because she used her expert hands, clean linens, hot water, and the Natives' and Africans' traditional herbs and practices, as well as Dr. E. D. Albright's medical guidance.

Adella's grandmother told her this: "Right after Emma told me (and no one else) what Judkins had done to her, her water broke in a flood. The contractions seized her, and she howled for almost two days." The girl's youth and narrow pelvis augured a risky birth, but Susan's fears of infection, hemorrhage, and what Dr. Albright called "fistulas" soon passed. Emma came through it only dog tired and a little torn up inside. She healed quickly, and her baby girl thrived.

Judkins was a thirty-three-year-old bachelor who figured he'd done no wrong, because like all of "the Hunts' people," Emma was his property and had no rights of refusal. He and most of the fellas that he'd grown up with usually "did it" for the first time either by poking their peckers in the cows or ewes, which felt "pretty durn good," or into the enslaved girls (or occasionally boys), which felt even better. By the time Judkins raped Emma, for almost two decades he'd been spewing his seed into the young ladies whom his family claimed to own.

The white men insisted, "It's them colored wenches what spread they legs and ask us in," while their wives sulked, seethed, or turned blind eyes, pretending they had no idea what was going on right under their noses or even between their own bedsheets. White women enjoyed some privileges, but their fathers' and husbands' legal, physical, and economic powers nonetheless enfeebled them.

Judkins and his ilk scoffed that "the dusky slatterns" wanted to be "mounted" sooner, rougher, and more often than "our ladies" did. White men agreed that protecting "their" young women's chastity, keeping them pure for the marriage bed, was an obligation and sacred duty. But there were no circumstances, they insisted and Georgia's statutes reinforced, under which a man could defile or "ruin" any woman of color, not even the youngest girl, be she enslaved or called free. According to law, and in practice too, none of them were thought to have any virtue worthy of honor, respect, or protection. State regulations iterated that no rape or other crime had been committed unless some outside malefactor "trespassed, without permission or the owner's consent," on a slaveholder's human property and "caused financial damage to the same."

Judkins Hunt maintained his proprietorship over Emma's infant, so she and her child contributed to his assets. Regardless of their paternity, such babies legally belonged to their owners, as did all the progeny of their livestock, and Judkins presumed he'd own this child forever. "Making" or breeding slaves cost a master much less than purchasing them, so morally, legally, and especially financially, Judkins reckoned, what was wrong with what he did in his own barn to his own property? Those commonly held beliefs notwithstanding, he found himself hesitant even to ask about the new arrival, though his slaves were abuzz. They knew that this baby was a "real" Hunt, and snickered, "It be as plain as the nose on her face."

A few weeks later Judkins moseyed into the kitchen and demanded, "What's her name?"

"I calls her Molly," Emma muttered, then turned away and returned to her saucepans.

Judkins left a rattle for Molly and a coin for Emma but came back often to play his violin and sing ditties that made the baby laugh. Emma watched Molly's happy face, caught flashes of her dimples as she clapped to her owner-father's fiddling. And sometimes Emma smiled too.

She stayed afraid and angry but saw that Judkins had fallen in love with his girl. Emma also wanted the money he gave her, so she hid the growing stash of coins in her pallet. Despite horrific memories of the assault for which she had no name, a broken tooth, and Molly herself, who proved that she "slipped and fell," Emma found herself liking Judkins Hunt—just a little.

It was hard not to. Most people in Hancock County acknowledged his foibles, even flagrant offenses, but Adella knew that he could be a charming rogue. His slaves also didn't care one bit for his plump pink bride, Rebecca Albright Hunt, whom he brought out to Nancy's Fancy a few months later. When their daughter, Penelope, called Neppie, was born a year after that, Emma didn't like her either. She grumbled that the bald newborn "look like raw buttermilk biscuits."

After Neppie's birth, Rebecca, who'd also had an arduous delivery, insisted on sleeping alone, in her own bedchamber. In that respect, she wanted nothing more to do with Judkins.

Emma continued as the Hunts' undercook until her mamma got so frail she barely could stand up, then Rebecca sent her out to the quarters and assigned her to slopping the hogs, while Emma took full charge of the big house kitchen. By the time her daughter, Molly, turned six, she too started cooking. Judkins smiled a lot because he ate royally and saw both of them every day.

Rebecca Hunt hollered at her "niggers" and slapped them if they didn't jump fast or high enough, and soon her daughter began behaving the same way. Little Neppie could be as sweet as syrup if her father was watching but as mean as a rattler if she was alone with her "tar babies": yanking their pigtails, calling them "my ponies," whooping "giddyap!" as she rode them up and down the carriageway. But Judkins and his mother, Nancy (Adella's white grandmother), didn't let Neppie do those things to Molly. All of the servants knew that Emma and Molly pretended to misunderstand "Miz Rebecca's" orders. They'd move as "slow as molasses in January," scorch their mistress's food, throw in too much cayenne or vinegar, "accidentally" break the crystal, and spit into the ladies' china plates if they were vexed: no need then to lace the sugar with arsenic.

Judkins didn't touch Emma again until she was seventeen, though he kept on trying—and finally she yielded to his persistence. The Hunts often hosted overnight guests at Nancy's Fancy, and the dishes rarely got cleared before nine, so Emma had to wait for the insistent bell rings that summoned her from the cramped room under the stairs if anyone demanded sherry or another of her delicious lemon tarts before retiring. And when Judkins whispered, "I want to stop by later tonight," Emma sent their daughter to sleep with her black grandmother out in the quarters.

Like her mistress, Rebecca, Emma didn't want another baby either and vowed that she'd never bring any more slaves into the world. So at twenty-two, when she found herself "in trouble" again, she went back to "Granny" Susan Hunt, who kneaded her belly hard and made her drink a bitter witch's tisane that she'd brewed from dogbane, slippery elm, and cotton root. It gave Emma horrendous cramps but two days later brought on a heavy clotted discharge. Many women, Susan told Adella, resorted to such means to protect their lives, health, and sanity.

In '65, almost all of Georgia's people of color were gratified that the North had won the war, but it was a bitter pill to swallow for the vanquished patriarchs, like the white Hunt men, because they faced major losses of property, prestige, and power. After the South's surrender, they had to admit that they didn't own black people anymore or have unfettered access to their labor and bodies. Those altered circumstances, however, gave white folks different advantages, since they no longer provided medical care, clothing, food, and living quarters (wretched though they'd been) for the "darkies." They could dismiss whomever they didn't want around, and Rebecca despised Emma because she heard the servants snickering behind her back and thought her mother-in-law, even her husband, preferred "outside" Molly to her own daughter, Neppie.

Mostly, Rebecca wanted to get Judkins's bedmate out of the house, so she made him a proposal. Young Molly, who'd become an excellent cook, could stay, but her mother had to go. And Emma negotiated her own bargain: she'd leave without any fuss if Judkins found new work for her and doubled the stash of coins she'd laid away so that she could move to a bungalow on Hunts' Hill, near where Judkins's brother Henry lived with his "barely colored" wife, Mariah, and their even whiter-looking children. The job Judkins arranged for Emma at Sparta's Old Eagle Tavern was tolerable enough, and Molly assumed full control over the kitchen at Nancy's Fancy.

On the evening in 1883 about which Adella's sister wrote her, in addition to his violin, Judkins took Emma a bottle of rye and a negligee he'd selected at a fancy shop in Milledgeville. He removed his hat, frock coat, cravat, vest, and boots, unholstered his pistol, and hiked his foot onto her table. Emma polished the crystal tumblers he'd given her and poured out two shots of whiskey. As they talked, she conjured up his favorites: corn-bacon chowder, fried chicken, ham steak with redeye gravy, biscuits, quince jelly, candied yams, and smothered collards. Between each course they downed a swig of rye, topped off the meal with a cobbler, then shared a cigar.

After that, Emma danced for him, twirling in her lacy new dressing gown and humming his favorite Stephen Foster songs as he fiddled. Finally, Judkins put away his violin, tickled her belly, covered her with licks and kisses, and wrapped her in a huge bear hug. Weary but eager, he pulled down his galluses, britches, and underdrawers, and he and Emma tumbled into bed.

"I'd sprinkled my sheets with lilac cologne," Emma later regaled her friends, "but that night, sweating bullets, drunk as a skunk, and happy as a pig in shit, Judkins was in midstroke and begging for more, when he hollered, 'Oh yes, my brown sugar angel!'" Then he collapsed on top of her like a punctured balloon, with his eyes wide open, but seeing nothing at all.

Although Emma was nearly fifty and her halo of dark hair was threaded with silver, she still was agile, yet she wriggled out from under Judkins only with great difficulty since he weighed 310 pounds, was as slippery as a greased pig, and definitely dead.

She ran over to the nearby cottage where Jenny Watkins (Robert Sayre's "colored" daughter) lived to awaken Jenny's "husband," Sheriff Rogers, and wailed out what had happened.

The sheriff returned with Emma, reclothed Judkins in his skivvies, shirt, and vest, tugged up her hefty Romeo's trousers, draped the jacket across his shoulders, placed the planter's hat on his head, and gently closed his eyelids. Using Emma's perfumed bed sheets as a sling, they toted the body out to Judkins's carriage. Figuring that he needed both medical and familial guidance, the sheriff drove the buggy over to the home of Rebecca Hunt's uncle, Dr. E. D. Albright. The doctor grudgingly agreed to keep the smiling corpse on some extra-large blocks of ice at his infirmary, then he and Sheriff Rogers headed off to inform "the ladies" out at Nancy's Fancy.

They reached there around sunup as Rebecca and Neppie were just stretching and yawning. E. D. Albright knocked, and the houseboy showed him into the parlor—the same room where Neppie had taught Adella to play the piano. As Sheriff Rogers waited in the kitchen, the doctor embraced his niece and her daughter, then delivered his less-than-totally-honest account.

By that time, Judkins and Emma's daughter, Molly, had started preparing breakfast. But when the sheriff told her what had happened the previous night, Molly burst into the living room sobbing as wretchedly as her white half sister. Outraged by that intrusion, Neppie wailed, "Shut your mouth, you dingy harlot. My daddy died, and the family's mourning in here." She seized and yanked a handful of Molly's crinkly hair and smacked her dimpled tan cheeks hard. Twice.

Molly didn't know what a harlot was but would not tolerate Neppie's abuse. The two women weighed about the same, though Neppie was a pillowy sack of cotton, while Molly was steely strong and five inches taller. She snarled, pounced, pinned Neppie down on the floral rug, and spit out words which, had she been thinking rationally, she'd never have uttered at all: "He was my daddy before he was yours, you fat pasty sow." But then realizing that she'd shattered a sacred taboo, Molly rolled off her half sister's soft belly and scuttled back to the kitchen.

Rebecca ignored the scrap and told the sheriff, "Keep him cold in town 'til Tuesday, then bring him out here. We'll put him in the ground, but there'll be no preacher, no mourners, no casket, and no wake. No funeral at all." She summoned Molly back in and snapped, "Pack up your paraphernalia, you mongrel bitch, and get your yaller ass outta *my* house straightaway."

Molly returned to Hunts' Hill with Sheriff Rogers and told her mother that Rebecca was refusing to have a funeral, but Emma shook her head and said, "Now that just won't do, darlin'." She took up a collection from family members and asked Mariah Hunt to write exactly what she decreed: words that she'd never forget. Emma purchased a granite slab from Sparta's memorial mason, who chiseled onto it the message Emma dictated and Mariah spelled out for him.

Sheriff Rogers, the mortician, and his crew of hirelings assembled at Dr. Albright's place early on Tuesday morning and heaved the large, sheet-wrapped body off the ice block and onto a hearse. An hour later they pulled into Nancy's Fancy and hitched their carts to Judkins's bug-eyed black iron jockey. Rebecca wrinkled her nose at the stench, examined her husband's beaming face and bloated body, then demanded, "Where are Mr. Hunt's boots, pistol, and violin, Sheriff? And where'd you get those putrid sheets?" Sheriff Rogers flushed but didn't answer.

Rebecca hadn't changed her mind about the funeral either and remained determined to have none at all. Thirty-five years had been long enough to tolerate her husband's shenanigans, so she ordered the mortician's "boys" to dig an extra-wide hole by the side of a cotton field two hundred yards from the big house. They rewrapped the corpse in Emma's perfumed bed linens and, without even putting Judkins in a pine box, slid the body down into the makeshift crypt.

After heading back to Hunts' Hill, Judkins's buddies shared a few words of farewell at Emma Hunt's observance, drank lots of whiskey, sang several of their friend's favorite songs, then placed his fiddle, boots, and pistol next to the granite slab that Emma had ordered and her neighbors laid down in the crawl space under her house. Its inscription read,

JUDKINS HUNT II

1814–1883

HE SLIPPED AND FELL

BUT NOW HE SLEEPS WITH AN ANGEL

Even after Judkins's death, the ruckus over J. M. Hunt's will dragged on. Then two years later, the death of Hancock County's cotton baron David Dickson rocked many Georgians, but the Hunts more than most others, because it raised issues so much like those that pertained to J. M.

The origins of that particular to-do dated back to 1846, when David Dickson (as Judkins Hunt had done to Emma) brutally deflowered a thirteen-year-old named Julia, who was one of his enslaved servants. As a result of that rape, Julia too had borne a baby girl. Her father-owner named his new slave Amanda, and later she became Adella Hunt's friend when they attended Atlanta University together. Mr. Dickson married for the first and only time when he was past sixty, but he and his young white bride, who soon passed away, had no children.

Following his wife's death and in consultation with his attorney, Charles du Bose, David Dickson laid out and dictated a final will. Except for a few minor sums that Georgia's "prince of planters" designated for a handful of employees, friends, and distant relations, the document specified that all of his assets (several hundred thousand dollars' worth) should go to his only child, Amanda.

Immediately after Mr. Dickson died, however, his white relatives contested the will, just as J. M. Hunt's white family had done. Mr. du Bose represented Amanda Dickson, and another local lawyer played a central role on the other side of the case. The attorney that the white Dicksons hired was Adella's cousin Tom Hunt, whom the Albright-Hunt sisters had retained to challenge J. M.'s will seven years before.

At first, the Dickson case progressed swiftly, with the curtain falling on its opening act when the probate court judge ruled in favor of the "designated colored heiress." But the white challengers appealed that decision to the superior court, where it went to trial early in 1885.

The core issues boiled down to these. First, the appellants claimed, the testator was stark raving mad when he'd drawn up the document. Second, his daughter and her "licentious" mother had exerted an "immoral influence" over him. Third, the petition contended, "this will is fatally flawed, and its implementation as written would generate results that are contrary to the best interests of all Georgians." What that final assertion really meant was that conveying such an unprecedented amount to a "darky woman," beyond any white men's control, threatened the ingrained racial, sexual, and social conventions that state authorities were struggling to maintain.

In addition to the press, litigants, and lawyers, many local folks attended the trial too, Adella's grandmother, aunt, mother, and sister among them. The case's disposition, they well understood, also might augur the outcome of J. M.'s similar and extended testamentary conflict.

Most facilities in Sparta weren't yet officially segregated, but everyone knew exactly where they were supposed to sit in the county's courtroom: "gentlemen" in the center section, "ladies" to one side in a three-row loge, and all people of color along with any white "spitters and sots" up in the balcony. But Adella's relatives seated themselves in the ladies' gallery, and even when Rebecca Albright Hunt exhorted the clerk to do so, he didn't try to remove them. He claimed not to know the younger women's "true" racial identities but spotted Susan Hunt as a "redskin squaw," shook his head, and told Rebecca, "I ain't taking on one of them."

Mr. du Bose introduced evidence showing that although pretty much everyone in Hancock County knew that David Dickson had "lived for years in a state of adultery with a colored woman," they'd tacitly accepted that arrangement and never spurned their "prince of planters." The Hunts' friends and neighbors had done much the same with J. M. and Susan.

The appellants' lawyer, Tom Hunt, however, exhorted the judge to direct his jurymen that "under the constitution and laws of the state of Georgia, sexual congress between white persons and negroes is forbidden. This entire document therefore must be invalidated." In fact, Georgia law did indeed prohibit both interracial marriage and all sexual relations (race notwithstanding) outside wedlock. Any will that bequeathed such assets to "an illegitimate, half-black child," attorney Hunt thus argued, "encourages illicit mingling and serves to undermine public policy."

But the judge cast aside those arguments as well. Rather, he instructed the jury that "due to the inalienable primacy of property rights, any man who is of sound mind may bequeath his worldly goods to whoever he chooses." The all-white, all-male, property-owning panel heeded those instructions, confirmed David Dickson's sanity, and reaffirmed the validity of his will.

As many observers, including Adella's white aunts by marriage, stomped out of the courtroom, Charles du Bose accepted the congratulations of a few well-wishers—Susan Hunt among them. She beamed, "You did a fine job, Mr. du Bose."

"Thank you, Miz Susan," he replied. "This is good news for Mr. Dickson's designated legatee and for your folks too. But remember, what happened here is only one chapter in this long book, and the folks who were denied today surely will take their case to our highest state court."

As Charles du Bose predicted, Tom Hunt promptly filed the white Dicksons' appeal with the Georgia Supreme Court's three member panel, headed by Chief Justice James Jackson, which met in Atlanta. And there again, attorney Hunt introduced his litany of objections to show how "all traditions of the past and hopes for the future of our Anglo-Saxon race are at stake."

And as soon as the introductory presentations wrapped up, Justice Jackson shook his grizzled head, pounded his gavel, and roared: "I'd rather die than uphold this abhorrent will!"

But that old vulture only prophesied and perhaps even accelerated his own demise, because three days later, still wearing his robes, he keeled over, dead as a doornail. No one was appointed to succeed him in a timely fashion, so the two surviving justices had to hear the rest of the pleadings and hand down a decision that would either confirm or deny the appellants' claims.

It took five months, but finally they too ruled that David Dickson had been fully compos mentis. White southerners impugned it, but the Constitution's Fourteenth Amendment iterated that for native-born Negroes, "distinctions between the races pertaining to citizenship rights have been abolished. Thus, whatever privileges accrue to a white concubine & her bastard, accrue to a colored woman & her bastard as well." The precedent set by the Dickson decision undercut every argument that the white Hunts' lawyer had used to circumvent J. M. Hunt's intent. Georgia's ultimate judicial entity had spoken, not just for the Dicksons but also for the Hunts.

Following J. M.'s death a decade before, Charles du Bose had petitioned Hancock County's probate court to sell "all Georgia Rail Road & Banking Co.'s stock in the estate of the deceased." The Hunts' internal bickering had long forestalled that pragmatic proposal, however, and only after the state's highest court upheld Amanda Dickson's similar claims did Rebecca Albright Hunt and her attorney, Tom Hunt, grudgingly raise the white flag of surrender. That's when Adella's grandmother Susan started receiving her long-overdue inheritance.

It wasn't a princely sum compared to the amount allocated through David Dickson's will, but it was far more than most white or virtually any people of color (an almost singular exception being Amanda Dickson herself) in Georgia had at that time. Each quarter annually, for the next three years, Susan Hunt would acknowledge its receipt with a bold "X" that she inked onto the chits, which confirmed, "Received of C. W. du Bose, Executor for J. M. Hunt, two hundred-thirty-six & 50/100 dollars, dividend from eighty-eight shares of Geo. R.R. stock."

Soon thereafter, however, attorney du Bose died. Susan Hunt and her descendants thus needed a new lawyer, and seeing no ready alternative, they retained their cousin Tom, who'd represented both their own white family and the white Dicksons. Tom had become an able practitioner too, and he negotiated a final settlement that all of the bickering Hunts accepted.

Susan received the stock sales' proceeds and a lot of real property—Fortitude included. Even when she bought an elegant phaeton and a pale horse that her daughters named Pegasus, Adella's grandmother thought she had more money than she'd ever want. Her mother and aunt also had gotten their legacies, but an equal portion still was due their absent brother, Jimmy.

Susan asked Adella to inform her son of his inheritance, and after receiving her letter, "Jimmy Pale Face" returned to Sparta. When he'd enlisted in the Union army in 1863, he became a white man and remained so. Now he lived in New York and was married and a father, though like many others who passed for white, he feared that the "secret inkwell" might spill over and reveal itself in his own child's skin color, features, or hair texture. But in his case, it didn't.

When he got to Sparta, where the family had assembled, Jimmy collected the thousand dollars his "stepfather," J. M. Hunt (who'd whipped him within an inch of his life), had bequeathed him. But staring at his relatives with those odd, mismatched eyes, he said, "I'm sorry I have to go, 'cause I love you, but if a fella has any choice, as I do, it's just too darn hard nowadays to be a colored man here in the U.S. of A."

Adella remained courteous but had to challenge him: "We have many battles to fight, Uncle Jimmy, but should always stay true to our families. Or are you abandoning us and the race altogether? Men such as you who've received much should give much in return."

But long before J. M. had fattened Jimmy's wallet, he'd permanently scarred his soul and his body, so Jimmy shook his head, said no more, and left Georgia. Adella, however, wondered what his white wife must have thought when she saw the hideous grid of keloid scars on his back that her grandmother had called "the burning bush." J. M. Hunt had bestowed those corporeal mementoes on his namesake as punishment for what he considered Jimmy's wartime treason.

As if to buttress Jimmy Hunt's concerns, a month later, "parties un-known" torched Hancock County's Bass Academy, where for fourteen years, a fortunate few of the county's children of color, including Adella and her younger siblings, had received a decent education. But any such enterprise, many white Georgians believed, made the "darkies" think too much of themselves and gave them "highfalutin notions." So they burned down the respected school.

And that railroad stock in J. M.'s estate still flummoxed Sparta's nosy parkers, because the white Hunts had no other such assets. Rather, they'd measured their wealth in acres and in slaves. They no longer could claim black people as property, farmland's value in Georgia had declined, and a range of economic and agricultural reversals diminished cotton's profit-ability.

But the source of J. M. Hunt's assets actually harked decades back, to when Nathan Sayre first had invested in the Georgia Railroad. As he'd pre-pared to travel abroad in 1850, he and Charles du Bose had drawn up a will, fearing that if he died in Europe, Georgia's courts wouldn't uphold the claims of any women of color, so they'd transferred the Judge's rail shares to J. M. and confirmed the pact with just a handshake. They agreed that when-ever Judge Sayre passed away, J. M. Hunt would care for Susan, and ulti-mately, he'd bequeath the stock to her. The white Hunts fought him tooth and nail, but J. M. honored that gentleman's agreement, then he did even more. He left his entire estate to Nathan Sayre's heirs, especially his "widow,"

Susan Hunt, who after the Judge's death became J. M.'s "wife," then his own "widow" too.

Henry Hunt Sr. also died that fall, and his niece Neppie Hunt, Adella's former teacher, wrested the funeral arrangements away from his wife, Mariah. Because her uncle "Big Henry" had been the only Hunt brother who'd borne arms with the Rebels, Neppie appropriated his body and had him buried in Sparta's town cemetery. Rev. Atticus Haygood delivered the eulogy for his old comrade-in-arms, and he did so while Henry's "colored" widow and children weren't even included in the service. The headstone that Neppie installed read,

CAPT. H. A. HUNT

1825–1889

CONFEDERATE SOLDIER

She also ordered a smaller foot stone. As with many others in Hancock County, it was inscribed "C.V.," meaning Confederate veteran.

County officials soon enacted an ordinance that restricted access to the main cemetery to whites only—except for the black people who drove the body carts, dug, weeded, and mowed the graves, and buried the dead. Adella and her siblings thus no longer were welcome to visit their father's or grandfather Sayre's interment sites. Following that affront, some of their neighbors swore that they saw vengeful "speerits" congregate in the graveyard at midnight under the blood-burning moon, writhing and howling to protest the prohibition. Several hours later, those silvery phantasms wafted away—until they furiously returned on that same date in the following years.

And in the town square, just across from the all-white cemetery, under the aegis of the Daughters of the Confederacy, the South's leading organization devoted to resurrecting the "Lost Cause," Neppie Hunt oversaw the erection of Hancock County's most pretentious memorial. It resembled many others that were being installed throughout the region and featured an obelisk much like the one that marked Judge Sayre's grave. Uniformed, rifle-bearing Rebel soldiers, carved in bas-relief, adorned two side panels of the granite cube below, which squatted atop five wide limestone steps.

Square-cut letters on one side spelled out, OUR CONFEDERATE DEAD, while on the opposite façade, a different message appeared, written in italic script. As Neppie often had intoned when she'd tutored Adella, its inscription, her paean to the Confederacy, read, *Georgia's was the word and theirs the will to die.*

When a work crew completed Susan's new home on Hunts' Hill, she left Fortitude, for the most part, and moved near her daughters. Adella's sister Lula Mae's children preferred store-bought clothes to those that their mother and grandmother usually made, and since they were Hunts (attorney Hunt's nieces), clerks in the local emporia sometimes let them try on such apparel. That courtesy almost always was denied to others of Hancock County's people of color.

After Adella's brother Henry Jr. had spent eight long years at Atlanta University, where he concentrated on academics in the fall semesters, then worked as a carpenter each spring, he finished as his class's top graduate. He married his patient fiancée, Florence Johnson, and they moved to North Carolina, where they both taught. Adella and Henry's sister Ella attended a nearby women's academy, and Sarah began teaching at Tuskegee Institute's Children's House. But their brother Maddy, a lifelong invalid, died, and after Bass Academy was torched, Tommy, their youngest sibling, moved to Alabama to live with Adella and her husband. Of Mariah's surviving children, only Lula Mae and Will remained in Sparta. Adella wrote her grandmother twice a month with news about all she was doing and knew that her mother or sister would read Susan those letters.

On a hot August morning, Adella later learned, her grandmother donned a straw hat, buttoned a calico blouse, knotted a bandana around her neck, and laced up her old buck hide boots. She slipped a corncob pipe in her pocket, tucked a Bowie knife into her belt, drove her phaeton down Hunts' Hill past her daughters' homes, and paused at the cemetery to share a few words with her white kinfolk interred there, then she crossed the courthouse square. Several black women called out, "G'mornin', Miz Susan," but some of the white ones whom she passed glowered or averted their eyes as she greeted them. They still considered Susan Hunt a "godless witch," and it rankled them no end that she was now decidedly well-to-do in her own right.

As she neared Fortitude, Susan paused at the graveyard by Shoulderbone Creek to talk with J. M., the other white elders, and their slaves who were buried nearby, then lingered in the shade of the giant oak where Capt. Judkins Hunt had laid out his wagon circle a century back.

Susan apparently unhitched, watered, then saddled her mount, Pegasus, in the Hunts' barn, where she and J. M. first had coupled as lusty teenagers. That also was where J. M. Hunt had brutally whipped his namesake, Susan's son, Jimmy, during the Civil War.

Several local folks recalled that they'd seen Susan astride Pegasus as he loped up the hill near Mt. Zion. The pale horse and its rider passed by Rev. Beman's old Presbyterian church, where the white Sayres, Watkinses, Albrights, and Hunts (but never Susan) had worshiped for decades. She paused at the crest, silhouetted against the late afternoon sun. One witness later reported that her tall, mounted figure appeared to rise and hover just above the ground as the intense summer heat dissolved the red clay road under her until it looked like a river of mercury.

In scarcely a moment, the clear sky turned slate gray. An inky funnel cloud thundered through, stripping leaves and severing branches, overturning carts, lifting wagon tarps and cabin roofs, sucking sheds from their underpinnings. Trash, fence rails, chicks, even piglets spiraled upward. Like an avalanche, a hailstorm (stones larger than pecans) sledge-hammered Mt. Zion.

At first, Adella's mother wasn't alarmed when Susan didn't return to Hunts' Hill for supper, since she sometimes bunked down at Fortitude, but after the weather cleared, Mariah sent her son Will to find his grandmother. He returned to report that during the twister, lightning split the Hunts' ancient oak. The nearby house burned to the ground, though not the farther-off barn with the phaeton in it. He assured his mother that Susan couldn't have been trapped inside.

Family and friends searched all over the county yet found nothing. Hearing of Susan's disappearance, Adella recalled Neppie Hunt's legends about the flying steed Pegasus, stories her grandmother had shared about the slaves who'd grown wings on their backs and soared across the Big Water to their homelands, and lore about the Cherokee tribe she called the Bird

Clan. But like her father, Osborne, who'd disappeared eighty years before, Susan Hunt simply vanished.

When the family finally abandoned hope of finding her, Adella wrote to share that news with her uncle—Susan's son, Jimmy—in New York City but heard nothing back from him. Then she returned to Hancock County with her siblings Tommy and Sarah. Adella had her children in tow, and she was pregnant again. Her ankles were swollen, her stomach churned, and her clothes stretched unattractively across her belly. The visitors hesitated at first but finally agreed to Mariah Hunt's sensible proposal that they sleep in Susan's unoccupied house.

Her first night back, Adella felt sick to her stomach and yearned for the white clay that her grandmother often sent to Tuskegee. After settling her toddlers in their great-grandmother's bed, Adella found what she sought on a pantry shelf: small cartons of "clean dirt." But what startled her was that the word UNAKR was printed in ink on each cardboard box. Mason jars filled the cabinet below. They'd been lined up alphabetically, with their pasted-on paper labels marked APPL SAWS, PEECH JAM, and PIKELS. She stirred a quarter cup of the UNAKR, or kaolin, into Susan's APPL SAWS, gulped it down, and her queasiness soon eased.

Toting a kerosene lamp, Adella poked around still more. She found the crate holding Judge Sayre's journals, a McGuffey's reader, and a number of novels, histories, and poetry anthologies. The Judge's bookplates, imprinted with "The Sayre Library at Pomegranate Hall," were affixed inside the covers. Alexander Walker's book titled *Intermarriage* and even law tomes had come from his mansion too. Many of the pages had been dog-eared, and notations in that same precise, bold print crammed the margins. Adella also found every letter she'd written to Susan. They'd been rubbed tissue-thin, tied with ribbons, and identified, FRUM ADELLA. Susan had arranged sixteen packets chronologically, one for each year since she'd left Sparta.

The unlikely truth dawned on Adella: at a time in her life (past eighty) when others—those few who were still alive—became timid and inflexible and aspired to learn nothing new, Susan Hunt had shared her bold endeavor with no one but taught herself to read and write.

Because they had no body, the Hunts couldn't put Susan's remains into the ground or designate an interment site. Adella and her mother called on their cousin, attorney Tom Hunt, but he wouldn't let them place any memorial in the graveyard at Fortitude or in the Hunts' plot at Rev. Beman's Presbyterian Church. Mariah scolded, "Shame on you, Young Tom! You know that Susan delivered you and saved your dear mother's life. You even drew up her will."

Tom nodded but reiterated what they all knew: "Susan Hunt was a pagan."

Then the Hunt women had a different thought. Why not ask the Ralstons, who'd bought Pomegranate Hall, if they might discreetly memorialize Susan somewhere on their property? Receiving the Hunt women on the porch since she'd never allow "colored folks" in her home as guests or equals, Mrs. Ralston pondered that request, and then to Adella's surprise, she agreed.

She and her husband considered themselves modern people who didn't believe in "ha'nts," but recently they'd heard inexplicable noises: doors that slammed when no breeze stirred the air, staccato rappings, and hushed sighs, like poetry breathed in an arcane tongue. "Long ago," their neighbors recalled, "Susan Hunt vowed that she'd return to Pomegranate Hall someday." Its new owners certainly didn't want "some avenging black-squaw spook" occupying their home. Mrs. Ralston told the Hunt ladies, "You can say a few words, sing some of your old slave songs, and pray for a while—outside, of course," as they placed an anonymous (at the Ralstons' insistence) marker in what had been Susan's glorious garden. Many of her pomegranate bushes remained, but the lawns were now a flawless jade velvet.

But what neither Adella, her sisters, nor the Ralstons anticipated was that as word of the upcoming observance spread around, scores of women, old and young, affluent and indigent, from the countryside, Sparta, and nearby towns, their complexions ranging from coffee brown to cocoa to palest vanilla cream, wanted to pay their final respects. Susan Hunt had cared for them through six decades. She'd facilitated, prevented, or sometimes safely terminated their pregnancies, delivered their babies, soothed the discomforts of menstruation and menopause, assuaged their melancholy, and more. Those women streamed down Pomegranate Hall's elm-lined driveway, past Judge Sayre's elegant verandah, on foot or straddling farm nags, steering mule-drawn wagons or ensconced in their elegant carriages. Mrs. Ralston couldn't have her servants shoo them off, since some of the white ones belonged to her own social circle.

Friends and family came from Hunts' Hill. Adella and her sisters knew that Susan wouldn't have wanted Rev. Lucius Holsey, the increasingly renowned preacher at Sparta's C.M.E. church, to pray over her, but Emma Hunt, Judkins's broken-toothed angel, led them in singing "Oh! Susanna." Even Stephen Foster's "darky" lyrics didn't rankle Adella that day. She recited the old prayer that Susan had taught her years before to denote such homecomings: "May the Great Spirit bless all of those who enter here and may a rainbow circle 'round your shoulder."

Mariah's daughters wished they had a photograph of Susan but knew that she, whom little frightened, was terrified by the camera's glass "eye," which, she'd believed, threatened to steal her soul. Mariah Hunt showed her girls the black-on-white silhouette of Susan, with its shred of red satin glued at the base of her neck, but Adella still didn't know its provenance.

On Adella's last Saturday in Sparta, she heaved herself into her grandmother's phaeton (her brother Will had retrieved it from Fortitude's barn), which Mariah said that Susan wanted her to have, then drove from Hunts' Hill to her old tutor Neppie Hunt's cottage near Pomegranate Hall. After her mother had died, Neppie sold the plantation where she'd been born and raised, and moved into town. The visitor knocked and called out, "It's Adella Hunt Logan, Miss Neppie."

Neppie was surprised to see a long-absent though familiar person at her front door, but fanning her damp pink face, she asked her former student to sit with her on the porch, where they shared some vanilla tea cakes and a pitcher of mint lemonade. They hadn't spoken since 1879, when Adella had left Hancock County for Atlanta University, although their vocation now was a point of common interest. Adella had heard that Neppie was donating her time, energy, and money to help the United Daughters of the Confederacy perpetuate the "Lost Cause" and also fighting the "demon rum" through her efforts with the Woman's Christian Temperance Union. (The local chapter had tried to burn down Sparta's Old Eagle Tavern.) But they didn't talk about Susan or discuss Neppie's preemptive role in the burial of Adella's father at Sparta's "whites only" cemetery. That shameful episode hung in the air, but Adella said, "What's done is done."

An hour later, Neppie coupled her farewell with a request: "Do you remember the name I used to call you?" Adella nodded. "Then please write me again . . . my Athena," Neppie pleaded.

After that, Will Hunt drove the sojourners over to Sparta's depot. They boarded the local to Camak Junction, where they transferred to the Georgia Railroad. Adella's belly clenched (she recognized the familiar onset of labor), and she broke into a sweat as she recalled the horrific train trip following her wedding. But she'd prepurchased their tickets, so they settled into the first-class car's sleek leather seats, thereby avoiding the discomfort, filth, dangers, and abuse that people of color usually endured. Thus, they rode west to Alabama masquerading as white folks.

Away from familiar locales where people knew and might expose them, anyone in the immediate Hunt family could shift his or her racial identity—if need be. Most of them remained within the African American community yet often hesitated when they saw the web of bluish veins that throbbed under the translucent veils of pale skin at the pulse spots on their wrists. But whenever Adella traveled around the South, she also never forgot how, without Judge Sayre's prescient investments in the railroad, many of their recent passages wouldn't have taken place at all.

Obstreperous Women

ADELLA'S CONTRACTIONS INTENSIFIED as she and the others boarded the Chehaw-to-Tuskegee wagonette. Her pelvis convulsed, and almond-scented amniotic fluid seeped from her unbidden as a ravenous beast clawed at her uterus. But Logan met their train and transported her to Halle Tanner Dillon's infirmary, where, despite unexpected difficulties, she bore a premature infant. The institute's termagant physician monitored Adella like a vengeful jailer and ordered her to stay in bed for two weeks. This wasn't called "labor" and "confinement" without good reason.

She didn't welcome her baby Ralph with much enthusiasm, and he proved unready for the harsh world he entered. A month later the whole family mourned when they buried him in Tuskegee's "family" graveyard, not far from Booker T. Washington's first two wives.

It took longer for Adella to move beyond the deep bereavement that followed the loss of her grandmother. A full year later, her brother Will, driving Susan Hunt's phaeton, and their cousin Alexander, following him in the new A, E, I, and O Hunt Brothers Funeral Home's horse-drawn hearse laden with many of Susan's possessions, arrived in Tuskegee. Alexander soon returned to Sparta, but the Logans had a job awaiting Will Hunt. He was a forty-year-old bachelor whose vocation until then had been as a butler and carriage driver, but as the son, grandson, and great-grandson of white Georgia farmers, he took to the agrarian work in Alabama as a duck to water.

Adella had to deal with all that came to her from Sparta, including the rugs and elegant furniture that soon graced her house alongside the simple stools, chests, and wood-framed mirrors that the school's cabinetry students crafted for them. She found the moccasins Susan had made for her years ago (the leather had become brittle and the silk linings crumbled into ruby dust), and she catalogued most of Judge Sayre's books for the institute's makeshift library. Each night that winter, as her family slept, she plowed through and learned from her grandfather's diaries.

And only a year later she gave birth again. Since Susan was gone, Mariah came to help her daughter care for the baby, whom she named Olivia for Booker T. Washington's second deceased wife. Adella appreciated her mother's support, but Mariah wasn't Susan and had worn widow's weeds from collar to anklebone since her husband and son Maddy had died. She turned to religion more than ever and advised Adella, "We must place ourselves in God's hands."

She meant well, but that phrase irritated her daughter. The new mother was exhausted too, because Olivia, crankier than her other infants had been, kept her awake every night with colicky bawling. Adella thus took advantage of Mariah's presence to nap during the daytime.

The Logans' home felt damp and chilly in the cooler months, so Mariah often rocked Olivia to sleep by the kitchen fireplace hearth. The babe in arms and her grandmother were dozing together there one late fall afternoon when a live ember rolled onto the hem of Mariah's long skirt. Junior and Ruth first smelled the smoke, ran in, and screamed, "Wake up, Granny, you're on fire!" Their cries roused Adella, who stumbled downstairs.

The house trembled as she entered the kitchen. A green aura suffused the room, and she saw a scaly apparition flap through the haze and alight atop the cast-iron stove, eying the golden cornbread that Mariah had baked and set out to cool. Cawing hoarsely, the creature circled the ceiling, then swooped down. Thrumming its wings against the older woman's chest, it ripped out hanks of silver hair, shook its scaly head, and wrenched the infant from her arms. Mariah spun like a top, then spiraled to the floor. Unable to find her lost voice or move her leaden limbs, Adella watched the fiend's putrid saliva extinguish the flames that had engulfed Olivia and her caretaker. It dropped her scorched infant into the sink like a sack of garbage, snatched a hunk of warm golden cornbread from the stovetop, then soared shrieking through the closed rear window. Adella never mentioned the Raven Mocker to anyone—if indeed she'd seen him at all.

Those gruesome images were the last she remembered until, jarred into wakefulness by a disinfectant's acrid stench, she resurfaced two days later in the institute's infirmary.

"Where's my baby?" she demanded, "and where's Mamma?"

Logan closed his eyes. Adella's sister Sarah, who lived with them, later told her, "that was when you began cursing and striking the poor man"— but she never remembered doing so.

Adella still was forcibly bedridden when her siblings and husband laid to rest a second infant. And not quite out of her earshot, Dr. Dillon warned Warren Logan about his spouse's "postpartum hysteria." ("*Quos deus vult perdere, prius dementat,*" Adella mused: "Whom the gods wish to destroy, they first make mad.") The physician also called her patient "randomly delusional," then grumbled, "Last night I had to strap your wife to the bed with canvas belts—a straightjacket—because she flailed at me and ranted about how she wanted to 'fly away.'"

During Adella's enforced absence from home, Logan brought in a crew of students to air out, scour, mop, and repaint the kitchen. One of them stashed in her bedroom chifforobe the singed skirt that Mariah had been wearing at the time of the tragedy. In its side pockets Adella found three items that her mother must have counted among her most cherished possessions.

First was the silhouette of Susan Hunt that the daguerreotypist had cut out at Mariah and Henry's 1852 wedding—a black-on-white paper profile with a shred of scarlet satin glued at the throat. Adella placed it on her dresser next to the second pocketed item: Mariah's only photograph of her father, Judge Nathan Sayre. The third memento was the note allegedly written by her uncle J. M. Hunt. But in fact, Mariah herself had composed it during the Civil War when she'd transported her brother, Jimmy, and their cousin Johnny for Susan to care for as they were being hunted by half (the white half) of the county following "The Great Darky Conspiracy in Sparta." It wasn't written in Mariah's familiar script, however, but as she'd often told her daughter, "I squared off and emboldened my usual handwriting to make it look like a man's."

At first, Adella thought that her mother had perished in the fire too, but in fact, under a doctor's care, Sarah had escorted her back to Georgia. Their sister Lula Mae wrote her siblings every week warning that Mariah's condition was deteriorating, then, a month later, sent the sadly anticipated cable: MAMMA LEFT US LAST NIGHT TO LIVE WITH JESUS. Adella's grandmother, two babies, and now her mother—all gone in little more than a year.

A few days later she joined family and neighbors who gathered in Sparta. Adella and her sisters had hoped to bury Mariah in the public cemetery next to her husband of almost four decades, but when they went to the courthouse to pursue that option, the clerk snarled, "I knows who you mongrel Hunts is, and no cullud can be buried there."

Rev. (now Bishop) Lucius Holsey conducted Mariah's service. He'd been her, Lula Mae's, and Ella's pastor and was renowned among Georgia's African Americans, and his oratory had vastly improved since he'd preached at Adella's uncle Judkins's plantation just after the war.

Garbed in a deep purple robe with his tan hands outstretched, Bishop (of the Christian Methodist Episcopal Church) Holsey looked skyward and began, "Beloved Lord and Your only son Jesus, we're jealous today because our sister Mariah has flown off to live with You forever. You wanted another angel, so she placed herself in Your blessed hands. Yea, death and chaos intermingle, 'til the immortal light shineth forth to raise Mariah from the funeral pyre on wings of flame." Given the circumstances leading to her mother's death, Adella considered his reference to "wings of flame" highly inappropriate. The Hunt family funeral home arranged the interment, and they laid her to rest in Sparta's Ebenezer Church's graveyard and marked the site with a simple headstone inscribed,

MARIAH LILY HUNT

1833–1894

HERS WAS A LIFE IN GOD

Adella also was aghast to learn that her Atlanta University colleague Amanda Dickson, another member of Bishop Holsey's flock and the country's wealthiest woman of their race, died that winter as she was returning from the North to her Georgia mansion. Rumors (unreliable though they proved to be) circulated through the grapevine and in the black press that white railroad workers, resentful that any such "highfalutin nigrah" could afford to engage a private car, had deliberately sidetracked her elegant conveyance. As the trainmen stood by, Amanda reportedly pounded on the locked doors and windows, struggled to breathe, then suffocated, as her leased facility, heated by a coal stove much like that which had sickened her when she and Adella had attended school together, became a virtual oven— and essentially roasted her.

Many people in Sparta and Tuskegee knew about Amanda Dickson's gruesome death as well as those of Adella's mother and baby. The latter tragedies felt like both personal and public failures. For months thereafter (to her husband's exasperation), Adella hardly could stop weeping.

She took some solace, however, in educating herself on the subject of woman suffrage. Through access to the ballot, she started to believe, people of color, especially women, hopefully might secure their fundamental civil rights. But most southerners, and a majority of northerners too, considered such aspirations preposterous. They deemed political participation "unnatural" for anyone of her sex, but she was both female and not white and thus doubly intended to remain in her "assigned sphere." The refusal of Sparta's clerk to let the Hunt sisters bury their mother in the town cemetery and the endemic abuse of and violence against African Americans throughout the South, reinforced by the burgeoning segregation of public facilities, strengthened Adella's resolve that acquiring and exercising that supposed guarantor of citizenship was essential.

As she read more, she learned that a quarter century back, white woman-suffrage advocates had become bitterly divided over the Fifteenth Amendment, which was formulated to ensure that race (though not sex) must no longer proscribe access to the vote. Shortly after its 1870 ratification, however, southern legislatures began chipping away at their new rosters of black male voters. They imposed poll taxes and "morality," literacy, and property requisites, although the franchise rights of most indigent, felonious, or illiterate white men soon would be legislatively protected by "grandfather clauses" that ensured that if their forebears had voted in the past, without renewed qualifications, they henceforth might do so as well. White officials manipulated voting policies, locales, and times of access, and white toughs menaced black men, trying to disfranchise them entirely. But a few of the school's male faculty nonetheless resolutely exercised their increasingly challenged access to the ballot. Each year as election time neared, Logan assured Adella that by casting his own precious vote he'd represent her interests as well.

In inclement weather, Logan unfailingly undertook fifty laps around the covered porch that encircled their home, and he wasn't in the least amused when his wife paced behind him reciting a stanza from one of her favorite poems, "Aunt Chloe," by the African American writer and suffrage advocate Frances Ellen Watkins Harper:

> Day after day did Milly Green just follow after Joe,
> And told him if he voted wrong to pack his rags and go.

Adella trumpeted her suffrage cause when- and wherever she had the chance, especially through the colored women's club movement. Like most of the women in her circle who were dedicated to "uplifting the race," she supported those collective efforts that sought to advance social and educational reforms among their people. Booker Washington, however, cautioned that "although the negro shouldn't be deprived of the franchise by unfair means, political agitation will not save him." He also tried to avoid altogether the "woman question," which he dismissed as a "hornet's nest." His wife belittled Adella's cause too. "At some point, our sex will be granted the vote," Margaret soothed any doubters, adding, "I'm not opposed to women voting, but the issue never keeps me awake at night." Many of her acolytes at Tuskegee Institute agreed that though voteless, if the third Mrs. Washington slept in peace, they could do the same.

By the mid-1890s Margaret Washington began her reign as "president for life" of the Tuskegee Woman's Club. She chaired several similar statewide and regional organizations and became a vice president of the new National Association of Colored Women. Adella joined the NACW too and attended most of its conventions, where she conceived, launched, and headed its dynamic suffrage department. Mrs. Washington, however, steamed and schemed year after year, waiting for the association's independent-minded members to relent and elect her as its supreme leader. She resented having to play second fiddle to anyone, except her remarkable husband.

Adella also wondered if, and under what circumstances, others of her race would attend the upcoming convention of the National-American Woman Suffrage Association—the recently reunified movement's foremost organization. Her friend Patty Winston had introduced her to the N-AWSA's work and mission. Patty planned to attend and urged Adella to join her. Because its leaders wanted to demonstrate that their cause was truly nation-wide, the organization would meet in January 1895 in Atlanta, Georgia, for the first time outside Washington, D.C.

It intrigued Adella that so many suffragists—she preferred that suffix, which denoted advocacy, to the diminutively gendered "suffragettes"—such as Patty lived near one another in upstate New York. A host of that region's senior suffrage advocates, Frederick Douglass, Susan B. Anthony, and Elizabeth Cady Stanton among them, had cut their teeth in political activism by participating in the abolitionist movement. Now the latter two compared women's woes to those of the slaves, although slaves, Adella knew, neither had benefited from nor had been able to take any solace in white men's supposed protections. Mrs. Stanton, however, haughtily protested that as a disfranchised white woman, she'd "had to stand aside to see Sambo walk into the kingdom first."

Adella also learned about Susan B. Anthony's attempt to cast a ballot in Rochester, New York, in the 1872 presidential election, followed by her trial and conviction. Adella's real hero, the former slave Isabella Baumfree, who'd reinvented herself as Sojourner Truth, tried to vote in Battle Creek, Michigan, that same autumn when the flamboyant Victoria Woodhull ran for president and selected Frederick Douglass as her putative running mate. But to Mr. Douglass's dismay, his friend Miss Anthony revisited her tirades that the Fifteenth Amendment, which he'd championed, "has placed a new class of voters, ignorant black men, over educated white ladies."

Few southerners shared the slowly increasing number of northerners' support of woman suffrage. Grey Columns' mistress, Nora Varner, for instance, sometimes invited Adella to her home for tea and even let her guest enter and leave by the front door. She also called her "Mrs. Logan," in defiance of Alabama's racial protocols, but when Adella asked her hostess to join her in Atlanta, Mrs. Varner demurred: "My husband wouldn't want me to do that."

When Adella had visited with her white cousin Neppie Hunt in Sparta after Susan vanished, Neppie had urged her former student to write, which Adella now did, hoping that Neppie also might want to attend the N-AWSA convention. She knew that her cousin worked on behalf of other reform efforts such as the burgeoning (its national membership topped 150,000) Woman's Christian Temperance Union—the WCTU. Under the aegis of Frances Willard, that group's president, many southern women campaigned against "the demon rum" in segregated chapters, where they denounced the reported brutishness, venality, and sloth of any and all imbibers. Neppie, however, didn't respond to Adella's letter about the upcoming N-AWSA gathering.

Adella was certain that any identifiable women of color, except for nursemaids, cooks, charwomen, or others who were restricted to menial roles, would be barred from the convention's hotel headquarters, yet she yearned to go but knew that she'd have to keep her racial identity carefully under wraps in those Jim Crow facilities. Such subterfuges made her anxious, though if she was to take advantage of this rare opportunity, she had no choice but to "wear the veil."

About a hundred official delegates, fewer than usual since most such advocates lived in the North and West, convened in Atlanta that winter. Other woman-suffrage sympathizers, as well as a slew of dissenters or doubters, also streamed in to listen, learn, and express their views.

On the afternoon Adella arrived, she visited the sales kiosk to buy items as slight as Frances Willard's new booklet, *How I Learned to Ride the Bicycle,* and as weighty as the third volume of Elizabeth Cady Stanton and Susan B. Anthony's *History of Woman Suffrage.* And as she was completing her purchases, she heard a familiar "Harrumph!" from across the room. Adella was surprised to see her cousin Neppie Hunt, and she nodded and discreetly waved.

As she awaited Miss Neppie's acknowledgment, Patty Winston introduced her to Susan B. Anthony. Because Adella had so admired Miss Anthony, she'd expected her to be a physical colossus, but she was of modest stature and held her gray head a bit askew. Adella later learned that was an attempt to compensate for her strabismus: a form of wall-eyedness. She knew that the great suffragist would be speaking at another nearby venue later that week, so she whispered, "I look forward to attending your address at Atlanta University but wish that you'd welcomed colored women other than those of us who can pass for white to your sessions here in the hotel."

Miss Anthony stared at (or past) her but didn't respond, then hastened on to greet others as Adella again glanced over at Neppie Hunt. She overheard the silver-haired attendee who was chatting with her cousin say, "I applaud your work on behalf of both the WCTU and our mighty Daughters of the Confederacy, Miss Neppie," and rightly surmised that she was Mary Latimer McLendon, one of Georgia's leading temperance crusaders and few backers of votes for women.

Neppie beckoned Adella to her side and said to her companion, "Mrs. McLendon, I'd like you to meet Adella Hunt Logan, a cousin of mine from Sparta who was one of my best students ever. She's married now and is teaching in Alabama." Ingrained prejudices and southern racial protocols kept Neppie from calling her "*Mrs.* Logan." She also didn't mention Tuskegee Institute, which was becoming the nation's best-known school for people of African ancestry.

"I'm pleased to meet you, Mrs. McLendon," Adella smiled as they shook hands, "and I certainly know your name and reputation." But she couldn't resist adding, "What a small world it is, since you are M. L., or Mary Latimer McLendon, whereas my sister is L. M., or Louisa Mae McLendon. Do you think your husbands might be related? And years ago, I should add, our mutual uncle married a woman whose maiden name was Latimer. Isn't that right, Miss Neppie?"

Neppie Hunt looked as if she wanted to sink through the floor, because she knew that Adella's sister Lula (Louisa) Mae's husband, Gilbert McLendon, was a dark-skinned mason in Sparta and also knew about J. M. Hunt's brief marriage to the long-deceased Marjorie Latimer.

M. L. McLendon squeezed Adella's elbow and said, "Wouldn't it be a lovely surprise if we turned out to be in-laws?" Then she added, "Miss Neppie, I'm hosting a private reception tomorrow. I'd like you and your charming cousin to attend." She jotted down the address and time but would have been horrified to know that she'd invited a "colored woman" to her home.

Adella courteously declined Mrs. McLendon's invitation, because the next evening she and Patty Winston trolleyed across town to Atlanta University for Miss Anthony's speech. She thrilled her interracial audience by urging the "weaker sex's" empowerment. "The people who clothe, feed, and house you think they have the right to dictate to you, so before you assume the luxury of marriage, take the time to earn your own money and buy your own home. Then your husband never can say, 'If you try to vote you must leave,' and cast you out. Young women such as you are starting to take their rightful places in the world," she concluded to fervent applause.

On the convention's final day Adella joined a small group of delegates who donned all-white outfits (she'd packed and wore her wedding dress) adorned with yellow satin sashes that had "Votes for Women" printed on them. They assembled at the hotel, then to protest the state's discriminatory suffrage laws, marched in symbolic silence to the capitol. Sparta's W. J. Northen, who'd endorsed Adella's admission to Atlanta University, recently had become governor, but to her relief, since there was a slight chance he'd recognize her, they didn't gain access to his office. She shivered in the chilly air, her heart pounded, her feet blistered, and she wondered how brave she'd be in the face of genuine danger but felt certain that although most Georgians opposed their campaign, as a "white lady," prevailing mores would ensure her physical safety.

Adella returned from Atlanta elated but exhausted due to the anxieties generated by her racial charade. She tried to assume a confident demeanor, but the lurking perils associated with such subterfuges took their toll. She'd also discreetly asked a few of the northern suffragists if they'd like to see Tuskegee and brought a few of them back with her, while Miss Anthony, who found time to address a very small, all-white pro-suffrage assemblage in nearby Montgomery, promised that the next time she came south, she too wanted to visit "Mr. Washington's school."

Patty Winston matched Adella's contribution to the N-AWSA, thereby making her a Lifetime Member. She thus became the association's first such member of her race anywhere, and the only one at all who lived in the ultraconservative state of Alabama. Thereafter she read every issue of its *Woman's Journal* and shared the N-AWSA's literature, rhetoric, strategies, and rare successes with her colleagues in the local, state, and national colored women's clubs.

But just a few weeks later, African Americans throughout the country were devastated to learn of Frederick Douglass's death, only a day after a different (and almost but not exclusively white) women's convention in Washington, D.C., where Susan B. Anthony had introduced him as her "esteemed colleague." Remembering his visit to the institute, everyone there mourned deeply, because they'd lost both their mighty hero and their beloved "grandfather." The "King of the Freedmen" was buried near Miss Anthony's home in Rochester, New York, a longtime breeding ground for progressive political activism, where he'd lived for many years as well.

Soon thereafter Patty Winston wrote Adella: *Aunt Susan regrets not having invited Mr. Douglass to her gathering in Atlanta last month, but she told me, "At least I had the opportunity to deliver my final tribute at his funeral."*

Adella felt obliged to correct her friend's misinterpretation. Miss Anthony told Patty that she'd opposed Frederick Douglass's attendance at her N-AWSA conference in Georgia because she "didn't want to see him humiliated." Yet more importantly, she'd feared that the dusky Titan's presence would deter a few wavering white southerners who otherwise might support her cause.

And inspired by Frances Willard's provocative booklet, which she'd recently purchased, Adella was determined to learn to ride a bicycle but presumed that Logan would object. When she raised the issue at supper one evening, she wasn't surprised when her husband fumed, "First, Mother, we can't afford such frivolous purchases; second, bicycles are dangerous contraptions; and third, those riders wear bloomers—and women in pants have no place on our campus."

As per Susan B. Anthony's counsel in her speech at Atlanta University, however, Adella did have money of her own, so she defied Logan and ordered from the Sears & Roebuck mail catalogue a broadcloth bloomer suit and a lady's Schwinn safety bicycle. She quickly mastered the device, relished her increased mobility (since she no longer needed to trudge across the large campus or accommodate her husband's schedule to use their buggy), and often quoted Miss Anthony's declaration: "I call bicycles freedom machines. They've done more to emancipate our sex than anything in the world. I rejoice whenever I see a woman pedaling by on a wheel."

And of far greater and more lasting import than Adella's new "wheels," the railways continued as major battlefields in the country's mounting struggles over racial segregation. A New Orleans *créole de couleur* named Homer Plessy had instigated one such initiative.

As with Adella and many members of her family, Mr. Plessy could pass for white if he chose to do so—although he usually didn't. Louisiana, however, classified him as an octoroon, and its laws specified that "anyone who has at least one-eighth African blood is a negro."

By purchasing a first-class ticket in 1892, Homer Plessy had deliberately challenged a new regulation that segregated in-state rail travel. When he was on his way to New Orleans that June, a railway official identified and arrested him. He was swiftly tried and found guilty. Judge J. Howard Ferguson upheld the statute, which iterated that "negroes traveling within Louisiana must not occupy passenger coaches reserved for whites." Over the ensuing four years, Mr. Plessy and his attorneys would appeal their case— ultimately to the nation's highest court.

Adella's birth family, though few others of the race, had profited financially as a result of the decision of Georgia's ultimate court a decade earlier in the case of *Dickson v. Dickson,* when its justices had ruled that the Constitution's Fourteenth Amendment protected the rights of all Americans— racial identity notwithstanding. She'd assumed that in similar instances, judicial precedent would result in similar outcomes. But in the 1896 *Plessy v. Ferguson* decision, the United States Supreme Court instead upheld Louisiana's new discriminatory regulation, ruling seven to one to do so, with a single abstention, John Marshall Harlan, "the Great Dissenter," voting no.

As a former slaveholder, Justice Harlan had opposed the late-1860s

Reconstruction amendments to the Constitution, but rumor suggested that he remained close to his light-skinned half brother (his father's "outside son"), whose mother the Harlan family had enslaved for many years. Like Homer Plessy, he too opted *not* to pass for white. Adella surmised that such an intimate affiliation must have influenced the justice's evolving legal thinking and opinions.

Despite Justice Harlan's dissent, the court's overwhelming majority determined that separate accommodations need not stamp "negroes with a badge of inferiority unless they choose to interpret those regulations in that way." Such facilities, they speciously argued, clearly "could be equal, and thus should result in no insult, hardship or inconvenience" to members of the race.

Outrages against men of color singed the institute too, and in mid-'95 two such events played out within days of each other. Each featured a John Alexander: one white and the other of predominantly African ancestry. The first incident centered around a brown-skinned widower, Tom Harris, who practiced law in Tuskegee. The white townspeople barely had tolerated his litigious profession in the past but responded more heatedly when he flaunted racial protocols by hosting a white female house guest. As an angry mob assembled, Mr. Harris tried to escape through the garden of his white neighbor—named John Alexander. A pursuer aimed his gun and fired, the agile Mr. Harris ducked, and the bullet meant for him instead nicked the elderly Mr. Alexander.

As Tom Harris fled, however, a rifle blast ripped through his thigh. His son bundled him into their buggy, and they careened down the back road to Booker T. Washington's residence. Responding to the late-night pounding on his door, the principal loudly (thinking that members of a white mob in hot pursuit might be listening) proclaimed, "No, young man, I will *not* harbor your father," but slipped him a scrap of paper with *See W & A Logan, first house to your right. Use rear entry.* scribbled on it. The fugitives crept over to the Logans' kitchen door. Adella showed them in and stashed their wagon in her barn. When torch-bearing vigilantes pulled up at the principal's residence a few minutes later, he assured them, "Yes, Tom and his boy came here seeking shelter, but I sent them packing. You know

I'd never challenge the will of Tuskegee's good citizens." The throng gradually dispersed as the Harris men cowered in the Logans' attic.

Adella stanched Tom Harris's bleeding and the next morning recruited Edgar Penney's wife, Eve, who was a nurse, to care for him. Cornelius Dorsette, their physician friend who lived in the state capital, responded
to Logan's cable: NEED PROMPT ASSISTANCE. BRING LARGE
WAGON TO TRANSPORT HEAVY PACKAGES TO MONTGOM-
ERY. Dr. Dorsette arrived the next day, then departed with the HEAVY
PACKAGES hidden under his tarpaulin.

The story spread like wildfire. Few people knew about the Logans'
role, but most of their race applauded Mr. Washington's action because
they heard that he'd aided an endangered comrade while also deflecting
racial strife. But those of a more militant bent charged that he'd "forsaken
a brother in distress." Some white Alabamians were glad to learn that the
institute's principal had "turned the scoundrel away," though many others
clamored for vengeance.

The mob that had wanted to lynch Tom Harris also smelled blood,
and a week later the black John Alexander suffered the consequences. The
injured white Tuskegeeite, perhaps a former owner (or father or half brother)
of the man who carried that same name, soon recovered from his minor
wound, while a band of hoodlums abducted the black victim . . . and more.

A Macon County sharecropper whispered, "They branded him with
cattle irons, Miz Logan, strung him up just for looking funny at a white gal,
then cut off his fingers, toes, and privates as souvenirs." Booker T. Washington made no public protest about John Alexander's lynching, which
occurred only a few miles from his campus, though he did amass and
maintain substantial files that documented similar race-based terrorism
elsewhere.

But more far-reaching than that murder, and more significant than
Mr. Washington's clippings folders of such criminality, was the new account
titled *A Red Record,* by Ida B. Wells, who'd recently married a Chicago lawyer surnamed Barnett. Adella first had admired her a decade before when
she'd resisted the conductor who'd thrown her off his train. She and Ida
Wells-Barnett also worked on behalf of common causes through the Na-

tional Association of Colored Women, but Adella considered her anti-lynching journalism her finest achievement.

Ida's exposé laid out white southerners' evolving excuses for sup-pressing African American men who they feared might defy them politi-cally, economically, and physically. When the bondmen were freed, mostly in 1865, many whites had protested that they ran amok. Then with the Fif-teenth Amendment's ratification, they argued that the new voters sought to establish "Negro domination." Those suspicions never materialized, but the conspiracy theorists revived another specious accusation: black men often violated white women, so those heinous crimes had to be avenged. Most offensive in the eyes of many southerners, Mrs. Wells-Barnett "in-solently" claimed that some such ladies voluntarily engaged in sexual rela-tions with black men. To demonstrate beyond any doubt that in just a small minority of cases had those men been accused of, much less charged with, tried for, or convicted of rape, she used as her documentation only accounts and statistics compiled by white authorities. Lynching (black women some-times were lynched too) might result from mere suspicions of burglary, chicken stealing, vagrancy, or "other mischief"—even for "being saucy to whites." The intent was to terrorize not just one specific individual but any people of color who might try to challenge the entrenched racial hierarchy.

The WCTU's leader, Frances Willard, Ida Wells-Barnett added, "fur-ther stokes the fires of violence." Miss Willard outraged women such as Ida and Adella when she wrote that "the colored race multiplies like the lo-custs of Egypt. Since the grog shop has become their base of power, our homes' safety is further menaced. Such situations demand hangings and burnings."

How someone who supported sanctuaries for abused women and suffrage for "the weaker sex" (and also promoted bicycle riding) could make such claims astounded Adella, so she declined to take part in Mrs. Wash-ington's formation of an all-black temperance chapter at Tuskegee Institute, though such apostasy distanced her from the school's first lady and her loyal entourage.

Adella never did know if Booker T. Washington read Ida Wells-Barnett's magnum opus, though she urged him to do so, but the speech he'd make at the World's Cotton Exposition in Atlanta that September 1895 soon would be heralded as one of the most pivotal in American history. A week before the institute's official party departed for that engagement, he asked his neighbor Adella, "Would you do me the honor of commenting on this draft of my presentation?"

She agreed and felt honored that he'd sought her advice, because he both respected her judgment and command of the language and had full faith in her loyalty to him and their school.

He primarily contended that in exchange for incremental economic progress and personal security, his people should accept racial segregation and political disempowerment—for the time being. That stance troubled Adella, but she expected that his oratory would appeal to upper-class southerners and the white masses, to northern philanthropists and industrialists (the institute's major financial supporters), and also to many of her own more hesitant or fearful people.

Booker T. Washington proposed to say this: *In all things purely social we can be as separate as the fingers, yet one as the hand in everything essential to mutual progress.* He'd used that metaphor in his published letter concerning the Logans' mistreatment on the railroad following their wedding. *Wise men of my race understand that agitation on questions of social equality is folly; that all privileges which come to us must be the result of gradual efforts rather than artificial forcing,* he went on. He was exhorting his people to demonstrate their worth to whites, so at some hypothetical future time, they might receive the benefits of full citizenship. In Adella's judgment, that was both a disturbing precept and a deeply flawed strategy.

The manuscript also encouraged Negroes and whites to *cast down your buckets where you are,* to generate economic progress through cooperative efforts. *There is as much dignity in tilling a field as in writing a poem,* he continued. True enough, though Adella hoped to see more poets and progressive, educated men and women become leaders of the race. She understood Mr. Washington's primary intent, but his persistent messages of appeasement made her uneasy.

The very next day, however, Margaret Washington vetoed Adella's presence in Atlanta, because, Logan tried to placate his wife, "It might provoke a problem, Mother, if someone mistook you for a white lady sitting among our official party mostly comprised of colored men."

What irony! She'd been able to attend the recent N-AWSA convention only because she looked white. Now her colleagues were barring her from another major event in the same city—and again because she looked white. So instead of possibly fostering "a problem" by going to what became Mr. Washington's most acclaimed address ever, Adella attended her youngest sister Ella's marriage in Sparta's C.M.E. church to a dark-skinned Romeo named Apollo Payne.

In weeks to come, many Americans applauded Booker T. Washington's message and strove to crown him as Frederick Douglass's worthiest, almost singular heir and "our nation's new king." Many people of both races began calling him "the Wizard of Tuskegee," and the following spring, the nation's most renowned university, Harvard, acknowledged his stature and escalating fame and bestowed on him a prestigious honorary degree.

J. H. Washington, who worked at the institute, was "the Wizard's" blood brother, Margaret Washington (Adella believed) his vengeful Lady Macbeth, and a few others maintained solid friendships with him, yet his unique relationship with Warren Logan, whom he often lauded as the "true builder and guardian of Tuskegee," endured and flourished. More than any others, Logan understood exactly how the Great Man performed his wizardry. If Logan started telling a familiar anecdote, Booker T. often intervened, delivered the punch line, and received the laughs and the accolades. Before people throughout the country recognized Mr. Washington's increasingly famous face, however, several awkward incidents had played out when the two of them stepped off a train together and a welcoming party initially assumed that Warren Logan, the taller, lighter-skinned man, was their guest of honor. Loyal Logan, however, always deferred to his longtime friend and leader: the incomparable Booker T. Washington.

Many white journalists lauded Mr. Washington's speech in Atlanta. One wrote, "Within moments the multitude was in an uproar. Canes were flourished, hats tossed in the air, Georgia's fairest ladies stood up and cheered, and the whole audience fell into a delirium of applause."

Adella's own people's views, however, meant much more to her.

"You have become our Douglass," one supporter said. Harvard's new PhD, W. E. B. Du Bois (his degree, the first doctorate that university awarded to one of their race, was earned and not bestowed honorarily, as was Mr. Washington's), whom the principal had begun courting to join their faculty, enthused, "Words fitly spoken, sir, and the solid foundation for a settlement between white and black."

Bishop Benjamin Tanner, Dr. Halle Dillon's father, who'd taught for a year at Tuskegee Institute's Bible school, first wrote, "Thank you, sir, for your recent utterances on behalf of our race," but later he confided to a friend, "We'll have to live a long time to undo the harm he's done to us colored men." And one of the few black newspapers that dared to criticize him bitingly editorialized that "if there is anything in him except the most servile type of Old Negro, we fail to see it."

Whether envying, praising, or very occasionally disparaging Booker T. Washington, few people could ignore him. By 1896, most Americans within the Logans' community and without felt ready to express their views—and usually to extol—the remarkable Wizard of Tuskegee.

Of the Genius and Training of Black Folk

TUSKEGEE INSTITUTE CONTINUED TO thrive in concert with Mr. Washington's burgeoning prominence, and one afternoon the following September, Adella answered a knock on her door. She opened it and saw a figure that resembled a stilt-like marsh bird perched on the porch rail. The lanky stranger hopped down, took three or four stutter steps forward, followed by one in retreat, then repeated that ungainly minuet. Bony ankles peeked out below his trouser cuffs, a limp, hand-sewn bow tie adorned his threadbare but immaculate dress shirt, and he wore a floral boutonniere on his lapel. In a high-pitched squeak, that dark, avian specter chirped, "I'm George Washington Carver, Mrs. Logan, and your husband suggested that I stop by to introduce myself."

Soon thereafter, Adella's sister Sarah brought Junior and Ruth home from the Children's House, and the newcomer spun out his tales as they listened spellbound, especially since Logan had shared little with them about his own early years of enslavement—nor had anyone else.

"I was born near a village called Diamond," their guest began, "and knew nothing of my real father and little about my mother, except that when I was a baby, she and I'd been kidnapped from the Missouri farm where we were slaves and taken to Arkansas when the border states became the Civil War's bloodiest arenas. Our captors murdered her, I was told, but a bounty hunter returned me to Moses and Susan Carver, the elderly white couple who were my owners and then became my only 'parents.' They even traded their prize racehorse to get me back. Ole Moses bathed, dressed, petted, and carried me on his shoulders but whipped me like a donkey if I misbehaved, while Miz Susan taught me how to launder, cook, garden, knit, and sew. Every night for six years I slept right between them in their bed, and they called me George Washington to honor our country's great white father. And my make-believe colored mother, a midwife named Mariah Watkins who lived nearby, showed me how to concoct her herbal cures."

Those accounts astounded Adella. A town named Diamond! A kidnapping, a murder, and an orphaned black baby who'd been ransomed for a racehorse! The names (Mariah Watkins and Susan) that their visitor shared and the former's vocation eerily replicated those in her own family. His height and affinity with nature enhanced his uncanny resemblance to Susan Hunt. He even said, "never waste anything," as her grandmother often had.

"As a child, I wanted to understand the essence of every plant, insect, bird, and animal I saw," George Washington Carver continued. Soon he'd develop paints, fertilizers, medications, and a variety of pastes from Alabama's cotton, milkweed, yams, and peanuts. But he almost never patented them, he insisted, because "knowledge belongs to all and shouldn't benefit one person alone." He'd also breed hybrid flowers, especially several exquisite amaryllis subspecies.

Most white Alabamians refused to call any black man "mister," and to counter that insult, their community termed members of its male faculty "professor," then abridged that word; so G. W. Carver became " 'Fess." " 'Fess's boys," Adella's brother Tommy among them, toiled away in his barns, gardens, and laboratory and often did their homework at his campus quarters.

"Don't forget, fellas," 'Fess playfully chided his acolytes, "I'll massage your shoulders and back if your muscles get achy from honest work but switch your buttocks if you're lazy."

He also mentioned a "cruel injury," a trauma sustained when he'd been abducted as a baby, but Adella tried to ignore the rumors about its perversity, as well as stories circulated by suspicious colleagues who gossiped about "his peculiar relationships with his favorite students."

After leaving Diamond he'd worked as a servant in several Midwest towns. He also became a skilled painter, yet he earned two degrees in botany as the only black student at a leading Iowa university—where he was denied dormitory accommodations and had to scour pots and eat in the basement kitchen. 'Fess came to Tuskegee to help his people develop their agricultural skills, but Adella also knew that no "white" college would hire him as a professor. Their new "blackbird" frequently visited the Logans' home, and he and Sarah Hunt began both complimenting and teasing each other, while Junior and Ruth sat on his lap and called him "Uncle 'Fess."

And within a year of meeting George Washington Carver, Adella crossed paths with another genius. She much preferred teaching, reading, writing, and even cooking to gardening; but 'Fess Carver had given her some seedlings that needed planting without delay, so she was wrist deep in topsoil one morning when she spotted an unfamiliar but nattily dressed gentleman standing on tiptoe and peering into the Washingtons' windows next door.

As a responsible neighbor, Adella walked over and asked, "Might I help you, sir?"

"Oh, excuse me," the stranger tipped his hat. "I inquired at the administration building as to where the principal and his wife's residence was and they directed me here. I'm Dr. W. E. Burghardt Du Bois, madam." He pronounced his surname Duh-*boys*. "Margaret Murray and I knew each other quite well at Fisk University, so I wanted to pay my respects before I departed."

"I'm afraid Mrs. Washington isn't here today," Adella briskly responded.

Recognizing his name, she knew that he'd initially applied to teach at their school but then rejected Mr. Washington's subsequent offers of employment. Out of courtesy, curiosity, or both, however, he'd come to visit anyway. Adella introduced herself and extended her hand. But instead of shaking it, he touched his lips to her earth-soiled, gloved fingertips, smiled and said, "It's my honor, Mrs. Logan," bowed deeply, and (she thought) clicked his heels.

Amused and intrigued by his awkward suavity, she asked, "Might I offer you a cup of tea at my home next door before you leave Tuskegee, Doctor?" He readily accepted her offer.

W. E. B. Du Bois was a few years younger than she but already balding. He had a waxed mustache and neat goatee, and in profile, his nose featured an odd, non-Negroidal hump, though he was decidedly brown skinned. He carried an elegant walking stick and wore suede spats and polished leather boots, the heels of which Adella deemed a tad too high for a true gentleman—although she speculated that he thereby was attempting to mitigate his obvious shortness.

"I was born and raised in western Massachusetts," he said, "where our white neighbors disparaged me as 'Black Willie,' but first hearing the slaves' sorrow songs performed by the traveling Hampton quartet [led at that time by her future husband, she interjected] introduced me to more than I'd ever known about my people's rich culture." At only fifteen, he'd matriculated at Fisk, where some of the students disdained him as a Yankee outsider and called him "Dube."

"Most of my classmates were more urbane and lighter skinned than I, and often shunned me, but Margaret Murray encouraged me," Dr. Du Bois told his hostess. Miss Murray's protégé ultimately prevailed at Fisk, then returned to Massachusetts two years later to earn a "full" bachelor's degree at Harvard University, where he continued for graduate studies. He admired the German culture that he encountered at a school in Berlin between his stints at Harvard and sprinkled his monologues with "*bittes*," "*dankes*," and various phrases he'd learned in Europe.

The federal government, he told Adella, recently had commissioned him to undertake some socioeconomic studies in her former home state, which would document and assess the impact of race on Georgians' lives. She described Dougherty County's town of Albany and its awesome river, her own schoolhouse and needy students, the forced labor wrung from the region's black detainees, and the crop lien system that financially and physically devastated so many of them. W. E. B. Du Bois affirmed that he was eager to begin his research very soon, especially, he asserted, "pursuant to your guidance and suggestion, Mrs. Logan, in Albany, Georgia."

Over the next few years, he'd occasionally return to Tuskegee and each time stopped by to see Adella Hunt Logan, informing her of his marriage and the arrival of his firstborn, and he sent her an autographed photo and a copy of his sociological study *The Philadelphia Negro*. Despite his outstanding academic credentials and that work's erudition and acclaim, its sponsoring institution, the University of Pennsylvania, refused to offer him an academic appointment.

And that first day, they also discussed Mr. Washington's recent "Atlanta Compromise" speech, which Dr. Du Bois initially had lauded but about which he, she, and others harbored increasing concerns. Adella told him she'd hoped to attend the event herself but didn't because "the powers that be" claimed that her presence as a woman who looked white, seated amid the institute's predominantly male, African American party, might have "created a problem."

"And how does it feel to be deemed 'a problem'?" her intriguing visitor teased.

As they got to know each other, the barriers between them further receded as Adella shared with Dr. Du Bois stories about her black, white, and red forebears, the pitiless expulsion of Georgia's Cherokees, and slavery's horrific legacies in the state.

"Please share with me more of your thinking on the 'peculiar institution,'" he added.

"Bondage in our country clearly was egregious, but also, I believe, more duplicitous than elsewhere, since the Founders tolerated or promoted it while supposedly endorsing equality for all," she said, "and I define it as the coercive possession or control of any people and the denial of their liberties to exploit them for production and profit, comfort, or even sexual pleasure."

He bristled a bit at that: "Might your definition of slavery apply to married women?"

"Very rarely," Adella smoothed his ruffled feathers, "and only when they must live exclusively to serve their spouses. But as Susan B. Anthony asks, 'Aren't women people too?' Therefore, Dr. Du Bois, shouldn't our civil rights be comparable to men's?" His puzzlement led her to believe that questions concerning women's citizenship hadn't previously occurred to him.

He continued his rigorous catechism by demanding, "Since the white majority oppresses us in so many ways, how ought we define ourselves, Mrs.

Logan? I myself feel a powerful double consciousness as both a Negro and an American, conjoined in a struggle to the death."

"As a corollary to that," she countered, "perhaps we women of color can claim a *triple* consciousness." He mulled over her theory, then asked if she felt isolated at Tuskegee.

"I'm content with my children, spouse, home, friends, and work," she answered. "I enjoy music, books, and a degree of intellectual stimulation here yet yearn to see more of the world as you have. Sometimes I rue our remoteness and feel that we're isolated in some sort of 'hither isles.' At least Frederick Douglass used those words when he visited us here four years ago."

"Now I understand," he smiled. "If these be Mr. Douglass's and your own so-called hither isles, Mrs. Logan, you surely must be the princess of this remote and secluded realm."

Locking horns with that genius unquestionably broadened her perspectives. She was sorry that he turned down Mr. Washington's repeated appeals to join their faculty, but as a result of his guile, or perhaps his increasingly conflicted regard for "the Wizard of Tuskegee," as well as friendships with a few select people at the institute, he continued his occasional visits.

Soon thereafter, however, Horace Bumstead, Adella's former professor who'd recently become Atlanta University's president, persuaded Dr. Du Bois to move south and teach there. It had become clear to everyone in their small world of black academe that no "white" university would hire him, although he had outstanding intellectual gifts to offer and unequaled credentials.

Anticipating his arrival but before he'd even relocated to Georgia, President Bumstead (who was white himself) convened a conference by, for, and about black people. It featured essays, panels, colloquia, and lectures that explored and analyzed "the Negro problem" or, as the phrase usually was writ at the time, "the negro problem." Adella capitalized the *N* when she either envisioned or wrote the word, though most white people and, following Booker T. Washington's early example, many of her race too rarely did. She deemed "Negro" as worthy of capitalization as "English,"

"African," or "American," however, and thus was pleased when she read the Atlanta University Conference's original published transcript. There was that capital N, smiling at her each time it appeared! But disappointed that she hadn't been invited to participate, she wrote Horace Bumstead, sharing both her praise and her concerns:

> *Let me congratulate you on your trailblazing Conference on the Condition of Negroes. Your participants brought knowledge, research skills, and diverse perspectives which cast new light on these issues, and I expect you and Dr. Du Bois to make this an important annual event. I appreciate that aspiration and only humbly suggest that it would benefit our school, the race, and the nation if you included more ladies among the participants, especially since our female alumnae equal men in numbers, and in their intellect, scholarship, and dedication as well.*

Pursuant to her sentiments, the following year Adella and a dozen other women were invited and contributed to the second annual congress, at which she delivered one of the featured lectures, titled "Prenatal and Hereditary Influences." To prepare that presentation, she returned to her grandfather Sayre's old tome, *Intermarriage,* by Alexander Walker. She'd first plowed through it when she'd received some of Nathan Sayre's books following her grandmother's disappearance and had been impressed by its progressive erudition in addressing interracial relations. She'd heard too that even Charles Darwin, prior to consummating his own endogamous marriage, had sought Dr. Walker's counsel, because the latter had warned about the "perils of reproduction between siblings or close cousins." His discussion of "the likelihood of supernumerary digits" brought to mind her own married "close cousins" and their six-toed, deaf and blind daughter. She better appreciated the late Judge Sayre's interest in Alexander Walker's analyses of "the crosses between Africans and Europeans, and between Africans and indigenous Americans, which," Dr. Walker had written, "have produced vigorous new races." Members of those supposed "new races" weren't the sly, feeble-minded, often barren mulattoes (mules?), quadroons, or *mestizos* that many white people anticipated, feared, and loathed.

Pursuant to the Atlanta University conferences and encouraged by Horace Bumstead, the Doctor (as she mentally designated Dr. Du Bois), and 'Fess Carver, Adella and her sister decided to attend the Chautauqua sessions on the island of Martha's Vineyard off the Massachusetts coast. Completing its curriculum a decade before during two summers at the Chautauqua's "mother ship" in upstate New York had earned Adella her bachelor's degree certification. Now she hoped to garner the qualifications needed for the master's level.

After two days on three rail lines, the sisters spent the weekend in Troy, New York, with Patty Winston and her ward, Della, who'd soon enter the Emma Willard School, then continued on to visit their brother Tommy. The previous spring he'd completed 'Fess Carver's advanced agronomy program at Tuskegee and, thanks to Mr. Washington's sponsorship, had moved to eastern Massachusetts, where he worked at the region's largest fresh produce market. Tommy was nicely situated, boarding in the town of Weston with its police chief O'Hara. As a memento to take back to 'Fess, he gave his sisters several packets of unique New England vegetable seeds.

Adella and Sarah proceeded from there to Boston, where they spent a pleasant morning with their friend Dr. Samuel Courtney, whose gracious, auburn-haired receptionist introduced herself as Georgia Fagain Stewart. Even the Hunt sisters didn't spot her as a woman of color, until knowing whence they'd come, she smilingly confided, "I attended Fisk University with both Maggie Murray Washington and 'Dube.' That's *Dr.* Du Bois now, I should say."

Having sent an advance letter of introduction, they visited the late Martha Merriwether Hunt's aging sister too. Ellen Merriwether shared with them how fondly she remembered their uncle T. J. Hunt's and her sister's wedding half a century ago and added, "Martha told me that she treasured your mother's friendship, Mrs. Logan, but slavery anguished her. She wrote about how some of those wretched slaves in Georgia, who looked as white as you, Miss Sarah, or I, had been sired by but then were abused, beaten, or even sold away by their heartless owner-fathers."

But knowing little of the Hunts' history or the South's racial absurdities, Ellen moved on to address a less contentious subject, sparing the sisters from trying to explain the inexplicable.

"I've saved the condolence note that your mother wrote during the war to inform me that my sister had passed away," Miss Merriwether told Sarah and Adella, and as a memento, she gave them Mariah Hunt's old letter. Then they bid her farewell and entrained to catch the late afternoon boat from Cape Cod headed out to Martha's Vineyard. Reading the message during that leg of their journey, Adella saw that her mother hadn't mentioned suicide but to save the Merriwethers' feelings had written only, *Our dear Martha died in a tragic riding accident.*

Their ferry, the paddle steamer *Monohansett,* bellowed like a tuba—its wake a blizzard foaming behind them. Once on the island itself, the sisters settled in at their rented gingerbread "doll's house," painted aquamarine, lavender, and gold, in the style known as Carpenter Gothic.

Twice a week, Adella sent her children colorful, linen-textured, deckle-edged picture postal cards of everything that she and Sarah encountered. They attended lectures and studied each weekday but on weekends rented bicycles, pedaled beside cornfields and cranberry bogs, drank the berries' medicinal, mouth-puckering juice, walked their "wheels" onto the rickety Chappaquiddick plank ferry and squinted eastward, trying to make out the nearby island of Nantucket, where their hero Frederick Douglass had delivered his first public address.

Adella ached for her little ones, reading with them, or sharing her grandmother's old stories about talking animals and the people who could fly. One evening Sarah mused, "Do you suppose I'll ever marry and have children, Sis?" She was twenty-nine to Adella's thirty-five.

When she queried, "Is that what you want?" Sarah nodded, "Though I fear that the object of my affections yearns for another." Adella speculated but didn't ask whom she had in mind.

The sisters' long hair tangled as they frolicked in the chilly surf. They collected conch shells, pebbles, and sea glass and basked like the sleek seals that lazed on the offshore boulders, as Adella rejected Neppie Hunt's bygone admonition to "carry a parasol to keep your skin pretty and fair by shading it from the sun." Rather, she blissfully became as brown as a raisin.

But they'd gone north to learn, so Adella pursued her quest to stake out a middle ground between the battling theorists who preached that either nature *or* nurture exclusively shaped the human experience. For her final essay, she conjoined Alexander Walker's findings with some of Sir Francis Galton's and Charles Darwin's. Many scholars and other polemicists had adapted the latter's theory of the "survival of the fittest" and used it "to explain the negro's recent precipitous decline." She rejected that premise, however, and plowed on to lay out what her professors at the Chautauqua deemed "a worthy start on the next leg of your advanced education."

Once back again in Tuskegee, Adella's gift mementoes included books for her children and, at Logan's insistence, a small offering for Mrs. Washington. Sarah and 'Fess Carver had corresponded frequently during their absence, and she presented him with a classic New England seafaring memoir, as well as the seed packets from their brother Tommy. Will Hunt also teased Adella, as only a brother would or could: "looks like you've put a little meat on your bones, Sis."

Will was right. After visiting the town of Tuskegee's leading physician in hopes of assuaging her atypical lethargy, she informed her husband and siblings that she was expecting again. Despite her prior siege of four pregnancies in little more than the same number of years and suffering the deaths of two babies, she and Logan agreed that it was time for another child.

Never thinking that his wife might be carrying a Paula or Paulette, Warren Logan wanted to name their new baby Paul, because he finally felt certain that Rev. John Paul Smith wasn't the man who'd sexually exploited his mother. Although Rev. Smith and his wife had owned several slaves and condoned and benefited from the institution, they usually had been supportive of Warren in his youth. Their son, who bore the name Paul too, had been Logan's close childhood companion. Adella, in turn, insisted that Patty Winston had to be her next child's godmother.

Adella also submitted her credits to Atlanta University, whose authorities agreed with those at the Chautauqua that her amassed course work should entitle her to be awarded a master of arts degree—after she'd been accepted by an academic mentor so that she could complete an original thesis. Employing all of her guiles, she persuaded Dr. Du Bois to serve as her advisor.

Meanwhile, Booker T. Washington's staunch Republican loyalty, combined with accolades for their acclaimed professor G. W. Carver from a great admirer (President William McKinley's secretary of agriculture) of him and his work, paid off handsomely for their school in the form of a historic December visit by the president and his wife. Patriotic bunting, flower chains, banners, and flags festooned the streets of Tuskegee and flanked the main road leading out to the institute.

President McKinley inspected the grounds, the choir sang old Negro spirituals, and the band played the national anthem and John Phillip Sousa's "King Cotton March." Nine hundred students bearing cotton bolls speared on cane stalks headed a cavalcade of farm animals, and a two-hour parade included mule-drawn floats that featured demonstrations of brick making, carpentry, blacksmithing, millinery, and more. The whole panoply reinforced Mr. Washington's escalating status as the country's best-known man of his race and convinced many hostile white Alabamians that his school would bring celebrity and especially dollars to their remote enclave.

Adella read everything she could find in preparation for meeting the first lady, Ida Saxton McKinley. She studied her portrait (which had appeared in several magazines) by the acclaimed photographer Frances Benjamin Johnston, and Patty Winston informed her that Mrs. McKinley was a clandestine suffragist. When the women affiliated with the school administration, their trustees' wives, and the town's leading white ones met her, Adella gave her name and said, "It's an honor, madam, and I applaud your support of votes for women, which is my crusade too."

Intrigued by her greeting, their guest responded, "I'm pleased to meet you and to hear that, Mrs. Logan, since I'd been warned that all white southerners oppose woman suffrage."

Adella didn't correct the first lady's misperception of her racial identity since to do so seemed awkward and ungracious, so she said only, "Many southern women are indifferent to expanding the franchise or believe that they must yield to their husbands' biases, but I was honored to meet your friend Miss Anthony at her convention in Atlanta several years ago."

"I remember she came south on that occasion," Mrs. McKinley nodded. "And this pretty girl must be yours," she said, smiling at Ruth, who was clutching Adella's skirt. In a wavering voice she added, "I've been ill for a long time, then my mother and daughters died the same year." Rumors abounded that Ida McKinley used narcotics to mitigate her melancholia and other ailments. "You're so fortunate to be expecting another child," she added, eying Adella's bulging belly. But before Adella could add that she'd also lost two babies, her grandmother, and mother in a comparably brief period, a Pinkerton guard dispatched by Margaret Washington denied her further access to the visiting first lady, whom he expeditiously returned to her husband's side.

With the Stars and Stripes, the gold eagle presidential banner, and Alabama's red-on-white state one, which evoked the Confederate battle flag, displayed behind him, Booker T. Washington stood at the chapel dais with Governor Joseph Johnston and President McKinley. It was a remarkable trinity: two elected white leaders and, between them, an eminent, gray-eyed, brown-skinned gentleman, "only recently risen from slavery," the governor solemnly intoned.

Mr. Washington addressed William McKinley, Governor Johnston, and the rest of the crowd, saying, "With the cooperation of white and black men, we welcome you to our humble institute where without bitterness, but with sympathy and friendship, southern and northern help, we keep working every day of every year, trying to do our best to honor our nation."

The president responded, "Your school enjoys a growing reputation for which I congratulate you. As the country's leading negro, you're planting here the seeds of good citizenship. By equipping your boys," he gestured toward the coeducational student body, "with humility and industry, many of them may hope to avoid the work house, police court, or chain gang." Booker T. Washington, and apparently he alone, President McKinley added, was "building in the rural South an experiment that may help to elevate your lowly colored people."

That event put Tuskegee Institute squarely on the map. And at least for the near future, virtually none of the race would challenge Booker T. Washington's burgeoning omnipotence.

Up from Slavery, *Off to the White House*

LITTLE COULD SURPASS TUSKEGEE'S FIRST presidential benediction, but the backstory had begun months earlier with the Spanish-American War, widely regarded as the pinnacle of the United States' escalating neocolonialism. In a reimposition and expansion of the seventy-five-year-old Monroe Doctrine, the U.S. Navy annihilated the Spanish armadas in the Caribbean and the Pacific and overwhelmed several tropic isles, and the country claimed as its new subjects myriad Puerto Ricans, Cubans, and, soon thereafter, Filipinos, whom the press dubbed "our little brown brothers." But those initiatives troubled Adella, and to the Washingtons' dismay, she not too discreetly supported a group of anti-imperialist Negro renegades including W. E. B. Du Bois.

As the nation's self-appointed "big brothers," a cohort of the State and War Departments, White House, and congressional leaders determined that a few of their newly claimed nonwhite noncitizens might benefit from acquiring some industrial, technical, or agricultural training in the continental United States. Pursuant to the presidential benediction recently bestowed on Tuskegee Institute, early in 1899 it was thus designated as the recipient of a boatload of Puerto Rican youths. Slavery on their island had outlived the South's "peculiar institution" by a decade, and most Caribbean "whites" treated darker-skinned people as inferiors, but not to the extent that race alone defined, demeaned, and singularly disadvantaged all "black" ones in the United States. With the Puerto Ricans' panoply of hair textures and skin tones, most of the institute's recently arrived wards might have been designated, in Alexander Walker's words, "a new race." But until they got to Alabama, they didn't know that African American students, staff, and faculty alone populated their new school. Nor did they fully realize, at first, the stigma attached to being identified as members of the "inferior" race. Compounding that cultural dissonance, they spoke or understood little English, and few people at Tuskegee knew more than rudimentary Spanish.

Those who were already at the institute felt under assault by the hostile Pablos, Josés, and Juans who hated the food, customs, regimentation, and inhospitable people whom they encountered. The "old" students complained that "the new boys smell bad, cuss in Spanish, carry knives, drink rum, and smoke in the woods," and they dubbed the islanders *cucarachas,* for the Caribbean's (and Alabama's) flying cockroaches. The recent arrivals, however, reappropriated that name as their own, captured scores of the vile creatures in cigar boxes, then released them under the door cracks of their tormentors' dormitory rooms. That swift retaliation led to a hostile detente.

The tense situation came to a head when several of the new arrivals' parents back on the island wrote Alabama's governor Johnston complaining that had they known in advance that Tuskegee Institute was "a school for negroes," they'd never have let their young people attend. The governor cabled Mr. Washington: I AM OUTRAGED BY THIS VIOLATION OF OUR RACIAL REGULATIONS. IF THE WHITE PORTO RICANS ARE NOT REMOVED WITHIN THIRTY DAYS THE INSTITUTES PUBLIC FUNDING WILL BE TERMINATED AND THE RESPONSIBLE PARTIES CRIMINALLY CHARGED. Pursuant to state laws, which directed that "colored and white students shall not attend the same schools," the "white boys" had to leave immediately.

Logan thus lined up the islanders in the quadrangle, where Alabama's superintendent of education inspected their ranks and plucked out the ones whom he deemed to be Caucasians. Those with lighter skins and straighter hair were removed from the premises but were neither transferred to a school for white Alabamians nor provided any means by which to return home. In the governor's eyes, however, his unanticipated "race problem" had been resolved.

Adella's baby, Paul Winston Logan, paler skinned and straighter haired than any of the ousted Puerto Ricans, arrived at their officially resegregated school soon thereafter—but one of Macon County's white physicians facilitated the delivery, not Dr. Halle Tanner Dillon. That pioneering female practitioner had remarried and laid aside her hard-earned profession to follow her new husband from his position at Tuskegee Institute's Bible school to a rural Louisiana parish. Once there, she bore three sons in rapid succession, then passed away in childbirth.

After Dr. Dillon's departure, students, faculty, staff, and their families went to the town doctor as needed. That presented a minimal hardship for Adella since the local practitioner winked at what he suspected was her designated race. She knew that such preferential treatment was unjust but guiltily accepted her inadvertent advantage. Yet for her darker-skinned colleagues who had to stand outside his office regardless of weather or the severity of their conditions and wait for hours as white patients streamed in and out, the experience was both humiliating and detrimental to their health. But after Booker T. Washington made several missteps in his efforts to circumvent that egregious situation, he found the right resident physician for the institute: Dr. John Kenney.

Some of Adella's friends, however, were less fortunate. Soon after her own Paul's birth, W. E. B. Du Bois's two-year-old son, Burghardt, died in Atlanta. He and his wife, both of them northerners who were naive about southern prejudices and practices, had been unable to obtain the services of a doctor with access to a hospital that would tend to his black patients' needs. Adella wrote her friend a letter of condolence but knew that nothing she said could be adequate.

On a happier note, Patty Winston came to Tuskegee for her godson Paul's christening. She also confided, "My ward, Della, has seemed morose of late, but I chalk it up to anxieties about her senior year at Emma Willard." Patty also urged Adella to join her in Washington, D.C., for the upcoming convention that would celebrate Susan B. Anthony's eightieth birthday. "As your race's only Lifetime Member of the N-AWSA," she asked, "wouldn't you like to bring greetings to Aunt Susan from the South's voiceless and voteless colored women?" Indeed, she would!

And meanwhile, Adella's youngest brother, Tommy—with his unusual, mismatched eyes—was thriving in Weston, Massachusetts. He hadn't changed his residence with the police chief since he'd first arrived there but had secured improved employment in a neighboring town's public gardens. The occupational upgrade, he reported, was better utilizing his agricultural skills, which George Washington Carver had inspiringly, demandingly, and lovingly nurtured. In 1899, he wrote his sister,

> *Still boarding at police chief O'Hara's house & thought for a while I'd try to become a copper too. But here you need a name like that to get those jobs, & one emerald eye don't make me Irish! Ha-ha! That reminds me, the other day I saw an "Injun" who scowled, pointed at me & said "evil eye." He shook his fist, hopped up & down, then spat on the ground. What do you think Granny Susan would've made of that harebrained performance?*

Adella hadn't shared with her brother their grandmother's legend that one light and one dark iris meant that back in the mists of time, some white man had violated a colored ancestress, or the weird gesticulations that constituted the ritual that was supposed to ward off the curse. Tommy continued:

> *You inspired me by earning the men's degree that Atlanta U. denied you, & soon I bet you'll get the higher one too. So I went to see the folks at U. Mass. in Amherst about entering their agri. program & laid out all that 'Fess Carver taught me. They say I can enroll anytime & they'll give me credit for those courses. Their profs appreciate 'Fess's sterling reputation & know he's a negro, but no one asks me if I might be a c—— man too. I never raise "the race question," of course, & as for "what I am," they don't ask me so I don't tell them!*

Adella promised to pay for Tommy's future studies at the University of Massachusetts.

Now that he lived in that state's eastern reaches, her youngest brother occasionally saw Mr. and Mrs. Washington in July, when some of the institute's northern donors made available to them a charming vacation cottage nearby. But that summer, those same benefactors, who'd become concerned about Booker T. Washington's overwork and resultant fatigue, instead sent the Tuskegee couple on a lavish, three-month European holiday—at no expense to themselves.

In Paris, they visited the expatriate painter Henry Ossawa Tanner, who was the late Dr. Halle Tanner Dillon's brother, and in England met distinguished diplomats, financiers, authors, and peers. Mrs. Washington even had tea there with Queen Victoria and Susan B. Anthony.

The Washingtons' new eight-bedroom mansion, The Oaks—also fully donor funded—was completed during their travels, and the Logan children "supervised" the construction work from their home next door. The school's instructors and students wired it for electricity, gas, and an internal bells system and plumbed, tiled, and equipped the elaborate kitchen (where the lady of the house rarely expected to set foot) and four bathrooms. Campus workers made and laid the bricks and did all of the framing, roofing, cabinetry, plastering, painting, and glazing. Booker T. Washington insisted that everything be done to his punctilious wife's specifications.

Margaret Washington also admired the Oriental-style Belgian rugs that first had graced Pomegranate Hall, Adella's mother's home, and then hers in Tuskegee. "They resemble," she cajoled Logan, "those that I yearned for but was too frugal to purchase on our European trip." Adella's husband (more magnanimous than she) insisted that they give the Washingtons one of those heirlooms as a housewarming gift, but the reluctant donor seethed when she overheard a visitor at The Oaks praise its elegance and their "first lady" didn't acknowledge its provenance.

Pursuant to her discussion with Adella during her recent visit, Patty Winston had written Susan B. Anthony suggesting that she invite Adella to speak at the N-AWSA's annual conference, and after Thanksgiving, she forwarded their unsettling exchange to her friend in Alabama. Patty's cover note said, *Miss Anthony clearly underestimates your intelligence, talents, and convictions, but she is so adamant that I find myself helpless to resist.* Then Adella read the enclosed letters.

Troy, New York. November 8, 1899

Dear Aunt Susan, [she was twenty years older than Patty]

Might a colored woman be granted a slot at the N-AWSA's upcoming gathering? I am thinking of my friend Adella Hunt Logan, who would like to speak about the importance of voting for her sex and race and bring our group greetings from her disadvantaged people in the South.

I introduced you to her in Atlanta back in '95, when she became a Lifetime Member, though you may not remember that encounter or receiving her letter soon thereafter.

Mrs. Logan, the wife of Tuskegee Institute's vice principal/ treasurer and a gifted teacher herself, is an informed and dedicated suffragist. She is a well-educated, well-spoken woman whose understanding and advocacy of our common cause profoundly impresses me.

Her hair is as straight as yours or mine, and she looks absolutely white but must call herself colored. She is the daugh-ter of a Confederate officer who "talked politics" with her from the time she was very young, and as a result, many civic issues remain of great concern to her.

She hopes to attend your January convention and says she would be honored to speak.

Susan B. Anthony's response had arrived soon thereafter.

Rochester, New York. Nov. 18, 1899

Dear Patty,

I certainly would like to have a colored
woman speak at our conference, and yes, I do
remember your Miss Logan's letter.

In part, Adella had written, *I am working with women who are slow to believe that they will get help from the ballot, but someday I hope to see my daughter vote right here in the South.*

Miss Anthony continued:

> Booker T. Washington's wife also mentioned her
> to me when we met last summer at Windsor Castle.
> If I knew that your protegee would astonish the
> natives and make the most biased Anglo-Saxons
> feel contrite, I'd invite her, but I cannot
> have speak for us a woman who has even a ten-
> thousandth portion of African blood who would
> be an inferior orator in matter or manner,
> because it would so mitigate against our cause
> and perhaps disadvantage her race as well. You
> will remember that both Mrs. Harper [Frances Ellen
> Watkins Harper, a gifted African American writer and reformer]
> and Frederick Douglass joined us in years past,
> and Sojourner Truth, the "Libyan Sybil," re-
> mains one of my heroes.

Adella mentally corrected that misspelling, since she knew—as Miss Anthony should have known—that Sibyls were ancient Greek oracles, whereas Sybil was a derivative name.

The letter went on,

> In addition, a few of our new recruits are
> Southerners, and I hope several such Congress-
> men and their wives will attend our next event.
> Thus, for me to bring straight from Alabama
> and seat on our platform a simple woman who is
> almost an ex-slave either would anger them or
> make them laugh.
> I would like to have join us a native of the
> South who had been bleached out by slavery's
> "sinful amalgamation." Nothing could match that
> as an object lesson which would embody the trans-

formation from property to personhood, from
chattel to citizen. That ex-slave, however,
would have to be the finest specimen [another spelling
error, not to mention Susan B. Anthony's repeated use of "Miss"
instead of "Mrs."] that I could find. Let your Miss
Logan wait till she is more cultivated, better
educated, and better prepared and can do our
mission and her own race the greatest credit.

Miss Anthony was both manipulative and bullying, and those attributes were helping to raise the country's awareness of her controversial cause, which had become Adella's too; yet she felt angry and hurt. But who could resist such a force of nature? Certainly not Patty Winston, who'd replied, *I must yield to your judgment, though you do not know Mrs. Logan as I do. You realize, as I did not, the prejudices one encounters even in our noblest reform movements.*

No, Miss Anthony didn't know her as Patty Winston did, and she'd swallowed whole and then regurgitated the old abolitionist rhetoric about female enslavement, sexual abuse, and the "plight of the tragic octoroon." She considered Adella a primitive entity: "almost an ex-slave." Slavery remained the nation's unresolved original sin, yet in some ways, that horror was separable from Adella's circumstances, since neither her grandmother nor her mother nor she (and certainly none of her white male progenitors) had been enslaved. And she didn't consider herself a victim of "sinful amalgamation." Adella worked hard, knew she was unusually privileged, and sometimes felt guilty about it, and she'd never passed through what Frederick Douglass had called "the blood-stained gates—the entrance to the hell of slavery." While recognizing both the misogyny and racial bigotry of many of the country's all-white, all-male elected officials, Susan B. Anthony nonetheless curried their favor in hopes of facilitating the introduction, passage, and ratification of a constitutional amendment that would secure women's voting rights nationwide.

Adella further wondered what Margaret Washington might have said about her to Miss Anthony when they'd reportedly chatted over tea with

Queen Victoria. But given that letter with its clear racist undercurrents, there was no way, even if asked, that Adella now would serve as her "object lesson." Thus, she didn't attend that year's N-AWSA conference at all. A respected and identifiable woman of color did speak briefly at the event, but Adella assumed that Susan B. Anthony herself had composed, or at least preapproved, her comments.

As an addendum, one day in mid-March, the Logans' mail sent over from the institute's postal office included a thick envelope, postmarked Washington, D.C. The enclosed card read:

> *President and Mrs. William McKinley*
> *request the pleasure of <u>Mrs. Logan's</u> company*
> *at a reception celebrating the eightieth birthday of*
> *Miss Susan Brownell Anthony*
> *at the White House*
> *Thursday, February 15, 1900*
> *2 p.m. in the East Room Respondez s'il vous plait*

Adella was livid. It was a full month past the date indicated. How could her invitation have been "mislaid" for so long? Then she saw that the envelope flap was rippled. It almost certainly had been steamed open and then resealed, and she suspected that Margaret Washington's hand was behind that otherwise inexplicable delay. Such violations of privacy didn't surprise her, however, since Booker T. Washington's brother served as the school's postmaster.

She'd read about the gala event in the *Woman's Journal,* which said that "Ida Saxton McKinley was too ill to attend, but on her behalf, the president gave Miss Anthony a bouquet of eighty lilies, which she carried in her arms as she presented to him each esteemed delegate by name." As an N-AWSA Lifetime Member and still its only one of color, Adella could have been such an "esteemed delegate" herself but never imagined that she'd be invited to the White House on her own. Mrs. McKinley, however, must have recalled their chat concerning Susan B. Anthony and suffrage from when she'd accompanied the president to Tuskegee the previous fall.

Adella suspected that Mrs. Washington had both poisoned the well for her with Miss Anthony and "misplaced" the invitation. She also speculated as to whether her own subterfuge, when (of necessity) she'd "passed" at the N-AWSA's 1895 convention in Atlanta, had nettled "Aunt Susan." Did the presence of someone who almost always identified herself as "colored" but looked as white as the majority make Miss Anthony feel ill at ease? As exemplars of black female authenticity, Adella found that dark-skinned, uneducated women such as Sojourner Truth could be easier for whites to pigeonhole and accept. As metaphorical "mammies," they could be demeaned, abused, tolerated, or occasionally appreciated as servants. But people who looked like Adella often disconcerted white women, in part because their very existence certified their own grandfathers', fathers', and husbands' repeated infidelities. She also knew, however, that adequate finances, influential friends, and her willpower and excellent education, combined with her ambiguous appearance, gave her unjustified advantages over many others of the race.

And not to be deterred from alternate paths toward cerebral development, Adella slogged along with her master's thesis. She formulated a scientific, historical, and intellectual synthesis by analyzing the work of acclaimed scholars who'd tried to assess the factors that shaped human social behavior and achievement. On one side were those who preached that "biology is destiny," whereas the opposing camp insisted that environment dictated virtually everything.

After completing her research, she organized, composed, and crafted several drafts that ultimately overflowed a dozen composition books. Then five evenings a week for three months, as Junior, Ruth, and Paul slept, and with her husband's sanction, she walked over to the institute's administration building to use his new Underwood front-strike-keyboard typewriter. He kept his office keys in their home study's desk, so each evening after completing her domestic chores, Adella removed and then later returned them to the same position in the top right-hand drawer next to her family's vital documents: their marriage license, diplomas, and receipts for Logan's poll tax payments—but no birth certificates, since Alabama didn't provide them for "black" babies.

During those nights in Logan's office, she taught herself to use his machine, practicing "a quick brown fox jumps over the lazy dog" on the unfamiliar keys. She slipped carbon paper between the onionskin pages behind the bond stock, rolled them onto the cylindrical platen, then at each line's end, flipped the silvery return lever and replaced the inked ribbon as needed. Even when she was typing at her speediest, making few errors and correcting those she did make using a rubber wheel eraser and tin shield, it might take her an hour to perfect a single page. When the mental strain exhausted her, she'd relax by scribbling in her diaries that she'd brought along.

She numbered each page at its bottom center, then clawed through a briar patch of citations, replicating the exact modes of reference that W. E. B. Du Bois had used for his PhD dissertation—which she'd recently heard that a female admirer had edited and typed for him.

Adella proofread and then reread her (hopefully) final version many times over and aligned it in a manila folder that she enclosed in a sturdy cardboard box. She addressed, tied, taped, stamped, and then mailed off the document and a backup copy accompanied by her cover letter:

```
Dear Dr. Du Bois,                    July 12, 1900
   Let me repeat the sentiments of condolence I
sent you and Mrs. Du Bois last year. As I know
from experience, nothing is more agonizing than
the death of a child. I hope that your work and
the recent birth of your daughter in some small
way may assuage the boundless grief associated
with that tragedy.
   You know, however, that I have other business
in mind. Enclosed is the original and a copy of
my original thesis. The Chautauqua Literary and
Scientific Institute credited me for the course
work required for the master's degree, but to
obtain it, I need your approval of my essay, and
if you see fit to send it along, that of Atlanta
University's president and trustees too.
```

```
        I await your comments, and remain yours,
    Adella Hunt Logan
    Adella Hunt Logan,
    Atlanta University, class of 1881
```

Then she waited. And waited. Finally, the Doctor's response arrived six months later. He opened with some poignant words:

```
        I received but failed to respond to your ear-
    lier letter of condolence. Many such messages
    came to me and my wife that are difficult to
    answer. Our new child, however, does help a lit-
    tle to console us through the pain. And I must
    believe that my beloved son is not dead but es-
    caped, no longer bound, but now free, yet still
    I ask myself: If one had to be taken, why not I?
```

Then he moved on to appraise her academic efforts.

```
        I know you to be an intelligent woman, other-
    wise I would not have consented to be your
    advisor, but I have found a number of diffi-
    culties with this thesis.
        Your methodology sometimes seems wanting,
    hence you revert to hypotheses that you fail to
    prove and fully document. Pursuant to these
    shortcomings and speculating too freely, your
    analysis at times becomes either naive or
    hyperbolic.
```

The letter went on in that critical vein for several paragraphs—but then its tone changed.

```
        Nonetheless, this thesis has its strengths,
    and reflects your rational and often-provocative
```

```
thinking. As I advised, you incorporated some
of the findings from my recent conferences, and
navigate fairly well the interrelationships
between economic, social, genetic, and environ-
mental factors to show how they may converge to
influence our people's health and welfare.
    Despite a few misgivings, I will give your
work to Atlanta University's Dean Myron Adams
for him to present to President Bumstead and
our Trustees. I require no revisions, and will
recommend that they bestow upon you the master
of arts degree. Given this school's lack of
accreditation formally to grant any such ad-
vanced academic recognition, the degree will
only be honorary, but your accomplishment is
worthy.
```

After slogging through Dr. Du Bois's opening page, Adella was re-lieved and delighted as she read his final sentences. When Dean Adams, President Bumstead, and the school's trustees received his endorsement and her thesis itself, they promptly approved granting the degree.

She wasn't even disappointed that it would "only be honorary," since the flaw was structural, social, political, and historical and due to no fault or shortcoming of hers. At that juncture, not one institution in the country that had been established to educate members of her race was accredited to grant graduate degrees in any academic fields. She'd also triumphed over the prevailing assumption that as a woman of color, she personified the antithesis of scholarship and intellectualism. Without further rocking the boat, she'd accept the honor at the June commencement exercises: Adella Hunt Logan, M.A. (master of arts). It had a very nice ring.

Some special attire was called for, so two days before the ceremony, she embarked on an urban shopping trip. First, she ventured to Rich's, At-lanta's elite department store, and splurged on a black taffeta gown with a gathered yoke, high collar, and full, leg-of-mutton sleeves. After it was fitted, she crossed the street to the Edwards Gallery, the city's most prestigious photographic studio, for a portrait session decked out in her new ensemble and wearing an enameled gold and pearl pansy brooch that had been her mother's. She had to pose as a white woman to receive the proper service at those establishments, but for once, she barely flinched as she did so. Logan didn't accompany her to Atlanta but later shared his displeasure with her "outrageous" expenditures.

Although she was gaunt and hollow eyed and, amid a recent tantrum, her two-year-old Paul had ripped out an earring and the lobe failed to heal properly, she nonetheless marched proudly in the procession and felt like a princess wearing her splendid outfit.

Following the ceremonies, President Bumstead hosted a lawn party at which Dr. Du Bois, adorned for the occasion in his crimson satin Harvard doctoral robes, came over, bowed, kissed Adella's hand, and purred, "Please accept my congratulations, Mrs. Logan. We've accomplished a lot together, have we not? And you're looking lovelier than ever."

Then he secured her silk-draped elbow and steered her away from the throng, saying, "I'd like to offer you some hospitality in my home, as you, my 'princess of the hither isles,' so graciously welcomed me at yours that day when I first went to Tuskegee as a callow stranger."

Adella was pondering his invitation when Dean Myron Adams intervened. He'd overheard the Doctor's familiar advances, frowned, and said, "Perhaps Mrs. Logan can accept your offer at a later date, *after* Mrs. Du Bois returns from the North, but others now are waiting to congratulate her." Then he reappropriated Adella's arm and guided her away as Dr. Du Bois briefly looked peeved but, in scarcely a moment, segued on to beguile another female attendee.

Months before her academic mission was complete, however, Adella had resumed her institute-based activism. She'd cajoled Mr. Washington, who almost never permitted "provocative" political endeavors at his school, and he'd let her debate team organize and carry out a campaign rally on campus. That singular student demonstration touted the reelection of President McKinley, who'd selected New York's governor, the Spanish-American War hero Theodore Roosevelt, as his running mate. Adella exhorted the

Adella Hunt Logan on the occasion of her receipt of an honorary master of arts degree from Atlanta University, June 1901. (Collection of the author.)

female participants to wear all white and tie on "Votes for Women" sashes as they held aloft their "Vote McKinley & Roosevelt" placards.

Most white Alabamians, however, remained hostile to any initiatives that might allow either her sex or black men to vote. One callous citizen declared, "I oppose giving women the vote because we can always club the colored boys away from the polls but wouldn't do that to our white ladies," while another railed, "I'm as much against Booker T. Washington voting as I am to voting by the coconut-headed, chocolate-colored little coon who blacks my boots each morning. Neither of them is fit to perform that supreme function and privilege of citizenship."

Such ambient presumptions contributed to the conception, introduction, passage, and swift ratification of Alabama's revised constitution. Its main intent, the governor boasted, "is to root out all elements of social interaction or equality between the races and to establish white supremacy subject only to the limits of the federal constitution." Soon, the number of registered African American voters in Alabama plummeted by 90 percent, yet Macon County claimed a disproportionate number of the state's small remaining black electorate—Adella's civic-minded husband among them. Mr. Washington's influence, wiles, and strategic deference to whites did help a little to protect the beleaguered civil rights of the institute's "privileged" gentlemen.

And despite Miss Anthony's previous rejection of her as a speaker, Adella remained dedicated to their common cause. She read virtually every article in every issue of the *Woman's Journal,* the country's leading pro-suffrage newspaper, then decided she wanted to write for it too. Her first of several successful submissions reported on the Southern Federation of Colored Women's Clubs' 1901 convention. Margaret Washington was that organization's first and only president, but instead of highlighting her role, Adella wrote instead, "The plenary session's main feature was a paper on Woman Suffrage delivered by Mrs. Warren Logan. She is a strong and articulate advocate of unqualified gender rights and handled her controversial subject with vigor and persuasion." She was fed up with repeatedly kowtowing to Mrs. Booker T. Washington.

The *Woman's Journal* rarely published any items by, for, or about

Negroes. Adella thus adopted the byline "L.H.A.," certain that few, if any, editors or readers would associate the "Mrs. Warren Logan" in her account with that discreet, reversed-initials alias. She hardly was alone in resorting to a deceptive moniker. Elizabeth Cady Stanton had often masqueraded (in print) as "Sunflower," while as a novice journalist, Ida B. Wells had used the noms de plume "Iola" and "Exiled." Many other women adopted pen names, so why not, she decided, Adella Hunt Logan?

Far outweighing her modest pseudonymous journalistic endeavors, however, Booker T. Washington's autobiography *Up from Slavery* was published that same winter. His "recipe for success" was for all of the race to follow his own example, work diligently, remain scrupulously law abiding, shrug off abuse, and never become impatient or angry. Yet as affirmative as his memoir was, it troubled Adella, though she wouldn't say that publicly, since most reviewers and other readers called it "inspiring," and at heart she remained loyal to the Great Man.

Mr. Washington detailed his early years living in a slave shack, sired by an unidentified but "blameless" white father and reared by a self-sacrificing mother (Adella was dismayed that he never even gave her name), whom he portrayed as unscarred by enslavement, sexual abuse, and stark poverty. Adella contrasted Booker T. Washington's maudlin depictions with those of Frederick Douglass, who'd stormed like Lear against the "peculiar institution." Instead, Mr. Washington depicted it as an obligatory "school" for his race's "primitive" people. Slavery, he claimed, had instilled in "my race" solid Christian morality, self-discipline, and work skills, all of which supposedly had to be learned from white men. He downplayed its physical, emotional, and mental cruelty, ignored the fact that it debased its subjects and put them at an irreparable financial disadvantage, and almost simpered about how the institution had similarly injured both the enslaved and their owners—which, he insisted, should nullify any residual resentment by his people. To prove that assumption, he cited the bondmen's reported loyalty to their masters during and after the Civil War. *Up from Slavery* discounted the country's rising segregation and dismissed antiblack violence as the isolated acts of a few venal individuals. "Troublemakers" who raged against race-based injustices, he added, only generated retaliation.

Its author also denigrated those whom he depicted as preening, foppish, "over-educated Negroes" and spun out derogatory tales about lazy jack-leg preachers or black pig thieves, whom he equally disdained. By contrast, he presented himself as the epitome of the manly, well-prepared but noncritical contemporary race leader and assured white readers that his people would remain loyal to them and "their" country. They must be deferential in their ambitions and expectations and never rashly demand either racial integration or political empowerment. Any bitterness they displayed only would erode white men's support and inherent goodwill.

Emulating through example, but far less in spirit, some of the narrative lines, structure, and phraseology from Frederick Douglass's autobiographies and deliberately evoking parallels between their lives, Booker T. Washington positioned himself as the "King of the Freedmen's" sole successor. He deliberately appealed to his northern benefactors and also tried to appease his white neighbors. But Adella feared that he gave the South's most venal officeholders and their followers free rein to continue their assaults on her people's bodies, minds, and civil rights.

He conceived the memoir himself, but his collaborator, Max Thrasher, a dedicated white journalist from New England who lived with the Logans during his long respites in Alabama, perfected it. B. T. Washington provided the biographical data and philosophical compass. Max, in turn, laid out, organized, and completed several drafts, which he returned to its subject for comment, then they reverted again to the deft Mr. Thrasher for a final polish so elegant yet simple that no one suspected that each fulsome phrase wasn't Mr. Washington's very own.

But early that October, tragedy struck the whole country when President McKinley was assassinated in Buffalo, New York. Everyone at the institute mourned but breathed sighs of relief and said, "Thank God it wasn't a colored man but a Bolshevik anarchist who'd killed him!" No one could blame this new national tragedy on "the Negro problem." It nonetheless felt like an intimate loss to Tuskegeeites, since William McKinley and his wife so recently had visited them.

Pursuant to Mr. Washington's maneuvering, the new president, Theodore Roosevelt, had been contemplating his own trip to their school, but after the murder, those plans had to be shelved for a while. What only the principal's inner circle such as Adella and Warren Logan knew, however, was that with guidance from his outer circle, the cadre of semi-influential men of color dubbed "the Tuskegee Machine" who operated on his behalf throughout the country, Mr. Washington began seeking a proximate occasion on which he could consult with "the Teddy Bear" in his den. His ambitions would soon be realized, because on the morning of October 18, 1901, President Roosevelt's secretary delivered to the Wizard of Tuskegee, who was visiting a colleague in the nation's capital, an invitation to dine at the White House that very evening.

Mr. Washington later claimed that he had no choice but to say yes to that presidential honor. Adella agreed but wondered how that acceptance was consistent with his supposed commitment to maintaining an "appropriate social separation" between the races. Yet what, she mused, could be remiss about one eminent American sharing a meal with another to exchange ideas and discuss significant national issues? On several occasions Frederick Douglass, the "King of the Freedmen," had been President Lincoln's guest, while Sojourner Truth had visited both Abraham Lincoln and Ulysses S. Grant at the executive mansion.

In clear-eyed hindsight, a number of observers theorized that the widespread disapproval that the event with Booker T. Washington generated arose largely because the meal took place in the White House's family dining room and included not only the president but his unmarried daughter. Many bigots considered interracial dining almost as offensive as interracial marriage, because, they argued, such social interactions hinted at the possibility of future sexual intimacy.

One critic denounced the dinner as an "egregious error that will result in the deaths of a score or more niggers who'll be emboldened by that mad act of a fool president!" Theodore Roosevelt's "rash decision to entertain that one nigger," another added, "will require our killing a thousand others before they learn their place again." Adella never acknowledged her "place," but why should any social faux pas merit a death sentence? The murders of "a score or more" or a thousand "niggers" and that of Booker T. Washington, however, seemed increasingly possible.

Over the ensuing months, the threats to Mr. Washington escalated—

Pinkerton guards began accompanying him everywhere—exacerbated by hostile ultimata, not only against him personally but against everyone at their school. Adella loathed the loaded rifle that Logan ("for the family's protection") stashed in their front closet, but she couldn't convince him to remove it. Many white folks who'd previously considered Booker T. Washington "a sensible darky" now raged about how he'd deceived them. The entire race must pay the consequences.

A couple of months after Tuskegee Institute's principal shared that controversial private meal with the United States' first family, Adella received an agonized letter from Patty Winston. She began,

> *I am so distraught I scarcely can contain myself. Last*
> *week Anna Leach, the headmistress at Mrs. Willard's seminary,*
> *summoned me to her office to say that she'd received an anony-*
> *mous letter charging that my ward, Della, is "of illegitimate*
> *birth and tinged with a touch of the tar brush." "Do you deny*
> *it?" she demanded.*
>
> *Of course, I could not do so, but asked why it mattered.*
> *She insisted she had no choice but to expel my dear girl for what*
> *she called "criminal deceit" and "flying under false colors."*
>
> *A sympathetic teacher took me aside and confided that the*
> *situation came about because some parents caught wind of the*
> *accusations and insisted that Della be removed from the school,*
> *citing "the danger of such exposure to our innocent daughters."*
> *Recently, I heard of a similar "revelation" at nearby Vassar*
> *College, but there, the administrators showed courage and*
> *allowed that young woman (a Virginia girl surnamed Hem-*
> *ings—her father probably one of Mr. Jefferson's quadroons) to*
> *receive her degree. Why not grant my child the same courtesy?*

Patty tried to fathom how that misfortune came about, adding,

> *Outside my family no one save you knew Della's "dark*
> *secret." Other than my nephew Ethan (and why would he wish*
> *us harm?) and her colored grandparents in Georgia, who*

scarcely can read or write, who suspected her Negro maternity?
Now she begs me, "I want to see Aunt Adella." I know that all
of you at Tuskegee are suffering in the wake of the venomous
responses by many of my people to Mr. Washington's engagement
at the White House, but might I impose on you and let her do
that?

Adella wouldn't trust her response to any possible misappropria-tion or delay at the school post office, so although she couldn't absolutely promise Patty Winston that white marauders in Macon County, Alabama, wouldn't attack them and their school, she promptly dispatched a telegram: DELLA WELCOME ANYTIME. TELL US WHEN TO EXPECT HER ARRIVAL.

ELEVEN

Minds, Bodies, and Souls

DELLA ARRIVED IN TUSKEGEE SEVERAL weeks later. Her guardian, Patty Winston, meanwhile had written Susan B. Anthony about the girl's expulsion from the Emma Willard School. Patty forwarded to Adella Miss Anthony's ensuing letter and the episode's aftermath.

Dear Miss Leach: April 20, 1902
    I recently learned that Della Winston, a
senior at your academy, was expelled shortly
before her expected graduation. Forgive my
intrusion, but that seems to me an excessive
reprisal for a happenstance that was neither of
Miss Winston's making nor knowledge and harmed
no one except the girl herself.
    I have spoken with several colleagues who
heretofore have been among your school's most
loyal alumnae and generous donors, Mrs. Elizabeth Cady Stanton among them. They share my
concerns. We know you would not wish to seem
intolerant, but while such accusations might
be untrue, appearances are critical.
    We thus urge that in your wisdom and charity,
you will find some way to acknowledge Miss Winston's successful completion of your curricular
requirements and bestow her diploma.
    In appreciation of what your school and you

```
have done to advance women's education, I ea-
gerly await your response.
```

Miss Anthony's epistolary arm twisting proved effective, and several weeks later a courier from the school delivered an envelope to Patty Winston. The accompanying note read, *We cannot readmit Miss Winston, but she hereby is granted her diploma, in absentia.* Patty forwarded the unexpected but welcome document to her ward at the Logans' home in Tuskegee.

Within several months of her arrival, Della Winston stood by Dr. John Kenney when Adella bore a third son, Walter Ogden Logan, whose middle name, his father insisted, must honor the influential and affluent white chairman of the school's board of trustees.

Della also took preliminary steps toward preparing for a nursing career by volunteering at John Kenny's infirmary and joining in his efforts to relieve the school's sanitary nightmares, which included open manure piles and infested barns, sties, slaughterhouses, and swamps. They tested the water supply and found that from reservoir to wells, pumps, and home faucets, it was dangerously polluted, which generated occasional outbreaks of cholera and typhoid fever. But citing the institute's "pressing monetary demands and limited funds," Logan and Booker T. Washington denied Dr. Kenney the resources needed to accomplish an effective cleanup. He'd also failed to restore the school's nursing program, which had fallen into neglect since Dr. Halle Tanner Dillon's departure, so Adella encouraged Della to enroll at Atlanta's Spelman Seminary, while the girl shared what she believed had generated her expulsion from the Emma Willard academy.

The previous fall, when Patty Winston's nephew Ethan Bullock had returned to visit his family in Troy, New York, Della began, "he sneaked into my bedroom one night and demanded that I perform an unspeakable act. When I spurned him, he twisted my arm behind my back and said, 'Girls like you always do such things.' Then he spat out, 'You'll be sorry you rejected me, you mongrel bitch'—though I hate repeating that ugly word."

Several weeks after Della rebuffed him, the anonymous letter revealing her nonwhite maternity had arrived at the Emma Willard school. Adella suspected that the bitter, insecure fellow must have spent much of the past eighteen years seething, and trying to avenge his late father Leo Bullock's excoriation of him as a "sissy Yankee pantywaist." Patty had reluctantly revealed to Della the name of her Negro mother (Essie Dwyer), though the young woman didn't know the sorry fact that Patty's late husband, Leo, was both her and Ethan's biological father.

Della wanted to meet her maternal grandparents, so Adella cabled her former co-teacher in Albany, Georgia, asking him about the Dwyers' receptivity to that request. He wrote back, *Sam Dwyer has died, but his widow, Emmaline, would be pleased to see her granddaughter.*

On the way to Spelman Seminary, Adella arranged a side trip to Albany. The dark-skinned Emmaline Dwyer and the pale girl embraced, laughed, and wept together. Then Della announced that in her grandmother's and late mother's honor, "whenever possible from now on, I'll call myself Della Winston Dwyer." Adella was touched to hear Della acknowledge that previously unknown racial heritage, despite her misleading appearance and long separation from the Dwyers. But the visit was brief, and they boarded an afternoon train to Atlanta, where Della enrolled as a "black" girl in Spellman's nursing program, using her newly assumed surname.

Soon after Adella returned home, the renowned photographer Frances Benjamin Johnston came to their school. Shortly before Ida Saxton McKinley accompanied the late president to the institute in 1899, Adella had become aware of Miss Johnston's work when she'd seen a splendid portrait she'd taken of the first lady featured in a national magazine. But Adella and Logan were especially impressed by and showed Mr. Washington the portfolio Frances Benjamin Johnston had recently compiled of Hampton Institute's people, work, and campus. They wanted everyone to know what their own school was accomplishing as well and urged the principal to contact her, as he promptly did.

Thus, in November 1902, Miss Johnston photographed Tuskegee Institute's agricultural, academic, and industrial endeavors, students, and faculty, including many portraits of Mr. and Mrs. Booker T. Washington and their family. When she'd completed the original contract, the Logans asked and, for a reasonable fee, she agreed to take pictures of their own children as well.

Miss Johnston and Adella also noticed that they resembled each other. They were about the same age and height, with similar features and comparably long wavy hair. "I guess we must be Snow White and Rose Red," their visitor laughed, acknowledging their slightly differing coloration: her eyes were blue and her hair sandy, while Adella was brown eyed and dark haired. Adella told Tuskegee's visitor that the Hunts had called her mother and sister those same names.

Mr. Washington also wanted Frances Benjamin Johnston to document a project that their institute sponsored at the nearby town of Ramer. The school was affiliated with their agricultural efforts, so Professor Carver would be Miss Johnston's official escort. But to ensure that no one would misread the dark-skinned man's relationship with a white woman and that she wouldn't have to travel alone, a chaperone was called for. Because Adella was a mature, respected matron who looked white, Mr. Washington entreated her to accompany the pair, and she readily agreed.

Late on a Sunday afternoon, 'Fess, Adella, and Miss Johnston boarded the wagonette that Macon County's wary African Americans still called the "Ku Klux local." After transferring at Chehaw and then riding another hour—the women in the pleasant "ladies" car and Professor Carver in the noisy, filthy, overcrowded Jim Crow one just behind the engine—their train pulled into the depot at Ramer. Adella knew that it was an unwelcoming "sunset town" where black people could work by day but couldn't sleep or reside except as household servants. Coming from their separate, segregated accommodations, they reunited with 'Fess Carver on the station's platform.

He'd expected one of his associates to meet them, but no such escort appeared as the station emptied of everyone except their interracial trio. Darkness had fully closed in when that gentleman finally arrived. He was deeply apologetic and told George Washington Carver, "I'm sorry, sir, but the folks what promised to board the ladies tonight just backed out on me."

As they were pondering an alternate plan, several dazzling streaks of light accompanied by the menacing rat-a-tat-tat of gunfire terrified them, and their greeter scurried off like a jackrabbit. The sight of the dark-skinned 'Fess Carver, who seemed to be on intimate terms with two "white ladies," apparently had enflamed some of Ramer's trigger-happy denizens.

They dropped onto the dusty boards, scraping their palms, elbows, and knees, soiling and tearing their clothes. Bullets whistled over their heads as 'Fess shielded Adella's body with his own. Finally, they crawled into the waiting room. A driver who was parked outside took them to the home of a black couple he knew who lived just beyond the town limits, and they agreed to let Miss Johnston and Mrs. Logan sleep in their attic. 'Fess clucked over his travel companions like a mother hen but departed at last and skulked around all night in the deep woods away from the roads, trying to divert the attackers' attention but also to stay beyond their murderous reach himself.

When the ladies ascended to the garret they'd share, they found themselves too keyed up for sleep. Rather, they rinsed their hands in a tin basin, then sat down to talk on the only bed.

Miss Johnston complimented Mrs. Logan on how bright, attractive, beautifully dressed, and well behaved her children were when she'd photographed them and also expounded on her own passion for recreational cycling. Adella agreed and shared Susan B. Anthony's quote in which she called bicycles "freedom machines" that, the famous suffragist insisted, had done more to emancipate women than "anything in the world." The photographer hadn't heard that quip before but quite enjoyed it and confirmed that she'd taken Miss Anthony's portrait too.

"What sort of subject was she?" Adella asked, telling her companion about their meeting at the N-AWSA's Atlanta convention but nothing of the ugly correspondence that surrounded her later rejection as a speaker at the gathering in Washington, D.C.—Frances Benjamin Johnston's home town. Miss Johnston, in fact, had photographed Susan B. Anthony on that very occasion.

"I hadn't imagined that Miss Anthony would be so vain," she chuckled, "and at first, she insisted that I photograph her only in profile so my camera wouldn't reveal that she was decidedly walleyed. But finally, I persuaded her to sit for several full-face portraits as well."

Adella persuaded the visitor to talk about some of her other projects. She'd recorded the activities of white students in the capital city's segregated schools and factory girls in New England, and a year before, she'd snapped the final images of President McKinley only an hour before his assassination. "Such amazing opportunities and remarkable pictures," Adella smiled, "from our first ladies, especially Ida McKinley, who visited us in Tuskegee, to politicians, international dignitaries, and performers."

"Indeed, but let me remind you, Mrs. Logan," Miss Johnston replied without any hesitation about flaunting her ascending reputation, "I am, in fact, the world's greatest woman photographer!"

Adella admired that unflinching self-confidence and felt honored that the "world's greatest woman photographer" had taken her own children's portraits.

Frances Benjamin Johnston revealed that she lived with a female companion in a cozy atelier, further admitted that she smoked and sometimes drank too much, and grinned: "To be honest, I yearn for a cigarette and a shot of whiskey right now." "When I'm on an assignment, I usually wear pants, which makes toting my equipment and negotiating rugged terrain much easier," she continued, "and when I dress that way, my friends call me 'Frank.'"

But Adella saw that the evening's ordeal had left Miss Johnston in distress, so she asked, "If it doesn't seem too personal, might I ease your discomfort with a neck and shoulder rub? My grandmother was a skillful healer who familiarized me with her massage techniques. I always carry a vial of witch hazel in my valise, as well as Professor Carver's emollient peanut oil."

"Oh, yes! I'd appreciate that," Frances Benjamin Johnston vigorously nodded. "After a day such as this, my neck throbs as if it's been clamped in a vise."

So standing behind the acclaimed photographer, who sat cross-legged on the narrow bed, Adella loosened her shirtwaist to access her work-strengthened shoulders. She swiveled and tilted her "patient's" head up and down, from left to right, then massaged her scalp, temples, jaw, and neck with lubricated fingers, knuckles, and the heels of both hands as she'd watched both her grandmother and 'Fess Carver do. She heard soft pops as she kneaded "Frank" Johnston's erector spinae, levator scapulae, and trapezius muscles. At first, it felt as if she had wire cables running through them and gravel in her joints, but soon her ashen skin became rosy, her pulse and breathing rates decelerated as her tautness yielded under Adella's ministrations. After half an hour, she gently tugged on the sojourner's earlobes and said, "I hope that helped."

"It did indeed, and I'll rest soundly now," Miss Johnston sighed and said, "thank you, Rose Red, I'm most grateful." Then she grasped Adella's left hand in her right one and pressed her lips to the vulnerable, blue-veined juncture where wrist meets palm.

They spoke little more but donned their night clothes, braided their hair, and settled into bed. Adella slept fitfully and dreamed of Jim Crow trains, "sunset towns," hostile gunfire, 'Fess Carver shielding her body, and the evening's unexpected intimacy with "Frank" Johnston.

The next morning Professor Carver rejoined them, and they agreed that attempting to reinstitute the Ramer project would be foolhardy. Instead, they traveled to a nearby locale where Tuskegee Institute sponsored similar efforts, and Miss Johnston put in a productive workday.

After Adella returned home and bade the photographer good-bye, she sent their filthy, torn garments to the campus laundry, where students were trained to mend, clean, and iron clothes, as well as the school's bed, bath, kitchen, and dining linens. Those girls, she often fumed, received no academic education beyond counting, measuring, and as their catalogue promised, "mastering the science of making soap and starch." But Margaret Washington, who oversaw the school's Women's Industries, insisted that those skills ensured that anyone who completed her program never would be unemployed. One afternoon a week, a young woman strode across the campus with a pannier balanced on her head to deliver a sweet-smelling bundle to the Logans' home.

Two weeks after Adella had sent over her extra-large load, she heard a rap at the usual hour. "Please leave it on the porch," she called out her bedroom window. But a more insistent knock followed. Adella marched downstairs and testily opened the door. There stood not only the usual delivery girl but, beside her, an attractive, mature, and well-dressed "white" woman.

"I'm Georgia Fagain Stewart, the new laundry directress, Mrs. Logan," the stranger began. "I'm sorry to bother you, but they gave me this package to bring from the postal office. Of course, we have your clothes and the family bedding, bath, and table linens too," she added, "and I've already mailed Miss Johnston's clean, mended garments to her home in Washington."

Mrs. Stewart shooed the student deliverywoman back to the laundry and handed Adella a flat packet that bore Frances Benjamin Johnston's name and return address. Expecting that it contained her pictures, Adella opened it. To her delight, it held not only several lovely photos of Junior, Ruth, Paul, and Walter with an invoice but also gift copies of the portrait she'd admired of Ida McKinley, another of Susan B. Anthony (in profile), and a third, which made Adella laugh, of an androgynous-looking "Frank" herself, dressed in men's clothing, grasping a bicycle's handlebars, smoking a cigarette, and sporting a pasted-on "handlebar" mustache.

An enclosed note read,

> *My dear Rose Red, Thank you for your caretaking that helped*
> *me survive the most terrifying night of my life. When you come*
> *to the capital city, remember that I'll have a comfortable bed*
> *and a glass of sherry wine awaiting you. Your friend, Snow*
> *White.*

But Adella didn't want to appear dismissive to this refined-looking woman who was waiting patiently, so she apologized: "Please excuse my distraction and come in, Mrs. Stewart."

Georgia Stewart readily accepted the offer. Adella sensed that the newcomer wanted both to chat and to see the interior of Tuskegee Institute's vice principal's home.

"You may not remember, but we met briefly three years ago when you and your sister visited Dr. Samuel Courtney in Boston," the visitor began as she curiously looked around.

The light dawned. "Thank you for reminding me," Adella said. "You were Dr. Sam's receptionist at the time, weren't you? I seem to remember that you attended Fisk University."

"That's right, and my daughter and I arrived here a month ago with my fiancé, J. Harris Bond," Mrs. Stewart continued. "He's your new academic director's administrative assistant."

Among the exacting terms of his employment contract, the Harvard-educated gentleman in question had demanded that he select and bring to the institute his own handpicked deputy. As a graduate of New England's foremost clerical school, J. Harris Bond perfectly fit the bill.

"Up in Boston about a year ago, Mr. B. T. promised me a position here as a teacher's aide, in your library, or as a dormitory matron, but Maggie would have none of it," Mrs. Stewart shook her head. "I think she read (and didn't like) the personal letters I'd written to her husband, so she overruled his requests on my behalf. Instead, she assigned me to this job under her direct supervision, though I told her that I knew little about either doing or teaching laundering." That reassignment didn't surprise Adella, however, since Mrs. Washington would have wanted to keep this beguiling woman right under her thumb, preferably in a somewhat demeaning position.

"Back at Fisk, I don't think I lorded it over Maggie the fact that my father was a builder in Montgomery," Mrs. Stewart's gossipy narrative gathered steam. "But we Fisk girls suspected that she'd never even met her ne'er-do-well Irish daddy. And you do know, don't you, that she fibs about her age? Her face is attractive enough, but she keeps getting thicker around the waist; and it's definitely not [she cleared her throat] the result of childbearing." Her observations were petty but true. "She has that bad hair too, and it's starting to go gray, though she tries to cover it up. I'm sure she resents you, since you're still so slim and your good hair's as dark as ever."

What an insidious gossip the attractive Georgia Stewart was! But Adella flatly rejected the use of such judgmental terms as "good" and "bad" hair. The fact that her sister's Rapunzel-like tresses, a part of their grandmother's Cherokee legacy, reached her hips, and the near idolatry of what actually was no more than dead protein cells, seemed ridiculous, although she knew that their "crowning glory" was a source of envy to other women and ridiculously worshiped by men.

With the floodgates open, Mrs. Stewart's stories surged forth. Adella found herself both horrified and guiltily hungering for more, but advised, "I think it's unwise for you to call Mrs. Washington 'Maggie.'"

"I'm careful what I say in public," Georgia Stewart shrugged, "but I first knew her as Maggie and still think of her that way. And didn't she smirk when I had to drop out of school after my fiancé and I 'made a mistake.' But we got married, of course, and I've never regretted it, because now I have my daughter, Carrie. Dube, you know, was Maggie's protégé at Fisk, since as a small yet very ambitious fellow, he likes having short, brainy women around him."

Adella gaped at those indiscreet disclosures from a relative stranger but remembered hearing the nickname "Dube" from Dr. Du Bois too.

"I'm sure you know that Mr. B. T. often goes to Boston to raise money and consult with Dr. Sam and his other advisors," Mrs. Stewart went on. "He and I got to know each other *quite well* back then. He'd hold my hand and say, 'I'd really like to help you, Georgia, since you've fallen on hard times.'" She was a clever mimic. "So in addition to asking for a job, I showed him the stories I'd written, and he asked his friends at the *Colored American* to publish them. Perhaps you've seen them: 'The Wooing of Pastor Cummings' and 'Aunt 'Ria's Ten Dollars.'"

The magazine of which Georgia Stewart spoke featured political and social commentary, essays, poetry, and fiction. It was the country's most prestigious, widely read periodical by, for, and about the race, and some of Booker T. Washington's Boston-based supporters financed, edited, published, and distributed it. Adella hadn't previously been aware of her visitor's writings but made it a point to seek them out since she and Logan subscribed to the journal. Alas, she'd find them among the most egregious "Negro dialect stories" she'd ever read. Mrs. Stewart totally failed to replicate the artfulness of deft writers of the race such as Paul Laurence Dunbar who'd mastered that difficult genre.

Georgia also told her hostess about her late husband. "He was brown skinned too, like my Harris. No offense to your very handsome Mr. Logan, but I want to be married to a dark-complexioned gentleman. I'd prefer not to have children who look as white as yours do and might have a hard time understanding, as it's often phrased, 'who they are.' I'd never want anyone to think that they'd want and try to pass for white or, someday, even *become* white."

"I assure you," Adella bristled, "no one in my family *wants* to pass for white. We do it only in unusual or dire circumstances, and my children definitely know that they're Negroes."

"Of course they do," Georgia Stewart agreed, "but think how often they'll have to explain themselves to others? You know how difficult that is. If white people find out about 'the secret inkwell,' those who'd first acted gracious suddenly shun and demean us, or worse. And other colored people claim that we're putting on airs and acting dicty or uppity, when we're not at all."

Everyone at the school knew about Adella's role in the misadventure with Miss Johnston and 'Fess Carver, so she asked her guest, "Given the temper of the times, doesn't it worry you to be seen in Alabama with a man like your fiancé, who's clearly a Negro, when you look white?"

"Maybe it should," Mrs. Stewart shrugged, "but I love dark men and still miss my first husband. He fell to his death, or perhaps someone pushed him. I've never known for sure."

After being widowed, she'd taught kindergarten near Montgomery with Sam Courtney's fiancée, then the two young women and little Carrie moved to Boston. Since Georgia Stewart was unqualified to teach in Massachusetts, when Dr. Courtney married, he hired his wife's southern friend to oversee his medical office, and she and her daughter boarded with his family.

"In addition to working as Dr. Sam's receptionist," Mrs. Stewart added, "at Mr. Washington's behest, I'd see to his son's needs every weekend since, as you know, he attends boarding school near Boston. I became his surrogate mother, making sure he did his homework, taking him to the dentist, church, and baseball games, seeing that his clothes were clean and mended, his shoes resoled, and the like. I think he respected me, but he often talked back to others and smoked whenever he could," she rolled her eyes. "He can be a very difficult young man! But I suppose one should expect that of a child who's really never had a mother," Georgia sighed as she delivered that thinly veiled critique of Margaret Washington, who, most Tuskegeeites knew, wanted little to do with her three stepchildren—and certainly wanted none of her own.

"Maggie rarely visited Booker T.'s son in Boston but sometimes came up by herself to see Dr. Sam," Georgia Stewart lowered her voice to stress her revelation's confidentiality, "and one time, I do believe, he performed a '*necessary procedure*' for her—right there in his office."

That statement almost floored Adella, but Mrs. Stewart smiled, shook her pretty head, and wagged her finger, "Of course, I never said such a thing to you or anyone else, Mrs. Logan."

Yet Adella wasn't altogether surprised, because gossip at the school swirled around Mrs. Washington's reported reluctance to perform her "wifely duties" and her "unexplained illnesses" during which Eve Penney discreetly nursed their "first lady." But Mrs. Stewart's story made Adella wonder if Maggie Washington had become pregnant, then "taken means," through Sam, so that she wouldn't have to give birth. She sensed that such a prospect horrified her neighbor.

Adella also saw a fortuitous opportunity and asked Georgia Stewart to join her at the National-American Woman Suffrage Association's meeting that would convene in New Orleans the following February. She wanted a woman to travel with her who either was or easily could pass for white. She'd first considered inviting Nora Varner again. Mrs. Varner was certifiably Caucasian and lived just down the road at Gray Columns; but when Adella had suggested that in 1895, Mr. Varner had opposed his wife's attendance at the controversial Atlanta meeting, so she wouldn't roil the waters by raising the issue again. Mrs. Stewart, however, was a mature and outgoing, racially unidentifiable woman who readily agreed to accompany her new friend.

The National Association of Colored Women had wanted Sylvanie Williams, its light-skinned *créole* leader in New Orleans, to represent their group at the N-AWSA event there; but some of the city's white women would recognize her, so she couldn't conceal her "true" racial identity. Ida Wells-Barnett protested that rebuff to Miss Anthony and finagled a promise for her personally to attend a meeting of the city's NACW chapter that Mrs. Williams headed. The N-AWSA wouldn't challenge state or local laws that banned interracial public gatherings, so as the chairwoman of the NACW's suffrage department, Adella took on the "invisible observer" role.

When Georgia Stewart and Adella left Tuskegee on the rail trip that headed west through Montgomery, they assumed their masquerades as white ladies. The train turned south at Vicksburg and wound through the sultry Mississippi River delta, with packed-earth levees banked to their right. In the canebrakes' swales, they saw bent, ebony-skinned sharecroppers, seemingly little removed from slavery, then passed Angola, Louisiana's ominous new penitentiary: a former cotton plantation thus named so that no one would mistake its incarcerated populace's racial identities. Their journey's final leg retraced the route to New Orleans on which Homer Plessy challenged the state's Jim Crow laws more than a decade before when he'd attempted to travel in a rail car designated exclusively for whites. For literary diversion, Adella had brought along a favorite book about their intriguing city of destination by Alice Moore Dunbar, a gifted *créole* writer.

She feared that some of the N-AWSA's suffragists might recognize her and report her presence to the authorities, so she and Mrs. Stewart would "lie low." Instead of joining the white women staying at the convention hotel, they'd sojourn in a private home, so they went directly from the railroad station to that destination. Their hostess, Sylvanie Williams (Alice Moore Dunbar's mentor), greeted and ushered them into her charming garden-side guestroom.

They awoke the next morning to the street *marchands'* musical clamor and, after being fortified by potent, chicory-laced coffee and eggy *pain perdu*, boarded one of the city's recently segregated trolleys to head across town. Before they left their hostess's home, Mrs. Williams had warned them that since the landmark *Plessy* decision, ruffians sometimes tried to drag racially suspect passengers off the "white" streetcars. So as a precaution, Adella carried her trusty hatpin.

To open the proceedings, Susan B. Anthony ceremonially turned over the gavel to Anna Howard Shaw, the N-AWSA's incoming president, then Carrie Chapman Catt, the outgoing one, said, "I want you southern ladies to know what an inspiration you are to us visiting northerners." Her words sounded welcoming, but Adella was uncertain as to their underlying intent, since Mrs. Catt and many other presenters spoke in an arcane but racially toxic language. Adella also wangled a private meeting with her, Mrs. Shaw, and Miss Anthony to reconfirm their reluctantly agreed to, upcoming engagement with Sylvanie Williams and her "colored" NACW associates.

Mary Latimer McLendon, whom Adella had met at the Atlanta gathering, spoke the next afternoon. Her advocacy of lynching and characterizations of black men "who've been wrongly empowered by the franchise" as "gorillas consumed by a brutal lust for white women," however, were so vile that Adella didn't pursue her suspicions, as she had back in 1895, that they might be related by marriage—ironically, either through the white Latimers or the black McLendons.

Grounded on the foundations laid almost four decades earlier by a senior generation of white female activists who'd opposed the Fifteenth Amendment, similar (and uglier) discourses suffused that year's presentations. Mrs. Catt revisited "Reconstruction's crime of bestowing the franchise on ignorant black men while denying it to white ladies." "In this new century," she continued, "women's enfranchisement alone will ensure continued white supremacy. There are many more American-born women than foreign-born ones, and nine of every ten educated southern ladies are white. The South must now look to its best Anglo-Saxon women as the means through which to maintain the superiority of the white race over the African."

On the convention's penultimate morning, a party that included Miss Anthony, Mrs. Catt, Patty Winston, Georgia Stewart, Adella, and several others set out from the hotel in chauffeured carriages headed to their destination: the Phillis Wheatley Sanitarium and Training School for Negro Nurses, where the New Orleans branch of the NACW always met. Clustered on that small building's balcony, a dozen cream-to-chocolate-skinned, white-pinafored-and-capped nursing students eagerly awaited their honored guests' arrival and greeted them with rousing cheers.

There at the city's only hospital that was dedicated to treating its darker-skinned residents, the white visitors joined that specially arranged meeting of the National Association of Colored Women's Phillis Wheatley chapter. It had convened that day pursuant to Ida B. Wells-Barnett's prior entreaties and Adella's recent deft maneuvering with the N-AWSA's leaders.

Sylvanie Williams was a co-founder and officer of the NACW. She'd also been a New Orleans school principal, but during the 1900 race riots, white marauders had burned down her educational domain, outrageously charging that it served as a weapons arsenal for the city's people of color. The Orleans Parish council retaliated by ending all public education beyond the fifth grade, except that provided for white children; but Mrs. Williams never conceded defeat, and the city's blacks, browns, and *créoles* hailed her as one of their most respected leaders.

As a *créole de couleur,* French was her first language, but after a brief *"Bienvenue, mes amies,"* she spoke in flawless English as she presented their guest with a lavish bouquet and said, "Some flowers are fragile and delicate, some are strong and hardy, some are guarded and cherished, but others are roughly treated and trod underfoot. The latter are our colored women, Miss Anthony, but when a person such as you honors us with her presence, it helps us to believe again in the brotherhood of man and sympathy of women." "Your organization often demeans us," Sylvanie Williams concluded, "but we will continue to pursue the rights of all women when, where, and however we can." Georgia and Adella applauded her eloquent remarks.

A young *créole* photographer named Arthur Bedou, who Adella thought resembled her brothers, was chronicling the event, so she introduced herself and said, "Since I've seen you so ably at work here, *m'sieu,* why don't you return with us to Tuskegee? I'm sure Mr. Washington would appreciate your skills, and you'd benefit from knowing him as well." Mr. Bedou readily accepted her invitation since he'd long aspired to enter the Wizard of Tuskegee's exalted orbit.

He thus joined Adella Hunt Logan, Georgia Stewart, Sylvanie Williams, and a dozen or so of the white N-AWSA conventioneers including Patty Winston, Susan B. Anthony, and Carrie Chapman Catt, all of whom traveled to Tuskegee as Miss Anthony had promised Adella eight years before. Those northern suffragists claimed that they "didn't want to miss the opportunity while so near to visit the country's most acclaimed colored school and meet its famous leader."

In Susan B. Anthony's honor, Mrs. Washington hosted an opulent luncheon at The Oaks, and later that afternoon their visitor addressed the student body. "You and your school inspire me," she declared in conclusion. She inspired them too, and the *Tuskegee Student* reported that "after she'd finished her apt remarks, every girl passed by to receive her hearty handshake."

Miss Anthony took Mrs. Logan aside to confide that she wanted to give the institute "a financial token" of her esteem and asked for Adella's suggestions as to its focus. (Neither of them, of course, mentioned Susan B. Anthony's disparaging correspondence with Patty Winston, who'd touted Adella as a speaker at the 1900 N-AWSA convention.) "We need wall maps, a globe, atlas, and telescope to help our students understand the universe beyond Alabama," Adella proposed. But intervening with her characteristic resolve and building on the "friendship" that dated back to the oft-cited tea with Queen Victoria, Mrs. Washington swept their guest away and persuaded her that the gift should be earmarked instead for a new program to be conducted under her own aegis: it would train a few of the school's girls to make brooms. Somehow, Adella concealed her dismay.

The year, however, started well with that visit. Adella donated the suffrage materials she'd purchased in New Orleans to the school's recently completed Andrew Carnegie Library, and her husband was thrilled to accept a second major gift epitomizing Mr. Carnegie's "Gospel of Wealth," which decreed that society's most affluent men should donate their surplus assets to benefit the "worthy poor." On the occasion of its presentation, the renowned industrialist said, "History will tell of two Washingtons, one white the other black, both fathers of their people." His princely donation included lifetime stipends for both Mr. and Mrs. Booker T. Washington.

Later that same month, Adella received her copy of W. E. B. Du Bois's new book: *The Souls of Black Folk.* Several things in it immediately struck her. The first was his coinage of so many dazzling phrases, especially the poignant query, "How does it feel to be a problem?" Similarly telling was his metaphor of "living behind the veil," suggesting that their people's survival often demanded that they maintain shrouded lives. He also advocated promoting a well-educated "Talented Tenth" to become leaders and insisted that "the Negro race, like all others, is going to be saved by its exceptional men." A noble goal, Adella agreed, but why only its men? "One ever feels his two-ness," Dr. Du Bois further wrote, "an American, a Negro, two souls, two unreconciled strivings, two warring ideals in one dark body, whose dogged strength alone keeps it from being torn asunder." Those were challenging ideas, stunningly articulated.

She deemed *Souls* a masterpiece. It blended politics, spirituality, history, and the arts and illuminated her own and the Doctor's *Black Folk* in all their joys and sorrows, strengths and frailties, victories and defeats. It immediately established its author as the country's leading African American intellectual, and Adella felt privileged to count him among her friends.

But his cavalier dismissal of her sex both disturbed and saddened her. Why didn't he acknowledge that Sojourner Truth belonged in the same pantheon as Frederick Douglass? He respectfully used his heroes' surnames but just fleetingly mentioned the Revolutionary era's brilliant poet Miss Wheatley and identified her only as Phillis. Other than that almost singular exception, he depicted women as oppressed mothers, covetous pursuers of lucre, naive babes in the woods, or the victims of sexual predations. When he wrote powerfully (as he unquestionably did) about the importance of the franchise for his people, he presented men alone as imperiled by that denial of a democracy's most fundamental source of political empowerment.

But more shocking to Adella and to others at the institute was the Doctor's excoriation of their principal in his scathing essay "Of Mr. Booker T. Washington and Others." She welcomed the brief introduction of him as "the leader not of one race but of two—a compromiser between the South, the North and the Negro. He is the most distinguished Southerner since Jefferson Davis." Although what person of color, she immediately thought, would want to be compared to the Confederacy's treasonous, slave-owning president? That, however, was just the beginning.

How might Dr. Du Bois's readers assess Booker T. Washington's counsel that black men should yield their already-restricted civil rights and pursuits of higher education? And what of his indictment that Mr. Washington "accepts the alleged inferiority of the Negro"? He charged that "the way for a people to gain their reasonable rights is not by voluntarily throwing them away and insisting that they do not want them," as, he claimed, the Wizard of Tuskegee counseled: "But so far as Mr. Washington does not value the privilege and duty of voting and opposes the higher training of our brightest minds, we must oppose him." "The white South," he added, "believes the educated Negro to be a dangerous Negro." He excoriated his subject's attempts to suppress dissent by scolding, "Hushing the criticism of one's honest opponents is a dangerous thing!"

But as devastating, though painfully correct, Adella feared, as that assessment of Booker T. Washington might be, another of the Doctor's essays felt more specifically pertinent to her. "Two hundred miles south of Atlanta lies Dougherty County, with ten thousand Negroes and two thousand whites," that reverie, titled "Of the Black Belt," began. Seven years earlier, that was precisely how she'd introduced the uninformed New Englander to that Georgia locale, already so familiar to her. "There is a humble schoolhouse nearby, perhaps ten by twenty feet, with two rows of un-planed benches," Dr. Du Bois continued. Yes, that was her modest, onetime school, and those were the exact observations that she'd shared. He'd probably later seen those things himself in and around Albany, Georgia, but described them precisely as she had to him.

With his government contract in hand, the Doctor had heeded her suggestion, gone to Dougherty County, visited its schools, homes, churches, workplaces, and jails, and conducted many interviews, during which he'd heard the black people's intermittently confident but mostly poignant stories. The Labor Department, however, had rescinded its agreement with him, so he folded his research into this essay, more eloquent than any that agency would have sanctioned. His disrespect in not even acknowledging Adella as a source of his information nonetheless gnawed at her. She only wanted a brief word of credit or thanks, but none ever came.

But W. E. B. Du Bois directed his most audacious assaults at Booker T. Washington and put the two men on a collision course that Adella correctly feared would escalate over time. A few Tuskegeeites, forewarned by that opening salvo, began covertly calling him "Dr. Dubious."

Adella and Logan, however, attended an unexpected dinner at The Oaks that July which the Washingtons hosted to honor Dr. Du Bois. At the behest of the school's academic director, a fellow Harvard alumnus, the Doctor had already agreed to lecture at their summer session. So despite the scathing portrayal of her husband in *The Souls of Black Folk,* Margaret Washington insisted on formally welcoming to the school her former (and now acclaimed) Fisk schoolmate, because he'd complimented her in his new book as "the energetic wife of the principal."

W. E. B. Du Bois both irritated and captivated Adella, but she generally disliked such compulsory social events, which inevitably included too many heavy, oversauced dishes. Those meals felt oppressive under any circumstances, but her late-term pregnancy made that one totally indigestible, although she did enjoy the honoree's clever repartee and the company, among others, of Rev. and Mrs. Edgar Penney and George Washington Carver, whose dinner partner that evening, as on many others, was Adella's sister Sarah. She also bristled at the practice of separating the sexes after such meals so that the gentlemen, Margaret Washington insisted, "can enjoy their cigars and serious political conversation while we ladies retire to powder our noses."

The Washingtons' pretentious gathering, Adella believed, sent her into early labor.

Adella's daughter Louise (for her sister Lula Mae, whose given name was Louisa) Thrasher (for Max Thrasher, Mr. Washington's collaborator on *Up from Slavery* who was also the Logans' dear, but recently deceased, friend) Logan was born several days later. Adella, however, failed to rebound quickly after her seventh parturition. Thus, she was confined in the school infirmary when her two-year-old son, Walter Ogden Logan, contracted cholera and died almost overnight.

She felt devastated and almost cursed, since three of her children had perished. Adella was enraged at everyone, from Dr. Kenney to Booker T. Washington to 'Fess Carver to her husband, for not remedying the school's polluted water supply. She felt guilty about not being at home for Walter and also about having been so determined to follow her grandmother's bygone directive to Judge Sayre: No more babies now! Time and again, she recalled W. E. B. Du Bois's poignant query, "If one had to be taken, why not I?" She tried in vain to console herself with his words about his own son's recent death from "Of the Passing of the First-Born" in *The Souls of Black Folk:* "Love sat by his cradle, and in his ear Wisdom waited to speak. Well sped, my golden boy, before the world declares your ambition to be insolence."

The recruitment of her brother to head the modest school in rural Fort Valley, Georgia, however, did help somewhat to console Adella. Following his Atlanta University graduation, Henry Hunt had taught for a decade in North Carolina. But Fort Valley's all-male, majority-white board of trustees recently had sabotaged the previous principal's efforts to establish a solid academic curriculum, then they ousted him to reshape "their" institute into an agricultural and industrial facility along the lines of the "Tuskegee model." Booker T. Washington was asked to nominate and approve "the agitator's" replacement, and he recommended Henry Hunt for the post. With that endorsement, Henry was quickly hired to serve as the new head of school, and Warren Logan was appointed to its board of trustees, where he'd serve as Mr. Washington's watchful "eyes."

Adella knew that her brother was brilliant, and it vexed her that he disavowed the truth about their relatively privileged upbringing and downplayed his "suspicious" Atlanta University credentials to get that job; but in the Age of Washington, anti-intellectual acquiescence became an integral part of institutional life for any ambitious men of their race. She was pleased that Henry would be nearer to her conjugal family, however, and promised to introduce him to Dr. Du Bois.

Meanwhile, as George Washington Carver and his scientific achievements became increasingly well known, rumors proliferated as to why he hadn't married. But few people knew much about his personal relationships, especially the long-standing one with Adella's sister Sarah.

After Rev. Penney's chapel service one spring Sunday in 1904, the institute's acclaimed agronomist called for Sarah at the Logans' residence, and they set forth on their weekly nature walk. But long before Adella expected her back, Sarah stumbled home alone, breathless and flushed, with her clothes in disarray and her long hair disheveled. She felt bewildered but told her older sister that, as they usually did, " 'Fess and I sat together on the stream bank and shared the delectable picnic lunch he'd prepared. The meal itself and the earthy smell that surrounded us almost intoxicated me, Sis," Sarah shook her head. "It must have clouded my judgment."

"I'd grown impatient, but what I did next embarrasses me to tell even you," Sarah went on. "You know how 'Fess loves my hair, so I unbraided and took it down as his arm lay across my shoulders. Then I tried to lower his head to my breast, guided his hand under my skirt, and placed mine on his thigh. Oh, dear Lord, what a mistake that was! But why was it being too forward when we've been strolling and courting—I thought—nearly every Sunday for how long now? Seven years, at least! Today, however, he shrank away in apparent horror, declined my usual invitation to join us for Sunday dinner, scrambled to his feet, and lurched off, dragging the picnic basket behind him and babbling about having to 'hurry back to check on some experiments at my laboratory.' I'm deeply ashamed and don't know what to say or think."

Nor did Adella, but she tried to comfort Sarah as best she could.

Sometime overnight, an envelope was slipped under the Logans' kitchen door. When Adella arose, Sarah handed her the letter and wailed, "Read what he says, Sis!"

Dear Sarah,   *May 14, 1904*

> *I hope you know how fond I am of you, but today's events showed me that I have not properly conveyed the nature of my feelings. You seem to have entertained thoughts of an increased intimacy between us, perhaps of our even entering into a domestic life together. But you must put such notions aside, because I am not a fit husband for you or anyone.*
>
> *As you know, I suffered greatly during my infancy, receiving grievous injuries that have plagued me ever since. I have loved my students, your brother Tommy among them, and often ask, how could any lady whom I might wed understand that they must be my first priority?—and that I would bring her bouquets of weeds, moss, and fungi instead of roses and have to leave home at four a.m. to converse with my "green people." (Feeble jokes, but true.) In some respects, our Great Creator made me unlike most other men. Occasionally I have taken*

pleasure in, but at other times feared or despised the baffling feelings that I harbor.

Then he acknowledged the disturbing import of appearance—especially skin color.

My horrific experience last year with Frances Benjamin Johnston and your lovely sister also made me dread the dangers that lurk here when a colored man (a colored gentleman!) is seen with a woman (a lady!) who is, or in your case appears to be, white. I fear for myself but would fear far more for your safety should we contemplate sharing a future together in this beleaguered region, these hither isles to which we have committed our lives.

Nothing could ever diminish my respect and deep affection for you or the Logans, who have taken me into your hearts and home. I hope you will understand that it is best for you to be a friend to this curmudgeonly scientist, but nothing more.

Your (and our dear and brilliant Adella's) devoted admirer,

Geo. Washington Carver

Rumors circulated as word leaked out about the "courtship's" dissolution. Why, several colleagues snickered, did 'Fess Carver pursue the "womanly arts" of painting, sewing, cooking, and music? Did his high-pitched voice suggest that he was a castrato? A few critics whispered that he was a "sissy," "freak," or "pederast" who "carried on" with his male students. Reports of "playful spankings," "suspicious massages," and "after-school frolics" infused those stories.

Others charged that the very light-skinned Hunts and Logans (the anagrammed Anglos?) opposed Sarah's relationship with 'Fess because of his dark skin. Not at all! Terminating the "romance" was entirely his decision, although after the horrific incident with Miss Johnston, as 'Fess acknowledged, they all better recognized the lurking dangers for a black man and a "white" woman who might be seen or, worse, try to wed and live together in the Jim Crow South. Her sister Ella's marriage to Apollo Payne had concerned Adella from the start, and recently that bumptious Lothario had taken up with a "real black woman" because he accused Ella of "putting on airs and disrespecting me and my race." When Ella protested, he'd blackened her eyes, after which she ousted him from their home—that she'd paid for. 'Fess's rejection mortified Sarah, but the Hunts and Logans said nothing of that sorry episode to anyone outside the family.

But just then, an unanticipated escape hatch opened for Sarah. The board chairman of a settlement house in Newark, New Jersey, wrote to both Booker T. Washington and W. E. B. Du Bois seeking candidates who might lead his new undertaking, which was providing shelter and counsel for the black migrants who were relocating there from the South. Due to the fame and reputations but escalating conflicts between Dr. Du Bois and "Dr." Washington, he wanted to hire "a politically neutral Negro," and Sarah Hunt had ties to both men. She quickly accepted the offer, packed her belongings, left Tuskegee Institute, and prepared to embark on a fresh life in the urban North.

Adella knew her family had much for which to thank Booker T. Washington. Logan had his secure post as the school's second-in-command, served on its board of trustees, and might be tapped as the new principal if the Great Man moved on. Mr. Washington had facilitated Henry Hunt's position at Fort Valley and Sarah's in New Jersey. He was the omnipotent master of a sprawling "plantation" where the Hunts and Logans lived. Adella was thankful he was their friend, because he and his wife callously crushed those whom they saw as either challengers or enemies.

One of Logan's duties as a Tuskegee Institute trustee was attending its annual meetings in New York City, where he urged Adella to accompany him that December. She agreed, among other reasons, because it would give her an opportunity to visit her sisters: Sarah, who'd moved to nearby Newark, and Ella Hunt Payne, who'd relocated to the big city after separating from her spouse. But now they could celebrate, since the wretched Apollo Payne had unexpectedly died and spared Ella the pain, embarrassment, expense, and legal nightmares of obtaining a divorce.

Warren Logan also had a new acquaintance in New York: Eugene Percy Roberts, a successful Negro physician who financially supported the institute. Logan cabled Dr. Roberts to inform him that Adella would be coming too. The doctor promptly responded and invited her and her sisters to dinner at the celebrated Rector's restaurant. He selected that establishment since it wasn't far from the Manhattan Hotel, where the trustees would be conducting their business, and he assured Logan that their well-dressed entourage composed of people of color would be courteously served.

Sarah ferried east across the Hudson River, while Ella bravely took the city's newly opened underground railway to meet them. The wiry, brown-skinned Dr. Roberts brought along his two younger brothers, and each gentleman presented each lady with his professional card.

When they entered the restaurant through Rector's unique new "revolving doors," the maître d' acknowledged and pocketed Dr. Roberts's discreet "donation" and ushered the physician and his guests to a well-situated table draped with a double-damask Irish linen cloth and set with fine silverware, crystal, and china. A few nearby diners stared or glared at the uncommon "interracial" sextet, but no one did or said anything untoward or protested their presence.

As they savored the impeccably served meal (champagne for all, the establishment's signature oysters and lobster Thermidor, followed by *crème Bavaroise*), E. P. Roberts told Adella about himself. He'd been born to an ex-slave couple and educated at Pennsylvania's Lincoln University, one of the country's oldest and best colleges for men of color, and graduated from New York's Flower Medical School. But no hospital in the city hired or offered full privileges to any doctors of his race, so to meet a serious need, he'd established a successful private practice.

After they finished dessert, Adella disgustedly mentioned the rats she'd seen scavenging about the streets. Dr. Roberts confirmed her observations and described the janitor who worked near his home and office. "He often sat on a stoop polishing his rifle—a real antique. That's an oddity in New York, where many men carry pistols but few have long guns," he explained. "I heard that he'd served in the Union army and was a dead-eye marksman, so he targeted our city's feral varmints from his elevated perch," E. P. Roberts laughingly shared that urban legend. "I never knew his name, but we called him 'the Huntsman.' He had one silvery and one copper-colored eye. It's a rare genetic deviation called *heterochromia iridum,* Mrs. Logan [Adella assured Dr. Roberts that she already knew that], but super-stitious people contend that it's evidence of a curse."

Adella gasped. Might "the Huntsman," with his mismatched irises, be her uncle Jimmy Hunt? She'd once seen the English rifle that her grand-father Nathan Sayre had given his son half a century ago and knew that Jimmy had lived in New York for some time. They'd corresponded about his wartime exploits, his inheritance, and deaths in the family, but she'd heard nothing from him in more than a decade. She shared her suspicions with Dr. Roberts and asked if she might meet the fellow, but he shook his head and said, "I'm afraid he's vanished."

"Vanished?" she asked in amazement, recalling both her grandmother Susan's and her enslaved great-grandfather Osborne's mysterious disap-pearances.

"Well, I assume he moved away or died," he smiled, "but 'vanished' is how we saw it."

Dr. Roberts's story distracted Adella, but as their party emerged from the restaurant, they were nonetheless in high spirits and ready to disperse to their various abodes, when a uniformed constable loomed up beside her and gruffly demanded, "Is dese coons bodderin' you?"

Adella was startled and taken aback but immediately tried to explain to the officer that the gentlemen were their escorts. As she did, however, he and another "copper" seized Sarah and Ella by their elbows and claimed that the Hunt women were resisting them. One muttered "streetwalkers" under his breath, while the other thrummed a nightstick against his thigh.

"Is you dolls carrying any weapons?" an officer demanded. Then his partner "patted her down," running his hands and a wooden baton under Adella's coat, across her breasts, even between her legs. Despite finding nothing dangerous (presuming they'd be safe that evening, she hadn't brought her usual defensive hatpin) and amid vulgar catcalls from bystand-ers, the "law enforcers" wrenched the doctor's and his brothers' arms be-hind their backs, locked cuffs onto their wrists, then wrestled them all into the back of a "Black Mariah" that screeched up to the curb.

They were driven to and herded into a nearby precinct house. At first,

Eugene Percy Roberts remained stoic and composed, but his suppressed anger almost boiled over when he and his brothers were accused of "soliciting ladies of the evening for illicit commerce." Another officer castigated the "suspicious white women" for "consorting and cavorting with negroes."

Dr. Roberts refused to be photographed or fingerprinted until the desk sergeant finally agreed to look at his professional card. Adella already had seen it, so she knew that it read, "Dr. Eugene Percy Roberts, 242 West 53rd Street." In the lower-right-hand corner was printed, "Medical Examiner, City of New York. The Honorable Seth Low, Mayor."

When the policeman read those words, his jaw dropped, and he halted the arrest proceedings. E. P. Roberts, in fact, was among the city's first licensed physicians of color, and he'd served for several years as an examiner for both the coroner's office and the police department itself. In addition, shortly after "the Honorable Seth Low" was defeated in his recent reelection bid, he'd joined Tuskegee Institute's board of trustees. Adella sharply informed their persecutors that the former mayor presently was attending a dinner meeting nearby with Booker T. Washington, her husband, and a number of their affluent and prominent white male colleagues. The incredulous officers reluctantly let Eugene Percy Roberts use their telephone. To their horror, the physician called Seth Low's home (the wealthy ex-mayor was one of the few New Yorkers who had a telephone in his private residence), and his personal assistant confirmed Dr. Roberts's identity.

A representative from the public affairs office finally arrived and offered the Roberts party the police department's "regrets for this unfortunate misunderstanding." He elicited their assurances that they wouldn't sue the city for false arrest, assisted Adella's sisters into a prepaid hansom taxicab that would take them to Ella's upper Manhattan apartment, and promised that Mrs. Logan and the Roberts brothers would be driven to their abodes (she to the Hotel Manhattan, the gentlemen to their nearby residence) in official city automobiles—as they were. Still quaking, Adella wondered what worse might have happened if their host hadn't been a rare, self-possessed, and well-connected municipal appointee who had friends in high places.

When former mayor Low heard the news, he sent her flowers at the hotel with a note of apology for her "infelicitous introduction" to his city. Since Booker T. Washington's dinner at the White House, many white people considered him an "arrogant darky" but knew that he was the country's most powerful one. Harassing a member of his inner circle wasn't a trivial matter.

Adella also didn't have the proper attire to withstand the wintry weather, so she was more than ready to return to Alabama, with the searing memory of a policeman's unwelcome touch on her body. She'd previously assumed that such encounters were limited to the South, where a more grievous outcome might have ensued: their escorts, even the ladies themselves, could have been lynched. She also wanted to head home because she had an ambitious project to undertake.

She'd read many pieces in the *Colored American* magazine, including Georgia Stewart's unfortunate dialect stories, and thought that should be the venue where she'd place an essay on woman suffrage that she'd been mulling over. She and Mr. Washington disagreed on many subjects, but she hoped that he'd endorse her endeavor with its publishers, as he promptly did.

It would be only a few pages, but Adella wanted to produce something significant. She guiltlessly poached a few ideas on political empowerment that Dr. Du Bois had proposed in *The Souls of Black Folk* and almost replicated her nightly ritual from five years before when she'd toiled away on her master's thesis. Logan's support for this new project, by contrast, was tepid at best, but each evening after supper and its cleanup, overseeing the children's baths, homework, and prayers, then settling them into bed, Adella walked over to his office to write.

She began,

```
We should heed President Lincoln's words:
"Government of the people, by the people and
for the people," but those requisites are only
partially realized if women have no vote. If
we are citizens, why not treat us as such on
questions of law and governance where women are
now classed with minors and idiots?
```

> Some observers claim that their husbands
> represent women at the polls, but what of those
> who have no spouses or have ones who oppress,
> abuse, or abandon them? What about the woman
> whose callous husband patronizes saloons, gam-
> bling dens, and brothels? She meanwhile stays
> at home to cry, to swear, or to suicide.

A melodramatic phrase, perhaps, but one crafted to capture her read-ers' attention, though she'd face considerable criticism that she'd even raised the *possibility* of self-destruction. Dr. Du Bois had warned, "take away the Negro's ballot, and behold the suicide of a race." But his metaphor referred only to depriving black men of their civic powers. "Fortunate" women of color such as Adella were meant to be keepers of the flame, para-gons for others, strong and pure in mind and body. Suicide, deemed a sin-gularly self-indulgent act, was maligned as a last resort for wealthy, "hyster-ical" white ladies. Suggesting even a whiff of depression, tears, or oaths was counterproductive: uplifting the race had to be the unyielding mission for women such as Adella.

She further asked,

> Why is it so difficult for liberty-loving
> Americans to apply their love of fair play to
> women? Many of our leaders, among whom Susan B.
> Anthony stands tall, know that empowerment
> through the ballot is critical in a democracy.

Adella had serious differences with the now extremely frail (Patty Winston recently had written her) Miss Anthony but felt increasingly mag-nanimous about her as she aged.

Delving deeper, she added,

> If white Americans with all of their advan-
> tages need the ballot, and they do; if it has

helped them, as it has; how much more do Negroes, male and female, need the defense of the
vote to help us secure and maintain our rights?

The main components of personal sovereignty
are wisdom and power, and the greatest power
any people in a democracy have is that which
they exercise at the polls. At present, few
women, especially colored women, can claim that
vital indicator of civic empowerment. This
writer, however, knows many of her own sex,
a number of them Negroes such as I, who are
prepared to assume the responsibilities and
rights of full citizenship. Those rights include casting our ballots, even perhaps one day
voting for other women and running for office
ourselves.

Her effort finally satisfied Adella, so she mailed it off, and the *Colored American* published it in its September 1905 issue. It identified her as "Adella Hunt Logan: Life Member of the National American Woman Suffrage Association" but didn't mention her long, close affiliation with Booker T. Washington and Tuskegee Institute. The Great Man had facilitated the essay's publication; but he clearly wanted to maintain his distance and remain neutral concerning such a controversial political statement, and "his" editors at "his" magazine complied with his wishes.

During the ensuing months, Adella received scores of comments, cables, and letters that criticized, challenged, or lauded her efforts. Patty Winston, Ida B. Wells-Barnett, Georgia Stewart, Sylvanie Williams, Eugene Percy Roberts, George Washington Carver, her siblings, and even virtual strangers expressed their support and approval, although W. E. B. Du Bois's cursory note, she thought, damned it with faint praise. She awaited even a brief acknowledgment from Susan B. Anthony, Carrie Chapman Catt, Anna Howard Shaw, or any others of their white N-AWSA colleagues who knew her, but except for Patty Winston's, she received none at all.

As the man who'd covertly sponsored the essay's publication, Booker T. Washington patted her shoulder but put nothing in writing, while his wife disregarded the article altogether. Logan resignedly shook his head and withheld any praise, but he didn't repudiate her work.

And by that autumn of 1905 she needed her husband's wholehearted support and encouragement more than ever, because, although she was loath to complain or yield to any infirmity, she had to admit that her physical well-being was definitely in decline.

Recalled to Life

DESPITE ADELLA'S INCREASINGLY problematic health and the debate that her suffrage article generated, the summer had gone well. She attended Georgia Stewart and J. Harris Bond's wedding, both her daughter Ruth and Georgia's daughter Carrie graduated from the Children's House and would start Atlanta University's preparatory program in September, and her brother Tommy completed his studies at the University of Massachusetts. Outlays for those initiatives strained the family's budget, but Adella deemed money spent on education to be well worthwhile and was overjoyed when Tommy received the unexpected offer of an adjunct teaching position in agriculture at the prestigious university in Berkeley, California.

But by autumn, she'd feel sporadically euphoric and energized but then become angry or forlorn. Her back ached, and her urine was often blood tinged, though she continued drinking the cranberry tisane that she'd first learned about on Martha's Vineyard, while Dr. Kenney self-consciously mumbled about "the benefits of a gentle douche following the act" and "decreasing the frequency of marital relations." Heeding his further counsel, Adella looked into going over to Spelman Seminary's new MacVicar Clinic in Atlanta to have her problem diagnosed and treated. Yet still she procrastinated, since Booker T. Washington finally had approved the plans that the institute's resident architect had drawn up to renovate and expand her leaky, pest-infested home.

After getting that project under way, she felt better about leaving, because her sister Sarah, hating Newark's frigid winter, the racism (though less directly threatening than in the South) she encountered when she told disbelieving northerners, "I am a Negro," and the sexual predations she was subjected to, returned to live with the Logans and teach again at the Children's House. In Adella's upcoming absence, "Aunt Sarah" would care for Paul and Polly.

Logan hoped to see his wife's health issues resolved with his minimal involvement, since he'd been charged with arranging for every guest, marcher, musician, farm animal, and float specified for President Roosevelt's momentous visit to the institute during his upcoming swing through the South. Some of Theodore Roosevelt's policies troubled Adella, but she was glad he remained a friend of their school and would include them in his itinerary even in the wake of the vitriolic and racist brouhaha that followed his controversial dinner with Mr. Washington at the White House. On October 24, 1905, shortly after the president delivered a brief speech at the all-white Alabama Female College near the Confederate war memorial that was nearing completion in Tuskegee's town square, his entourage rolled into their campus around noon.

After several rousing musical numbers and an acclamatory introduction by Booker T. Washington, the distinguished visitor began, "I've known about Tuskegee Institute for many years but had no idea that I'd be so impressed when I finally came here." An auspicious overture to be sure!

"It's important that the negro makes himself useful and becomes educated, because ignorance is the most wasteful crop our country can raise," President Roosevelt continued. "I urge you to join hands with Alabama's white people to support law and order and avoid yielding to criminality, especially the crimes perpetrated by men of your race." Few whites resisted characterizing black men as sexual predators. "You must bide your time and prove yourselves worthy by showing self-control," the president concluded to applause from the enthusiastic, mostly black crowd. That sentiment replicated Booker T. Washington's oft-repeated dicta.

Logan's carefully organized plans went off without a hitch. Theodore Roosevelt smiled admiringly as he shook Adella's hand, and she observed, as did a number of others, that he and her husband undeniably resembled each other. But pleading poor health, she skipped the ensuing luncheon at The Oaks, where she'd have been served at the usual demeaning "second seating for ranking Negroes" after the institute's white guests had finished their meals.

As with almost every aspect of southern life, discrimination and poverty limited the availability and quality of health care for the race, but the MacVicar Clinic was better than most such facilities. It had thirty-one beds and a capable workforce of African American nurses. Several black male doctors (Spelman's first physician, Sophia Bethea Jones, had long since left) oversaw the treatment of its predominantly female patients, while two white ones from nearby Grady Hospital served as visiting consultants. For major procedures, those men occasionally transferred patients of color to their own establishment but attended all "visible" ones in the hospital's understaffed, overcrowded, and unsanitary Jim Crow facilities.

But by the time Della Winston had completed her first semester at Spelman, she realized that its nursing program was primarily geared to preparing girls to work, almost as servants, in white Georgians' homes or to become medical missionaries in Africa. They almost never could acquire state licenses or secure professional jobs in the Jim Crow South. With her diploma from Emma Willard in hand, she thus trolleyed across town to Grady Hospital's imposing new 125-bed Italianate building to convince its admissions panel that she satisfied its entry criteria. Della iterated, however, "I only can attend your program for half of each year."

To explain that proviso, she spun out a tale about a spinster aunt with whom she traveled during the other six months and hinted that the wealthy dowager might send a hefty donation to the facility in gratitude for admitting her niece. Using that leverage, from August until January, Della would study and work at Spelman as a woman of color and from February through July as a white one at Grady. Somehow, she was successfully pulling off that arduous charade.

Grady's most proficient surgeon, Della determined, was William Stokes Goldsmith, who also consulted at MacVicar, and soon she became his favorite trainee. She told him about her "ailing godmother," but not until she'd sworn him to secrecy when she explained that despite their appearance, Georgia law categorized them both as Negroes. Though surprised by that revelation, the doctor wanted to continue nurturing Della's talents, so he agreed to maintain the subterfuge and help as best he could. He'd meet with Mrs. Logan, assess her condition, then perform at Grady whatever procedures might be indicated. Only by assuming her racial masquerade would Dr. Goldsmith's new patient have access to the best medical care available in the Deep South.

Della shared with Adella everything she knew about William Goldsmith: "He specializes in genito-urinary tract, kidney, and uterine disorders, bases his diagnoses on symptoms, clinical tests, and the patient's medical history, not race or sex, and doesn't disdain poor people and Negroes, especially colored women, as most white practitioners do. And I'm certain that he'll call you *Mrs.* Logan. He also employs scientific language to explain his findings," Della advised, "so when he uses words that start with reno-, nephro-, or pyelo-, he's referring to your kidneys. The lithos he'll probably mention are calcifications within the body, and section means to slice into and repair a damaged organ. Most important for you, he occasionally performs nephrectomies. Very few surgeons can do that!"

"Dr. Goldsmith won't undertake any major surgery at MacVicar and makes certain that his operating room at Grady is scrupulously clean," she went on. "He insists that everyone on his surgical team scrub thoroughly before they even enter the premises. They all must use face masks and cover every strand of hair, and his equipment, floors, and walls get swabbed down twice daily with mercuric chloride. He doesn't just wear an apron but puts on a full, fresh white suit and new, disposable rubber gloves for each operation. And he makes the most elegant sutures," she rhapsodized, adding, "I want you to look at his hands. They're so unusual!"

First, Adella went to MacVicar for diagnostic tests, and the technicians found blood, pus, calculi, and indications of an acute infection in her left kidney, but the other one seemed to be functioning satisfactorily. For a preliminary evaluation, she met with Dr. Goldsmith at his Grady Hospital office, then returned to MacVicar to await her procedure. Other than the white surgeon and Grady's discreet black ambulance driver, who shuttled her back and forth, no one outside Spelman and its affiliated clinic would know that Adella Hunt Logan was "a colored patient."

As per Della's instructions, Adella studied the doctor's hands. They were rock steady, with exceptionally long fingers. After assessing her test results, he said, "In my operating room, Mrs. Logan, I'll position you in a supine lithotomy posture: knees flexed and elevated, with your feet in stirrups [the pose a woman usually assumed for childbirth], and one of my interns will shave and thoroughly cleanse your mons pubis and pudendum to assure a sterile procedural site. Then we'll lightly sedate you so that I can suction out any minimal calculi through the perineum. It's wise to start with the least invasive procedures, but once you're on my table, I must maintain the option of continuing, without interruption or delay, to perform any more radical incursions."

Failing the initial option's success, Adella would be turned on her right side and fully chloroformed. "To determine the extent of your pyelonephrosis, I'd make a vertical posterior incision starting just below the last sinistral false rib," Dr. Goldsmith added, "remove any lithos and perinephritic abscesses, then if needed, I'll perform a partial or complete nephrectomy."

"I remain skeptical about the efficacy of my profession's new blood-typing protocols, so I prefer not to transfuse my patients," he continued. "The kidneys are highly vascular, so you'll lose a lot of blood during the procedure, but I'll not let you exsanguinate. It's preferable that you be anemic for a while than that I compromise your health with an incompatible source. A white woman might thrive on a Negro man's blood, or vice versa, whereas your own sister's could be toxic for you." That information surprised Adella, but she yielded to his experienced counsel. Lastly, he introduced his anesthetist, who rasped, "I'll be your sweet dreams man."

She'd brought along many books, her diary, and stationery and each evening wrote a few lines and letters, and read a chapter from Alice Moore Dunbar's *Violets*. Several years ago, Miss Moore had married their brilliant and troubled poet laureate, Paul Laurence Dunbar, but recently she determined that she had to escape his escalating alcoholic rages. After Alice's midnight flight, her husband had returned to his mother's welcoming arms, where he now awaited an agonizing, tubercular death. Adella nonetheless knew that Mr. Washington had commissioned Mr. Dunbar to compose a dedicated ode for the institute's upcoming twenty-fifth-anniversary celebration.

She also wrote Patty Winston. *By the time you get this Logan should be here, and if he makes up his mind to it, I will be able to move ahead.* In her suffrage article, she'd protested that "in questions of law and governance, women are classed with minors and idiots." Thus, both the hospital and surgeon, she knew, needed her husband's permission for her to go under the knife.

Her letter continued,

> *Such requirements infuriate me. I need this operation, I will pay for it, and I am neither a minor nor an idiot. Do you know Alice Moore Dunbar's work? She writes this: "Marriages might be made in heaven but are consummated here on earth based on the man's desire to possess the woman, as a child wildly desires a toy." My husband doesn't need my approval for his medical procedures, yet I must have his for mine. So under the law, Logan "possesses" me—as if I were his "toy" or even, God forbid, his slave.*

Logan tore himself away from his work, went to Atlanta for a day, signed the papers that provided his formal consent to his wife's procedure, then bade Adella farewell. Early in January, she placed herself in her doctor's very large and, she felt confident, extremely capable hands.

On the morning of the operation, Grady's orderlies transferred her from her warm bed to a cold gurney that clattered through the halls to the operating room. A bevy of worshipful white male medical students who'd paid to see William Goldsmith perform his miracles watched from a banked gallery that overlooked the surgical theater. Blinding lights blazed down, and a steel tray covered with medieval instruments of torture glittered on a metal table near Adella's head as the team commenced. First, a whiff of ether, its scent like cane syrup, from the cone pressed firmly over her nose and mouth, then the room and its sundry occupants drifted away.

Alice Moore Dunbar's words surged back: "Deafening reverberations steeped the senses in sonorous melodies as I lay, arms outstretched, in an infinite waste of water." Adella tried to swim upward, but a veritable Sargasso Sea ensnared her. "I'm borne along by the mass of hair floating around. An unknown force presses my face. Centuries swallow me up in the gulf of eternity until I arrive at a sublime quiet in the stark white hall where

I lie," her semiconscious literary reverie continued, "then the agony begins anew as the heart springs back to life."

Before she could articulate her own words, Mrs. Dunbar's further interceded: "I clutch at the monster with superhuman strength, fling him off, and rise, throbbing with consciousness and pain. It wasn't opium or a nightmare, but chloroform." The "monster," however, morphed into Adella's "sweet dreams" anesthetist, who drawled, "Say 'hello' to me, Miz Logan," and she did.

For several days, throbbing pain and waves of nausea besieged Adella as she lay in a darkened hospital room, where Della Winston returned her rings to her left hand, looped the French coin on its slender chain around her neck, monitored her vital signs, pressed under her behind, then removed, emptied, and sterilized an enameled bed pan, shampooed and braided her long hair, cleaned her body and teeth, spoon-fed her broth, and watched over her as she slept. Dr. Goldsmith came by each morning, and as her discomfort ebbed, he began removing the surgical tape, outer dressings, drainage tubes, gauze packing, catheters, and finally the fifty-six silk stitches that comprised the precise, seven-inch vertical seam on the left side of her back.

Adella's sisters and her daughter Ruth visited several times, but she couldn't take the chance that any identifiable associates of color might be ousted from the hospital themselves or expose her own designated racial identity, which would necessitate her relocation to Grady's Jim Crow ward. A couple of friends recently had experienced such health-threatening indignities. Dr. Du Bois heard about her hospitalization from Atlanta University's (white) Dean Myron Adams, who stopped by every day to ensure that Adella had whatever she might need.

Three weeks after the operation, William Goldsmith pronounced Adella stable enough to be transferred to Spelman's MacVicar Clinic for further recuperation. Her industrious spouse visited only once, but since her darker-skinned colleagues were now welcome, George Washington Carver came over from the institute several times, even bringing her an exquisite oil rendition that he'd painted of his newly named hybrid *Amaryllis Adele Hippeastrum.*

Then her brother Henry and W. E. B. Du Bois turned up at MacVicar the same afternoon. Adella had been promising to introduce that cerebral duo for several years, and soon they were happily sparring over knotty ethical, political, and philosophical conundrums. The Doctor marveled at how the Hunts almost always chose to identify with the race to which only one of their eight great-grandparents "officially belonged." He termed them "Voluntary Negroes." What a pair they made: milky-skinned Henry, nearly six and a half feet tall, and "Burghardt," nut brown and almost a foot shorter. Only their facial adornment was virtually identical: two dark waxed mustaches that sloped at the same angle and topped neatly trimmed, triangular Van Dyke beards.

At Adella's exit conference, Dr. Goldsmith laid out procedures for her ongoing recuperation. "Your incision is healing nicely, Mrs. Logan. Use the anodynes I prescribe as little as possible and try to walk two miles a day." Then turning to her medical chart, he frowned: "I see that your urinary tract problems began shortly after you married and became sexually active. Since you're forty-four with only one kidney and already have experienced seven parturitions, it's imperative that you *not* become pregnant again. Doing so might put an untenable strain on your remaining organ, which thus far is functioning well, but it would be life threatening if that one were to fail."

Then he veered off to address a current political debate: "I'm appalled by the restrictions imposed under the Comstock Laws, which impose fines, threaten the loss of our medical licenses or even imprisonment, and prohibit the dissemination of what federal inquisitors call 'obscene fertility suppressants.' I call them contraceptives! Many such health-enhancing items, as well as our best gynecological textbooks, can't even be sent through the U.S. Mail anymore."

"But," he cleared his throat, "as to your own case, I advise you and your husband to curtail the frequency of sexual intercourse and always employ prophylactic measures. In lieu of the proscribed condoms, my patients sometimes cut the fingers from surgical gloves to use as contraceptives. Here's a brand-new pair—the largest size available—of my own. I want to see you again in six months," he concluded. "Please contact my office for an appointment."

She readily agreed and thanked Dr. Goldsmith for his well-intended, latex-rubber farewell gift—which she knew that Logan probably would not accept and certainly not use.

Once Adella was back at Tuskegee, her friend Eve Penney, a capable nurse, came over each morning to tend to her convalescent needs. And during her extended absence, the work on their renovated and now much less bird- and insect-infested home also had been completed, with its additional bedrooms, second bath, upgraded kitchen, and enhanced, Carpenter Gothic porch painted in the rainbow of colors that she'd first admired years before on Martha's Vineyard.

And Logan was putting final touches on the upcoming production he was orchestrating to commemorate the school's twenty-fifth anniversary. To celebrate that gala event, Patty Winston boarded one of the Pullman Company's cars on Andrew Carnegie's private conveyance, which would transport from New York City to central Alabama a hundred of the institute's wealthy and influential supporters. Students were ousted from two dormitories to house their Negro visitors, a few distinguished visitors stayed at the Washingtons' mansion, more returned each night to the awaiting Carnegie train, and still others (whites only!) slept at Dorothy Hall, the school's gracious new guesthouse.

Along with a contingent of government dignitaries, Frances Benjamin Johnston joined the caravan in Washington, D.C., and both she and New Orleans's Arthur Bedou photographed the occasion. Miss Johnston sent Adella a note saying,

My dear Rose Red, I'm sorry I can't spend time with you during this brief, busy trip but often think back on that horrendous night in Ramer when you so wondrously restored my well-being. Warm regards from your Snow White.

As per Dr. Goldsmith's instructions, Adella took daily walks with Patty Winston, who confided, "My fellow passengers have been speculating about the two veiled women who never leave their train suite. They're rumored to be that monstrous Anthony Comstock's nemeses, the free-love

advocate Victoria Claflin Woodhull Martin and her sister, Tennessee Claflin Bartels Cook," Patty laughed. "I think that sexually emancipated women
frighten men more than do female voters. You'll remember that Mrs. Woodhull ran for president back in '72 and tapped Frederick Douglass as her
potential second-in-command, and people have gossiped for years that
Tennessee Claflin used to be Mr. Carnegie's amour. That, in particular,
explains their presence!"

Such frivolity concerning the suffrage movement's most flamboyant
advocates distracted them and was preferable to mourning, as they also did,
Susan B. Anthony's recent death. "I can't forget how she treated me in advance of the 1900 N-AWSA convention," Adella shook her head, "but I'm
honored to have known and worked with that giant on behalf of our common cause."

At the formal anniversary observances, the institute's choir performed
the old slave spirituals they treasured and the school's white benefactors
demanded as representative of their "authentic negro culture," as well as
the recently deceased Paul Laurence Dunbar's new lyrics—"Tuskegee, thou
pride of the swift-growing South"—that were sung for the first time that day
to the strains of "Fair Harvard." And fair Harvard's President Charles Eliot
himself delivered the keynote address.

Tuskegee Institute had been operating for a quarter century. Facing
opprobrium, defiance, and worse, the faculty and administrators proved
that, pretty much alone, their people could successfully operate one of the
country's most notable institutions of its kind. By that time, they had forty
buildings, electrical and gas lights, indoor plumbing, a postal office, a fire
brigade, a few telephones and motorized farm vehicles, and the institute's—
its principal's—new automobile, which Logan and others of the male faculty soon learned to drive. Tuskegee sometimes still seemed to Adella an
outpost, more in the "hither isles" than the main channels of American life,
yet compared to the miseries that surrounded them in the rural South, she
knew how fortunate they were. But most regrettably in her estimation, their
school could point to few significant academic achievements.

That spring Adella also received welcome news in the wake of a major
seismic occurrence.

Dear Sis,   *Berkeley, Cal. May 15, 1906*

I know you've read about the great S.F. earthquake, so I wanted to assure you that I am safe & sound. Three weeks ago, however, violent shaking tossed me out of bed at 5 a.m., & for the next several days I looked across the bay & watched & smelled that beautiful city burn.

Adella was grateful to receive that reassurance from her brother Tom. He continued:

Sarah has kept me up-to-date, so I know you're finally home after your operation. I spoke with a physician here at the U. who confirms that kidney removal is very rare & very serious! Especially dangerous if you were to become pregnant again, but I'm pretty sure you don't want more children. You were wise to transfer to Grady Hospital for the procedure, though I know you hate to "misrepresent" yourself. But sometimes we have to do that.

His new institutional affiliation also exhilarated Adella's brother.

I'd never have gotten this great job without 'Fess! He taught me more about agronomy than anyone at the U. of Mass but hope he understands why I can't boast about or even mention my education at "the famous Tuskegee Institute." Thinking of your friend Dr. Du Bois too. He's really brilliant with his Harvard PhD & all, but if white universities won't hire those two, they'd never hire me. I'd lose my position here if anyone knew I was a c—— man & I love teaching at Berkeley.

By the way, the dean of our agricultural college (yes, my boss!) is also named Thomas F. Hunt. We're getting to be friends & wonder if we might be related. (Ha-ha!)

I remain ever grateful for your generosity in paying my

many school bills, & how you always stressed the importance of
education.

Love always from your "baby" brother, Tom

Late that summer Adella wrote Dr. Goldsmith's office in Atlanta
and made an appointment with him for her final postoperative evaluation.
Shortly before her scheduled departure, however, the fates intervened.

Rabble-rousing newspaper accounts about a rumored sexual attack
on a white woman by a black man triggered turmoil in that city. Hordes of
vengeful whites rampaged through the streets, chasing, mauling, beating,
stabbing, and shooting their darker-skinned neighbors. They ransacked
black businesses, set trash and house fires in "colored" neighborhoods,
dragged African Americans off trolleys, attacked women, children, and the
elderly. After three days, the governor called in the state militia, which finally quelled the riot. Among other prejudicial acts, the police arrested not
so much the perpetrators but a dozen or so Atlanta University–affiliated
gentlemen, some of whom concluded that the assaults on members of their
community resulted in part from their acquiescence to Booker T. Washington's policies of appeasement. More and more, his challengers began calling the "Great Man" the "Great Accommodator."

Dr. Du Bois, on the other hand, rejected passivity and wrote, "I
bought a double-barreled shotgun and two dozen rounds of shells. If white
marauders had invaded the university grounds where my family lived, I
would have sprayed their guts on the grass without hesitation."

Though deeply shaken by the Atlanta riots, Adella knew she had
much to be grateful for. She lived in a comfortable home surrounded by
four healthy children, her successful, diligent husband, other relatives, and
supportive friends. As Logan neared fifty, his sexual demands had diminished somewhat, and in her midforties, the possibility of another pregnancy
seemed remote. In addition, after months of recovery and rehabilitation, her
health had clearly improved. That follow-up appointment with Dr. Goldsmith simply would have to wait.

THIRTEEN

Live Not on Evil

SOON AFTER CHRISTMAS, DR. SAMUEL Courtney and his
wife came to Tuskegee from Boston. They joined Warren and Adella Logan,
Booker T. and Margaret Washington, John Kenney, and several other school
leaders at a celebration in the home of Rev. Edgar Penney and his wife, Eve.
Ruth Logan had returned from Atlanta University's preparatory program,
the Penneys' daughter and their student boarder Cherie Rideaux were there
too, and the three girls served the meal.

Eve had prepared the traditional New Year's Eve feast. The guests devoured her collard greens and "golden" cornbread, both symbolizing money,
which they always needed; white rice, representing virtue; glutinous pigs'
feet, auguring travel; and for wisdom and foresight, black-eyed peas, which,
as much as the South's former slaves, had been pirated from West Africa.

After downing a second plateful, Booker T. loosened his cummer-
bund and launched into one of his familiar homilies. "The pig's my favorite
animal," he began. "At heart, our people are farmers, and I want colored
boys everywhere to have the same opportunities to raise hogs as our youngsters do here at the institute. Our country folks tell me, 'Since yuh taught
us how tuh raise dem hawgs, Mistuh Washin'ton, we don' has tuh steal 'em
no mo.'" It was one of his favorite "darky stories." He guffawed and slapped
his thigh as his friends tolerantly smiled, knowing he'd crafted that folksy
tale to evoke hearty laughs from appreciative white audiences.

"It's better for our people to visit a pig farm than to vacation in Europe's storied cities," he concluded, as if virtually any of their race, even in
that room of gainfully employed, well-educated ones, had such options, except the Washingtons themselves, with their donor-sponsored international

travels. Everyone dutifully applauded their leader's monologue, however, and toasted the continuing success of the man and the institute that they genuinely loved.

Eve presented her acclaimed pound-of-butter, pound-of-sugar, pound-of-eggs, pound-of-flour vanilla cake. The gentlemen clipped, lit, and puffed their cigars, while the ladies enjoyed a cup of eggnog or second glass of champagne, except for Margaret Washington, who peered over her gold-rimmed pince-nez, pursed her lips, patted her crinkly chignon, and eschewed the merriment, sweets, and spirits alike. Adella somewhat spitefully speculated (but only to herself) that despite Mrs. Washington's commitment to the segregated Alabama Woman's Christian Temperance Union, in the privacy of her home, she sometimes quaffed a stiff jolt of bourbon.

Logan and the ladies played bid whist, while Adella, Sam, and their host enjoyed a game of anagrams. Edgar Penney became "Dry Green Pea," Sam Courtney was "Same Country," and Adella Hunt Logan again declared herself "Dull Anglo Athena," although her colleagues laughingly protested, "You'll always be our goddess of wisdom but never 'dull' and rarely 'Anglo.'"

She also threw in some palindromes: "'Live not on evil' should be emulated, my friends. My cousin taught me that old adage, and Reconstruction's 'Egad, no bondage,' is another I like!"

"Here's a current one," Edgar Penney chimed in: "A man, a plan, a canal, Panama." That referred to President Roosevelt, whose "gunboat diplomacy" had appropriated a four-hundred-mile stretch of the Central American isthmus and created a new nation. The canal was T.R.'s engineering colossus, while Mr. Washington continued cultivating his support of their school.

As the evening wore on, old stories were retold. Rev. Penney recalled the evening when he and Eve, who'd been sweethearts at Atlanta University, "were mistaken for the KKK" when they'd sneaked into President Ware's garden to spoon in his wisteria arbor. At first, they'd been discreet, but then their youthful passions got the best of them. They became noisier than they'd realized, and Edmund Asa Ware heard a rustling outside his bedroom. He had reason to fear the Klan, since marauding night riders some-times ventured right into Georgia's capital city. As an acclaimed institute of higher learning for Negroes, his school could be a ready target of their ire.

Wielding his rifle but dressed only in a cap, nightshirt, and slippers, Atlanta University's president had peered out his window. "I hear you scuf-fling around in my yard, you cowardly miscreants," he'd shouted into the darkness. "Come out and show yourselves before I shoot!"

"We were horrified at being discovered," Rev. Penney continued. "Our clothes were disheveled, faces flushed, and hair rumpled as we emerged from the arbor spluttering apologies. President Ware was furious but re-lieved to see that we carried no rifles or torches and wore no white hoods. As we cowered on the porch, he lectured us about how 'your irresponsible behavior threatens our school's reputation and safety.'" Edgar Penney de-lighted in reliving that incident, and everyone at the party (except Margaret Washington) laughed and enjoyed it too. Ultimately, the amorous duo re-ceived only a couple of demerits, which soon were deleted from their tran-scripts, and reports of their escapade went no further.

Old friends embraced at midnight, summoned in the new year, and toasted its promise. Logan and Adella sauntered back across campus, slightly tipsy but having enjoyed a delicious and diverting respite from their ongo-ing responsibilities. Then they celebrated on their own.

Several weeks later, Adella was working on a new faculty evaluation assigned by Mr. Washington as her three-year-old, Polly, napped. Since Tuskegee neighbors often dropped by unannounced to share joys and sor-rows, gossip, books, or recipes, she wasn't surprised to hear a knock at her rear door. But that afternoon it was neither a friend nor a contemporary but, rather, a pretty youngster with blond, corkscrew curls, whom Adella didn't immediately recognize.

"Don't you remember me, Mrs. Logan?" her visitor asked. "I'm Che-rie Rideaux, the Penneys' boarder."

Then Adella recalled that they'd met at the New Year's Eve celebra-tion and said, "Oh, of course, Cherie. Please excuse my hesitation, but what brings you here today?"

The girl caught her breath, then began weeping: "Last week I overheard Mrs. Penney tell the reverend you're the only one here who's not afraid of Mrs. Washington. That's why I came."

Between soft sobs, she spoke in a Gulf Coast lilt that combined standard English with a *créole* patois. Adella didn't confirm or deny Eve Penney's assumptions about her fearlessness but said, "I can't help if you don't compose yourself, so blow your nose. I'll fix us some tea."

"I'd rather have sherry," Cherie replied, pronouncing the word much as she did her own name. But Adella insisted she couldn't give wine to a student, so the girl agreed to the tea and sat down at the Logans' kitchen table. Once she began speaking in earnest, she scarcely paused.

"My mother died two years ago in New Orleans, then *mon oncle* Armand, who became my legal guardian, sent me here last September to enroll in the millinery course. But the troubles started months before that with my first painful *régles menstruelles*. That's when *mon oncle et ma nounou* Celeste took me to see Dr. Gregoire Galleon," the girl explained. "He's well known back home because he cares for a number of *les jeunes filles* in Storyville."

Nounou Celeste was the Rideaux family's retainer, while Storyville was New Orleans's "red light" district, where some of the "*filles publiques*" were even younger than Cherie. But if Gregoire Galleon could successfully treat those girls who often endured brutal assaults and accidental or deliberate "miscarriages" and might suffer from any number of sexually transmitted miseries, he surely could cope with Cherie's rather unexceptional adolescent menstrual distress.

"At first, I had to stay in bed several days each month with *la dysménorrhée*." That scientific term that Cherie threw in surprised her hostess. "But then the doctor said he'd treat my cramps with what he called 'internal massage' and *hypnotisme*. He also told my guardian that he'd studied in France with a *protégé* of Dr. Mesmer. Do you know that name?"

Adella assured her that she did know Franz Mesmer's name and something of his work. She'd also read about how Austria's Dr. Sigmund Freud occasionally employed similar methods.

"This is what happened when I was alone with Dr. Galleon in his office," Cherie resumed her account. "He used his gold watch fob like a pendulum, swung it back and forth, and whispered, 'Close your eyes, breathe deep, and relax.' I must've fallen asleep, because the next thing I knew I woke up all sweaty and panting. The doctor was sweating too. He sniffed his fingers that looked sticky with blood and something else—I didn't know what. Then he smiled and said, 'I massaged your girl parts real good, *ma chère* Cherie. Don't you feel better now?'"

"I did feel better because my cramps had eased a bit, but after three more sessions with *hypnotisme*, *nounou* Celeste told the doctor that I was leaving New Orleans for Tuskegee. At first he got very angry but finally said that by repeating the conjurations he showed me, I could treat myself with massage as he did and bring on the same sort of deep sleep. Last fall *mon oncle* wrote Mrs. Washington telling her I was in poor health, so she arranged for me to board with the Penneys, because she's a nurse and he's the chaplain. For a couple of months, things went all right over there, but then I started getting these letters from my physician." The girl pulled from her pocket and held out several sheets of pale-blue stationery covered with a bold, black script. She said, "I want you to read this one, but Mrs. Washington took the others."

"Are you telling me that she stole your personal letters?" Adella asked.

Cherie nodded and went on, "She told me, 'I'm in charge here and can take anything at all from you while you're at the institute.'" But Adella wasn't really surprised, because she recalled how Margaret Washington almost certainly had read the private correspondence that Georgia Stewart had sent Booker T. from Boston and further believed that she'd intercepted some of her own incoming mail—especially her unexpected invitation to the White House.

Adella was hesitant though curious as she agreed to Cherie's unusual request. "*Ma chère Cherie*," she read aloud from Dr. Galleon's letter. "*You belong to me alone. Don't let anyone else treat you while you are away at school, but more internal massage as I did before will relax you and do you good. Undress, get into bed, and touch yourself as I did,*" the voyeuristic doctor went on and Adella read in shock, "*then enjoy what was so good for both of us last summer. You must write and tell me about it. No one else shall have you, ma chère Cherie.*"

Appalled by that evidence of Gregoire Galleon's prurient malpractice, Adella put down the torrid missive and fanned her face as the girl resumed her account. "The way he massaged my girl parts did help to relieve my cramps, so maybe he's a good doctor, but he's a bad man. And in addition to his letters, other, different things began getting bad too." Cherie paused, inhaled, then blurted out, "A month ago, Rev. Penney began making *les gestes d'amour* to me."

At first, Adella thought she'd misheard and shook her head: "Oh, no, that can't be true!"

"Oh, *yes*. It's true," the girl insisted. "He asked me, 'Don't you want a little magic in your life, Cherie?' He held up a copper coin between his thumb and forefinger and said, 'A penny for your thoughts.' First, he made it disappear, then pulled it out of my sleeve. After that, he whispered a very long word that I can't quite remember. 'Presti-' something, I think."

Adella swallowed hard, then said, "Perhaps he used the word 'prestidigitation.'"

"That's it," Cherie gratefully affirmed. Adella never could forget how Edgar Penney had cried out, "Prestidigitation!" while he performed the same "magic" coin tricks when he'd visited her school in Sparta. How could Cherie have made up from whole cloth that very specific and singular story?

"But his trickery got worse. On the Saturday before Christmas when Mrs. Penney and their daughter went shopping, he called me into his office and put my letter next to him on the settee. When I reached over to pick it up, he grabbed my arm, pulled me down, and began caressing me," Cherie paused as Adella gaped. "Then the next day he came into my bedroom, squeezed my breasts, and said, 'Your face is red, so I know you want me as much as I want you.' He reached under my skirt and only stopped when he felt the wetness between my legs, realized I had my monthly bleeding, and said, 'I'm sorry, dear Cherie. I didn't know you were unwell.'"

"I hoped it was all a mistake," Cherie continued, "but he kept trying to do things like that whenever he had a chance. I had to tell someone, Mrs. Logan, and I stand by my story in the eyes of God." Then she crossed herself. Twice. She was clearly a devout Catholic.

"When I told Mrs. Washington what he'd done, she got very angry. She stuck her red face right into mine and said, 'You're lying, you little hussy!'" The girl shook her head, "But I'm not lying, and I'm not a hussy. I called her a bully and an ugly *créole* name, but I don't think she understood me. She said I'm to blame for the letters, that I sweet-talked Dr. Galleon and made love with him. But I didn't do that with him or with anyone else."

As much as the story horrified Adella, it somehow had the ring of truth, and Mrs. Washington certainly could be a bully. She also was curious about that "ugly *créole* name" that Cherie said she'd called the school's lady principal. Yes, Edgar Penney had performed those same "magic" tricks for decades. Yes, he used the phrase "a penny for your thoughts" and the unusual word "prestidigitation." And yes, he could be flirtatious, but to make such vile advances to a female student for whom he served in loco parentis was another matter entirely and almost beyond belief. Cherie interrupted Adella's troubled reverie to plead, "I don't want to go back to the Penneys' house, Mrs. Logan. Please, may I stay here with you for a while?"

That request took Adella by surprise, and she almost said no; but after briefly evaluating the uncomfortable circumstances, it became clear that she had to reconsider and act immediately.

A few years before, Adella recalled, an incident that presaged Cherie's story had roiled Tuskegee's campus. A student had charged, "Rev. Penney fondled my breasts and tried to kiss me." Adella had been stunned, since she'd become reacquainted with the reverend whom her old teacher at Sparta's Bass Academy had invited there long before to inspire his students. At that long-ago time, she and her classmates had enjoyed his "magical disappearing coin trick" (a penny, of course) and other entertaining deceits. But a few days after the first institute student had made her ugly accusation, she reneged and confessed that she'd concocted the story to persuade her parents to remove her from school because she'd been miserably homesick. But now Adella wondered if the original version might have been true.

No matter how deceitful that particular girl might have been, clergymen, teachers, and medical practitioners, even more than others, Adella believed, had to scrupulously refrain from exploiting their positions of power and trust to abuse or manipulate vulnerable young people.

And clearly, she had to act quickly. "My toddler's name is Polly," she said. "If you'll stay here in case she wakes up, I have to check something out. But I won't be gone for long." Cherie nodded in agreement, then Adella left and bicycled over to the Penneys' home.

When Eve Penney saw Adella's tortured face, she immediately suspected what might have happened and gasped, "What did Cherie tell you?" She'd already heard the girl's accusations. "We're devastated by that lying little hellcat's accusations. Edgar's locked himself in his study. He won't come out or eat, sleep, pray, or even speak with me," she moaned.

"I know this is dreadful for you, Eve," Adella took her hand, "but Cherie wants to stay at our house for a while. That might ease the situation for your family. This doesn't mean that I believe her." She wouldn't tell her friend how very credible parts of the girl's story did seem.

When Adella returned home, Cherie was curled up on the porch swing with sleepy Polly quite content on their visitor's lap, sucking her thumb and twirling a tendril of limp tan hair.

As the investigation into Cherie Rideaux's charges unfolded, accounts of Edgar Penney's supposed past misbehavior arose, including the incident that had amused them at his home about how Atlanta University's President Ware had threatened to shoot Edgar (Adam) and Eve when he'd caught them canoodling in his "Garden of Eden." Mrs. Washington's suspicious mind and sharp tongue distorted the young couple's eager petting into a possible sexual assault by Edgar.

Both of the Penneys denounced Cherie's "seductiveness and untruths" and proclaimed Edgar's innocence. But Eve was an honorable woman and an impeccable professional who'd never reveal anything that, when she'd been Margaret Washington's nurse, she might have learned about the school's first lady's "female problems" or the "necessary procedure" that Adella had heard rumored in order to extort Mrs. Washington into taking a more accommodating position—a position that assigned any misconduct to Cherie alone.

Edgar Penney needed to defend himself and his reputation, so he quickly enlisted the support of Horace Bumstead, the president of Atlanta University, where the reverend served as a longtime trustee. President Bumstead, in turn, lambasted Booker T. Washington for maligning his advisor's integrity. He searched the school's archival records but found no suggestion of any untoward behavior when Edgar had been a student there more than thirty years ago and asked, "How can you sabotage a colleague's spotless reputation based on rumor alone?"

Despite some misgivings, Adella brought Cherie's personal belongings—a few clothes, eau de cologne, a gold cross on a chain, and a French Bible—over to her home. At first Logan was incensed and demanded, "Why did you get us involved with that depraved child, Mother?" But ultimately, he conceded, "In everyone's interests, I suppose she had to leave the Penneys."

Cherie often wet the extra bed that Adella put in Polly's nursery. The smell of urine pervaded the Logans' second floor, and their new laundry director (Georgia Stewart Bond had left when she remarried) sent them a note of complaint: *You're sending us too many dirty sheets!*

The girl was a somnambulist too. Cherie would pad around the Logans' dark hallways after midnight, still sound asleep. And Adella began having her own nightmares, in which a malevolent policeman assaulted her or she struggled to escape the long-deceased Leo Bullock.

Cherie told Adella that her people had been *gens de couleur libres.* At a Quadroon Ball, her mother had been introduced to the white man who ultimately became Cherie's biological father. She and others of New Orleans's elegant women of color sometimes entered into legally binding agreements called *plaçages.* Such contractual concubinage previously had set them apart from slaves, and in the twentieth century, those contracts still helped to financially protect them and their children. Adella told the girl that her own grandfather had urged his daughters to "know the law and use the law."

Egged on by his wife, who continued excoriating both Edgar Penney and Cherie, Booker T. Washington called the student "hysterical and prone to fantasy" and said he had to expel "that promiscuous, lying troublemaker." Logan, in turn, negotiated a formal separation settlement between the school and Rev. Penney, who admitted no guilt but submitted his resignation.

Ultimately, "the best interests of Tuskegee Institute," personified by Principal and Mrs. Washington, prevailed, as Adella always assumed that they would. Booker T. Washington's skirmish with Atlanta University's Horace Bumstead made Edgar Penney and Cherie Rideaux mere pawns in an ongoing and escalating political, ideological, and financial chess match over who'd shape the future of Negro education. All that mattered, it seemed, was maintaining the school's and the Washingtons' reputations and success.

In April, Cherie's uncle Armand Rideaux came to take her home. Trailing behind him was the girl's *nounou* Celeste, whose red, polka-dot *tignon,* Adella thought, made her look quite like Aunt Jemima, the "happy negro slave" whose grinning image now promoted sales of a prepackaged pancake mix to white folks who claimed to be nostalgic for "the good ole days."

Armand ranted that Cherie had shamed his family, then slapped the girl's face. *Nounou* Celeste cringed but didn't seem surprised. Adella protested, but Monsieur Rideaux snapped, "She's my ward, not yours, madame, and she's incorrigible." He was courteous to Logan but never proffered a word of thanks to either of them for sheltering his niece. Polly understood little of what was going on but wept when she realized that her "new big sister" was leaving. Cherie hugged her protector, then kissed her good-bye and said, "You're *ma nouvelle maman.*"

Adella took her aside, asked her to write, suggested that she keep a hatpin handy, and urged, as her own grandmother often had, "Stand up straight and look them right in the eye."

As per the termination contract with Tuskegee Institute's executive council, from which Edgar Penney had been hastily removed, he and his family, though shunned by most colleagues, were permitted to stay in their house through spring semester, and with President Bumstead's unyielding support, he retained his prestigious advisory position as an Atlanta University trustee.

The reverend had avoided Adella since she'd first harbored his accuser, but one afternoon while Eve and their daughter were packing up the residue of their shattered lives, he dropped by the Logans' home. Recalling their New Year's Eve's parlor game, he sighed and shook his now unkempt and much-grayer head: "'Evil did I dwell; lewd did I live,' my friend."

She paused, then responded with a more concise palindrome: "'Live not on evil,' Edgar."

He nodded, turned away, descended the Logans' steps, and trudged off down the street.

Eve understood the difficult bind that Adella had been in and wanted to bid her a more extended farewell, but it was a wrenching encounter since they'd been through a lot together.

"At first, I was at a loss, which I'm sure you understand," Eve said, "but I'm grateful that you took that wretched girl off our hands. And now, Edgar and I need to move along."

Adella would never repeat to Eve the reverend's final words, which she interpreted as his mea culpa. She could have been mistaken, however, and perhaps, she thought, they had some alternate meaning. But she only added, "I was glad to do what little I could to ease the situation."

Eve Penney clasped Adella's hand, then reverted to her professional caretaker's role, placed a palm on her brow, felt her pulse, and palpated her slightly distended abdomen. Then she frowned and said, "You seem a bit flushed and feverish. I can't be certain, but is it possible that you might be expecting again? You really should stop in to see Dr. Kenney one day very soon."

Adella gasped. But frankly, her periods had been spotty and random since her kidney removal. She'd assumed that their irregularity heralded the onset of menopause yet now had to admit that perhaps she'd been living in a state of self-denial for the past few trying months.

In keeping with Dr. Goldsmith's warnings when he'd removed her kidney, Adella's pregnancy was fraught with pain, intermittent bleeding, and other difficulties. With the exception of a fiftieth birthday party she orchestrated for Logan, she pretty much closeted herself at home.

She also informed her husband that she planned to name their unanticipated baby for Atlanta University's Dean Myron Adams. He was W. E. B. Du Bois's colleague who'd been instrumental in untangling his school's red tape to facilitate the issuance of her master's degree. He'd also rescued her from the Doctor's seductive overtures on the day of that degree's bestowal and, furthermore, had visited her often and seen to her various needs during her postoperative weeks at Grady Hospital. To the Logans' surprise, however, it wasn't Myron at all, but rather Myra Adele, whom they affectionately called My 'Del, who made her unexpected debut.

FOURTEEN

Reckless and Insubordinate

AT FORTY-FIVE, ADELLA'S EIGHTH delivery depleted her, but as if My 'Del sensed her mother's frailty, she was the perfect baby: healthy, serene yet spirited, with piercing turquoise eyes.

Patty Winston spent the following Christmas with the Logans, and Adella divulged (yet again) that "the change" was upon her, characterized by frequent insomnia, heart palpitations, mood swings, and irritability. Despite her drenching night sweats, she rejoiced that she was finally shaking off "the curse." Soon she'd no longer be deluged by the loathsome "red tide."

Just after the new year, however, she was perplexed to read Mr. Washington's declaration in the *New York Times* that "women's moral and intellectual development doesn't involve the privilege or duty of voting, and they would not exercise any greater influence upon the larger world if the responsibility of participating in politics were imposed upon them." Adella considered his statement almost nonsensical, but soon he clarified that evasive stance and added his name to a list of prominent educational leaders opposed to woman suffrage.

Far more favorable in her opinion, Dr. Du Bois relocated from Atlanta to New York City, where he joined the leadership team of an interracial vanguard, mostly composed of white northerners, who committed their money, energy, and intellects to challenging Jim Crow and pursuing civil rights. In 1909, they founded the National Association for the Advancement of Colored People (the NAACP), and soon the Doctor would begin editing and publishing its monthly magazine, *The Crisis: A Journal of the Darker Races*. He dropped Adella a persuasive note urging her to support what he called "The New Abolition Movement," as she did, though based on past experience, she expected that someone at Tuskegee Institute's post office had spotted the Du Bois name on an envelope, then steamed open and read his letter of solicitation before delivering it to her home.

Within a month, however, all of that faded in importance when Adella again visited John Kenney's office hoping he'd prescribe something to alleviate her uncomfortable "menopausal symptoms." When the physician completed his examination, he beamed, "You shouldn't use any anodynes right now since you're not going through the change at all. Congratulations! You're expecting another little stranger. I expect that your baby will arrive in mid-August."

The room swirled around. When she caught her breath, she shrieked, "Tell me that's not so, John. I'm forty-six years old! By your projected delivery date my second child will be packing for college. You know how painful and frightening my last pregnancy was."

Adella wrote Patty Winston,

> *Do you remember when you were here at Christmas and we thought I was going through "the change"? Well, that's not the case at all! I'm pregnant again and need to get this awful situation taken care of. I'm furious with Logan. How inconsiderate even the best men can be! You were wise to remain a "spinster" after your husband's death.*

When Dr. William Goldsmith had performed Adella's nephrectomy, he'd warned her never to become pregnant again. In that respect, she'd failed. Worse, she'd now failed twice. He'd told her that any pregnancy challenged the kidneys, but with only one of them, the dangers to a woman's health drastically escalated. She also knew that for a physician to recommend "illicit birth control" was a minor transgression, but performing a therapeutic abortion was quite another matter. Though agonized by that dire option, she was convinced that ending this "work of the devil," as many called such later-in-life conceptions, was essential for her own survival and best for her family, so she decided to seek Dr. Goldsmith's assistance again.

But when she cabled his office in Atlanta, a clerk at Grady Hospital replied that he'd left its employ.

Adella told her husband nothing about the source or depth of her anxiety but scavenged the recommended herbs and stirred up her grand-mother's old "foolproof" abortifacient. Even ingesting that vile tonic, how-ever, failed to produce the desired outcome. She also pummeled her stom-ach hoping to induce a miscarriage, but to no avail, the result being only some gruesome and painful bruises. Cowardice alone kept her from hurling herself down a staircase or resorting to the dangerous coat-hanger or knit-ting-needles techniques. But then she recalled what Georgia Stewart Bond had suggested: Dr. Samuel Courtney once had performed a "necessary pro-cedure" for Margaret Washington at his office in Boston. By coincidence, her physician friend was coming to Tuskegee in a few days.

When he arrived, Adella pulled him aside and blurted out, "John Kenney tells me I'm expecting again, Sam. I heard through the grapevine that on rare occasions you'll perform therapeutic abortions. With only one kidney, I'm terrified that this pregnancy endangers my life. I'm altogether too old for this, I'm already feeling ill, and we simply can't afford another child."

He looked aghast. "I take the Hippocratic oath very seriously, Adella. I cherish life and know that you do too. I'd only consider such a radical measure in the direst of circumstances and couldn't do it at all without your husband's consent. What does Logan say about this?"

She fell into his arms howling like a madwoman: "I haven't even told him I'm pregnant. I'm living through this nightmare, he's not! You took care of Maggie's 'problem' several years ago, didn't you, Sam? I'd bet dollars to doughnuts that Booker T. never gave you his approval for that procedure." She knew that she was unfairly taunting Sam Courtney and pressing him to do something that was clearly controversial and perhaps illegal.

"Who told you that?" he demanded, but she loyally wouldn't reveal her friend Georgia Stewart Bond as her source. Then Sam shook his head: "Honestly, Adella, who could deny Maggie *anything* she'd absolutely set her mind on doing?" Adella recalled Cherie Rideaux's words: "Mrs. Penney told the reverend you're the only one here who's not afraid of Mrs. Washington." Margaret Washington, it seemed, even had intimidated Dr. Samuel Courtney.

"Without Logan's agreement, my hands are tied," Sam went on. "Despite your kidney removal, I doubt that this pregnancy is really life threatening. Please do whatever John Kenney suggests, but cable me right away if any problems arise. After the baby's birth, come up to Boston. If you still want me to, I can perform a new surgical procedure to ensure that you won't have to go through this again. Until then, I'm sure Logan will be supportive."

But when she told her husband, he said, "First, I'm too busy to deal with all this drama; second, your hysteria over this routine situation is unwarranted; third, you have a fine physician right here; and fourth, babies are always a blessing." Adella withdrew in wounded silence.

Her nausea continued unabated. She vomited each morning for months and ate little but her grandmother's recommended applesauce-and-kaolin-chalk slurry that "friends" whispered made her children's complexions so pale. She thought she looked like a skeleton toting a watermelon. Her usually bony toes became gross pork sausages that she barely could squeeze into her shoes, her back throbbed, and urination was agonizing. Those were unequivocal symptoms of compromised kidney function.

She feared she might die. What would become of her children? She refused to share the marital bed and lay sleepless every night on the parlor sofa, scribbling in her diary, *A man's sole motivation may be the gratification of his physical passions. . . . By yielding to one's murderous thoughts might one become a murderer?* The embryo that gnawed at her innards was a mistake, but could she *become a murderer?* The time window for the solution she pursued soon passed, however, so she only could try to survive her unwelcome circumstance as best she could.

But despite a harrowing and life-threatening pregnancy, her new son arrived on schedule with little "drama," and he was her most beautiful baby ever, with deep dimples, green eyes, and blond curls. The photographer Mr. Bedou had become a good friend, so she named the baby Arthur, although frankly, he scarcely interested her.

But Patty Winston had been her conspirator in organizing an upcoming itinerary, so as soon as Adella got up and around, she informed Logan, "Patty and I have made plans," and fled.

She cabled Sam Courtney, then traveled to Boston, where a nurse scrupulously sterilized everything in his procedure room. To perform what he called a "tubal occlusion," the doctor sedated her, made a lower-abdominal incision, clipped and sutured her fallopian tubes, then stitched her up. Considering her age, he'd been reluctant to do so and asked, "Are you quite certain about this? The likelihood of your becoming pregnant again is very slight, you know."

But after two "change-of-life babies" Adella refused to take any more chances, and the innovative operation, Sam promised, should make it impossible for her ever to become pregnant again. Equally important, she and her physician made that decision together, without asking for or receiving her husband's permission. What a great victory and profound relief!

Adella stayed with the Courtneys during a ten-day recuperation in Boston; then Ruth joined her, and she helped her daughter settle in at Dudley Sargent's Normal School for Physical Education across the Charles River in Cambridge. Ruth was a large girl—tall, broad shouldered, and somewhat prone to "baby fat"—so Adella hoped that the school's arduous sports agenda and courses in physiology, anatomy, and nutrition would help to harness her untapped muscle and brain power.

In 1881, Dr. Sargent, a novice professor at the Harvard Medical School, was assigned to monitor all of the university's athletic activities. Seven years later, however, Harvard's Board of Overseers denied him tenure after he joined its president, Charles Eliot, in (unsuccessfully) advocating the discontinuation of its popular football program, which they both excoriated as "a cause of violent fisticuffs and grievous injuries." As Dudley Sargent gradually distanced himself from Harvard, he began to focus on educating and preparing physical education teachers. He expanded those efforts into a three-year degree program, which soon became a certified normal college. By the time Ruth arrived in the early fall of 1909, the institution had about a dozen young men and several hundred female students. Its first black one, a Bostonian named Alfreda Armstrong, had entered a year ahead of Ruth, and the girls became close friends.

Patty Winston had organized every detail of the jaunt's next leg. She'd learned that the controversial Austrian psychoanalyst Sigmund Freud was coming to the United States to deliver five lectures and receive an honorary degree at Clark University in Worcester, Massachusetts. Clark's president, Dr. G. Stanley Hall, was an American pioneer in that field, and he'd invited Dr. Freud to commemorate the twentieth anniversary of Clark's founding. Patty persuaded her Alabama friend that attending the program would be a stimulating interlude that would inform their interests in the arcane workings of the mind and also address their concerns about ways that male physicians often ignored, degraded, mistreated, or misdiagnosed women. She and her German driver, Heinrich Kraus, would motor 140 miles east from Troy, New York, to Worcester, Massachusetts, in her new Model T Ford, so on September 8, Adella boarded a westbound train for the short trip from Boston to join them.

A decade before, Patty Winston had given Charlotte Perkins Gilman's controversial novella *The Yellow Wallpaper* to Adella, and in the final letter she'd written before her friend departed from Tuskegee, Patty suggested, *In light of Dr. Freud's upcoming lectures and your own, understandable postpartum "tristesse," you'd be well served by reading it again.*

Its narrator is a nameless woman, beset since the recent birth of her child with "nervous depression and a hysterical tendency." "Such a dear baby, yet I cannot be with him at all," she mourns. Her overbearing physician husband insists that she take a long "rest cure," during which he forbids her either to see her infant or to "touch pen or pencil," although Mrs. Gilman crafted the story as a series of entries in her protagonist's handwritten journal. She's locked in a room, the walls of which are overlaid with a bilious yellow paper, and soon comes to believe that other women are trapped behind that covering, whence they're struggling to escape. Even as the diarist claws at the paper in a vain attempt to free them from their "cages," she feels increasingly secure in her own confining "prison," loses touch with reality, and descends into madness.

While rereading the book on the train, Adella noticed two gentlemen seated nearby who seemed to be discussing it in German. She overheard them mention Clark and Dr. Hall and surmised that they must be Sigmund

Freud and a companion. Adella nodded and bade them *"Guten Tag"*—her limited familiarity with their language mostly consisted of words and phrases that W. E. B. Du Bois had strewn around over the years. She gave her name, identified herself as *"eine Lehrerin,"* and addressed her bearded fellow traveler as Herr Doktor Freud.

He pointed to Adella's reading material and asked, "Do you think that Charlotte Gilman's *fraulein* is neurasthenic, Frau Logan?" *The Yellow Wallpaper* hadn't yet been translated into German, but several American colleagues, Dr. Freud continued, had written him citing the book's pertinence to his own work on "female hysteria and neurasthenia."

"The author's central premise is that her protagonist has been oppressed by her domineering husband and poorly served by his officious medical colleagues," Adella responded.

She feared that her chance acquaintance might be offended, disagreed, or didn't fully understand her, however, so that ended their exchange. But as they debarked from the train half an hour later, she approached him on the platform and haltingly said, *"Schön Sie zu treffen,* Herr Doktor Freud. I look forward to hearing about your work at the upcoming lectures but thought you might like to read Mrs. Gilman's book yourself." She held out the slim volume to him.

He took it, tipped his hat, smiled, and said, *"Ya, danke sehr,* Frau Logan." Then he turned away to greet Clark's President Hall, Worcester's Mayor James Logan, and several other local dignitaries who'd assembled at the station to greet their esteemed guest.

Worcester had long intrigued Adella since it was known among "feminists"—a recently coined term for the cadre of "aggressive" women who (like her) were considered the antitheses of "feminine"—as the site of the first National Women's Rights Conference back in 1850. That groundbreaking gathering had been attended, among others, by her heroes Frederick Douglass, Sojourner Truth, and Susan B. Anthony. But except for that history, the amusing coincidence that the mayor was named Logan (he wasn't related), and Clark University's modest presence, Adella found little to recommend that grimy industrial city.

The next day, Patty's chauffeur, Heinrich Kraus, drove them from their hotel over to the campus, where the symposia would be held in the dark, wood-paneled library of its main academic building. After parking the auto nearby, and at Patty's insistence, he returned and took a seat between Adella and his employer.

Every other morning at eleven, Adella pulled out a pen and spiral notebook, as Sigmund Freud embarked on an hour-long lecture. She reconstructed her synopses of his presentations, titled in toto "The Origins and Development of Psychoanalysis," from her own and Patty's scribbles, Herr Kraus's assistance, and the translations in Worcester's daily newspapers. Dr. Freud was most comfortable speaking German, so he used it almost exclusively, since much of the predominantly male, largely medically trained audience was familiar with that language.

After thanking his hosts for inviting and honoring him, Dr. Freud introduced his subject by explaining that what he called his "talking cures" were far from new: "In part, I consider myself an interpreter of dreams, as other men before me have done for centuries."

"In analyzing my patients' dreams and subconscious thoughts," he went on, "I find that purses, cabinets, and the like represent passive female sexuality, while guns, spears, and cigars are male associated, or what I call 'phallic symbols.'" Adella considered her own nightmares in which a policeman forced his nightstick between her legs, another generated by her dread of the shotgun that Logan stashed in their front closet, and often, strange visions of flying and falling.

"More than a century ago," Dr. Freud added, "a number of European physicians began experimenting with what they called 'hypnotic somnambulism.'" He'd used hypnosis himself and, for a while, believed it to have some therapeutic value. But he'd come to consider that technique unreliable and potentially dangerous. Unscrupulous practitioners, he admitted, sometimes abused such methods. Adella thought back on Cherie Rideaux's grim experience with "mesmerization" that her predatory New Orleans doctor had used to (mis)treat her.

Sigmund Freud further expounded on "the centrality of sensual impulses and memories" but admitted that even some of his staunchest supporters complained that he vastly overstressed the critical importance of sexuality. "Most patients," he explained, "resist being candid in that respect, and almost no one reveals his full erotic life even to a trusted friend."

"Infants," he continued, "bring sensuality into the world with them, but in time, they usually redirect their initial autoerotic desires to a nurse or parent. It becomes detrimental to their further development, however, if they remain fixated for too long on their earliest objects of affection. Emotionally healthy people transfer such feelings to others as they mature, yet they also can retrogress, which may result in what I call 'inversions' or 'exclusive homosexuality.'"

Sigmund Freud disparagingly called persons who maintained those romantic, same-sex preferences into adulthood "inverts." Hearing that explanation, Adella's thoughts turned to a dear friend who she privately believed might be so inclined.

"Psychoanalysis may help us understand and possibly surmount this strange propensity," Dr. Freud concluded his penultimate lecture. "It may enable an appropriate redirection for a patient's residual puerile desires— or then again, it may not."

"Many people cope successfully with childhood memories," he began the final one, "but others have a difficult time doing so. Why, I ask myself, do similar conflicts sometimes allow for and support sound mental health but alternatively may lead to debilitating neuroses?"

Dr. Freud paused a moment, then said, "*The Yellow Wallpaper.*" Adella gaped, dropped her notepad, and prodded Mr. Kraus, who helped translate the lecturer's next words for her: "This is the story of a troubled *fraulein* who's denied therapeutic help, loses control over her impulses, and regresses to a state of infancy as repressed conflicts lead her toward total dysfunction. I struggle to understand what women want and how their psyches differ from men's, and this book may help me. I hadn't read it until recently, but a few days ago, a generous *Lehrerin* gave me her copy." Sigmund Freud nodded to acknowledge Adella's presence as she flushed with pride.

She and Patty Winston attended all five lectures with others of the equally impressed, undecided, ambivalent, or scornful assemblage. When that momentous serial event concluded, Heinrich Kraus drove Adella and

Patty back to Troy in her new forest-green touring car, with its tan leather upholstery, handsome brass side lamps, and Vanadium steel fittings. The September weather was splendid; so he lowered the pleated "convertible" hood for them, and they enjoyed the sunshine and breezes as they motored along at an exhilarating thirty-five miles per hour.

Adella spent the weekend with her friend, then Mr. Kraus took them west to Rochester, where they laid flowers on Frederick Douglass's and Susan B. Anthony's neighboring graves.

Patty Winston left Adella in that city, where she boarded a sleeper train and two days later arrived back at Tuskegee to resume her customary household management, spousal duties, and child care, certain that she better understood her resistance to dealing with the realities of her life. The Prodigal Mother had returned, though she'd pay dearly for her temporary defection.

Logan was furious that she'd "run away," Paul and Polly ingested some of his hostility, but My 'Del was happily oblivious. At two months, Arthur didn't recognize his mother at first, and when she tried to hold him, he wailed for his aunt Sarah's familiar arms. His middle name, Adella decided, had to be Courtney, after her physician in Boston who'd been her recent savior.

Baby Arthur was healthy, but Warren Junior, who was attending Howard University, "the Capstone of Negro Education," wrote to his parents saying that he'd felt inexplicably weary for some time. He'd received a tentative diagnosis of tuberculosis, so he returned home for further evaluation. Dr. Kenney performed a second series of tests and deemed Junior's condition less serious than they'd first feared. After six weeks of rest, he felt strong enough to return to school. Pursuant to that crisis, Adella and her husband laid aside most of their recent conflicts.

And soon thereafter, the school received thrilling news: former president Theodore Roosevelt agreed to join their board of trustees. That triumph reflected Booker T. Washington's burgeoning reputation and influence. His name also had been mentioned as a potential cabinet member during T.R.'s presidency and now was again in William Howard Taft's. If such an appointment were made, Mr. Washington would be the first acknowledged person of his race to be so recognized. In the wake of those speculations, Logan admitted to Adella that if an honor like that were bestowed on the Great Man, his own aspiration was to succeed him as principal.

On an otherwise unmemorable Sunday in March 1911, however, Mr. Washington's ambitions suffered a serious blow. He'd gone to New York as part of a speaking and fund-raising tour, and around nine on the evening of the eleventh, near his usual temporary residence at the Manhattan Hotel, he boarded an underground municipal train, then got off at a station a mile or so further north, near the city's Central Park. He'd later claim that Logan had sent him a telegram providing the name of the institute's new independent auditor and the address of the building where his uncle lived. They were supposed to meet at his apartment that evening. The block in question, however, was tawdry, and a seedy burlesque hall stood just across the street.

As an assortment of residents and visitors entered or left the apartment house, Mr. Washington repeatedly rang an inner doorbell, then paced outside awaiting his appointment's arrival. After an hour, a heavyset white man who'd been lurking under the theater marquee charged over and demanded, "What do you want, you blackguard?" He snatched a walking stick from a passerby and mercilessly pummeled his victim while pursuing him eastward down the sidewalk. As he fled, Booker T. Washington, who'd only recently been released after a medical checkup at the Battle Creek Sanitarium, pleaded for mercy.

The assault culminated at the park corner, where a plainclothes policeman identified himself and brought it to a halt, at which point the attacker charged that "the black scoundrel" had accosted several white women, including his wife, greeting her with a presumptuous, "Hello, sweetheart." Although the badly bloodied Mr. Washington obviously was the victim, the young assailant claimed that the "colored fella" had been the aggressor and demanded that he be arrested. At that point, a pair of uniformed patrolmen arrived and took both men into custody.

At the nearby station house, the police officers started to book them. Mr. Washington had repeatedly given his name, but the authorities hadn't believed him; and only after a tense hour or more did he finally provide what they considered to be adequate proof of his identity.

The desk sergeant reluctantly agreed to charge the actual aggressor, a German American named Hugo Ulrich, with battery and let Booker T. Washington make a telephone call. He reached the chairman of Tuskegee's board of trustees, New York's former mayor Seth Low, who arranged for an ambulance to take him to Flower Hospital, where the Logans' friend Dr. Eugene Percy Roberts helped the interns examine, clean, stitch up, and bandage him. When Dr. Roberts escorted Mr. Washington back to the Hotel Manhattan, a group of advisors assembled and began preparing a press statement that would cast the most positive light on the evening's events.

But a couple of days later, the auditor whom Booker T. Washington asserted that he'd expected to meet said that he knew nothing of such an engagement, and neither the original nor a copy of any letter or telegram confirming their purported appointment could be produced. That perplexed Adella, since Logan and the principal usually were scrupulous about such minutiae.

Several critics charged that Mr. Washington had gone to the building for a tryst with a white amour or a prostitute. Perhaps he'd been intoxicated. Admittedly he drank on occasion, despite Margaret Washington's purported commitment to total abstinence, but as far as Adella knew, he never did so to excess. He'd also recently sullied his own credibility by passing along scurrilous hearsay that Dr. Du Bois and several colleagues "of the African type" had been seen "carrying on with cultured white ladies attired in low-cut gowns." Their community's epic internal feud was becoming more acrimonious than Adella had thought possible.

In Booker T. Washington's time of need, however, most of the race ultimately pulled together. Even Dr. Du Bois acknowledged that "in unity there is strength," so he and his organization, the NAACP, agreed to stand shoulder to shoulder with his frequent antagonist.

It would've been regrettable enough had the incident just simmered down and come to a discreet finish at that juncture, but it didn't. Flower Hospital's interns and Dr. Roberts submitted sworn statements that Mr. Washington had been stone-cold sober when they attended him on the night of the assault, but Hugo Ulrich refused to disavow his accusations of drunkenness.

When a prosecutor finally brought the case to court six months later, the defendant testified, "The *schwarzer* insulted my wife, so I had to drub him." Despite solid evidence as to the white man's guilt, a panel of judges found the charges against him "unproven."

The "Ulrich affair" unjustly tarnished Booker T. Washington. Despite his longtime patronage, the Hotel Manhattan's management refused to let him stay there anymore, with the clear message, "negroes create problems and no longer are welcome in our establishment."

Many suspicious supporters feared that the episode was part of a conspiracy to destroy Mr. Washington's reputation or even kill him, but others argued that it provided further evidence that rebutted the supposed efficacy of his policies of accommodation. Adella frankly hoped that the attack itself and his subsequent travails would prompt him to speak out more forcefully about how racial violence might erupt at any time or place. Even in "progressive" New York City, which more than the South held Jim Crow in abeyance, the nation's most illustrious and respected person of his race, whom friends and supporters lauded as the Great Man but detractors began disparaging as the Great Accommodator, was suspect, imperiled, and even lynchable.

FIFTEEN

The Princess and the Pen

DESPITE THE BRUTAL ATTACK AND UGLY accusations against Booker T. Washington, and his ensuing misadventures in New York, Tuskegee Institute and its leader survived. In addition to Teddy Roosevelt, Mr. Washington had been courting Chicago's Julius Rosenwald—president of the renowned Sears & Roebuck company and a rising colossus in the country's Jewish philanthropic community—to join his board of trustees. Early in 1912, Mr. Rosenwald agreed to do so, although he already was an NAACP supporter and thus had placed one foot firmly in the Du Bois camp. Adella and his wife, Augusta, soon found a pleasant commonality with each other in that "Gussie," as friends called her, had a daughter named Adele. Mrs. Logan also helped to persuade Mrs. Rosenwald about the merit and import of suffrage, which, the following year, the state of Illinois legislatively granted to most women—in most instances.

Adella returned in June to Cambridge, Massachusetts, for Ruth's graduation from Sargent College, where the previous spring, Alfreda Armstrong had completed the program. Tuskegee immediately had hired Miss Armstrong as its first girls' physical education teacher. She and Dr. John Kenney soon began courting, and they'd become engaged. Prior to Ruth's commencement exercises, the sight of perspiring (sweating, actually) young women had made Adella feel ill at ease, but the athletics demonstrations that Ruth and her classmates presented were exhilarating. Her pudginess had melted away, and she'd become a taut, muscled Valkyrie.

Following that celebration, the Logan ladies went south to Virginia's Hampton Institute to participate in the National Association of Colored Women's annual convention. Jennie Booth Moton, one of Margaret Washington's loyal protégées, was the event's hostess, and she welcomed the organization's many delegates to the historic school. For more than a decade, her spouse, Major Robert Russa Moton, had served as Hampton's commandant of cadets, its second-in-command and dean of men, since an elderly white Yankee doddered along, clinging to the institute's helm.

That summer, after sixteen years during which Mrs. Booker T. Washington maneuvered and plotted to seize the NACW's reins of power, she finally was elected as president of that influential women's group dedicated to "racial uplift," which by then incorporated hundreds of chapters and had thirty thousand members nationwide. Her first official act reconfigured the leadership team, and she removed Adella from the chairmanship of the vibrant suffrage department, which she'd proposed, founded, and steered. Margaret Washington reassigned her neighbor to head what Adella considered a less prestigious committee that dealt with rural conditions. To justify that decision, Mrs. Washington cited "Mrs. Logan's extensive work with Professor Carver."

Ruth considered that action an affront to her mother, while Adella suspected that the proximate reason which prompted Mrs. Washington to do so was that shortly before she left Tuskegee, she'd received a letter from Dr. Du Bois, asking her to contribute an essay for the *Crisis*'s upcoming issue dedicated to woman suffrage. She guessed that Tuskegee's suspicious "first lady" had certainly seen, and probably read, that solicitation from her husband's critic.

As soon as they returned, the school hired Ruth as its second girls' physical education teacher and also hosted the National Medical Association (NMA) convention. Inspired by Mr. Washington's Atlanta Compromise address, which advocated "voluntary separation," a score of the country's black medical practitioners had founded that organization in 1896. They'd also done so because the much-larger American Medical Association, if it included them at all in its directories that listed many doctors beyond those who were members, sought to stigmatize physicians of their race by placing the designation "col'd." next to their names. Its constitution included no specific, racially discriminatory membership qualifications, but many state medical organizations did so; and participation in the AMA's national activities required a local affiliation and sponsorship by a number of members in good standing. The respected "white" association thus declined (or refused) to offer membership to any physicians of color at all. So much, Adella thought, for rosy predictions that the country, as exemplified by one of its most prestigious professional organizations, was trending toward racial inclusion and opportunity. Many black doctors seethed at that institutional exclusion, but few of them openly complained, since Jim Crow restrictions were endemic, expected, and often tolerated throughout the country.

John Kenney sponsored, organized, and oversaw that NMA event at Tuskegee Institute, where several hundred medical professionals, New York's Eugene Percy Roberts among them, convened for a week of meetings, presentations, collegial dining, and the like. Dr. Roberts even asked Adella Hunt Logan, as an informed layperson, to address a panel he chaired where she laid out some ideas she'd been mulling over that might enable poor women to obtain prenatal care for themselves and annual medical examinations for their children.

From Adella's perspective, however, the convention's climax was the suffrage parade that she and Ruth organized. Bearing "Votes for Women" placards, a contingent of the female faculty and students dressed in white and sang the new lyrics Adella had written to the tune of "Comin' Thro the Rye." Many conventioneers joined them in the revised first stanza, which went,

> If a body pays the taxes, surely you'll agree
> That a body's earned the franchise, whether he or she.

That informative and festive gathering also provided an opportunity for Ruth Logan and Dr. Roberts to get to know each other better. Adella heartily supported their nascent relationship but feared that their dashing new band leader, Capt. Frank Drye, attracted her daughter far more.

She also thought long and hard before accepting W. E. B. Du Bois's request for her to submit an article for his monthly magazine that fall. He planned to dedicate an entire issue of *Crisis* to the debate over women voting. Logan grudgingly tolerated his wife's passion for an expanded suffrage, but her overt support of the NAACP frankly embarrassed him, because no one else at the institute belonged to the organization. The entire state of Alabama, in fact, had only one very small chapter, and that a hundred miles away. Given Mr. Washington's vitriol toward Dr. Du Bois, and vice versa, Adella assumed that her husband would oppose any contribution she might make to his journal, yet she ultimately resolved to move ahead. She didn't share with Logan what she'd be working on, but she requested and received his permission to use his office typewriter again and titled her new effort "Colored Women as Voters."

She began typing:

    Every day increasing numbers of colored women
    study civics but are convinced that their ef-
    forts would be more telling if they had the
    vote. The fashion of saying, "I do not care to
    meddle with politics," is rapidly disappearing
    among these women because politics meddles con-
    stantly with them.

    When colored juvenile offenders are ar-
    raigned, judges rarely offer them clemency be-
    cause they belong to an impotent class. Rather,
    they throw those youths in with adult criminals
    so they come out hardened, not chastened, by
    their imprisonment. Such authorities recognize
    few obligations to our voteless citizens, and
    having no vote or power, mothers who plead on
    behalf of their sons need not be heeded.

Eighteen years before, she'd become the National-American Woman Suffrage Association's first Lifetime Member of her race, but as she shaped her October 1912 treatise, she proudly acknowledged,

    More and more colored women are participating
    in civic and political activities, and women

```
who believe that they need the vote also see
that the vote needs them.
    We should re-read our Constitution and the
Declaration of Independence every year. This
much is certain: We Negroes believe in equal
justice regardless of race, color, creed,
class, or sex and eagerly await the day when
the United States truly shall have a government
of the people, for the people, and by the peo-
ple—including its colored women.
```

Adella received both praise and considerable acrimonious criticism for her essay, and its appearance in "the enemy's" journal distanced her from a number of Tuskegee colleagues who unequivocally supported Booker T. Washington in his power struggle with W. E. B. Du Bois.

Over the next months, demonstrations encouraging woman suffrage played out in many venues. In particular, an alliance of activist associations organized the largest such march in the nation's history, which would take place in Washington, D.C., on March 3, 1913, the eve of Woodrow Wilson's inaugural. It was meant to raise the public's and the incoming president's awareness of their cause and sway him to support it. But bitter racial conflicts soon emerged.

Adella regretted that she couldn't attend but wrote Ida B. Wells-Barnett in Chicago and several friends in the nation's capital urging them to do so. *It seems outrageous to me that there will be a float for the nation's Indians but none for us Negroes,* her letters protested.

The white organizers stipulated that any African Americans who wanted to take part should walk at the rear, but the *Woman's Journal,* which covered the event in depth, scarcely mentioned that prejudicial directive. As directed, members of several Negro sororities from Howard University reluctantly agreed to voluntarily separate themselves in order to participate, but Adella was pleased to learn that with a few of her white friends' collaboration, Mrs. Wells-Barnett desegregated the Illinois contingent by stepping into the main line of protesters.

Eight thousand supporters marched, and many times more observers watched men throw stones, trash, and insults, as members of the District's all-male, all-white police force turned their backs or even cheered the assaults on the participants. What a difference from the 1895 event in Atlanta when Adella had known that as a "southern lady," her "whiteness" would protect her.

Nor were such demonstrations limited to the United States. That June, she read about the English suffragette Emily Wilding Davison, who leapt from the grandstand to throw herself in front of the king's racehorse on Derby Day at Epsom Downs. A dozen behemoths trampled her on the track, crushing her skull. Was it an act of suicidal martyrdom or a tragic accident? Was Miss Davison calling attention to her cause when she tried to affix a suffrage rosette to the horse's bridle? Many countrymen vilified her as "a reckless anarchist who endangered the royal mount." (The British, Adella heard, cared more about animals' rights than women's rights.) Whatever her motivations might have been, Emily Davison died four days later as the result of her injuries.

Later that month, Dr. John Kellogg, accompanied by a dietician, a nurse, and a trainer from his sanitarium in Battle Creek, Michigan, visited Tuskegee. When Mr. Washington had gone to "the San" for a recent medical assessment, Dr. Kellogg promised that he'd come south to inform their physical education and kitchen staffs about their principal's exercise and nutritional needs. While there, he exhorted everyone at the school to modify what he denigrated as their "'possum and pork" preferences and to adopt a diet featuring more whole grains, fresh fruits, and vegetables.

Dr. Kellogg's visit coincided with the dedication of the school's first real hospital, named John Andrew, for Massachusetts's former abolitionist governor who'd been its major donor's grandfather. For years they'd made do with a small infirmary, but the well-equipped new facility was vital not only to the growing institute itself but also to many black people in and around Macon County, Alabama, since the nearby "white" hospital often refused to treat them at all.

John Kellogg also urged Booker T. Washington to avail himself of a vacation dedicated to rest and relaxation, so early in September, he and his brother, Dr. Kenney, Logan, and several others of the school's "leading men" headed south to Mobile Bay for a two-week fishing retreat.

By then, Adella believed that her support of the NAACP bespoke her commitment to an assertive approach toward the nation's racial inequities, but even in the face of ongoing reversals, her husband insisted that the Wizard's continued adherence to accommodation ultimately would generate social, political, and economic progress. Dr. Du Bois, on the other hand, vexed her for different reasons. Yes, he was brilliant and progressive, albeit arrogant and duplicitous. Every month she hardly could wait to plunge into a new issue of *Crisis,* to see what would thrill, challenge, or infuriate her, but the grotesque fairy tale that he published in October 1913 took her by surprise.

When she and W. E. B. Du Bois first met sixteen years before, he'd asked how she felt about living and teaching at Tuskegee, and she'd quoted Frederick Douglass, who'd described the institute as "some sort of 'hither isles.'" "If these be the 'hither isles,'" the Doctor had suavely maintained on that prior occasion, "you must be the princess of that remote and stygian realm." Now, to her dismay, he titled his latest opus "The Princess of the Hither Isles."

His protagonist was a "pale gold Princess" who lived in a fictive domain called the "green and slimy Hither Isles," where she was tyrannized by "the white and tawny King of Yonder Kingdom." To a discerning reader such as Adella, that depiction clearly suggested a person of mixed race. "Niggers and dagoes!" the tyrant excoriated his subjects, "curling his long mustache" and puffing on a cigar. Mr. Washington was clean shaven, but the Doctor's literary portrait, she thought, evoked Logan's bountiful whiskers and both men's enjoyment of "a good smoke," not to mention the symbolic cigars that occupied Sigmund Freud's erotic dream cabinet.

"Shuffling through the slime, a beggar man, bald, black and bent, entered the Kingdom," Dr. Du Bois's legend alliteratively plunged on. The compassionate Princess saw in his face "the suffering of endless years," but the King snarled, "I hate beggars, and he's a nigger too." Adella loathed his repetition, even, she thought, his possible sanction of that vile and disparaging word.

The King continued wooing the Princess and promised her riches galore if she became his queen, yet yearning to stay with the vagrant, she refused. Anguished by her conflicts, she "stood in mad amaze, and snatched her own red heart" from her chest. "From the soul of the Princess welled a cry of dark despair. Poised on the crumbling edge of that great nothingness she hung, hungering with her eyes and straining her fainting ears against the awful splendor of the sky." "Don't be a fool!" the King thundered, but the deranged woman heard other, more compelling voices, and "feeling the throbbing warmth of heaven's sun . . . the Princess leapt."

W. E. B. Du Bois never disclosed his story's derivation or the inspirations for his dramatis personae, but recognizing his vitriol toward Mr. Washington, Adella assumed that his gold-hungry King was a fictionalized portrait of the Wizard of Tuskegee or even of her husband as the institute's treasurer. That, combined with his prior designation of her as "the Princess," led her to conclude what had motivated him. He'd appropriated the information she'd shared about Albany, Georgia, and used it without thanks or attribution in *The Souls of Black Folk*. She hadn't challenged the provocateur at that prior juncture, but now she'd no longer hold back.

> *Burghardt,* [in this instance she wouldn't address him as *Dear Doctor*]
>
> *You know that pursuant to your urging and in the face of profound approbation from my friends and colleagues here at our school, I joined, and continue my financial, moral, and vocal support of the NAACP. I read* The Crisis *faithfully and, at your request, contributed my essay "Colored Women as Voters," which you published last year—I've heard to wide acclaim.*
>
> *Thus, I consider it a personal affront that in your most recent issue you misappropriated the phrase I shared, "the Hither Isles" (as I designated Tuskegee in a* private *conversation), and call your suicidal heroine "the Princess," as you referred to me. Even if no one else knows that history, I do, and I find this a disrespectful breach of our long friendship. But enough of that.*

My pique notwithstanding, I enclose a photo of four of my children, which you might like to include in your next Children's Issue. This group portrait, taken a decade ago, is the work of Frances Benjamin Johnston, acclaimed as "the world's greatest female photographer." If you decide to use it, I ask only that you identify neither the subjects nor the photographer by name.

Adella signed, sealed, and stamped her letter, went to the post office, and mailed it off.

She also, however, had reason to think again about Cherie Rideaux, because each New Year's Eve since the girl had been expelled from the institute for her supposed "untruthfulness and debauchery," she'd written Adella on the anniversary of the occasion when they'd first met.

In 1910, Cherie told her mentor, *I had to retain a lawyer, because I no longer could endure the demands that my guardian made—much like Rev. Penney's, you might have guessed.* She'd heeded Adella's counsel to "know the law and use the law" and brought suit against him. Her cause prevailed, and a civil court in New Orleans had declared her an emancipated minor.

The following year she shared other news: *For some time, a well-situated gentleman here has been courting me, and on February 12, he and I will wed. Might you and Polly join us to celebrate our marriage?*

She couldn't accept Cherie's invitation but sent her a silver-backed hand mirror as a wedding gift. The young woman warmly thanked Adella, but two years later, she revealed that although she and her husband both wanted children, so far, she'd failed to conceive.

Adella also mentioned an upcoming milestone in her own life, and Cherie responded with a promise: *a surprise for you and your daughters.*

It was a special occasion indeed, because several days after Christmas of 1913, Adella and Warren Logan would celebrate the twenty-fifth anniversary of their marriage. Ruth and Junior were gainfully employed, so as a gift from themselves and their younger siblings, they ordered and presented her with a small (for travel, Ruth explained) sterling-silver coffee set: a two-cup pot, sugar bowl, and cream pitcher, with *1888–1913* etched on the side of each piece.

Margaret Murray Washington, however, astonished Adella when she announced that she wanted to hold a reception at The Oaks honoring her and Logan—although she made it clear that she'd done so pursuant to her husband's insistence. The Logan children, the whole Washington clan, and much of the institute's senior faculty would be included, while Will Hunt and the Varners from Gray Columns were among the other local guests. Logan's half siblings and Adella's three sisters joined them too, and Henry Hunt and his wife, Florence, arrived from Fort Valley, Georgia. Their youngest brother, Tommy, however, regretted that he couldn't make it from California. He wrote, *Sis, I appreciate the invitation, but it's an expense I can't afford. I must tell you, I've recently become engaged to a Canadian girl and have told her nothing about our "invisible" ancestry.* Patty Winston attended too, and the photographer Arthur Bedou and the NACW's Sylvanie Williams traveled north together from New Orleans. The institute's board chairman, Seth Low, accepted the Washingtons' invitation as well, as did the Julius Rosenwalds.

The seamstress who'd created Adella's wedding dress still had her shop, so she stitched up an elegant ivory satin gown and bolero jacket for her that featured embroidered paillettes and a deep drape across an asymmetrical, ankle-length skirt, as well as Ruth's long dress and My 'Del's and Polly's short, organdy ones. Little Arthur wore a dark velvet suit with a bow tie, lace collar, and cuffs. Logan and Junior both donned handsome formal cutaways and Paul a stylish tuxedo. Yes, the family's outfits were entirely— symbolically, perhaps—black and white.

Before the guests arrived, Arthur Bedou aligned two of Adella's Oriental rugs from Pomegranate Hall (her husband had given Mrs. Washington the third as a housewarming gift) under their feet and photographed the whole family on their multihued Carpenter Gothic porch.

That gala affair at The Oaks included music, dancing, dining, and multiple toasts with raised glasses of fruit punch—many of which had been "spiked" in the Washingtons' kitchen. George Washington Carver emotionally saluted Adella as "brilliant and beautiful," while Booker T. Washington again lauded Warren Logan as "the real builder and guardian of Tuskegee."

In the rear, from left to right, Warren Hunt (Junior), Adella, Warren, Ruth, and Paul Logan. In front, from left to right, Louise (Polly), Arthur, and Myra Adele (My 'Del) Logan. Taken on the front porch of the Logans' home, Tuskegee, Alabama, on the occasion of Warren and Adella's twenty-fifth wedding anniversary, December 1913. (Collection of the author; original photograph by Arthur Bedou; reproduction photograph by Mark Gulezian.)

Adella appreciated Cherie Rideaux's gift and wrote to express her thanks.

> *My beaded bandeau, Ruth's egret tiara and the little girls'*
> *hair bows are beautiful. Just before the reception, the N.O.*
> *photographer Arthur Bedou took photographs of our family. I*
> *gave him your name and address and directed him to deliver a*
> *copy to you when he returns and develops his images. My sincere*
> *regards, with a hug from Polly for her "big sister" Cherie.*

But the institute had also temporarily lost its most prominent trustee: Theodore Roosevelt. First, there was his run for another presidential term on the ridiculous Bull Moose Party ticket. That campaign was an abject failure and split the traditional Republican vote (Logan admitted that, out of personal and institutional loyalty, he'd "gone moose"), which had resulted in the erudite but wily and frankly racist, southern-raised Democrat Woodrow Wilson's victory. The ex-president attempted to restore his swashbuckling but damaged self-esteem following that political debacle by undertaking a bold adventure. He traveled to South America with a scientific expedition to explore the Rio da Dúvida: the River of Doubt, a major tributary of the Amazon. His journey began in December 1913, so he couldn't attend either that winter's gathering of the trustees or the Logans' concurrent anniversary celebration.

When former president Roosevelt returned to the institute for the next round of meetings, he was still suffering from the debilitating aftereffects of malaria and a painfully septic leg wound. At the executive session, he nonetheless distributed to each of his fellow trustees, copies of *Through the Brazilian Wilderness,* the newly published account of his epic expedition.

"The mightiest river in the world is the Amazon," he held forth. "It flows from the Andes to the Atlantic, but no geographer heretofore has mapped out its primary tributary, the Rio da Dúvida, which itself is longer than the Rhine." Theodore Roosevelt, one of his sons, and their intrepid team left automobiles, telegraph lines, and even oxcarts behind, paddled dugout canoes, and slept in hammocks, as raging currents swept away two of their *camaratas* and several pack mules. They admired parrots, toucans, and orchids, ate fresh-picked bananas and papayas, shot caimans, fended off scorpions, and, T.R. added, encountered "wasps the size of sparrows and razor-tusked, white-lipped peccaries that looked like survivors of the Oligocene Age."

At a reception at The Oaks that followed the trustees' formal sessions, the former president spied Adella and hastened over to chat. The palindrome that she'd recently heard, "A man, a plan, a canal, Panama," distracted her, but she listened attentively as he rehashed his swashbuckling adventures. Margaret Washington peevishly observed their tête-à-tête for a few minutes, then intervened. But glancing back over his shoulder as the school's "first lady" swept him away, the ex-president grinned and said, "Perhaps one day we'll paddle together along the Rio da Dúvida, Mrs. Logan. Did I tell you that the Brazilians are renaming it the Rio Teodoro?"

She had to smile. Though perhaps not quite his old self, the man was incorrigible!

Adella again thought about how much he and Logan resembled each other. They'd even been born the same month of the same year. ("Twins separated at birth?" she mused.) Logan was a scant inch taller, with curlier hair almost the same shade as Mr. Roosevelt's. His eyes were gray, whereas the former president's were blue. Despite his rigorous outdoor life, he was extremely pale skinned, while Logan's complexion was creamy; but the two men's similar wire-rimmed glasses and impressive mustaches reinforced the underlying physical resemblance.

Adella had no reason to suspect that the esteemed Roosevelt clan had been "sullied" by any suspicious "tar brush," although some of the United States' renowned "white" families surely were. She pondered the legacies of Thomas Jefferson's purported Hemings progeny, Justice John Marshall Harlan's "colored" sibling, the Caribbean-born Alexander Hamilton's probable mixed ancestry, her own kin's rumored links to his namesake, the Confederacy's vice president Alexander Hamilton Stephens, and Logan's reported paternal connection to Senator Henry Clay. But the possibility of any quantifiable, physical realities of race confounded her. What bound her to her people, she knew, was less genetic than it was deeply grounded in familial bonds of affection and their shared culture and history, while the country's prejudicial laws, prohibitions, and practices further entrenched her in the bosom of the black community.

But such hypothetical musings, Adella knew, accomplished little. And since Margaret Washington had removed her from the leadership of the NACW's suffrage department and put her "out to pasture," charged with overseeing its committee on rural conditions, she vowed to become that cause's most effective possible spokeswoman. And Mrs. Washington's assertion that her affiliation with George Washington Carver warranted the changed assignment did have a solid foundation. They'd collaborated for a decade on behalf of Alabama's struggling country people by addressing critical aspects of their work lives, diet, health, and overall well-being. Now Adella's friend would provide her with a more formal outlet for her advocacy.

Early in 1914 'Fess Carver started compiling and editing a journal he called *The Negro Farmer*. Even more than he had at the Logans' anniversary celebration, he praised Adella as "a beautiful mother and treasured friend, who tirelessly helps the southern farmer and his family."

Her first article, "Food and Cooking," warned that although children, pregnant women, and manual laborers, in particular, needed ample nourishment, "overeating can be as detrimental to good health as undereating." She urged rural women to substitute fresh produce for fried foods, limit their consumption of sweets, and make economical use of leftovers. "What is more healthful and tastes more delicious," she asked, "than a roasted chicken, followed the next day by croquettes or hash, then a nourishing soup stock made from the carcass?" Adella got little satisfaction from other domestic tasks but saw feeding one's family as "an art, a science, and essential yet satisfying work. It is the branch of housework that brings one the most pleasure, and the poor can set a beautiful table and eat as well as the rich. Mix brains with your cooking, ladies, and your grateful husband will say, 'Thank the Lord, and bless the food and the cook.'"

Her ensuing contributions, however, ventured farther afield. In "Better Homes for Better Farmers," she wrote, "Concerns about privacy tell us that even the simplest abodes should have separate rooms for boys and girls to sleep in and for the purposes of 'courtship.' Despite a family's limited circumstances, even humble dwellings need potable water, and poor children, as much as any others, should have access to annual medical examinations and health care."

She urged rural black women to petition their local boards of health, state representatives, even United States congressmen and senators for essential constituent services. Such recommendations, however, were considered troublemaking, and she worried that she might only be exhorting the South's neediest, most vulnerable, and often illiterate citizens—if they honestly could claim citizenship status at all—to tilt blindly at windmills. But she remained determined and tried to ignore her colleagues' fears, opprobrium, and disapprovingly raised eyebrows.

And her family's lives plodded along. When Alfreda Armstrong Kenney became pregnant, Ruth took over the girls' physical education program. Logan continued working too hard, their son Paul headed back to Atlanta University's preparatory program, and the younger children attended Tuskegee's primary school. After graduating from Howard University, Junior had moved to New York City, where, following in his father's footsteps, he took an accountant's job and, in his mother's, he enrolled at New York University to start work on a graduate degree. His health still concerned Adella, but she didn't expect the letter that arrived just after Christmas.

Junior felt exhausted. He'd lost weight and had a persistent cough, so he'd made an appointment with Dr. Roberts to undergo a new round of tests. The results confirmed that the treacherous tuberculosis, which his physician called "the White Plague," had returned. E. P. Roberts persuaded Junior that returning to Tuskegee to recuperate in the Logans' home with access to John Andrew Hospital's facilities was where and how he'd get the care he needed.

Her son's decline deeply distressed Adella, then she received another letter from Cherie:

> *My dear Mrs. Logan,*   *New Orleans, December 31, 1914*
>
> *It took almost a year for M. Bedou to deliver the photo-graph from your 25th wedding anniversary celebration, but well worth the wait. I cherish it, and you all look beautiful.*

Little good news from me. Last summer my physician informed me that the old problems with my womb prevent me from ever bearing children. When I told my husband, he said that if I couldn't give him an heir, I was of no more use to him. The diocese here (our civil courts serve women somewhat better) granted him a declaration of nullity on the (false!) grounds that I had concealed my infertility, and affirmed his demand that I no longer use his name.

But I opened my own chapellerie and already have loyal customers, so I will never go hungry. If you come, no, when you come to my city, I will make you a beautiful hat.

I hope that you and your children all are well. Je vous aime.

Your "autre fille," Cherie

No, all of Adella's six children were not well, but thankfully, most of them were.

Firestorm

ADELLA WOULD HAVE ENJOYED A GETAWAY, but visiting New Orleans wasn't in the cards, because right from the start, daunting obstacles confronted her that winter when she turned fifty-two.

She did, however, sit several times for a formal portrait by the visiting African American painter William Edouard Scott, who was "in residence" at the institute that spring, as did George Washington Carver, Booker T. Washington, and a few others of the school's officials.

She could go no place for very long, because Junior had returned home from New York after his tuberculosis recurred. Many physicians, and laypersons too, referred to it as "the Negro disease," but ironically, Dr. Roberts called it "the White Plague." Junior spent his days dozing on the family's porch in a combined state of languor, ennui, and underlying terror. Adella knew she shouldn't blame her husband, though his mother's death from the same insidious malady seemed the likeliest source of her son's predilection toward that ultimately fatal affliction. Most people called it "consumption." Yes, she had to watch her eldest child slowly being consumed.

And despite her erratic relationship with W. E. B. Du Bois and his deepening friendship with her brother Henry, he didn't ask her to contribute an essay on woman suffrage for his upcoming second issue of *Crisis* dedicated to that subject. His apparent rejection grieved her, especially since he (and she too) had received considerable attention for her previous piece.

In his fable "The Princess of the Hither Isles," Dr. Du Bois misappropriated the words Adella had shared with him, and she'd castigated him for that. She'd also sent him the photo taken by Frances Benjamin Johnston

Adella Logan, oil portrait by William Edouard Scott. Started 1915; completed posthumously, 1918. (Collection of the author; reproduction photograph by Mark Gulezian.)

that he'd featured in his recent Children's Issue, but she'd heard nothing from him since, although as per her explicit instructions, no caption next to the image identified either the photographer or the subjects (Warren Junior, Ruth, Paul, and Walter Logan) by name and, also as she'd insisted, he did return the original to her.

Walter had died, but the others were pleased to see their younger faces in the magazine. Logan, however, berated Adella for sending the photograph to Dr. Du Bois, and Mrs. Washington (who scoured the journal to monitor his endeavors) scolded, "I was shocked to see your children in *The Crisis* and must remind myself to separate your acts from your husband's."

Then an unforeseen rift with her sister Sarah heightened Adella's malaise. George Washington Carver often came over to collaborate on a proposed recipe book intended to inform Alabama's ill-nourished rural people about nutrition. They'd toil for hours, peeling, chopping, sautéing, stewing, and baking, and they squabbled or laughed about the soufflé that emerged from Adella's oven a sodden sponge and the leaden rye, barley, and winter-squash muffins that even 'Fess's swine refused to eat. Just after he'd left the Logans' home late one afternoon that spring of 1915, Sarah snapped, "Our distinguished scientist clearly prefers your company to mine."

Adella was stunned and said, "Not really, Sis, but you know he and I have collaborated for years on these nutritional efforts. And he's the children's 'Uncle 'Fess,' almost our brother."

"That's not it at all," Sarah's voice level and agitation escalated. "George thinks you're lovelier and smarter than I or, frankly, any other woman. He speaks adoringly of you, hangs on your every word, and even named his exquisite hybrid *Amaryllis Adele Hippeastrum* for you! No indeed, he spurned me because he's always been in love with my own captivating sister."

Silence wasn't in Adella's nature, and she wanted Sarah to understand and not cast blame.

"He and I are dear friends, but when you revealed your amorous feelings, he was at a loss because he couldn't similarly respond. Yes, he fled from you, but even more, I think, he feared that people at our school would condemn his [she paused to select the right word] 'preferences.'"

"This is difficult to say, but I've become increasingly certain that those who stir George's blood, who make his heart pound and yearn for romance and intimacy, aren't women but men. You should read what Sigmund Freud says about what he calls 'inversions.' Plato, Leonardo da Vinci, and Walt Whitman, all men of genius, were like that too," Adella continued. "*I* didn't divert George's passions. He withdrew because he couldn't bear to deceive you. That's who he is, no matter what you, I, or anyone else might think or want to do about such predilections."

Sarah gasped, then spat out, "Dr. Freud's a charlatan!" Certainly, many people agreed. "You're maligning George and insulting me. I won't listen to more of your hateful lies."

She stormed off and stayed with a friend for several days. When Sarah returned, she reaffirmed her devotion to her nieces, nephews, and Logan, but turned an icy shoulder on Adella.

And what else could Adella say about Professor Carver? When they'd first met, she'd considered him a nearly virtual, though darker, reincarnation of her grandmother Susan. She also couldn't forget his almost maternal protection of her when white gunmen had attacked their interracial travel party during the terrifying misadventure with Frances Benjamin Johnston.

Adella often faced criticism for her own "unwomanly" opinions and behavior yet knew that she remained attractive to men. Over the years, others, including Dr. Du Bois, Rev. Edgar Penney, perhaps Frederick Douglass, Booker T. Washington, and even President Roosevelt had flirted with her or eyed her lustfully. But never her dear friend George Washington Carver, with his high-pitched voice, interests and skills in the "womanly arts," and his intrinsic fastidiousness.

He didn't seem drawn to other women either, yet she thought she'd observed his eyes light up and his posture change when he encountered an especially charming fellow. Hadn't she also seen him cringe, fearing that others might notice those prohibited attractions? She recalled Sigmund Freud's statement, "Almost no one reveals his full erotic life even to a trusted friend."

Who else had Adella known with similar inclinations? She thought of Frances ("Frank") Benjamin Johnston and their chance intimacy that horrendous night in Ramer. Miss Johnston often donned men's clothing and shared her domestic quarters with a female companion—an arrangement sometimes joked about, tolerated, or alternately condemned as a "Boston marriage." And what of Susan B. Anthony, whose deep passion for Elizabeth Cady Stanton their detractors lampooned and scorned as a "frustrated romance"? Critics disdained such women, labeled them lesbians or Sapphists, and disparaged their (even Adella's) "masculine mind-set."

But the few people who spoke at all about such things usually considered men who physically or romantically desired others of their own sex more perverse and even dangerous than similarly oriented women and lambasted them as "queers," "buggers," "faggots," and worse.

As for George himself, some of Sarah's colleagues at the Children's House gossiped about "that pervert who tries to corrupt our boys." But Adella believed that his accusers mostly were jealous, because he was the school's most acclaimed, revered, and also best-paid teacher—though he cared little about money and often failed even to cash or deposit his paychecks.

What might it suggest if the sadist who'd kidnapped the enslaved infant during the Civil War had "surgically neutered" him? Could it have warped a sensitive child's development if a "doting grandfather" had cosseted and stroked him too often, too intimately and for too long? Or were George's "different" penchants inborn and immutable? Adella simply didn't know.

Before the spat with Sarah, she'd never articulated her intuitions about 'Fess Carver with anyone and had spoken to few about Dr. Freud, but she knew that many people mistrusted and disparaged "that wily Austrian Jew." Her friend Patty Winston, Mr. Washington, and several of his trustees or their wives (Gussie Rosenwald among them) had been treated at Battle Creek's renowned sanitarium, and "the San's" kingpin, Dr. John Kellogg, who'd recently visited the institute, was one of many physicians who excoriated or dismissed the excessive eroticism that they protested permeated all Freudian theories, analyses, and therapeutic practices.

Adella, however, could deal privately with her speculations about Professor Carver's "aberrations," her son's illness, and the schisms with Dr. Du Bois and her sister. The Alabama legislature's refusal to allow any woman suffrage issue even to be placed on the ballot that year, on the other hand, was a public matter. Not that she'd ever felt optimistic that the all-male, almost exclusively white electorate would approve such a measure had it come before them. She wasn't even certain what her husband would have done, but she believed that those men at least should have been allowed to debate it fully and then vote. But the state's paternalistic (even misogynistic) legislators defeated the initiative early on and quashed that possibility.

One Alabama newspaper characterized woman suffrage as "the most dangerous blow aimed at white supremacy and the peace and happiness of the people of Alabama since the Civil War."

She took several day trips to Montgomery that spring to monitor the suffrage debates and try to collar some representatives in the capitol's hallways, hoping to persuade them of her cause's justice, import, and urgency. On each occasion, however, Adella's efforts were thwarted when officials whom she approached first asked politely, "and where do you live, ma'am?" When she said "Tuskegee," they eyed her suspiciously, then suddenly had to hasten off "to deal with some pressing business." They'd been forewarned to be on the lookout for "Booker T.'s crazy, white-looking suffragette." Alabama's handful of pro-suffrage white women (who'd barred her from joining their very small, all-white Alabama Equal Suffrage Association) knew her too and either turned their backs or threatened to have security guards remove her from the Jim Crow galleries.

By midsummer she felt increasingly distraught. Sometimes she'd stay awake all night, writing, reading, cooking, or just fretting, then at dawn, collapse in total exhaustion. She treated family and friends harshly, felt anxious, and suffered from bone-rattling panics. Dr. Kenney performed a host of tests at John Andrew Hospital but found no underlying physical causes.

Early in September, however, the campus was quiet since the students hadn't yet arrived. Much of the faculty was away too, especially Booker T. Washington, Logan, Dr. Kenney, and several others who'd gone south for their annual retreat on the Gulf Coast at a spot called Coden-on-the-Bay. Just over half a century ago, the country's last, felonious slave ship, the *Clotilda,* had smuggled a boatload of captive Dahomeyans to that remote debarkation site, whence they'd been auctioned off to toil in the cane, rice, or cotton fields. Even now, when the tide ebbed, observers could catch glimpses of the spectral schooner's charred, half-sunken skeleton bobbing in the shallows. For the past three years, the visiting gentlemen from Tuskegee had listened to the old tales shared by its lone survivor, who still lived in the nearby enclave called Africatown. The day after Logan reached that legendary destination, he dutifully wrote Adella:

Dear Mother,   Coden, Alabama. September 1915

*Last night a driver brought us from the station to our
fishing camp, and this morning I looked out on the familiar,
idyllic seascape. Tomorrow we'll re-visit Africatown, then with
next week's full moon, we'll pull out our binoculars and try to
spot the Clotilda's ghostly remains.*

*We'll fish or hunt every day, take long waterside hikes,
ride horses, eat well, and sleep soundly, and since John Kenney
is with us, we'll have competent medical care, if needed. That's
especially important for Booker T., whose well-being concerns
us all.*

*I'm glad I came despite your "problems," because I believe
my presence is critical to our leader's contentment. I'm hopeful
he'll come home feeling fit again, though he's been advised to
return to Battle Creek for a thorough re-appraisal by Dr.
Kellogg. Should you need help in our absence, John Kenney says
that his new head nurse, Nella Larsen, is the best he's ever had.*

But for now, please be my good girl while I'm away.

So "*Mother*" tried to suppress her "*problems*" and be Logan's "*good
girl,*" but she seethed that, once again, he'd put "*Booker T.'s well-being*"
ahead of hers and their family's.

Junior needed her attention, however, and Arthur's hair had to be cut
before he started first grade in two weeks. Adella found the institute's barber lethargic, so she devised a different plan. She dressed and groomed
herself and her youngest, lest some white person dare to suggest that they
looked slovenly, then she went to the barn and hitched a horse to her grandmother's vintage phaeton, which the school's carriage makers had repaired
and refitted for her several times. Their Dalmatian pup Vulcan leapt in beside her and Arthur, and they set off on an overcast afternoon.

One of the bargains that Booker T. Washington had struck with Macon
County's officials was that their citizens always were welcome at the institute for any events that featured the renowned and talented visiting per-

formers (black and white), lecturers, and politicians who often enhanced their otherwise drably insular lives. On such occasions, the locals were invited to sit, dine, or even stay overnight in the campus's comfortable "whites only" guest facilities. In return, the county's civic authorities grudgingly allowed a few of the school's male faculty to vote.

In addition, people from the institute supposedly wouldn't be endangered if they ventured into town, but if they did so, they were directed to travel only via the designated back road and, once there, to comply with all state and local Jim Crow laws, customs, and demands. But instead of veering off onto that sanctioned byway, Adella continued along the prohibited primary traffic artery. Montgomery Road, the route for which she opted, was macadamized and more direct.

Passing Gray Columns, the Varner mansion, then continuing into Tuskegee's commercial district, she tied up the dog and tethered her horse, then she and Arthur crossed the courthouse square. A rifle-bearing granite Confederate soldier that stood sentinel atop a memorial pedestal erected and sponsored by the United Daughters of the Confederacy dominated the town's central plaza. They entered the nearby, glass-fronted barber shop, sat down, and waited to be served.

A tobacco-chewing "cracker" eyed them suspiciously for several minutes, then slammed his talc, towel, strop, and razor onto a shelf and demanded, "Ain' chew fum out at duh school?"

What should she say when she'd been asked so directly? It was one thing, as her brother Tommy declared, "if they don't ask, I don't tell," but another to flat out lie. She couldn't do it.

"Yes, we're from the institute, and I want to get my son's hair cut. He's sitting there, as good as gold," she pointed to her neatly dressed, blond-haired, green-eyed "King Arthur," who was quietly reading a book on the grimy couch.

"We don' do no pickaninnies' nappy hair," the proprietor barked.

Adella caught her breath. Oh, Lord no! He'd called her beautiful child a pickaninny.

"Why not? My son's hair is less nappy than yours, and except that it's cleaner, it's no different than that of your other customers," she snapped back.

"It's my shop an' it's duh law, dat's wye, an' don' git sassy wid me," the barber snarled. "Yew an' yuh boy bettuh git," he jerked his thumb, "cuz Ah don' wan' no trouble, aunty."

Aunty? White southerners often insulted older women of color by designating them as such instead of respecting them with surnames. Was she angrier because the lout denied her patronage by discriminating against her boy and all others of the race or because he considered her old? Not at all! She was in her early fifties, still trim, with almost no gray hair, although the other day a stranger had asked her twenty-three-year-old daughter Ruth if Arthur were her son.

"Who are you calling 'aunty'?" her tone sharpened. "Please show some respect, sir. I'm '*Mrs.* Warren Logan,' wife of the institute's vice principal and treasurer."

"Ah don' give a rat's ass who yew or yuh cullud fella is," the ghoul hissed, "an' lak ah say, *aunty,* yew betta git, 'cuz Ah don' wanna call duh *po*-lice. But Ah'll do it ef Ah has tuh."

There was nothing to gain and possibly serious peril for them in further resistance, so she grabbed her bewildered son by the collar and turned on her heel. As they left, the barber slammed and bolted the door behind them, though Adella heard coarse laughter from within.

While they'd been inside, the sky had turned gunmetal gray, then the leaden clouds broke. A silvery devil's pitchfork of lightning illuminated the street and silhouetted Macon County's looming Confederate war memorial statue—which disconcertingly reminded Adella of her father. Exactly three seconds later, thunderbolts crashed around them like a wagonload of falling bricks. Her armpits moistened, goose bumps rose, her gums and tongue tingled, and she tasted metal.

Because Arthur was too small to leap over the gutter that quickly became a two-yard-wide maelstrom, Adella ordered her son to remove his footwear, but as he blissfully splashed through the swirling water, she shouted, "Get in here right now!" His glee became mixed with terror as he watched his shoes, like toy boats, bob away downstream. With herculean strength, Adella reached down from the buggy, seized his elbow, and whirled him upward in a precipitous arc.

As Arthur strove to gain a secure handhold, his fingers caught in his mother's long hair and demolished her carefully groomed upsweep. Clutching and bruising the boy's upper arm with one hand and gathering the reins in the other, Adella whipped her horse into a gallop. She was certain that the unpaved byway that the institute's residents were supposed to follow had become a quagmire. She thus returned along the same prohibited route by which they'd come.

Their venture had started out in near sunshine only an hour before, so Adella had brought along no rainwear. As the downpour intensified, she sought shelter nearby at Gray Columns. She rang the bell, did so several times more, and Cora Varner's uniformed housemaid finally responded. The young woman knew Mrs. Logan from previous visits but was unwelcoming that afternoon, gaped at Adella's disheveled coif, cut her eyes, and mumbled, "My mistress ain't here."

Adella doubted that was true and expected that both Mrs. Varner and her servant had seen her arrive uninvited. "Go to the back door!" "Sit in the back seats!" "Use the back road!" and similar insults rattled in her head. She spat out an undeserved epithet at the girl, again climbed into the phaeton next to her trembling son and their dappled, black-and-white dog, and drove on.

Dr. and Mrs. Kenney's home also was nearer than her own, so several minutes later, Adella pulled up there and pounded on the door. Alfreda Armstrong Kenney immediately answered.

"I found this pretty child wandering around in the roadway all by himself. As you can see, he's barefoot and soaking wet, as am I. Won't you help us, please?" Adella implored.

The "soaking wet, pretty child" started to cry. He didn't know what to make of the wild-haired, wild-eyed woman who'd metamorphosed from his beloved protector into a stranger.

Alfreda showed them in, hugged and dried Arthur, settled him at her kitchen table with milk and a ginger snap, brewed tea for Adella, and suggested that she use the bathroom facilities to towel off and repair the damage to her coiffure. She couldn't manage even those simple tasks, however, so she sat immobilized where she was, looking, she feared, like a crazed Medusa.

Alfreda knew Ruth would return as soon as her pre-school-opening workday finished, so when the downpour eased, she drove Arthur and Adella home. Ruth greeted them at the door.

"Your mother seems confused, and I have no idea what happened to your brother's shoes," Alfreda Kenney whispered. Ruth nodded, thanked her friend, then bade her good-bye.

Ruth prepared supper and began getting Polly and My 'Del settled in for the evening. Adella stroked and kissed Arthur, but he remained mystified about their misadventure, especially his mother's baffling harshness. Then "Aunt Sarah" read her nephew a story and put him to bed.

Adella went to her room, reread Logan's letter, and realized that might partially explain why she'd behaved as she had that afternoon. He'd been selfish and hurt others, especially her. "Mother" was responsible for correcting the children's behavior, like taking away a toy or privileges if they talked back or neglected their lessons. Similarly, she occasionally needed to correct her husband too. So she stripped to the bone, swiftly redressed, and rebraided her hair—thinking again that such long, unwieldy tresses might be more trouble than they were worth.

And she had a mission. She rummaged in her chifforobe, pulled out several volumes of her diaries, and stuffed them into a satchel. Years before, when she was editing and transcribing her thesis, she'd liked to peruse and annotate them during her evening work breaks when she was typing in her husband's office. Perhaps she'd revive that ritual. Then she removed Logan's cluster of brass keys from their home desk's top drawer—exactly where he always kept them.

She left by the rear door, let Vulcan out of his kennel, and together they crossed the street to the main campus. Riffling through the keys, she identified the one she sought, opened the administration building's outer portal, turned right, and walked down the silent central corridor. Logan's workplace was still next to what had been her library niche but now was his secretary's domain. She located another familiar key, unlocked the inner door, and entered the empty room.

Even in the near dark Adella saw that everything was in shipshape order. Hoping not to attract the attention of the watchman who oversaw all of the campus's fifty buildings, she turned on no electric lights but retrieved from a corner shelf and lit Logan's emergency kerosene lamp with one of his sulphur friction matches. After a few seconds, a soft glow suffused the office.

In her husband's top desk drawer, she found a colorfully decorated cardboard box with "Hecho a mano en Puerto Rico" printed on it. It held the cigars given to Logan by some of their now very content and appreciative (all brown-skinned) students from that island. Raising the lid, she took out a Colorado Maduro, clipped its end, licked the wrapper, then lit and—choking a bit—began puffing on the fragrant tube. She'd never smoked one before but had watched her husband do so after dinners at The Oaks when, as Margaret Washington dictated, the gentlemen "can enjoy their cigars and serious political conversation while we ladies retire to powder our noses."

Warren Logan's candlestick-style telephone, address book and message pad, a neat row of fountain pens, the crystal and silver inkwell set that she'd given him for his fiftieth birthday, and a green, leather-cornered blotter occupied his rolltop desk's writing surface, and the vertical compartments at its back contained dozens of alphabetized, precisely aligned manila folders.

What might be expendable? Adella pulled out a file marked "Coden 1915," opened it, and found several notes that Logan and Mr. Washington had exchanged over the previous weeks.

```
Mr. Logan:
I hope Mrs. Logan is feeling better. Will her
health allow you to come to Coden with us this
September? BTW


Mr. Washington:
Dr. Kenney and I re-evaluate her condition
every day. I greatly appreciate your concern
and patience. WL
```

A week later, the principal asked his second-in-command for an updated report, then from only six days ago, a carbon copy of another read,

```
Mr. Washington:
I am pleased to confirm that Mrs. Logan's im-
proving health will indeed allow me to join you
and the other gentlemen at Coden. WL
```

Adella tossed that entire file into her husband's previously empty trash basket.

A nearby folder was marked "Angela Kurtz (Johnson)." It contained half a dozen items in an exchange that had started the previous June and pertained to the institute's possible employment of a woman of that name as a kindergarten teacher. As soon as Mr. Washington received her personal letter of inquiry, he'd forwarded it to the Children's House director, who informed him that she'd already reviewed applications from several other candidates whom she'd much prefer to hire. They all had far more impressive credentials than "Mrs. Johnson."

Angela Kurtz, a member of Howard University's class of 1911, and B. T. Washington first had met there, since, as one of its trustees, he often visited that school. Junior's stretch at Howard had overlapped with Miss Kurtz's, and he'd told his mother that she was "quite fetching but not very sharp." After graduating, she'd married the otherwise unidentified Mr. Johnson and had a son, but she soon divorced and reassumed her "maiden" name for both herself and (much more surprisingly) for her son. Tuskegee Institute, however, never employed divorcées, because their example, it was feared, might cast a shadow over the whole institute's morality. That was a harsh judgment, but since they clearly had better-qualified applicants, why hire this woman?

Yet Booker T. Washington remained adamant. A follow-up note to "WL" read,

```
Please resolve this problem for me. BTW
```

As usual, Logan resolved BTW's "problem." Tuskegee Institute hired Angela Kurtz, and she and her son recently arrived there. Adella decided that the "Kurtz (Johnson)" file also was dispensable, so she added it to the others. If Logan were to understand and amend his misbehavior, like the children, he too needed to have some of his possessions taken away.

But Adella realized that those folders alone wouldn't accomplish all that she wanted to do, so she ripped out dozens of pages from the diaries she'd brought along and tossed them in as well. Cotton also was flammable. Her mother often had described how Hancock County's cotton fields became oceans of fire when Sherman's troops had set them aflame on their late-1864 rampage through Georgia. So Adella tore off her broadcloth skirt's bottom tier, then the upper one, added her shirtwaist, the half-smoked cigar, and a little kerosene, lit another match, and tossed it in as her pyre began to smoke and crackle, then blaze. She leaned back in Logan's desk chair to watch, dressed in her camisole, petticoat, bloomers, stockings, and shoes. Years ago, her tutor and cousin Neppie Hunt had admonished her that it was unladylike ever to go barefoot.

As a firehouse dog, Vulcan started howling. "Come on, boy, it's time to go home," she soothed as they exited the smoky office. She locked its door behind her, then the outer one that opened directly onto the driveway, left the Administration Building, and turned back down Montgomery Road.

As Adella neared home, she saw Ruth looking out the parlor window. She called out and saw her daughter's body jerk as she heard and then spotted her. Ruth burst from the house and hurtled across their front yard and the street. She looked beyond Adella's shoulder and saw the Administration Building's two glowing, first-floor windows, realized they were those in her father's office, and demanded, "What happened just now, Mamma? You look and smell really strange." Then the strapping young woman swept up Adella and, with Vulcan barking behind, carried her home and ordered Sarah, "Ring up the fire station and the hospital immediately!"

A fire engine soon clanged along the main road and screeched to a halt in the turnaround. Four men climbed down, unrolled a canvas hose, screwed its metal coupler onto a hydrant, and having been greeted by the frenzied watchman, entered the Administration Building. Dozens of curious observers mingled between the Logans' house and the campus. Junior succumbed to a debilitating coughing fit as smoke wafted across the street and into his bedroom, and Adella's younger children crept from their beds to watch the noisy scene unfolding outside their window.

Half an hour later Sarah responded to the doorbell. Adella heard an unfamiliar voice followed by footsteps ascending the staircase, then a rap and the question, "May I come in?"

"Yes, please do," Ruth said to the crisply uniformed, tan-skinned visitor.

"I'm Nella Larsen, Dr. Kenney's new head nurse at the hospital," the woman introduced herself and shook hands with the Logan women. "What seems to be the problem?"

"We have no problem," Adella shrugged. "I'm afraid my daughter has overreacted."

Ruth frowned, "May I have a private word with you, please, Nurse Larsen?" and drew their visitor into the hallway. Adella overheard her daughter quietly say, "What with all the commotion outside, you must be aware of the fire at the Administration Building. Well, half an hour ago, my mother left there reeking of tobacco, kerosene, and smoke. I'm not certain what ensued while she was away from the house, but I found her wandering along Montgomery Road wearing only her shoes and undergarments."

The two young women returned to the bedroom. Adella yawned and said she was exhausted; so Miss Larsen prepared a cup of "special tea," and soon Adella was dead to the world.

When Adella finally awoke, she realized that she'd slept through the entire night and the following morning. Then nurse Larsen administered another tonic, and she fell asleep again.

The next time she awakened, Logan stood scowling across from the bed. She hadn't known he'd returned from Coden, and anger seemed to outweigh any concerns about her. She tried to explain. "You know I've been ill. You behaved irresponsibly when you cast aside your family obligations and left us, so I had to administer some discipline. You must realize that."

But shaking his head, he stalked out of the room, muttering, "No, Mother. No, no, no!"

Dr. Kenney also had arrived back at the institute, and he directed Nella Larsen to continue checking on Adella. She found the new nurse to be pleasant, efficient, and also inquisitive.

Over the next few days Miss Larsen told her patient that she'd attended but been expelled from Fisk University for protesting the school's rigid dress code, then for two years she'd lived in Denmark, her mother's home country, before moving to New York City, where she'd recently graduated from nursing school. She'd met Dr. E. P. Roberts there, and he'd recommended her to Dr. Kenney at John Andrew Hospital. Despite her first-rate training, she felt unsure how she'd be accepted in their community, which was loath to embrace newcomers. Nella Larsen liked her profession well enough but loved literature even more and hoped one day to write fiction.

"Perhaps I'll create a heroine based on you, Mrs. Logan," she smiled. "She'd be a beautiful and clever but troubled Negro woman who looks white. I'm thinking about calling my story 'Passing,'" she mused. "Do you think that's a viable idea and a good title?"

"It could be quite compelling, Miss Larsen," Adella assured her. "Have you read any earlier novels about very light-complexioned colored women, such as Frances Ellen Watkins Harper's *Iola Leroy* and even H. L. Hosmer's frankly mawkish *Adela, the Octoroon?*"

"Yes," she nodded, "I've read those and several others. My father was a mulatto from the Caribbean and my mother is a white European, so I think I can articulate the inherent racial complexities. But now, Mrs. Logan, you need to rest. We'll talk more tomorrow."

Adella hounded Ruth for reading materials, so she brought the latest *Woman's Journal,* some library books, and more. That week's *Tuskegee Student* included a brief item that reported, "A small blaze broke out last Wednesday evening in the treasurer's office, which the institute's fire brigade efficiently extinguished. Mr. Logan was away with Principal Washington on their annual fishing trip at Coden-on-the-Bay, but when a cable informed him of the incident, he returned to assess the situation. Fortunately, the damage was slight, and little of value was destroyed."

Adella wouldn't be long without other visitors. Her brother Will stopped by, Henry came over from Fort Valley, her sister Lula Hunt McLendon arrived from Sparta, and Ella Hunt Payne came all the way from New York City. Her brother Tommy couldn't attend what he called "the family reunion," but wrote, *Wish I could join you, Sis, but our fall semester is starting next week & I'll lose my job if I'm not present and prepared. Hope this "U.S. Grant" will help.* He'd enclosed a fifty-dollar bill, though Adella didn't know what "help" it might be intended for.

Logan remained irate and wanted Adella to acknowledge the problems she'd generated, so he showed her some recent correspondence between Margaret and Booker T. Washington:

```
Dear husband,                    Sept. 28, 1915
   During your absence in Coden, Mrs. Logan made
trouble for us again, and again she has endan-
gered our well-being. You know best, of course,
but I'd suggest you write and ask Dr. Kellogg
to admit her to his Sanitarium at Battle Creek.
Whatever you decide, act quickly and do not be
swayed by old friendships.
MMW                                      cc: WL
```

Logan insisted that Adella read his carbon copy of Mr. Washington's follow-up letter:

```
Dear Dr. Kellogg,               October 4, 1915
   If you see fit to approve this proposal, I
will advise our vice principal and treasurer
Warren Logan to send his wife to your facility
for treatment as soon as possible.
   You met Mrs. Logan when you visited us two
years ago. She is one of our most loyal and
capable teachers, but has become distraught and
run down nervously of late. Our Dr. John Ken-
ney, however, finds no significant problems with
her physical health.
   I must be frank. I realize that objections
might be made to having a colored woman come
to your Sanitarium as a patient, and Mrs. Logan
would be the last person who would choose to
```

sail under false colors, but if no one calls
attention to the fact that she is a Negro, no
one would guess it from her appearance. The
same is true of her daughter Ruth who would
accompany her.

Ruth Logan is a graduate of your colleague
Dr. Sargent's college in Cambridge, and now she
directs our girls' physical education program.
Perhaps she might benefit your trainees by sharing her expertise in ladies' sports while she
is with you.

I would be grateful if you could admit Mrs.
Logan to the San and do what you can to restore
her health. We benefitted greatly from your
previous trip to Tuskegee and hope you will
return soon again. I often tell my colleagues
how much I learned when I attended your Race
Betterment Conference last year.

I look forward to your response to this
urgent request.
Respectfully yours,
Booker T. Washington
Booker T. Washington, Principal
ccs: MMW, WL, JK

Mr. Washington's apparent sanction of the "Race Betterment," or eugenics, movement distressed Adella. Its supporters argued that "the best
people" should reproduce prolifically, but only within their own races,
whereas "society's dregs" must be deterred from having children at all.
Fervent eugenicists advocated involuntary sterilization of the physically and
mentally "defective," especially members of the "Darker Races." A few elit-
ists among her own people, such as Dr. Du Bois (for Adella, nothing better exemplified his sporadic "dubiousness" than this fleeting flirtation with
eugenics), supported such efforts in part, while trying to ignore the move-

ment's inherent racism. Others whom Adella admired, among them Margaret Sanger, a white nurse who in the face of fierce opposition to her controversial crusade tried to disseminate information on how women might regulate their childbearing, also espoused the morally repugnant eugenics initiatives. Adella, however, feared that slippery slope, and she rued Booker T. Washington's peripheral involvement in the crusade, as well as its advocacy by Battle Creek's Dr. Kellogg.

John Kellogg quickly agreed to Booker T. Washington's proposal, but at first, Adella resisted being sent away. Her siblings and husband, Dr. Kenney, even Patty Winston and Gussie (Mrs. Julius) Rosenwald, however, urged her to go, citing the benefits of two months' rest, a rigorous diet, exercise, and various therapies. So she yielded to their concerted pressure, which exiled Adella Hunt Logan from Tuskegee and sentenced her to an unwelcome interlude as "Dull Anglo Athena": a drab, deranged "white" woman. Only two weeks after Mr. Washington sent off that letter, she and Ruth left Alabama's balmy autumn and headed to chilly, unfamiliar Michigan.

SEVENTEEN

Exile

ADELLA AND HER DAUGHTER TOOK THE wagonette to Chehaw, changed trains, traveled west to Montgomery, then north to South Bend, Indiana, where they transferred onto the Western and Central Michigan line that veered off to Battle Creek. They shared a cozy roomette in a Pullman sleeper car where gracious, uniformed Negro attendants pulled out and turned down their upper and lower berths each evening, made them again the next day, kept "the Tuskegee ladies" well supplied with pillows and fresh bed, bath, and table linens, brought meticulously prepared meals to the compartment, and served their morning coffee from Adella's silver anniversary travel pot.

But their exchanges weren't always congenial. Frank Drye, the institute's bandmaster, was wooing Ruth, and when prodded by her mother, the young woman conceded that he made her heart pound. Adella scolded, "You have to stop panting over him like a bitch in heat."

Ruth's jaw dropped. "It's true!" Adella shrugged, then embarked on a pragmatic maternal discourse as she urged her daughter to consider instead Dr. Eugene Percy Roberts.

"E. P. Roberts is extremely intelligent and also one of New York's wealthiest colored men, while Captain Drye, though handsome, is as poor as a church mouse. But Dr. E. P. clearly is in love with you. Didn't he give you that initialed gold Tiffany locket for your last birthday? He's kept his prestigious mayoral appointment and has inveigled the city into hiring its first colored policeman. He supports suffrage and civil rights and works with both the NAACP and the National Urban League, which, as you know, is led by the admirable Ruth Baldwin, for whom you, my dear, were named.

I bet he'd buy you a fine house in that up-and-coming Negro neighborhood called Harlem. You'd have the resources you need to work on the causes that you care most about. I've told you that years ago I wrote Susan B. Anthony saying, 'I hope one day to see my daughter vote right here in the South,' but it would be all right with me if you lived—and, of course, voted—in New York City instead. Or perhaps," Adella slyly needled her daughter, "you'd rather heed the Book of Ruth, 'Wash thyself and anoint thee, put thy raiment upon thee, and get thee down onto the floor.'"

"Don't go quoting the Bible at me, Mamma," Ruth fumed. "And as for Dr. Roberts, yes, he's smart and rich, but he's short, and almost as old as you are. I want children, and he doesn't."

"I'll give you My 'Del and Arthur," Adella joked (or did she?), "and you certainly don't want to become a broken-down brood mare as I am."

"That's ridiculous," Ruth retorted. "You need to get better, but you're hardly a broken-down brood mare; and the little ones already miss you terribly and eagerly await your return."

But Adella continued unfazed: "On the subject of procreation, you should read Margaret Sanger's newsletter, the *Woman Rebel*. She exhorts us to become 'mistresses of our own bodies' and to 'awaken our spirit of revolt against everything that enslaves us.' I agree with that dictum, don't you? But get it while you can. Our autocratic postmaster general has started confiscating her journal because he claims that its 'racy' contents violate the Comstock Laws."

"Enough of that," Ruth snapped, "though I did write Dr. Roberts to inform him that we're going to Battle Creek, and he thinks highly of Dr. Kellogg and the San. I also should tell you that I asked our new kindergarten teacher, Angela Kurtz, to help Aunt Sarah care for the children while we're away. Her little boy will be a nice friend for Arthur, and she'll play bid whist with father on Saturday nights." Ruth smiled, knowing that such pastimes bored her mother to tears.

"What could you have been thinking?" Adella retorted. "She's divorced and a fallen woman! I don't want her son anywhere near Arthur or having her play cards with your father."

"That's ridiculous, Mamma! I'm sure it'll be for the best—and it's done now. Besides, you always lecture others about narrow-mindedness. How often have I heard you say, 'Divorced women shouldn't be condemned because they extricate themselves from intolerable situations'?"

"True enough, but Junior thought poorly of her when they attended Howard together," Adella tartly concluded. They spent the next few hours in icy, intergenerational silence.

When their train pulled into Battle Creek, they taxied to the Sanitarium, registered, and were ushered to their spartan quarters. Despite its lofty reputation and bucolic environs, it was one of the most formidable edifices they'd ever seen: an ominous mountain of gray granite.

The Seventh-Day Adventists, an evangelical denomination that eagerly awaited "the Rapture" and Jesus's long-promised second coming, had opened the hospital shortly after the Civil War. A decade later, when they learned about Dr. John Kellogg's excellent surgical skills and lofty ambitions, they hired him, and he rose quickly through the medical and managerial ranks. Sojourner Truth had been one of his early patients there, and rumor had it that he'd tried to graft his own white skin onto her black backside, which had been oozing with bedsores.

Dr. Kellogg's unorthodox convictions, however, abounded, especially his sanction of sexual intercourse exclusively for the purpose of procreation. He preached that "the dispersal of vital bodily fluids depletes one's energies." Adella wondered if he might be, in Dr. Freud's new vocabulary, an "invert," since he and his wife boasted that they never copulated at all. Thus, they had no biological children but (preposterously!) had reared almost forty foster ones.

The original facility had burned to the ground in 1902, with rumors of the conflagration's genesis being a faulty furnace, Dr. Kellogg for the insurance, or even arson by one of his crazed, adoptive sons. But a gigantic new fireproof "Temple of Health" soon rose like a phoenix from the ashes. A few of the poor, many of the rich and famous, performers, politicians, and even royalty flocked there. John Kellogg's "inspirational" directives displayed throughout the hospital read, INHALE! EXHALE! EXERCISE! MASTICATE! DIGEST! ELIMINATE! REST!

Sojourner Truth had been a Battle Creek resident for years and tried to vote in 1872, so Ruth and Adella made a pilgrimage to the dilapidated cottage where their hero had lived and died. But at the nearby cemetery they found only a rotting wooden marker inscribed with the barely legible query, "Is God dead, Frederick?"—referring, of course, to Frederick Douglass.

"She's almost the only Negro woman whom Miss Anthony and Mrs. Stanton even cited in the *History of Woman Suffrage*," Adella indignantly shook her head. "They often quoted her words, 'If colored men get their rights and not women, they'll remain our masters and things will stay as bad as before.' If Sojourner actually said that, and I'm not at all sure she did, the white suffragists thought that it justified their own shameful opposition to the Fifteenth Amendment. How duplicitous even the best of them could be!" Ruth nodded to appease her righteous mother.

Acknowledging Mr. Washington's renown and letter of introduction, Dr. Kellogg personally welcomed the Logan women to his facility. To epitomize his legendary chastity, the snowy-haired John Kellogg dressed in seraphic garb: a bedazzling three-piece white suit, shirt, tie, belt, socks, and even shoes. He introduced them to Adella's personal physician, Mary Hunter Newlove, who arranged for laboratory analyses of her new patient's blood, urine, and "fecal excretions," and specified every detail of her therapies, diet, sleep, and exercise routines.

That onerous regimen included daily yogurt colonics and warm wax enemas to purge Adella's intestines, and deep tissue massage administered by a Swedish behemoth who roughly rubbed her from head to toe with almond-, citrus-, mint-, or coconut-infused oils. The seven-inch scar from her nephrectomy intrigued the masseuse, whose rigorous manipulations navigated the sensitive interstices between pleasure and pain, as well as those between her vertebrae.

In the gymnasium, Adella hung upside down on a vertical wall rack to stretch her spine, rhythmically swung a pair of Indian clubs, and endured jarring "mechano-vibration" treatments to stimulate her circulation. Hydrotherapy in the ladies' swimming pool was barely tolerable, while pinpoint water hoses nearly flayed the tender skin from her abdomen. One jovial attendant assured her, "Our heliotherapy will help to relieve your gloomy moods," but Adella flatly rejected the recommended "uplifting group laughter sessions." She rode a bicycle around the grounds or, on rainy mornings, pedaled indoors on one of Dr. John Kellogg's bizarre new cycling contraptions that went absolutely nowhere. Given the leader's blanket rejection of any Freudian or other analytical or restorative therapies, however, the San offered no counseling or "talking cures" at all. Tobacco, stimulants, intoxicants, sugar, and condiments were forbidden, and all edible flesh was deemed "filthy carrion." Adella picked at the bland mealtime offerings of purées, roughage, and herbal beverages and yearned for just one cup of strong coffee served from her own silver pot, a slice of crisp, salty bacon, or a single bite of any well-seasoned food.

Dr. Newlove exhorted Mrs. Logan—who grudgingly agreed—to rest for an hour each afternoon in the Palm Court, a five-story crystal palace that constituted the San's architectural epicenter. Date and areca palms, banana trees, and giant ferns abounded, and Adella thought she spotted some ruby pomegranate globes dangling like Christmas ornaments from the emerald shrubs.

A python slithered through the manmade jungle, then a chameleon shifted colors and ballooned out his throat at her. *Cucarachas* hissed across the aviary's upper reaches, while hairy tarantulas scurried below. A drab peahen waddled beside her gaudy mate, who strutted past with his feathery pride-and-joy adorned with *heterochromia iridum* "eyes" fanned behind him. Then a long-tailed female monkey pissed on a high branch to declare her readiness. She lifted her rosy rump to welcome the priapic male, who sniffed and promptly mounted her. Her barks goaded him on as he snorted, whinnied in climactic satisfaction, swung away on ropy lianas through the green canopy, descended, then defecated on a fallen tree trunk. When that gnarled "log" grunted and lumbered off to submerge itself in a nearby morass, however, Adella realized that it must be an Amazonian caiman. Might she encounter more such reptiles, she giddily mused, if she were to accompany "el Presidente Teodoro Roosevelt" along his daunting River of Doubt?

She evidently laughed aloud, because Ruth's "Wake up, Mamma!" shattered her reverie. Adella insisted that she hadn't been asleep but expressed her disgust at the copulating primates.

"You needn't worry about the monkeys," Ruth tried to reassure her, "because the attendants showed me where they're securely caged down-stairs in the basement laboratory."

Adella, however, warned, "I'm sure that most of them are where they belong, my dear, but not these randy creatures." She looked and pointed upward, but the elusive pair had slipped away.

Dr. Kellogg and his colleague Dr. Dudley Sargent, the president of Ruth's alma mater, promoted similar fitness routines, so while Adella endured her therapies, her daughter "earned her keep" by teaching ladies' basketball to the San's female trainees. Since those sports tutorials occupied much of Ruth's days, Adella usually saw her only at meals. Everyone dressed formally for dinner, when eight "guests" sat around each linen-draped, candlelit table in the top-floor atrium as fawning uniformed waiters attended them. They ordered from elegant menu cards that listed a monotonous array of the sanctioned diet: avolena, brumose, maltol, nuttolene, vegetable mushes, wheatose, zwieback, and the like. Stimulating conversation thus was essential.

"I understand that you and Miss Ruth have just joined us from the South, Mrs. Logan, so perhaps you'll share your thoughts on the negro problem?" her dinner partner "Captain" began.

"What 'problem' is that, Captain?" Adella tartly retorted as Ruth covered her eyes.

"Oh, don't be coy, madam," he conspiratorially squeezed her hand. "I refer to colored men's moral laxity and venality, especially the brutal crimes they commit against white women."

"I have a suggestion," Adella said as five heads snapped 'round to receive her southern wisdom: "Perhaps our government could mandate that at least for one generation, every Negro must copulate with a white person, and vice versa. White men always had their way with female slaves and still often do with their vulnerable servants. Few of our countrymen have deemed those liaisons much of a problem. But this proposition also would require black men to have intercourse with white women."

"What a curious joke, Mrs. Logan," Captain's eyes bulged and his mustache twitched as their tablemates squirmed. "We Yankees should admit that slaveholders sometimes used to have, er, 'illicit congress' with wanton colored women, and unsavory mulattoes and quadroons have resulted from those tawdry encounters, but I must have misunderstood you. You're not seriously proposing that our white ladies have, er, 'relations' with black fellas, are you? I hesitate even to mention such a thing in mixed company, but think of their primitively large, er, 'members.'"

"Yes, Captain, that's exactly this proposal, though I have no grounds for comparison."

"Oh, Mrs. Logan," he spluttered, "I wasn't for a moment suggesting that you did."

"No matter," Adella went on. "A woman of ill repute might evaluate any racially based variations in size better than I, though most reputable scientists downplay those differences. But if you think that Negroes' *penises,* the word you hesitate to use, are overly large, do you suggest that white fellas'—yours, for instance, or those of the other gentlemen here [she gestured around the table]—are extremely small?" Captain coughed and flushed brick red as she continued.

"I should point out that a woman's love tunnel, Venus flytrap, honeypot, or whatever you choose to call her vagina plays a more critical role as the birth canal than in sexual congress," Adella continued. "And childbirth itself requires a much-greater stretching of that orifice than intercourse with a male 'member' of any size. Imagine forcing a bowling ball through one of your nostrils, Captain, then you'll understand what happens during parturition. I've experienced that agonizing miracle nine times." Her male tablemates flinched and reflexively touched their noses, while the mothers among them, though shocked, hid their experienced smiles. Ruth, Adella could see, desperately wanted not to be there at that moment—or even to be her daughter.

Adella continued without a pause. "You should read the works of scientists such as Charles Darwin on the survival of the fittest and Gregor Mendel on hybridization. Dr. Alexander Walker is less well known, but he too demonstrated how inbreeding often generates weakness in humans much as it does in plants and animals, while cross-breeding tends to strengthen the progeny. If my 'miscegenation proposal,' if you choose to call it that, were imposed, soon perhaps, we'd have a handsomer, stronger, smarter, and more moral race in our country or, instead, no races at all. After a generation or two if we had no more white people, would we also have no more of what you characterize as venal black men either? Where, then, would be your 'Negro problem'?'"

Captain gawked, cleared his throat, grumbled about "race mixing," then turned aside to choke down his unpalatable food. But Adella knew that although she'd negatively impacted his digestion, which gave her some degree of guilty pleasure, as "Dull Anglo Athena," a deracinated moral weakling, she'd concealed herself yet again behind her convenient veil of whiteness.

One woman who sat two chairs away seemed nonplused by the conversation's erotic and politicized content. She tried to redirect the conversation by admiring Adella's hair. "I wish that mine was as thick, long, and lustrous as yours, Mrs. Logan," she smiled: "What's your secret?"

Rather than frankly attributing it to her mix of African, Native American, and European antecedents and undoubtedly generating even greater alarm, Adella thanked the woman but added, "I'm thinking about cutting it extremely short as many French women recently have started doing. It's considered *très chic* in Paris nowadays. What's your opinion?" Her well-intended tablemate was rendered speechless. If race and sex were chancy conversational topics, Adella's brief discourse on a lady adopting a "foreign" boyish bob seemed equally shocking.

The following evening, the obsequious dining-room host ushered the Logan ladies to a corner table for two.

The most critical component of Adella's treatment began several days after that dinnertime debacle, once her colon and lungs had been fully cleansed and her strength, endurance, and flexibility upgraded during her first week and a half at the San. It was electrical shock therapy.

Dr. Mary Hunter Newlove tried to assure (or delude) Adella that it wouldn't be painful, but she'd have endured almost anything to get her emotions back on an even keel. So early one morning halfway through her second week, she was rolled on a gurney to a chilly basement cell where a vacant-eyed, slack-jawed woman with a crimson drizzle on her lower lip was being wheeled out. The nurse gave her a "soothing drink," fastened a bulky diaper around her rump, and winked, "just in case." She and a male attendant checked and recorded their patient's vital signs, strapped her wrists and ankles to clamps on the tabletop, placed a rubber "bit" between her teeth, rubbed a dab of petroleum jelly on each temple, and tightened a steel and leather "cradle" around her skull. Then the man warned, "Steady, Mrs. Logan. I'm gonna pull the switch now."

The lights hissed, flickered, and dimmed. Silvery streaks flashed behind Adella's eyelids as a corporeal firestorm assaulted her. She smelled scorched hair, tasted salt, copper, and bile, then knew nothing more until she reawakened with a horrific headache, feeling vertiginous and nauseated. The technician posed a couple of questions—place of residence, date of birth—that she answered easily. She flummoxed him when she first insisted that her name was "Dull Anglo Athena" but then obediently amended that response to "Adella Hunt Logan." When he asked her to tell him the date, day of the week, or what she'd eaten for dinner the previous evening, however, she was stumped. He assured her, "Some short-term memory loss is common after a treatment, but it'll quickly pass, and soon you'll start feeling and thinking much better, indeed."

At first, finding the right word was frustrating, but one that she dredged up to describe her post-shock images was "etiolated": whitened or bleached out. The sky seemed hardly blue, and the surrounding fields looked scarcely green. They were strewn throughout with nonroses and unviolets. As Dull Anglo Athena, Adella saw everything in drab grays and tans.

But the electro-technician had been right, and after a few days the missing puzzle pieces began slipping into place. No sooner had they done so, however, than it was time for another session in that torture chamber, where Adella returned thrice more. Yet after five weeks out of the prescribed eight, she noticed a little improvement, as if she were afloat on somewhat calmer seas. But even as the crocs, *cucarachas,* and fornicating monkeys retreated from her electrically benumbed brain, so did the dazzling images that she loved, and her vivid, insomniac cognition.

Then the unthinkable happened. Before leaving Alabama, she and Ruth had known that Booker T. Washington had been feeling less robust than usual. But on November 11, they heard from Eugene Percy Roberts, who'd joined the team of physicians who'd been called in to attend the Wizard of Tuskegee in New York, that Mr. Washington had collapsed during a speaking tour in the Northeast and was immediately hospitalized. For several months, Dr. Roberts, among others, had been urging him to revisit the San for a checkup as he'd done before, but the time for precautionary measures apparently had passed. E. P. Roberts's cable read, RETURN HOME IMMEDIATELY. MR. WASHINGTON MORTALLY ILL. HE LEAVES NYC FOR TUSKEGEE TODAY.

By the time they received that message, Booker T. Washington, accompanied by his wife and Dr. John Kenney, both of whom had hastened north to join him the day before, boarded the private Pullman car that Andrew Carnegie provided, and departed for Alabama. If the consulting physicians' prognostications were correct, he'd die there—and very soon.

Adella had completed only half of her prescribed course of treatment, but she and Ruth flung their belongings into their suitcases and boarded the next train headed south. A car, driver, and the inconsolable George Washington Carver met them at the whistle stop north of Tuskegee.

Their chauffeur followed the same route that the ambulance from the institute's hospital had taken the previous evening carrying Mr. and Mrs. Washington and Dr. Kenney. That trio had arrived at The Oaks near midnight on November 13. "Family members," including Warren Logan, were summoned to Booker T. Washington's bedside, and in one of his final breaths, Adella's husband later confided, the Great Man whispered, "Take care of our school, Angela Kurtz, and her boy, my friend." Shortly before five the following morning, he passed away at his home in Alabama, where for thirty-four years he'd exhorted his people to cast down their buckets.

EIGHTEEN

Flight

WAS IT POSSIBLE THAT BOOKER T. Washington was gone, not just on one of his frequent expeditions but forever? Wasn't he the incomparable and, yes, immortal Wizard of Tuskegee?

A number of the race suspected foul play. And why ever not? Perhaps malicious white men or jealous black ones murdered the Great Man. Over the past dozen years, Pinkerton agents had thwarted several attempts on his life, and more than a few conspiracy theorists believed that the 1911 attack on him in New York City had been part of a nefarious plot, not "just a mistake." But in fact, rational diagnoses indicated that a lethal confluence of hypertension and arteriosclerosis brought about the renal failure that precipitated his sudden demise. His passing set Adella atremble as she considered how easily her own single kidney might betray her.

Sarah Hunt greeted her sister and oldest niece, sobbing inconsolably both over Booker T. Washington's death and also because, pursuant to Ruth's well-meant but ill-advised strategy, she'd had to deal with Angela Kurtz in their absence. "Polly and My 'Del feel wretched," Sarah shook her head. "Her son, Harland, is only a toddler, but he smashes Arthur's toys and then throws a tantrum if anyone tries to correct him. She acts as if it's her house, not ours, and you won't believe how overprotective she's become with Logan, but I think he enjoys her attentions."

Adella found that Angela Kurtz had alphabetized and shelved her books, reorganized her kitchen pantry, and even, the usurper blithely informed her, "cleaned out and reordered your closets." But Adella had no opportunity to discuss that inappropriate behavior with her husband.

Messages arrived from around the state, the country, and the world, most of them directed to Logan, as acting principal. They came from former presidents Roosevelt and Taft (though not President Wilson), Andrew Carnegie, Julius Rosenwald, Harvard's Charles Eliot, and many other dignitaries who couldn't get to Alabama in time for Booker T. Washington's burial.

Tears flooded Tuskegee Institute, and black crepe shrouded each door. An agonized cook eviscerated himself with a butcher knife, howling, "I can't live without him. He was my God!" as geysers of blood spewed across the central kitchen's stoves, counters, sinks, walls, and floor.

Across the side lawn from the Logans' home, the Wizard's body lay at The Oaks in a simple wooden casket. On the morning of the funeral, J. H. Washington (the Great Man's brother) and Warren Logan led a solemn procession accompanied by muffled drums that slowly snaked through the campus over to the institute chapel, where the student choir sang "Lead Kindly Light" and other old spirituals.

Fifteen hundred mourners, half of them white people who occupied most of the reserved seats, pressed inside for the service, while thousands more black-garbed, black country folk stood outside and wept disconsolately in the rain. Tuskegee's mayor attended and asked his town's merchants, including those who routinely abused, insulted, or refused to accommodate anyone from the institute, to close their shops for the day, as many of them did.

Logan knew that although Adella and Booker T. Washington had locked horns at times, they'd remained friends, so he honored her request to speak briefly at the grave site in the small "family" cemetery where the Great Man would be interred in hallowed ground a few yards from the Logans' three deceased children. Margaret Washington didn't object either, because she had more pressing matters to deal with. She'd been flat-out blindsided because her late spouse's newly accessed testamentary documents (Warren Logan was the executor) instructed that he be buried next to his second wife, Olivia, who Adella and many others knew had been the love of his life.

Adella delivered a brief tribute with which her colleagues were unfamiliar, and had they known its origin, they wouldn't have let her do so. It was a reverie composed by Dr. Du Bois, who'd sent her a copy when a mutual friend had died. Despite the two men's conflicts, Adella believed that both Booker T. Washington and W. E. B. Du Bois genuinely aspired to uplift the race, but in different ways, and she thought that the Doctor (as she often called him) would approve of his (unaccredited) words' inclusion: "We thank thee, O Lord, for the gift of Death," she read, "for the silence that follows the jarring noises of the world. We saw the passing of that Great Man and must not forget the legacy he left behind. We are richer for his sacrifices, truer for his honesty, better for his goodness."

But soon after anonymously quoting Dr. Du Bois, Adella was appalled to read his harsh public indictment that "we must lay upon the soul of this man a heavy responsibility for the consummation of Negro disfranchisement and for the even harsher enforcement of the color caste." The Doctor minimally tempered his latest diatribe by conceding that Mr. Washington "was the country's most acclaimed Negro since Frederick Douglass," but that otherwise vitriolic defamation, with the body scarcely cold in the ground, affronted Adella.

Once again, Warren Logan held the institute's reins of authority in his steady hands. He also continued planning the memorial service that would take place on Sunday, December 14, for the Great Man's many friends, associates, and admirers from around the country who'd been unable to attend the funeral itself. That major public event would be followed by the institute's trustees meeting in executive session, where the primary item on their agenda would be to determine who would succeed the inherently unsucceedable Booker Taliaferro Washington.

Gloom permeated the campus, but although Adella remained angry at the Doctor for his ugly obituary and was further aggravated by her exclusion from his magazine's second "Votes for Women" symposium, she distracted herself by reading every article in that recent issue of *Crisis,* which featured a striking image of Sojourner Truth's ebony-hewn visage on its cover.

Despite the pervasive doldrums, Adella hoped that her younger children still might enjoy a somewhat festive holiday season. Her brother Will thus took them into the woods to gather pine cones, cut holly branches, and chop down a fir tree. Toting the small hatchet from his toy toolbox, six-year-old Arthur (whose latest passion was his open invitation to "conduct science experiments" with 'Fess Carver in his laboratory) trotted alongside his long-legged uncle.

Adella didn't join them, however, because she was mulling over the letter she'd received from Julius Rosenwald's wife, Augusta. When Booker T. Washington had informed her that "Mrs. Logan is ailing," "Gussie" Rosenwald had sent a generous personal check. Adella thanked her profusely and applied the money to her hospital costs. Now her friend wrote this:

> First, welcome back from Dr. Kellogg's Sanitarium, and I hope you're feeling better. But what could have been worse than returning to face the agony of Mr. Washington's passing? My husband and I are devastated here in Chicago and know that you at Tuskegee are even more so.
>
> I wrote Mrs. Washington expressing my condolences and concerns for the institute's future. She replied immediately, and that's what I need to share with you.

Gussie followed that with a paragraph she'd copied from Margaret Washington's letter:

> Since you raised the matter of succession, I must be candid. Warren Logan is a loyal soldier but hardly the leader Dr. Washington was. In other circumstances, his familiarity with the school under my husband's tutelage might have made him a logical successor, but you and I understand a spouse's importance. As you know, Mr. Logan's wife was recently hospitalized. My late husband described her condition as "run down nervously," but it's worse than that: she has taken total leave of her senses! One of her recent exploits left our administration building in flames. She promotes immediate access to the ballot for all women and indiscriminate racial integration, and she demands services in our town as if she were white. Her acts and beliefs resemble those of the Bolsheviks. I share this reluc-

tantly since she's a friend, but her deterioration necessitates the removal of her husband from the Trustees' consideration to succeed Mr. Washington.

Gussie Rosenwald's own words resumed:

> *When I shared Mrs. Washington's response with my husband, I found that she'd written much the same to him, but his letter also includes the following: "In my estimation, no one but Hampton Institute's R. R. Moton is qualified to become Tuskegee's next principal. He is an experienced administrator who is dedicated to my late husband's goals of industrial and agricultural training for the race, and he advocates gracious accommodation with our white friends. His wife, a refined and modest woman, also will suffice as the Institute's new 'first lady.' Your fellow trustee President Roosevelt, you know, already has publicly declared his endorsement of Major Moton for the position."*

Mrs. Washington, Gussie's letter concluded, *clearly is not, as she claims, your "friend."*

A "Bolshevik" who'd "taken total leave of her senses" was she? ("*Quos deus vult perdere, prius dementat*": "Whom the gods wish to destroy, they first make mad," Adella again mused.) Margaret Washington's missive, however, correctly pointed out that she *did* advocate universal suffrage and equal access to public facilities, education, and health care, regardless of race, sex, or class. But she felt a crushing guilt that her openly stated beliefs, among other "sins," apparently had destroyed her husband's chance to assume the position he'd long aspired to.

So there she was that horrific autumn. Her oldest son had returned home to recuperate for a month, which was stretching toward a year. Junior was dying, and no woman should have to bury a child—though she'd already buried three. She'd alienated her sister by supposedly (Sarah still believed) usurping George Washington Carver's affections and embarrassed her daughter Ruth during their recent interval in Battle Creek. Grinding guilt almost paralyzed her.

Booker T. Washington, her longtime friend, neighbor, and employer, had died, and collective grief nearly suffocated the institute. Dr. Du Bois had apparently rejected her and also made unconscionable statements about the late Great Man. Woman suffrage, her abiding political cause, recently had met an ignominious defeat in the Alabama legislature. Her sterilization and the "change of life," she believed, had left her a wretched pile of debris: weak, haggard, quarrelsome, and absent the supposed central purpose of womanhood.

Though weary in body and mind, Adella busied herself with the usual holiday plans. In the weeks leading to the trustees' summit, she polished her mother's Fiddlehead table silver and began soaking currants in rum for holiday fruitcakes. She brought down from the attic the children's black Santa, carved in the school's carpentry shop, and silver balls, bells, and an angel for the tree top. Performing those familiar tasks felt essential to maintaining her equilibrium.

She scribbled in her diary too:

Friday, December 10. Still agonizing over Gussie R's letter from Mrs. B. T. about how I would not do as the Institute's first lady. Perhaps I did ruin Logan's chance to fulfill his ambitions to lead our school. Can I repair the damage? I keep thinking back on the phrase I wrote a decade ago: "to cry, to swear, or to suicide." But I have to be practical. More chores await me, and I must go to the Children's House teachers meeting at Huntington Hall this a.m. As a founder, I feel obligated to do so, though the newcomers natter about me whether I'm present or not. Things remain somewhat testy with my dear sister, who'll attend too, and I don't look forward to sitting in the same room as Angela Kurtz.

Adella trudged across campus to the main academic building and climbed to the fourth-floor conference room. Her sister Sarah and Miss

Kurtz had taken seats at the front (but not near each other), and two young teachers were whispering as Adella arrived. She wasn't certain but thought she heard one of them snicker, "She came home from Battle Creek crazier than ever, and all the while our new temptress was dallying with her husband." How dare they gossip like that?

She listened to tedious reports about student discipline and extra funds needed for special projects and wondered how My 'Del's and Arthur's routines over at the Children's House might be occupying them. Polly was in her sixth-grade classroom on Huntington Hall's third floor and Ruth down in the basement gymnasium. She'd stop by to see them when the meeting adjourned.

But soon, Adella began feeling agitated and short of breath. She no longer could sit still, so she crept from her back-row chair, escaped her long-winded colleagues, ascended another flight, and entered an unoccupied classroom. Hungrily seeking fresh air, she crossed between the empty desks, unlatched and tugged open a heavy window sash, and leaned out over the wide sill.

She must have clambered onto it too, because she found herself perched on a droppings-splattered ledge on the top floor of the institute's only five-story building. Adella had invaded their domain, so a family of vengeance-bent, blue-black crows angrily flocked around, screeching in her ears. Their talons raked her hair as she harked back to her grandmother Susan's Raven Mocker and the apocryphal story she'd called "The People Who Can Fly."

Under the direction of Capt. Frank Drye, uniformed band members had lined up in the quadrangle below to rehearse their musical program for Mr. Washington's memorial service two days hence. Clusters of black-clad white dignitaries and institute friends, Gussie Rosenwald and Patty Winston among them, also had assembled. They'd arrived at Tuskegee well in advance of the observances and sat with others in a graceful arc of wicker lawn chairs, whence they enjoyed the impromptu concert. Adella pulled out a handkerchief and waved, but they didn't see her.

Her thoughts turned to Emily Wilding Davison, who'd leapt in front of the king's horse at Epsom Downs two years ago. She also recalled W. E. B.

Du Bois's phrase from "The Princess of the Hither Isles": "Poised on the crumbling edge of that great nothingness she hung, hungering with her eyes and straining her fainting ears against the awful splendor of the sky."

Adella paused there for a moment on her own "crumbling edge of nothingness," swaying to the band's rhythmic cadence.

A door hinge creaked. Sarah had come looking for her and saw her silhouetted against the "awful splendor of the sky." She raced to the window and clutched at Adella, trying to drag her back inside. Her vise-like grip bruised her older sister's ribs and arms. But protesting that she needed air, Adella tried to shake Sarah off, and thought, "INHALE! EXHALE! IN-HALE! EXHALE!"—the San's droning mantra. Then she wrenched away.

She stepped up and out. As Dr. Du Bois had written, "the princess leapt." First, she soared like an eagle, then glided down past Polly's classroom window. Were those her sweet girl's splayed hands and ashen face that she saw pressed against the glass? One of the band's trombonists later said that he'd seen "Mrs. Logan's long, black witch's skirt balloon out like an umbrella or a parachute." Then, without warning, it treasonously tangled up between her legs and somersaulted her head over heels. Thank goodness, she fleetingly thought, she'd put on a fresh petticoat, bloomers, and stockings that morning. One shoe dropped off as she fell faster.

The musicians and Tuskegee's eminent guests watched openmouthed or screamed.

Seventy years later, a girl who'd been hanging upside down on the parallel bars in her physical education class that morning recalled hearing a loud thump in the concrete window pit just outside the basement gymnasium, followed by her teacher's agonized shriek as Adella's daughter Ruth peered through the iron security grill, then spun around and raced outside.

After the Fall

ADELLA AWAKENED ON A COT IN AN unfamiliar room. Her hair was sticky and matted, her head was swathed in cotton gauze, and a widening scarlet halo stained the starched pillow slip.

A distraught student standing just beyond the open door wept, "Miz Ruth, she heard something heavy hit the cement. Our phys ed teacher ran out wailing, picked her mother up, and just began carrying her off when 'Fess Carver pried Miz Logan out of her arms, put her into an ambulance, and took her to the hospital. That thick cushion of long hair must've saved her life."

Adella heard the marching band's cymbals, xylophones, drums, and horns blaring in rhythmic retreat as she looked at Ruth, Sarah, and Logan, who'd gathered at her bedside.

"What have you done now, Mother?" her husband demanded.

"You tell me, Logan," she tartly responded. "Where am I, and where's the Doctor?"

"You had a bad fall, Mamma, and you're in John Andrew Hospital," Ruth explained. "Dr. Kenney's getting ready to examine you."

"But he isn't the Doctor" (Adella meant Dr. Du Bois); she pointed across the room.

"You know me. I'm John Kenney, and yes, I am your physician," the faintly familiar brown-skinned gentleman who was wearing a starched white jacket assured her.

Sarah whispered, "Here's the Old Paris cup with your name on it, Sis. I've brought you some hot cocoa." Then she sobbed, "Was it my fault because I got so angry with you?" What could Adella say to relieve her sister's anguish? Nothing, she feared, and drifted off.

When she reawakened, her children had gathered too: Junior, Ruth, Paul, Polly, My 'Del, and her precious little King Arthur, as well as the three lost babies.

Dr. E. P. Roberts had his arm around Ruth, who said to her mother, "I'm so sorry about that debacle with Angela Kurtz. You know I meant well, but I was wrong about her."

Angela Kurtz's son, Harland, sulked nearby. Adella's youngest boy raised his toy hatchet over the toddler's head, but his agile mother intervened and walloped Arthur down to the floor; then she turned and quietly said, "I warned you, Logan, we'll have to send your little demon away."

Lula Mae Hunt McLendon had come from Hancock County with Adella's old teacher, her cousin Neppie. Their youngest sister, Ella, arrived from New York and their brother Tommy from Berkeley, California, though he'd sworn he'd never again return to the Jim Crow South.

A host of medical professionals also crowded into the room. In addition to Drs. Kenney and Roberts, Samuel Courtney had come from Boston and Halle Tanner Dillon from wherever she'd gone. Adella couldn't remember. The San's Drs. Kellogg and Newlove were there too, as was Grady Hospital's surgeon William Stokes Goldsmith.

The bevy of nurses included Della Winston Dwyer and dear Eve Penney, who'd apparently never left the institute at all. A white-pinafored delegation from the MacVicar Clinic arrived from Atlanta, while another group represented New Orleans's Phillis Wheatley Training School for Negro Nurses. John Andrew Hospital's own Nella Larsen was overseeing Adella's care. She squeezed her patient's hand, smiled, and whispered, "I've started writing my novel, Mrs. Logan, and know what will happen to my heroine. Shall I tell you how it ends?"

"No thank you, Nella," Adella answered. "I like surprises, and I'll read it soon enough."

Three ministers vied to pray over her. First, Rev. Cyrus Francis arrived from Atlanta's "Big Church," where she'd graduated and married. Then came Bishop Lucius Holsey, who urged, "Your mother put herself in God's hands, Mrs. Logan, now you should do the same." But Rev. Edgar Penney interrupted, winked, and grinned at Adella: "Prestidigitation, my friend!"

Best of all was seeing her Daddy-longlegs, her mother, and especially her grandmother Susan, who rubbed Adella's cheek and said, "I know you're not feeling well, my precious, so have some of these healing pomegranate seeds." She held out a handful of translucent rubies.

Then pointing to a small, silver-haired, silver-eyed man, Susan asked, "Have you met the Judge yet? And your great-aunt Della Sayre Watkins is here too." Her grandmother gestured to the pale woman standing by Judge Sayre. "Did you know that you and I are exactly the same age now, Adella?" she said. "You've done honor to the name, and I hope it's done well by you."

Cherie Rideaux glided in wearing a stylish straw boater and carrying a shiny hatbox. "Let's try on this chapeau I made for you. See how lovely you look?" Cherie smiled and held up the silver-backed mirror that had been Adella's wedding gift, but she scarcely could see herself in the darkening looking glass.

Georgia Stewart Bond was there too with a slim, tan-skinned girl whom she introduced as her younger daughter, Wenonah. "Let's make sure that she and your Arthur get to know each other, and very soon," Georgia said. Adella nodded and readily agreed.

In the corner, their New Orleans hostess Sylvanie Williams seemed to be formulating some shrewd strategy with Ida B. Wells-Barnett when Cora Calhoun Horne walked in carrying a gorgeous, honey-colored infant in her arms. She said, "This is my granddaughter Lena, named for my sister. I'm worried that she'll get into trouble in the wicked city and want to send her to your brother Henry so that she can grow up in peaceful Fort Valley, Georgia."

"Of course, Cora," Adella replied. "And look, Henry's just arrived! I'm sure he'll take care of Lena. Our grandmother used to warn that 'good looks can be a curse for a colored girl.'"

Several trustees had come over from their meeting. Theodore Roosevelt split away from the group and boomed, "Are you ready to explore the Rio da Dúvida with me, Mrs. Logan?" His resemblance to her husband still startled Adella; but she'd navigated her own Rivers of Doubt for so long that she didn't want to undertake another such adventure, so she gingerly shook her aching head and said, "I'm flattered, Mr. President, but no thank you."

A mighty quartet stood by the window: Susan B. Anthony, Sojourner Truth, and Frederick Douglass were talking with George Washington Carver, who excused himself and stutter-stepped over to Adella's bedside. "I'm sketching out a double portrait for a new mural," he confided. "It'll depict Mr. Washington, our mighty fallen oak, standing next to you, my perfect, exquisite amaryllis." But he seemed conflicted, and tears streaked his dark cheeks as he turned away.

Then Dr. Du Bois, that bantam snake in the grass, tap-danced in and across the room. He grinned and roguishly probed, "You literally interpreted the words in my 'Hither Isles' fable, didn't you, my princess?" He and Adella's brother Henry embraced, but their cousin Neppie Hunt scowled and scolded, "She's not your princess, sir. She's my Athena and never dull."

The Doctor and Henry chorused in response: "Oh, no indeed, ma'am! She's *never* dull."

"So, Henry, my favorite Voluntary Negro," their "dubious" friend began his usual patter, "you, your sister Adella, and others of your ilk puzzle me. You look and speak like elite white southerners, so why do you choose to live as black people? I know that after first being treated respectfully, you've often been insulted and ostracized because you insist on identifying with the 'lesser race.' But thousands of others who look like you choose to do otherwise, and do so every day. Why flaunt your colored ancestry simply because white folks find it so important to know and thus to label and demean you? Don't you have the right to be judged and respected as they are, simply as human beings? Why not just sit back and bask in the grand deception?"

"I speak for Adella as well as myself, Burghardt," Henry responded, "when I say that to represent ourselves as anything but Negroes would've made us miserable, since as such, we've had opportunities to do battle on the highest plane. If we'd followed those easier routes, would we have gleaned the same satisfactions that we have because we choose to traverse life's rougher roads? Most of the Hunts have never regretted standing proudly with the race to which only one of our great-grandparents officially belonged. We understand, but pity more than we condemn those who opt to do otherwise. Joining hands to help our people advance is vital. Adella and I know that bigotry and poverty breed ignorance and shattered lives, but by trying to alleviate the travails of this generation, perhaps we can improve the opportunities for those who follow us. We walk now so that they can fly. You, my friend, understand better than most that we share so much: our history, music, lore, food, and sacred beliefs. One's world mainly is composed of family and friends, and neither of us would abandon our loved ones, cast off the bonds of affection that enfold us, or try to create new places for ourselves in an alien universe. Attempting to erase, ignore, or denounce our Negro heritage can't be the answer." That debate, Adella expected, never would be resolved. She also wondered how in years to come Henry's very light-skinned children, and her own, would negotiate those daunting ambiguities.

Arthur Bedou and Frances Benjamin Johnston gaped in the presence of so many luminaries and worthy subjects. Those dogged photographers tried to position President Roosevelt, Mayor Seth Low, and Julius Rosenwald alongside Dr. Du Bois, George Washington Carver, Susan B. Anthony, and Booker T. Washington. Yes, both the eminent suffragist and the Great Accommodator—the Wizard of Tuskegee—were there as well.

"Did I see Sojourner Truth and Frederick Douglass pass through a few minutes ago?" the trouser-clad "Frank" Johnston asked as she gently massaged Adella's neck and shoulders.

Mr. Bedou clapped his hands, trying to command everyone's attention, and said, "Please, friends, let Miss Johnston and me take just one photograph of all of you together. You don't even need to smile, but this is historic and must be preserved. Negro history as American history! Negro history *is* American history!"

Led by Capt. Frank Drye, Tuskegee Institute's smartly uniformed band marched through again. Then Mrs. Booker T. Washington lurched in, struggling to keep time with the unrelenting cadence. Her face was flushed, her stocky figure draped in deep-red widow's weeds, and she preened in her bejeweled fool's gold crown. "The first two imposter queens passed away decades ago, and now our mighty and irreplaceable leader is gone too. But long live the Dowager Queen Margaret!" she crowed. "Step aside, Mr. Logan, and step lively, Major Moton, you'll soon become Tuskegee's new black prince, but not our king. And you and your wife must *never* try to oust me from my palace," she warned, then reeled across the room and out the door.

Patty Winston had returned to the bedside, where she stood next to her adopted daughter, Della Winston Dwyer. Adella whispered, "Just ignore the red queen. She's far too loud in so many ways. And please promise me, my dear friend, that you'll burn the rest of my diaries."

Patty nodded and squeezed Adella's hand as her wayward nephew Ethan Bullock skulked in. He sidled over to his half sister Della and snaked his arm around her hips. She shrank away as he fondled her buttocks. Patty Winston watched silently for a minute, then drew a tiny Philadelphia Derringer from her purse and pressed its nose into Ethan's ear. Adella heard a soft pop-pop and saw his jaw go slack and his momentary expression of disbelief as buckets of blood and "gray matter" splattered the room. As her visitors gaped, Ethan's knees buckled, and he slowly sank onto the chilly, gray-green linoleum in a wrinkled heap of well-tailored clothes.

Following that preposterous to-do, the band's metronomic, bass-drum-driven, seventy-two-beats-per-minute pulse beat gradually decelerated, then faded into silence.

"What a Strange Thing Is 'Race,' and Family, Stranger Still"

I INHERITED ADELLA HUNT LOGAN'S stories, or at least the right to tell them, because my father, Arthur Courtney Logan, was her last-born baby. My paternal grandmother was forty-six years old when she learned that she was pregnant—yet again. With only one kidney, her health was tenuous. She was ill, frightened, and depressed, and she agonized about the impact that another child would make on the family's finances and her own well-being. If she even survived. Yes, my father was the one whom, I know from reading Adella's letters, she *did not want*. That was the pregnancy she wished to terminate, and I think she should have been able to make that choice for herself. Her daughters, the remarkable women who helped rear me, believed that too. If their mother had been successful in that effort, however, Adella's story might never have been told, or at least it wouldn't have been told by me.

Her death was a pivotal moment in the lives of many of the people around her. In mid-1915, Dr. John Kenney had hired Nella Larsen as John Andrew Hospital's new head nurse, and when Adella "went crazy" that September, Miss Larsen oversaw her care. Over time she intermittently pursued that profession but also became a literary luminary of the Harlem Renaissance. Like Adella Hunt Logan herself, Clare Landry, the heroine of *Passing*, Nella Larsen's aptly titled novel, is a light-skinned African American who looks white. Larsen wrote this about her protagonist's tragic demise: "Clare stood at the window. . . . One moment she'd been there. The next she was gone." Had she "deliberately leaned backward? It was an accident, a terrible accident."

I later learned that the circumstances surrounding Adella's death so outraged her son Paul, who was only sixteen at the time, that he'd challenged in court (though unsuccessfully so) his father's testamentary spousal right to serve as his wife's executor. Less than two years after Adella's own "terrible accident," her daughter (my aunt) Ruth Logan married Dr. Eugene Percy Roberts. They moved into an elegant Harlem brownstone, which later was my second home.

For a long time, Adella's children didn't want much to do with their father because they'd heard and reluctantly believed that he'd been involved in a romance that prompted their already-vulnerable mother to take her life. When Warren Logan married the woman in question, in part substantiating the prevalent scuttlebutt, it seemed impossible for the younger generation to forgive that apparent transgression. Warren soon sent his youngest child, Arthur, north to live with Ruth after he reportedly threatened to split open his stepbrother's skull with a toy hatchet.

From my childhood, I remember rare visits from my punctilious grandfather, born into slavery, who served for half a century as Tuskegee's treasurer. He lived into his late eighties and continued coming to New York City to attend the institute's annual trustees meetings. Only after refusing for two decades did his daughters finally let him bring his second wife into their homes.

I've re-created Adella's story from dry accounts and both incontrovertible and notably tall tales. I've culled information from census, court, school, and church records, journals and other archives, books our family read, music we listened to, games we played, food we prepared and shared, and the people whom my elders loved, admired, and honored, or disdained and mistrusted. I also have a striking oil portrait of a dark-haired woman, who could almost be one of John Singer Sargent's subjects. But no, it's Adella Hunt Logan, painted by a contemporaneous African American artist named William E. Scott. It now hangs on my apartment's entry wall, whence she watches over me.

On shelves and in drawers, files, and cabinets, I've stashed photo-

graphs, letters, silver spoons and porringers, baby cups, and more. Learning about and using such treasures suffused my childhood, as did my antecedents' wisdom, opinions, sorrows, and joys.

In time, I began teaching and writing history, and immersed myself
in the primary and secondary sources that reference both the celebrated
and anonymous players who populated my grandmother's world. I ventured
across various landscapes, neighborhoods, and cemeteries and explored
the halls, chambers, and galleries of the old southern courthouses, schools,
hospitals, and residences that I describe here. I visited the Logans' house
at Tuskegee Institute that survived into the early twenty-first century. It was
the home nearest to The Oaks, the stately mansion that's now a museum
that memorializes Booker T. Washington's extraordinary life and legacy.

Much of the Hunts' old acreage in Hancock County, Georgia, lies
beneath the surface of a manmade lake, but most enthralling for me was
Sparta's magnificent Pomegranate Hall, which I explored several times before its deranged owner burned it almost to the ground, along with its resident ghosts, who surely included my antecedents: Nathan Sayre, and Susan
and Mariah Hunt.

In search of Adella, I telephoned, exchanged letters and emails, formally interviewed, and casually chatted with scores of relatives, friends, and
virtual strangers who'd crossed paths with the Hunts and Logans over many
years. Their words, wisdom, and rumors enrich my stew.

I've conflated various characters, conjured up a few others, and sometimes altered names to avoid confusion or duplication and especially to protect the innocent. While "Cherie Rideaux's" courage in the face of repeated
authoritarian sexual coercion, for instance, is well documented, that wasn't
her real name. I created dialogue, reconfigured or eliminated many incidents,
or combined, paraphrased, and edited myriad other very real letters, essays,
and articles, as I tapped into their meaning, intent, syntax, and verbal energy.

I've also made up several incidents and compacted others. I've done
so, however, to clarify the story and never to obfuscate the overall and underlying truths as they pertain to my family. I'd not presume to do that if
I were reconstructing and recounting someone else's story but believe that
it's legitimate in telling my own.

Four years after her crusading "black" suffragist mother died, Ruth Logan Roberts celebrated the ratification of the Nineteenth Amendment, which assured women's right to vote. She lived with her physician husband in that awesome New York home, where she held political and cultural salons in the storied era when Harlem was in vogue and for decades thereafter.

In her big kitchen, Ruth taught me, her niece (but only child), to make "Tuskegee pound cake" and how to roll marbles of yeast dough in melted butter and place three in each muffin tin for fancy cloverleaf yeast rolls for fancy Sunday dinners. But I still chow down on the pigs' feet, black-eyed peas and rice, collards, and cornbread that constituted the family's New Year's feasts and conjure up Ruth's apple-onion-sausage-pecan Christmas stuffing and summer succotash.

During my early years, my aunt Louise, a stalwart educator called Polly, came twice a week to her brother Arthur and sister-in-law Wenonah's apartment to read to and then with me. I heard—but not from Polly, because the story was too agonizing for her to retell—that when she was twelve, she'd seen her mother, with her long, black skirt a parachute, sail past her classroom window at Tuskegee Institute. No one ever knew for certain if Adella Hunt Logan jumped, fell, or tried to fly away.

For some time, Myra Adele, often called My 'Del, the Logans' youngest girl, who was both brilliant and beautiful, as was her mother ("a true beauty who hailed from Sparta, Georgia," one source described her), wanted to be a concert pianist. She was certainly talented and accomplished enough to do so, although she ultimately pursued a very different profession. Myra often played beautifully for me on one of the family's Steinway baby grand pianos.

Despite the disbelief and taunts Myra faced when she revealed her race to white people, as well as the sexual harassment she endured, she completed many years of medical training and became a surgeon, who, I learned, but not from her, was the first of her sex *ever* to perform open-heart surgery. She also was the only married woman whom I remember from childhood who used her "maiden" name and, more meaningful to me, drove a car when her spouse didn't.

For one of my early Christmases, Myra and her artist husband, Charles

"Spinky" Alston, gave me a pedigreed puppy bred by Ralph Ellison, a family friend and author of the epic novel *Invisible Man,* which pseudonymously evokes Booker T. Washington and Tuskegee Institute. "Spinky" created book and magazine covers and other illustrations featuring Sojourner Truth, Booker T. Washington, Frederick Douglass, George Washington Carver, W. E. B. Du Bois, and other champions of the race, and he sculpted the noble bust of Rev. Martin Luther King Jr., another friend of the Logans, which President Barack Obama first displayed in his Oval Office.

I know that Adella escorted her daughter Ruth to college in Boston in September 1909 but only have speculated that she went from there to nearby Worcester to hear Sigmund Freud's landmark lectures at Clark University, then laid flowers on Frederick Douglass's and Susan B. Anthony's graves in Rochester, New York—as the latter's spiritual feminist heirs still do. On one occasion, however, Myra told me that Dr. Freud's methods and teachings so motivated her that (prior to entering medical school) she'd earned a graduate degree in psychology.

Before most women could vote, Adella, who'd grown up in a house built by slaves, exhorted readers of her political essays to reexamine the U.S. Constitution every year—as we heard eloquently stated during the 2016 presidential campaign. More than a century ago, my grandmother also urged her friends to march for universal suffrage in Washington, D.C. I'm certain that she and her daughters, who protested all manifestations of racial discrimination and supported women's reproductive rights, would have joined the massive peaceful demonstrations in our capital city and elsewhere throughout the country more than a hundred years later.

In 1895 in Atlanta, and at rallies Adella organized in Tuskegee, she wore white to protest women's denial of political empowerment, as did Brooklyn's African American congressional representative Shirley Chisholm when she ran for president in 1972 and sixty-six Democratic congresswomen (with many more to come) did again in 2017 to signify that their voices would not be silenced. Reconstruction's Fifteenth Amendment supposedly guaranteed all male citizens the right to vote, but only in 1965 did the federal Voting Rights Act do very much to assure southern black women's suffrage. I cringe at the venal voter suppression efforts that once again threaten those hard-won rights but also think of how exhilarated Adella would have been to help elect an African American, or any woman, to her country's highest offices. In her children's eyes and mine too, few civic sins top failing to vote.

Here's an old "race story" that my devilishly handsome, pale-skinned, green-eyed father told me. Early in World War II, and in the face of escalating civil protests against Jim Crow, he went to an enlistment station to sign up for his country's segregated armed forces and informed the conscription officer that he was an African American physician. "Then we can't enlist you, Dr. Logan," the dumbfounded man stammered. "Since you're eight years out of medical school, military regulations require that we assign you the rank of captain. But you tell me you're a colored man, so we can't do that, because if you held that rank, we'd have to give you command over a number of less senior white doctors." How shocking is that?

My father also introduced me to the quixotic proposal I've imagined Adella suggesting to a tablemate at the Battle Creek Sanitarium, where Booker T. Washington had exiled her to "cure" her mental distress after she'd set a fire (yes, my grandmother, the deranged arsonist, really did that!) in Tuskegee's administration building. Her son Arthur (tongue in cheek?) suggested that for several generations, all supposedly white Americans should be required to have children only with Negroes, and vice versa. After that mandated foray into "interbreeding," our country would have no more "black" people and no more "white" ones; then we could join hands to eliminate racial prejudices, discrimination, and the resultant social and economic disparities. Perhaps, my usually sanguine father speculated, a "new race" would improve on its inbred predecessors.

And what of my uncle Paul Logan, who came once a year from "way out west" to see his siblings in New York City? He'd graduated from Pennsylvania's "colored" Lincoln University, then earned a master's degree in forestry from Cornell, sponsored by his godmother, who lived nearby. While there, Paul was recruited by, joined, and then worked for thirty years with the United States Forestry Service, where he never spoke the revealing words "I am a Negro." But perhaps that was understandable in his green, but all-white, world of tall trees, conservancy, and fire prevention.

Two generations later, much of the world heard my daughter, Elizabeth Alexander, deliver her poem "Praise Song for the Day" at President
Barack Obama's first inaugural, but I believe her most insightful work illu-
minates family and race. This is how she retells Paul Logan's story:

> Sometimes I think about Great-Uncle Paul who left Tuskegee,
> Alabama to become a forester in Oregon and in so doing
> became fundamentally white for the rest of his life, except
> when he traveled without his white wife to visit his siblings—
> now in New York, now in Harlem, USA—just as pale-skinned,
> as straight-haired, as blue-eyed as Paul, and black.

He did, after all, move to Oregon, where Negroes couldn't legally reside until after 1926.

I spoke to my uncle Paul's widow only once, and on the telephone, so
she didn't see my tan skin and curly hair. Responding to my queries more
graciously than I deserved, she told me that her late husband had burned
his family memorabilia. Yes, he'd deliberately incinerated all of his ancestral
legacies. The only incident about his mother that Paul ever shared with his
wife, she added, was that President Theodore Roosevelt had attended her
funeral. What a story! And surely a true one, because T.R. definitely was in
Tuskegee the days right after Adella died.

My great uncle—Adella's brother and W. E. B. Du Bois's bosom
buddy—the NAACP's Spingarn medalist Henry Hunt, was as white looking but black thinking as his favorite sister. And yes, he really did help to
rear Lena Horne in bucolic (but deeply segregated) Fort Valley, Georgia. In
1935, Franklin Delano Roosevelt summoned Henry to join the "Black Cabinet" in Washington, D.C., where he died three years later. In an essay titled
"The Significance of Henry Hunt," "the Doctor," whom I remember visiting our apartment during my years growing up in "Harlem, USA" and whom
my relatives did indeed jokingly call "Dr. Dubious," celebrated his great
pal's life and achievements by rhetorically asking, "Why, if only one of his
eight great-grandparents was black, did Henry Hunt identify himself as a
Negro, when the easier route would be to become the white man that his

appearance proclaimed?" Dr. Du Bois referred to his recently deceased compadre as a "Voluntary Negro." I've recycled and paraphrased that appellation, those thoughts, and Dr. Du Bois's fitting eulogy for Henry Hunt.

I think too of my great-aunt Sarah Hunt, who had that legendary hip-length hair. I heard whispers about her thwarted romance with George Washington Carver, and as have many others, I came to believe that " 'Fess" Carver rejected her because he was gay—though no one used the word with that meaning in those years and rarely spoke of such "perversions" at all. But Sarah's beloved motivated her brother Tommy to pursue a career as an agricultural educator. Thomas F. Hunt taught for decades as a specialist in arboreal propagation for the University of California in Berkeley, where his employers, coworkers, friends, and even, I suspect, his wife and their Berkeley-educated sons (who, though they presented themselves as Caucasian, looked "blacker" than their black-identified Hunt and Logan cousins) never knew that he was anything but the white man he appeared to be—although by "becoming white," Tommy severed virtually all ties to his siblings. Professor Carver taught and guided Thomas Hunt into that career. He encouraged my uncle Paul Logan to enter the world of sustainable forestry, welcomed Myra and Arthur to his laboratory, and inspired both of them to become physicians. But he also broke Sarah's heart.

The Logans remained devoted to G. W. Carver. In the early 1940s, my father and aunts subwayed to midtown Manhattan to see the visiting scientist, who'd been both their teacher and dear "Uncle 'Fess," and they showed me their commemorative half dollars that featured Carver's and B. T. Washington's profiles. My family had mixed feelings about Mr. Washington but rolled their eyes, shook their heads, and called his widow, Margaret, "a very difficult woman." R. R. Moton, who assumed Tuskegee's principalship, never did try to oust Mrs. Washington from The Oaks.

Through decades of education combined with considerable mother wit, Adella's children became wise and very adept at their professions. They also loved books, food, music, and cerebral games and understood and tapped into the power of words, as had their mother. But sometimes my aunts cussed like troopers, and as their newly "liberated" lives allowed, they drank hard liquor and smoked as much as the men in their circle did. Then they died too soon from lung cancer and emphysema. And at sixty-four, my father—like his mother—jumped or fell to his death.

For all of them, "the race" and our struggles for empowerment remained in the forefront. With dollars, energy, and brainpower, they supported the NAACP, National Urban League, Southern Christian Leadership Conference, League of Women Voters, Planned Parenthood, and other organizations that fought for equality and justice and to protect and expand human rights. They especially deplored the ways that public policies, from slavery through Jim Crow, voter repression, and other legal and illegal atrocities, threatened African American lives and well-being.

Most of the people whom the physicians in my family treated were little known, but Dr. E. P. Roberts and his "virtual children" (E. P. was old enough to be their father), Myra Adele Logan and Arthur Courtney Logan, also cared for a number of their community's luminaries. In some circles, however, they were excoriated as "pinkos" during the Red Scare 1950s, when they became pioneers in group medical care by assuming leadership roles in the New York Health Insurance Plan's Upper Manhattan Medical Group, a new HMO that my father's longtime patient and friend Edward "Duke" Ellington later immortalized in his composition titled "U.M.M.G." Seventy years after Adella Hunt Logan died, when I began seeking and reading her words in earnest, I found that she too had envisioned and advocated basic health care for all.

I was everyone's daughter, so I acquired both her children's strong convictions and their memorabilia, among them a pierced gold French coin dated 1850, a hinged jewel box filled with family wedding rings, a teaspoon with "Adella" etched in the bowl, her small, silver anniversary coffee service, a crewel-covered foot stool made in Tuskegee's carpentry shop, a china cocoa cup adorned with her name glazed in gold leaf on its side, and also the compelling portrait.

To reconstruct Adella's story I found, read, edited, and excerpted her writings on health, inheritance, race, governance, suffrage, and more. Her quest for empowerment, especially for women and racial minorities, suffused her life. I've included but paraphrased much of her correspondence with Emily Howland (whom I renamed Patty Winston because I merged several entities to create her composite character), the derisive letter from

Susan B. Anthony, and Booker T. Washington's obsequious 1915 entreaty to John Kellogg at the Battle Creek Sanitarium in which he insisted that Adella would readily don a mask of whiteness in her time of profound emotional distress so as not to offend the racial sensibilities of Dr. Kellogg's white patients.

I still remember my first trip to Tuskegee when I was fifteen. My mother, Wenonah Bond Logan (the daughter of Adella's friend the novice suffragist Georgia Stewart Bond, who shared her own stories, because during my childhood she lived with us in New York), and I sojourned at Dorothy Hall, the institute's longtime guest house where even "privileged Negroes" like us were not accommodated for decades. I don't know when that changed, but do recall the huge hissing cockroaches (*cucarachas*) that buzzed our room and strafed me as I huddled under the bedcovers one night and vowed—yearned!—to make a speedy escape from Jim Crow Alabama and its menacing vermin.

But I was warmly welcomed there and also in Hancock County, Georgia, as a long-lost cousin. I climbed to the top floor of the building at Tuskegee Institute from which Adella flew, fell, or jumped. And in the intimate "family" cemetery, I paid silent tribute at the cluster of gravestones memorializing B. T. Washington and his three wives, George Washington Carver, Adella and Warren Logan, their son Warren Junior, and their daughters Louise and Myra and Myra's husband, as well as markers that commemorate my uncles and an aunt who died too young and whom I therefore never knew. I also observed with righteous aversion the Confederate monument (which now has been sensibly relocated to a private cemetery), a tribute to the secessionist Old South, that for a century loomed over the nearby town square, as well as the comparable one in Sparta.

Adella's life was unlike any other I've encountered, and I was challenged to find, understand, and evoke the early generations of Sayres, Hunts, and Logans but especially my paternal grandmother, who still speaks to me in a voice as familiar as that of an old friend. Bit by bit, story by story, I came to understand how she and her legacy dominated my father's and his siblings' lives. Would they have appreciated the anagram I crafted for their mother that characterizes her as Athena? And would Adella have smiled and thanked me too? I hope so.

I have no solid proof that Adella had the peerless relationship I've detailed with her Granny Susan, but it seems likely. I also wonder whether Susan Hunt's reported proficiency as a healer might have skipped two generations, then inspired her great-grandchildren Arthur and Myra Logan to become physicians. It's quite possible, as I propose here, that Adella was both bullied and motivated by a white cousin, because she explicitly acknowledged such an unnamed relative as a critically important teacher in her early life. She could have read her grandfather Sayre's diaries too and kept one of her own. I don't know that for sure but like to think that she did.

In the decades after Nella Larsen wrote *Passing*, African American women spoke to us eloquently through the novels of Anne Petry, Toni Morrison, Alice Walker, Gloria Naylor, and others. But those are fictive accounts of endurance and survival—or not. Adella's story, by contrast, situates a remarkable, certainly flawed, but very real "black" heroine in the center of an intricate, female-crafted quilt that unfolds and stretches over slavery and its violent termination. Here I've detailed her struggles to survive across the ensuing half century in the Jim Crow South.

My collage includes healers, hero(in)es, haters, scoundrels, teachers, students, reformers, farmers, and presidents. And I've assessed the ideological power struggle, perhaps the most iconic *ever* in our community, between Booker T. Washington and W. E. B. Du Bois, as well as the related (and still unfinished) struggles for women's empowerment personified here by Sojourner Truth, Ida B. Wells-Barnett, Susan B. Anthony, and especially Adella Hunt Logan.

My daughter, Elizabeth Alexander, has taken some of these stories and reconfigured them with poetic luster. One of her works includes the phrase I use to reference Adella's belief that "learning is the only true religion." Another concerns false friends at Tuskegee who gossiped about how she ate chalk (kaolin clay or "unaker") during her many pregnancies to make her babies' skin white. Elizabeth's previously quoted poem titled "Race," concludes,

> What a strange thing is "race," and family, stranger still.
> Here a poem tells a story, a story about race.

I've taken a few liberties with the details yet believe that I've fully respected the demands of both my academic profession and my heritage as I listened to and learned from what family members, associates, even strangers wanted me to hear and, I think, to repeat. I've tossed, stirred, and blended together hard facts with the gifts of love, lore, and imagination.

"But is it true?" you still might ask. Indeed so, although truth like beauty lies in the eye of the beholder, and Adella Hunt Logan's story may have other beholders who observe the same people, places, and events from their own perspectives and draw different conclusions. This is my family memoir, and I encourage them to share their stories as well.

Rationale, Methods, Sources, and Notes

This memoir is grounded in stories that the elders shared as I was growing up and the many interviews (mostly chats and unrecorded conversations) that I conducted over the ensuing decades. That backlog of oral history supplies many of the book's underpinnings and details.

As to what's "true" and what's not, I flatly disagree with the hogwash that unscrupulous pundits recently have been feeding us about that subject. Of course, there are truths and lies! But profoundly frustrating for diligent historians, we sometimes find ourselves faced with bottomless chasms, or seemingly impenetrable walls, when we realize that we've observed or stumbled onto deeper truths than conventional methodology and traditional sources can thoroughly document. There's little question that these blockages and lacunae especially plague us when we try to document the lives of women, people of color, those with limited literacy, and the otherwise disempowered and disenfranchised whose voices have been habitually, deliberately silenced.

Some occurrences that I stumbled over seem so incredible that they need a compelling backstory to explain them. I've supplied many of them and use these notes to explain when, where, why, and how I did so. While stirring in a healthy dash of literary imagination, I provide sources, details, and contextualization about the places and events I describe and the characters I portray. This should not, however, be construed as either a comprehensive bibliography or a roundup of standard academic citations.

In 1892, Anna Julia Cooper, one of my most revered African American foremothers, wrote, "What is needed, perhaps, to reverse the picture of the lordly man slaying the lion, is for the lion to turn painter." So, not to be thwarted in my efforts to present Adella Hunt Logan and her story in its complex entirety, this lioness has "turned painter."

I've struggled throughout over the racial designations I use. "Negro" and "colored" now feel dated, but "black" or "African American" sometimes seem anachronistic when referencing the nineteenth and early twentieth century. I always capitalize "Negro" if I'm using it myself and when it appears as such in an original source. Otherwise, I've tried to assess when, whether, and why I imagine a particular person would have conceived the word, using an upper- or lower-case *N*. The correspondence and published writings I pored over also have given me insights into how I think my antecedents' and their colleagues' conversations and voices sounded.

In reference to the title, I explain the phrase "Princess of the Hither Isles" in chapter 15 and its notes. The character "Jim Crow" originated in the 1830s as the onstage persona of a wily white actor who performed in blackface. By the late nineteenth century, it came to personify the segregationist initiatives that legitimized a brutal racial caste system in the U.S. South.

Introduction

My article "How I Discovered My Grandmother . . . and the Truth about Black Women and the Suffrage Movement" first was published by *Ms.*, in November 1983, and reprinted in Darlene Clark Hine, ed., *Black Women in American History*, vol. 1 (Brooklyn, NY: Carlson, 1990). My maternal aunt, Caroline Bond Day, wrote *A Study of Some Negro-White Families in the United States* (Cambridge, MA: Peabody Museum of Harvard University, 1932), and the Peabody Museum is the repository for the correspondence, charts, photos, and hair samples she amassed for that innovative and controversial anthropological study while she was an undergraduate and then a graduate student at Radcliffe College. She conducted her research at Harvard University under the tutelage of Earnest Hooton, one of the country's leading anthropologists, though not Harvard but Radcliffe (its women's college) granted her degrees.

Certainly, "scientific racism" has a long, tawdry, and destructive history. Such theories have been shamefully used for political, social, and economic advantage. I flatly reject any arguments about one's inherent superiority or inferiority that his or her supposed racial "genetic makeup" might suggest.

My earlier books that touch on or recount my heritage are *Ambiguous Lives: Free Women of Color in Rural Georgia, 1789–1879* (Fayetteville: University of Arkansas Press, 1991) and *Homelands and Waterways: The American Journey of the Bond Family, 1846–1946* (New York: Pantheon Books, 1999). As I accumulated new and sometimes differing information, I've altered a few dates and names from those as I previously recorded them. I also included some family stories in my essay about the intertwined legacies of racism and sexism in "She's No Lady; She's a Nigger: Abuses, Stereotypes, and Power from the Middle Passage to Capitol (and Anita) Hill," in *Race, Gender, and Power in America: The Legacy of the Hill-Thomas Hearings,* ed. Anita Faye Hill and Emma Coleman Jordan (New York: Oxford University Press, 1995).

Also see Terrence D. Smith and Sally J. Zepeda, "Adella Hunt Logan, 1863–

1915: Educator, Woman's Suffrage Leader, Confidant of Booker T. Washington," in *The Varieties of Women's Experiences: Portraits of Southern Women's Experiences in the Post–Civil War Century*, edited by Larry Eugene Rivers and Canter Brown Jr. (Gainesville: University Press of Florida, 2009).

I'm indebted to Daria Willis-Joseph for her PhD dissertation, "Adella Hunt Logan: Educator, Mother, Wife and Suffragist" (Florida A&M University, 2007). Her insights into Adella's life show impressive sensitivity and insightfulness. She shared with me her strong conviction that Adella had kept a diary. At first, she thought I was keeping it from her. I wasn't, but she convinced me about the existence of such a personal journal, which I've incorporated here to help me tell Adella's story.

For her portrait, see my notes for the afterword.

1. The People Who Can Fly

My favorite retelling of this traditional story appears in Virginia Hamilton, *The People Can Fly: Black Folktales* (New York: Dragonfly Books, 2004). Similar versions appear in Native American and African American lore. It evokes Christian theology, intergenerational family ties, and potential empowerment of the oppressed or silenced. It also suggests flight as a metaphor for liberation and homecoming.

2. Susan's Stories

Nothing about the ways by which Susan Hunt negotiated her position in Nathan Sayre's Georgia household discounts the malevolence of the slave society in which her family lived. In a *New York Times* op-ed on June 16, 2018, Annette Gordon-Reed, who brilliantly chronicled the somewhat analogous Jefferson-Hemings saga, wrote, "People tell me they think it is ridiculous that Sally Hemings, Thomas Jefferson and their children could be a true family, . . . [but] they had a life together, however bizarre that life may appear to us today." Neither that story nor my less familiar account of the Sayre-Hunts, to use Gordon-Reed's further words, "drains a single drop from the evil of slavery." One significant difference from Sally Hemings's experience, however, is that Susan Hunt was a rare *free* woman of color in the antebellum South—no matter how much her sex and her mixed racial heritage might have constricted that freedom. Regardless of the intimacy and reported affection in the Jefferson-Hemings relationship, slavery was always an intrinsically coercive institution, and men, then and now, also have societally reinforced powers that are often denied to women. No one should be restrained in or forced into any relationship (no matter how widely accepted or "normalized") that is characterized by institutional, physical, legal, or economic dependency. Only recently have our laws acknowledged that sexual acts with any imprisoned or otherwise restrained person *never* can be consensual or that rape within a legally sanctioned marital relationship is even possible. Economic and gender hierarchies and power inequities remain deeply entrenched in our country and around the world.

In addition to Adella's imagined conversations with her grandmother Susan, I created Nathan Sayre's diary as a storytelling device, but lots of hard data document his career, family and home, books, and other possessions, especially as they're revealed in his will.

A number of (white) members of the Daughters of the American Revolution trace their lineage and membership documentation back to Virginia's Capt. Judkins Hunt. Until fairly recently, that organization had no African American members at all. In recent decades, however, it has admitted a few new members who can trace their lineage back to black men who fought in that war, but I've been unable to ascertain if it now accepts candidates of color whose lineage is not traced through documented marriages but rather through "illegitimate" conjugal relationships between white men and African American women, enslaved or not.

In recent years, the historical information on Hancock County posted online by Eileen McAdams has been extremely helpful. The most definitive published sources are Forrest Shivers, *The Land Between: A History of Hancock County, Georgia, to 1940* (Spartanburg, SC: Reprint Company, 1990); John Rozier, *Black Boss: Political Revolution in a Georgia County* (Athens: University of Georgia Press, 1982); and Elizabeth Wiley Smith, *History of Hancock County* (Washington, GA: Wilkes, 1974). Smith asserts that the white Hunt family had five hundred slaves. That's an overstatement, but according to the 1860 U.S. Census, and according to law, the Hunt brothers and their spouses and children altogether claimed to own more than two hundred black people. In lieu of "slaves," I try to use the words "enslaved" or "held in bondage," in my attempt to clarify that it was an enforced condition and never fully defined who those individuals were.

Ira Berlin's *Slaves without Masters: The Free Negro in the Antebellum South* (New York: Oxford University Press, 1975) remains the classic on nonenslaved African Americans. Also see "Free Black Women in the Antebellum South," by Virginia Gould and me, in *Black Women in America: An Historical Encyclopedia*, ed. Darlene Clark Hine, Elsa Barkley Brown, and Rosalyn Terborg-Penn (Brooklyn, NY: Carlson, 1993).

Much (in addition to Caroline Bond Day's seminal study) has been written about "race mixing" in our country. Melville J. Herskovitz, *The American Negro: A Study in Racial Crossing* (New York: Knopf, 1928), is another valuable classic, and Joel Williamson's *New People: Miscegenation and Mulattoes in the United States* (New York: Free Press, 1980) adds to the discussion. More recently, Daniel J. Sharfstein's *The Invisible Line: Three American Families and the Secret Journey from Black to White* (New York: Penguin, 2011) is a fine contribution. For triracial history, see especially Charles M. Hudson, ed., *Red, White and Black: A Symposium on Indians in the Old South* (Athens: University of Georgia Press, 1971); and Arica L. Coleman, *That the Blood Stay Pure: African Americans, Native Americans and the Predicament of Race and Identity in Virginia* (Bloomington: Indiana University Press, 2013).

The material that recently has become available online about Cherokee foods, medical practices, pharmaceuticals, and the lore that surrounds them is legion, and the legend of the Raven Mocker appears more than any other. Cultural historians, anthropologists, and folklorists have noted many similarities in the stories told by eastern Native Americans and those of African Americans. The word "unaker," as the Cherokees designated white clay, may be a distortion of a Native American one by early English people in this country who hoped to use it in making fine pottery.

The names of Cherokee Mariah Lily, as Mariah Hunt was called, and her sister, Sue Rose, appear in the Mount Zion Presbyterian Church's baptismal records at the Georgia Department of Archives and History (GDAH) in Atlanta. In Hancock County's courthouse, I accessed Nathan Sayre's and J. M. Hunt's wills and the supplemental materials that provide documentation of Sayre as an early investor in the Georgia Railroad and Banking Company. After J. M. Hunt died, that stock appeared among his assets.

The progenitor's name passed down in the Hunt family was Oscar. But the similar one Osborne means "bear." I wanted to suggest that Susan Hunt believed that after the disappearance of her enslaved father, he was transformed into the constellation Ursa Major. In addition to Oscar, several Alexanders, Edwards, and Isaacs appear among the "colored" Hunts. I refer to the Hunt brothers as A, E, I, and O, and think "Li'l Susie" was Sue Rose Hunt's only daughter. During Reconstruction, the Hunts founded, owned, and operated the funeral home that served Hancock County's African American community until World War I. As part of the Great Migration north, seeking better opportunities and hoping to escape the worst of Jim Crow, many of the Hunts moved to Chester, Pennsylvania, where the family business still maintains its services.

Several legends concern the ancestral "curse" supposedly revealed by irises of different colors, *heterochromia iridum* (though it's not a genetic verity that it occurs only among people of mixed racial ancestry), and the rituals that are meant to ward it off. I, however, also use this rare aberration as a metaphor for people of mixed racial heritage. My cousin Wanda Hunt McLean alerted me to the appearance of that phenomenon in the Hunt family.

The egregious treatment of enslaved girls such as "Tilly" by white women who were inherently complicit in perpetuating the "peculiar institution" should not be diminished or overlooked. For thorough examinations and analyses of them, see Catherine Clinton, *The Plantation Mistress: Women's World in the Old South* (New York: Pantheon, 1982); and Elizabeth Fox-Genovese, *Within the Plantation Household: Black and White Women of the Old South* (Chapel Hill: University of North Carolina Press, 1988), among a number of other studies.

I made up the names Fortitude and Nancy's Fancy (and, in chapter 5, Flint-lock), although most "big houses" in the region did have such appellations. I also searched in vain for tangible remnants of the Hunts' early homes. Some of them now lie under water in a manmade Hancock County lake, and as indicated in chapter 7, others burned down. A century later, however, I visited several of the extant cottages on Hunts' Hill that were built by African Americans in the late 1800s.

For Nathan Sayre's legislative career and other aspects of early Georgia law, see especially Oliver H. Prince's multivolume *Digest of the Laws of the State of Georgia . . . to 1837* (Athens, GA: Prince, 1800–1837).

Information about and photographs of Pomegranate Hall now appear on many websites and in books, notably, John Linley's *The Architecture of Middle Georgia: The Oconee Region* (Athens: University of Georgia Press, 1972). Mary Moragné's diary, *The Neglected Thread: A Journal from the Calhoun Community, 1836–1842*, ed. Delle Mullen Craven (Columbia: University of South Carolina Press, 1951), includes an account of Miss Moragné's visit with her cousin Nathan Sayre at Pomegranate Hall, descriptions of his daughters—though she never identifies them as such—and her attendance at a concert at the Sparta Female Academy where two musically talented little girls, whom she snidely called "Turkish houris," performed.

The Georgia-based artist Sterling Everett did this lovely rendering of Sparta's Pomegranate Hall and also sent me one of its last silver-plated door escutcheons. The mansion was abandoned after being gutted by fire (arson) in 2001. Only an overgrown, rotting shell now remains. I visited it several times in the 1980s and '90s, and the "secret apartment" that Judge Sayre incorporated for Susan Hunt and their children was especially intriguing. Susan's suite was decidedly less servile but nonetheless resembled the living quarters near the master's boudoir at Monticello that Thomas Jefferson designated for his enslaved consort, Sally Hemings.

I've slightly reconfigured the biographies of Nathan Sayre's siblings.

Judge Sayre made out his will shortly before his 1850 trip to Europe. The Steinweg family "Americanized" the company's name to Steinway when they moved their operations to the United States a few years later. I have the gold French coin (it hangs on my daughter's charm bracelet), dated that year, and assume the Judge brought it home from his overseas travels.

The only known photographs of Judge Sayre and his daughter Mariah Hunt (I've never seen one of Susan Hunt) appear in Caroline Bond Day's *A Study of*

Some Negro-White Families in the United States. I heard a description of Mariah's sister, "Young Sue Rose" Hunt, from her great-granddaughter Romie Turner, who further told me that her father called the white James Hunt Jr. "J. M." Milledgeville's Joseph Miller was the only daguerreotypist in that part of Georgia, so I assume he took the photo of Judge Nathan Sayre and perhaps one of Mariah too.

I scoured the U.S. census records (including the agricultural and slave censuses) for Hancock County, from 1790 through 1880, and Nathan Sayre did indeed oversee and certify the one in 1840, which lists neither Susan Hunt nor their children. That's not surprising, since free people of color, who occupied tenuous positions in what was meant to be a rigidly bifurcated, slave/free, black/white society, often were ignored or hidden. The names, ages, residency, places of birth, and so on for folks of any status or race in that era are helpful but often contradictory.

At the GDAH, I accessed the few microfilmed copies of the *Sparta Ishmaelite,* Hancock County's newspaper. Random issues are also available in the University of Georgia's archives.

I can't swear that Judge Nathan Sayre performed the marriage ceremony for his daughter Mariah and Henry Hunt at Pomegranate Hall, but as recently as the 1980s, African Americans in Sparta insisted to me that they'd been legally wed. Such unions, however, were unsanctioned at that time, and officiators could indeed be prosecuted and punished. The right for those of differing races to marry throughout the country was only assured by the U.S. Supreme Court in 1967, in the aptly named case of *Loving v. Virginia.*

I have one of Mariah's coin silver spoons by Milledgeville's silversmith, Otis Childs, and can pinpoint the time of its crafting and her wedding date with relative certainty. I've imagined and used the black-white-red silhouette of Susan as a metaphor for the Hunt family's triracial heritage.

Documents that accompany Nathan Sayre's will detail the posthumous auction of his estate and include a list of his books—most intriguing, Alexander Walker's *Intermarriage; or, The Mode in Which & the Causes Why Beauty, Health & Intellect Result from Certain Unions, & Deformity, Disease & Insanity from Others* (New York: J. and H. G. Langley, 1839). I've assumed that some such books were passed down in the Hunt family. A marble obelisk in Sparta's main cemetery confirms the dates and places of Sayre's birth and death.

Rev. C. P. Beman, the first president of Georgia's Oglethorpe College, delivered Judge Sayre's 1853 eulogy. Hannah Rozear, a resourceful Duke University archivist, sent me an image of the only extant copy of that sermon. For many decades, two Beman brothers and one of their sons were clergymen in Hancock County, but for reasons of clarity and simplicity, I've merged them into one character. Also, the family that intermarried several times with the white Hunts was surnamed Albright, not Alfriend. In addition to Dr. "Albright," E. M. Pendleton was the Sayres' long-time physician. I've also combined those doctors' personas.

In Sparta, I heard rumors about the Hunts' "blood ties" to the family of Alexander Hamilton Stephens, the region's most famous citizen. Although Stephens championed slavery and ballyhooed African Americans' innate inferiority, as with the Sayres and Hunts, several free people of color lived under his aegis. See my notes on him for the next chapter.

Helen Tunicliff Caterall's *Judicial Cases Concerning American Slavery and the Negro,* vol. 3, *Judicial Cases Concerning Georgia* (Washington, DC: Carnegie Institution, 1932), is an encyclopedic source for legal documentation of the struggles over slaves and slavery. Don E. Fehrenbacher's *The Dred Scott Case: Its Significance in American Law and Politics* (New York: Oxford University Press, 1978) is the most acclaimed examination of that egregious decision.

3. The Hunts' War

In various Georgia archives, I came across several sad instances when illicitly freed black people in the late antebellum era couldn't survive as such and asked to be reenslaved by former owners and also found that one of the Hunts had emancipated several "faithful slaves" in his will.

One version of Laura Alfriend's (Albright's) "incineration" during a celebration of the state's secession in a county adjacent to Hancock and her subsequent symbolic martyrdom appears in Jonathan M. Bryant's *How Curious a Land: Conflict and Change in Greene County, Georgia, 1850–1884* (Chapel Hill: University of North Carolina Press, 2014).

On Stephens, see Thomas E. Schott's *Alexander H. Stephens of Georgia: A Biography* (Baton Rouge: Louisiana State University Press, 1988). Various sources use slightly different wording for his statement about the inherent inferiority of African Americans, but it is widely credited as providing the philosophical underpinning for the eleven southern states' secession and the ensuing "War of Northern Aggression." Those sentiments ultimately outweighed Stephens's reported respect for and long friendship with Abraham Lincoln.

The January 1863 Emancipation Proclamation claimed to liberate only "people held in slavery in the rebellious states" and not those in the "loyal border states," whose continuing support the president needed. The "rebellious states," of course, considered themselves part of an autonomous country, the Confederacy, and felt no obligation to conform with that dictum.

Smallpox inoculations were performed by lay practitioners, nurses, and licensed physicians in rural and urban venues throughout the United States, starting in the early 1800s.

In October 1863, the *Milledgeville Southern Recorder* and the *Atlanta Intelli-gencer* reported the "emeute" in Hancock County. Also see J. William Harris, *Plain Folk and Gentry in a Slave Society: White Liberty and Black Slavery in Augusta's Hinterlands* (Middletown, CT: Wesleyan University Press, 1985). I have no solid proof that Jimmy Hunt and Johnny Watkins participated in that insurrection, and I've imagined Jimmy's letters. Several of the county's few but unidentified free peo-ple of color, however, were reported among the rebels, and I did find records of Georgians named James Hunt and John Watkins who enlisted with the Union forces at Vicksburg, Mississippi, late that year. Oral history also indicates that Adella's "Uncle Jimmy" ran away during the Civil War and ended up in New York City. Most of my information about "Young Sue" comes from conversations with her direct descendants, my cousins Lorin, Charity, and the late Charles Hunt.

I inherited the "daughter's birthright" diamond, given to Mariah Hunt by her husband when Adella was born. That reportedly was the jewel in Adella Hunt Logan's engagement ring mentioned in her will, which is archived in the Macon County, Alabama, courthouse. Mamie McLendon Thomas, Adella's niece, de-scribed a similar one that had belonged to her mother.

The activities and movements of Adella's father, Henry Hunt, during the Civil War are difficult to iterate with precision. He enlisted as a sergeant in mid-1861, switched units, and then, as indicated by his tombstone's inscription, ended up a captain. I've speculated that he and Rev. Atticus Haygood knew each other because they served together with Linton Stephens's Hancock Grays, the county's most renowned unit. Henry certainly was on home leave and impregnated his wife, Mariah, in the spring of 1862, because Adella was born the following February.

My account of this celebration of the Civil War's conclusion comes from George Rawick, Jan Hillegas, and Ken Lawrence, eds., *The American Slave: A Composite Autobiography,* supplement, series 1, vol. 4, *Georgia Narratives* (West-port, CT: Greenwood, 1978), as detailed in an interview with Henry Rogers, who'd been enslaved in his childhood at Judkins Hunt's plantation. The thousands of interviews that constitute the collection were conducted in the 1930s as a major project of the federal Works Progress Administration.

Rev. and later the Christian Methodist Episcopal Bishop Lucius H. Holsey was pastor for members of the Hunt family. I have relied on his *Autobiography, Ser-mons, Addresses and Essays of Lucius Henry Holsey, D.D.* (Atlanta: Franklin, 1898).

4. School Days

For background in this chapter and the next, see Edmund L. Drago, *Black Politi-cians and Reconstruction in Georgia: A Splendid Failure* (Athens: University of Georgia Press, 1992); and Jacqueline Jones, *Soldiers of Light and Love: Northern*

334 Rationale, Methods, Sources, and Notes

Teachers and Georgia Blacks, 1865–1875 (Athens: University of Georgia Press, 1982). I've conjoined the experiences of several Freedman's Bureau teachers who worked in or near Hancock County and found the letter about the Hunts' cousin Ida Watkins in the GDAH archives, incoming state legislative correspondence. The Ku Klux Klan atrocities in Hancock and its surrounding counties were very real indeed.

Adella Hunt Logan often mentioned that she'd received some early education "of a private nature," provided by a relative in Sparta. For more on that, see my notes for the afterword. At that juncture (the 1870s), Neppie Hunt was the only teacher in the Hunt family, so I assume that she was the one who tutored her precocious "colored" cousin.

All of the region's residents who bore the Alfriend (Albright) surname were related, and they claimed Pocahontas and John Rolfe among their antecedents. Wyndham Robertson's compilation *Pocahontas, Alias Matoaka, and Her Descendants through Her Marriage at Jamestown, Virginia, in April 1614 with John Rolfe, Gentleman* (Richmond, VA: Randolph and English, 1887) lists Alfriends (Albrights) and Hunts in Hancock County, Georgia, and Logans (as discussed in chapter 6) in North Carolina among those descendants.

Rowena Hunt Bracken, the daughter of Adella Hunt Logan's brother Will, shared with me Adella's admonition to her that "a lady must never let a man see her bare feet." I attribute that assertion as well as the palindromes and anagrams to Neppie Hunt's teachings.

My book *Ambiguous Lives* provides more information about Sparta's early schools for Negroes. Atlanta University's archives had the letters of recommendation for Adella's college scholarship.

5. Trains, Rains, Pedagogy, and Savagery

For Amanda Dickson, see Kent Anderson Leslie's superb *Woman of Color, Daughter of Privilege: Amanda American Dickson, 1849–1893* (Athens: University of Georgia Press, 1993).

The Edmund Asa Ware and Horace Bumstead Papers at Atlanta University's Robert Woodruff Library and Clarence A. Bacote's comprehensive *The Story of Atlanta University: A Century of Service, 1865–1965* (Atlanta: Atlanta University, 1969) provide detailed information and many stories (including the one quoted here about "Sambos" and their "cannibal sires") concerning that school during Adella Hunt's years as a student and her ongoing affiliation with it. Information in the *Bulletins and Catalogs of Atlanta University* is vital to this chapter and the next. They and many other institutional records from the late 1800s are now available online. The Sparta Academy's R. (Richard) H. Carter and Tuskegee Institute's

Rev. E. (Edgar) J. Penney are listed among the members of Atlanta University's small college class of 1875.

Most information on the Calhouns and Hornes comes from Gail Lumet Buckley, *The Hornes: An American Family* (New York: Knopf, 1986); and Buckley, *The Calhouns: From Civil War to Civil Rights with One American Family* (New York: Atlantic Monthly Press, 2016). Gail, Adella's classmate Cora Calhoun's great-granddaughter and Lena Horne's daughter, and I first met through our families as children, then became friends when we attended Radcliffe College.

W. E. B. Du Bois coined the phrase "Talented Tenth" to designate a critical leadership caste that he thought would consist of gifted, well-educated, and hard-working Negroes.

Adella definitely was one of her class's top students. Thus, she would have been among the five graduation speakers in 1881. I've re-created that talk using her ideas and words found elsewhere. The phrase "soldiers of light and love" referred to Reconstruction's white teachers from the North, as laid out in Jacqueline Jones's book (see my citations for chapter 4) of the same name. I assume that Rev. Atticus Haygood based his 1881 commencement address at Atlanta University on the chapter "Schools for Negroes," which I've paraphrased here, from his book *Our Brother in Black: His Freedom and His Future* (New York: Phillips and Hunt, 1881).

Most of my description of Albany, Georgia, comes from "Of the Black Belt," an essay in W. E. B. Du Bois's *The Souls of Black Folk* (Chicago: McClurg, 1903), which provides considerable information about Dougherty County. Since he was unfamiliar with the rural Deep South when he met Adella (although he'd spent two midteen years in Nashville, Tennessee), I believe that she steered "the Doctor" toward that county, which she knew well. The Institute of Southern Jewish Life has a substantive online entry about the immigrants of their faith who settled in Albany before the Civil War, and accounts of the Flint River's floods are legion. Frances Butler Leigh's *Ten Years on a Georgia Plantation since the War* (1883; repr., New York: Negro Universities Press, 1969) includes the story of a black Georgia child who yearned to turn white.

The most authoritative, acclaimed historical study of the white South's onerous convict lease system is Douglas A. Blackmon's *Slavery by Another Name: The Re-enslavement of Black Americans between the Civil War and World War II* (New York: Random House, 2008).

The woman whom I call Patience (Patty) Winston Bullock is a composite character but is largely based on Adella's friend and fellow suffragist Emily Howland, who became her son Paul's godmother. See, especially, Judith Colucci Breault, *The Odyssey of a Humanitarian: The World of Emily Howland, 1827–1929* (Millbrae, CA: Les Femmes, 1976). Adella's extensive correspondence with Miss Howland is included in the microfilmed Emily Howland Papers at Cornell University. I've based the "Bullocks'" backstory on similar ones about Yankees who relocated to the Reconstruction South. I often heard the "a pretty face can be a colored girl's curse" adage and analogous accounts about (fortunately) thwarted sexual assaults on members of my family.

W. C. Green continued teaching in Albany, Georgia, for many years after Adella Hunt left. Several reports mention that Atlanta University's President Ware tried to hire her in 1883.

6. The Hither Isles

I know that Adella left Albany precipitously but do not know why or the exact date in June 1883 when she arrived at Tuskegee. I've speculated that her arrival coincided with Portia Washington's birth. Ruth Ann Stewart's *Portia Washington Pittman: Booker T. Washington's Daughter* (Garden City, NY: Doubleday, 1975) is the best biography, but Roy Hill's *Booker T.'s Daughter: The Life and Times of Portia Marshall Washington Pittman* (Washington, DC: Three Continents, 1988) also deserves mention. Considering me a trusted Tuskegee "insider," Mr. Hill shared some of Portia's suspicions, as well as her family and institutional secrets.

The historiography about Booker T. Washington is legion, but it is dominated by Louis R. Harlan's *Booker T. Washington: The Making of a Black Leader, 1856-1901* and *Booker T. Washington: The Wizard of Tuskegee, 1901-1915* (New York: Oxford University Press, 1972 and 1983). The latter concludes with a capsule account of Adella Hunt Logan's tragic death. The biography itself is supplemented, in fourteen volumes, by Louis R. Harlan and Raymond W. Smock, eds., *The Booker T. Washington Papers* (Urbana: University of Illinois Press, 1972-1988). They published only a small portion of the immense collection (additional parts of which can be accessed online) from the Library of Congress's manuscript division. Unless otherwise indicated, my information here and in ensuing chapters has been culled from those sources. Several times in his biographies Harlan mentions an unidentified "neighbor's home." I've interpreted that as the Logans' residence, which was located across a wide lawn from the Washingtons'.

Also noteworthy are Samuel R. Spencer, *Booker T. Washington and the Negro's Place in American Life* (Boston: Little, Brown, 1955); Michael R. West, *The Education of Booker T. Washington* (New York: Columbia University Press, 2006); Robert Norrell, *Up from History: The Life of Booker T. Washington* (Cambridge, MA: Harvard University Press, 2009); and Raymond W. Smock, *Booker T. Washington: Black Leadership in the Age of Jim Crow* (Chicago: Ivan R. Dee, 2009).

In 1985, I visited St. Mary's County, Maryland, and saw the church where

Warren Logan taught and the sharecropper's cottage where he lived, which the 1880 U.S. Census pinpoints.

My aunts told me that their father, Warren Logan, spoke "in outline form," "using bullet points," befitting the meticulous accountant he was. They also joked about the "morning constitutionals" he took circling their porch on inclement days. Many online sites picture Gray Columns, the Varner mansion near Tuskegee Institute (now University), which is reminiscent of Pomegranate Hall. In recent years, it's become the home of the school's president in lieu of The Oaks.

Christine McKay shared with me her excellent research into Warren Logan's genealogy. In several letters and telephone calls, members of the North Carolina Smith family whose grandparents had held Pocahontas and her son, Warren, as slaves shared stories with me. Mary Watson Smith's published diaries are available on the Greensboro History Museum's website.

Archivists at the University of Virginia confirmed that Henry Clay Warren was a student there in 1856 and 1857, then abruptly left, I suspect when (and possibly because) he was charged with impregnating Pocahontas. "Poky" nonetheless thought well enough of Mr. Warren to name their son for him. He returned to Kentucky months before baby Warren, who later took the surname of his African American stepfather, Parker Logan, was born into slavery. I've used this information to imagine and reconstruct Warren Logan's letter to Adella Hunt about his conception. Apparently, Warren originally did think that Rev. Smith was his biographical father, but the white Smith family stuck with the University of Virginia story, which (since I've been able to identify the "Kentucky student" whom they specified) I now believe too. J. Stephen Catlett's fine article on Warren Logan, "From Greensboro to Tuskegee: One Life," in the *Greensboro (NC) News & Record*, February 2, 1992, was helpful too. Hampton University's archivists also provided me with documents about and photographs of my grandfather.

Robert Francis Engs's *Educating the Disfranchised and Disinherited: Samuel Chapman Armstrong and Hampton Institute, 1839–1893* (Knoxville: University of Tennessee Press, 1995) and James D. Anderson's *The Education of Blacks in the South, 1860–1935* (Chapel Hill: University of North Carolina Press, 1988) lay out the strong ties between Hampton and Tuskegee Institutes and those schools' common philosophies and methodologies. Atlanta University and Tuskegee Institute exemplified the competing ideologies about how best to educate African Americans in the late nineteenth century. Atlanta University adhered to an approach based on the model of New England higher education, while Tuskegee Institute (like Hampton) cast aside such "elitist" notions and mainly trained its students to become proficient at "practical" agricultural and industrial skills—for occupations that, in many cases, were becoming obsolete.

I took the name *"Darkwater"* from the title of W. E. B. Du Bois's 1920 collection of essays, poems, and short stories, subtitled *Voices from Within the Veil* (repr., New York: Schocken Books, 1969). It seems fitting for the squalid communities where formerly enslaved black people such as Pocahontas Logan and her family relocated during Reconstruction.

Concerning Adella's library books at Tuskegee Institute, I couldn't resist mentioning H. L. Hosmer's *Adela: The Octoroon* (Columbus, OH: Foster and Follett, 1860).

During my childhood, my aunts, Adella Hunt Logan's three daughters, had most of their clothes made by a personal dressmaker. I've assumed their mother did as well. The image of Adella in her wedding dress taken by the photographer Thomas Askew comes from the collections of the Herndon Home in Atlanta. Her 1888 marriage to Warren Logan is documented in the GDAH archives for "colored" unions, and I have her wedding ring. In 1884, John D. Rockefeller endowed the Baptist Female Seminary and renamed it to honor his wife, Laura, née Spelman. Samuel Courtney's account of a perilous railroad journey such as that when the Logans returned from Atlanta to Tuskegee appears in the *Booker T. Washington Papers,* along with Mr. Washington's published response. A photograph shared with me decades ago by Hampton's archivists identifies the Logans' home as "The Rookery."

The pervasiveness of women's deaths in childbirth was appalling well into the early twentieth century. The frequency of such tragedies didn't diminish significantly until the 1920s, and even a century later, maternal and infant mortality rates in the United States among African Americans and Latinas still parallel those in scarcely developed countries. In part, I attribute Adella Hunt Logan's escalating depression to her repeated childbearing.

The best source on Ida B. Wells-Barnett is Paula J. Giddings's resonant *Ida: A Sword among Lions; Ida B. Wells and the Campaign against Lynching* (New York: Amistad, 2008). Also see the memoir of Wells-Barnett's daughter Alfreda M. Duster, *Crusade for Justice: The Autobiography of Ida B. Wells* (Chicago: University of Chicago Press, 1970). Some of the Dusters (Ida B. Wells-Barnett's great-grandson Ben and his family) live in the same apartment building as I do and shared the story about their fierce antecedent's corrupt white lawyer.

On Halle Tanner Dillon and others of her ilk, see Ruth J. Abram, ed., *"Send Us a Lady Physician": Women Doctors in America, 1830–1920* (New York: Norton, 1985).

For information about Dr. Dillon, Alice Dunbar-Nelson, Frances Ellen Watkins Harper, Nella Larsen, Sojourner Truth, Margaret Murray Washington, Olivia Davidson Washington, Phillis Wheatley, Sylvanie Williams, and organizations such as the National Association of Colored Women, see especially Darlene Clark Hine, Elsa Barkley Brown, and Rosalyn Terborg-Penn, eds., *Black Women in America: An Historical Encyclopedia* (Brooklyn: Carlson, 1993). Social activism such as Adella's was prevalent among those of her sex and race, as detailed in Darlene Clark Hine and Christie Anne Farnham's essay "Black Woman's Culture of Resistance and the Right to Vote," in *Women of the American South: A Multicultural Reader, ed. Farnham* (New York: NYU Press, 1997); Rosalyn Terborg-Penn and Janice Sumler-Edmond, eds., *Black Women's History at the Intersection of Knowledge and Power* (Acton, MA: Tapestry, 2000); and Paula Giddings, *When and Where I Enter: The Impact of Black Women on Race and Sex in America* (New York: William Morrow, 1984).

The blind and deaf baby was the daughter of Robert Sayre's grandson, Felix Rogers, and his first wife and cousin, "Li'l Susie" Hunt. In 1919, Adella's sister Sarah moved to Los Angeles (she reportedly wanted to marry Warren Logan and raise the Logan children, but that was not to be), where she married the recently widowed Felix, who also was her own and Adella's cousin, and cared for his motherless children. Arthur Silvers shared much that he remembered about his stepgrandmother Sarah Hunt Rogers, who helped rear him too. Arthur also gave me the Old Paris porcelain cup that Sarah had taken to her new home in California after she left Tuskegee.

The legends and science about dirt-eating (geophagia, *cachexia Africanus,* or pica) are legion. It's often derided as a "primitive tendency," but in fact, kaolin clay is mineral rich, is soothing to the intestinal tract, and protects against harmful toxins. My daughter Elizabeth Alexander's poem "The Dirt-Eaters," in her *Antebellum Dreambook* (Minneapolis: Greenwood, 2001), was inspired by rumors that her great-grandmother Adella Hunt Logan "ate clay to make her babies so white."

I can't imagine that Adella didn't read Charlotte Perkins Gilman's acclaimed feminist captivity novella *The Yellow Wallpaper* (Boston: Rockwell & Churchill, 1892).

Henry Ossawa Tanner, Halle's brother and Bishop Tanner's son, who in 1891 emigrated to France, was one of the first African American painters to achieve international acclaim.

The works by and about Frederick Douglass are innumerable, starting with his three memoirs published in 1845, 1855, and 1881. I consider William S. McFeely's *Frederick Douglass* (New York: Norton, 1995) the best biography to date. Philip S. Foner's *Frederick Douglass: A Biography* (New York: Citadel, 1964) is a solid runner-up, but David W. Blight's *Frederick Douglass: Prophet of Freedom* (New York: Simon and Schuster, 2018) surpasses all that preceded it.

I give repeated examples of how most white southerners refused to use surnames and honorifics for African Americans and called them "boy," "gal," "uncle," or "aunty," and I also indicate how black people resented and tried to resist those demeaning references. On the other hand, even now the use of "Aunt" and "Uncle" among African Americans to reference respected elders is more prevalent than it is in the majority community.

7. Vanished

Mamie McLendon Thomas, who grew up in Sparta, Georgia, told me that her mother, Lula, and her aunt Adella frequently corresponded and that the Hunts, virtually alone among Hancock County's African Americans, usually were courteously served by clerks at local stores.

The best work I've found about enslaved children is Wilma King's *Stolen Childhood: Slave Youth in Nineteenth-Century America* (Bloomington: Indiana University Press, 1995). On women held in bondage, see especially Deborah Gray White's classic study *Ar'n't I a Woman: Female Slaves in the Plantation South* (New York: Norton, 1985).

In Sparta, I heard many stories about Judkins Hunt II, including those of the gravestone under his African American mistress's home and his wife dumping his body into an unmarked grave. The Georgia Hunts called anyone who exhibited profligate behavior "a Judkins."

Ample oral history as well as the many documents that accompany J. M. Hunt's will and its long-delayed settlement testify to the decade during which the white Hunts challenged Susan Hunt's and her descendants' rights to their duly designated inheritance.

My family used the phrase "secret inkwell" to mean a "hidden" genetic legacy—tightly curled hair, broad features, or somewhat darker skin—that might expose the existence of a black ancestor. Those characteristics sometimes appear in the children of people who look white themselves, as genetic traits can easily "skip a generation."

Even in the wake of electoral gains by Sparta's African Americans, segregationist habits remained so entrenched that in the 1980s black people there who'd warmly welcomed me "home" expressed their dismay when I ventured (by myself) into the "white cemetery." Unless it's recently been moved, the Confederate war memorial still dominates the town square.

I've speculated about the circumstances surrounding Susan Hunt's "disappearance." Throughout Hancock County and at numerous websites, I searched in vain for any grave marker for her. Decades ago, however, I discovered an overgrown unmarked granite cube, about ten inches in all dimensions, which seemed to be deliberately positioned in the grounds of Pomegranate Hall, but I don't know for sure if it commemorates the mansion's first female resident. I don't think, as has been suggested to me, that it was a property-line marker. Ralston, moreover, was not the surname of the people who purchased the mansion from the Sayres in the 1870s.

8. Obstreperous Women

The late Rowena Hunt Bracken told me that her father, Will Hunt, arrived in Tuskegee around 1890, ran the Logans' pine-lumbering and turpentine-making side venture for many years, and married a pretty, dark-skinned local woman, Eliza Green. His white friends and associates, Rowena added, didn't believe Will was African American and couldn't understand why he married Miss Green, " 'stead o' jes' beddin' her down."

Adella's second "lost" child's name was Cecilia, not Olivia, but since my Logan relatives insisted, "we all were named for family friends and associates," I've called her Olivia because I couldn't identify anyone whom Adella and Warren were close to who carried the name Cecilia. Several times at Tuskegee, I heard the horrific story about the Logans' baby who died with her grandmother in a kitchen fire. That seems to coincide with the time when Adella first became intermittently delusional, so I incorporated her presumed visions of the Raven Mocker.

Frances Ellen Watkins Harper's poem "Aunt Chloe," quoted here, is included in her *Sketches of Southern Life* (Philadelphia: Henderson Bros., 1891).

For an earlier examination of the tensions that Adella's political activism engendered in the Logan family, see my article "Grandmother, Grandfather, W. E. B. Du Bois and Booker T. Washington," *Crisis*, February 1983.

Leaders and members of the National Woman's Suffrage Association and the American Woman Suffrage Association became bitterly divided in the late 1860s over the exclusion of women from the Fifteenth Amendment, and they only united, for added institutional clout and political advantage, as the National-American Woman Suffrage Association in the early 1890s.

The most thoroughgoing work on black women's involvement in suffrage efforts is Rosalyn Terborg-Penn's mighty *African American Women in the Struggle for the Vote, 1850–1920* (Bloomington: University of Indiana Press, 1998). Also see my essays "Adella Hunt Logan and the Tuskegee Woman's Club: Building a Foundation for Suffrage," in *Stepping Out of the Shadows: Alabama Women, 1819–1990*, ed. Mary Martha Thomas (Tuscaloosa: University of Alabama Press, 1995); and "Adella Hunt Logan, the Tuskegee Woman's Club, and African Americans in the Suffrage Movement," in *Votes for Women: The Suffrage Movement in Tennessee, the*

South, and the Nation, ed. Marjorie Spruill Wheeler (Knoxville: University of Tennessee Press, 1995). A significant recent piece on the subject in the mainstream press is Brent Staples's op-ed "The Racism behind Women's Suffrage," *New York Times,* July 29, 2018.

Nell Irvin Painter's uniquely insightful *Sojourner Truth: A Life, a Symbol* (New York: Norton, 1996) evokes the subject of her study more through archetypal literary and visual representations of her than from unreliable, often contradictory biographical data.

Kathleen Barry's *Susan B. Anthony: The Biography of a Singular Suffragist* (New York: Ballantine Books, 1988) is probably the famous suffrage advocate's most acclaimed biography. Ann Gordon, ed., *The Selected Papers of Susan B. Anthony and Elizabeth Cady Stanton,* 6 vols. (New Brunswick, NJ: Rutgers University Press, 1983–2003), includes letters by and about Adella and records of her signed copies of three volumes of Anthony and Stanton's epic *History of Woman Suffrage.* Elisabeth Griffith did full justice to her subject with *In Her Own Right: The Life of Elizabeth Cady Stanton* (New York: Oxford University Press, 1984), although she and I disagree significantly on Cady Stanton's views about race. Though Stanton claimed to advocate solidarity among supporters of an expanded suffrage in the late 1860s, her reference to "Sambo" can't be excused simply as commonly used language. On Victoria Claflin Woodhull and her sister "Tenny," see Myra McPherson's *The Scarlet Sisters: Sex, Suffrage, and Scandal in the Gilded Age* (New York: Twelve, 2014). More about that pair appears in chapter 12.

The National-American Woman Suffrage Association's convention reports now can be found online and document Adella's life membership starting in 1895. The Atlanta University *Bulletin* for that February details Susan B. Anthony's visit to the school. *The Woman's Journal,* the suffrage movement's most significant periodical, is not yet available online. At the Library of Congress's rare book division, I slogged through every issue during the period that Adella participated in such activities and stumbled on her pseudonymous but easily identifiable articles.

Here I use "wearing the veil" as a metaphor both for passing for white and for African Americans' need to conceal their innermost selves and to find protective coverings that might allow them to accommodate, resist, or circumvent endemic racism. W. E. B. Du Bois brought the phrase into common usage in *The Souls of Black Folk.* See my further notes for chapter 6.

I don't know any full biography of Frances Willard but have read extensively about her and the Woman's Christian Temperance Movement. Early in 1895, the WCTU published Willard's *A Wheel within a Wheel; or, How I Learned to Ride a Bicycle.* One Tuskegeeite whom I interviewed remembered Adella as an enthusiastic cyclist. Miss Anthony's quote on cycling appears widely, using slightly differing wording. I very much like Peter Zeutlin's online article "Women on Wheels: The Bicycle and the Women's Movement of the 1890s" and Lynn Sherr's *Failure Is Impossible: Susan B. Anthony in Her Own Words* (New York: Times Books, 1995).

For one of the Supreme Court's most egregious civil rights decisions, see Charles A. Lofgren, *The Plessy Case: A Legal-Historical Interpretation* (New York: Oxford University Press, 1987).

In addition to Tom Harris, a handful of African American lawyers practiced on an ad hoc basis throughout Alabama in the late 1800s, but the first one sanctioned by the state bar association was only certified in 1937.

The given name of Ella Hunt's husband was Berzilia, Brasilla, or Brazilia Payne. In light of those varied spellings and his reported dashing looks, I substituted Apollo.

9. Of the Genius and Training of Black Folk

Tuskegee Institute's Children's House pioneered early childhood education in the South.

The classic early study of Carver is Rackham Holt's *George Washington Carver: An American Biography* (New York: Doubleday, Doran, 1943), which was published shortly after his death, but the most comprehensive scholarly biographies are Linda O. McMurry's *George Washington Carver: Scientist and Symbol* (New York: Oxford University Press, 1982) and more recently Christina Vella's *George Washington Carver: A Life* (Baton Rouge: Louisiana State University Press, 2017). Audio recordings of Carver attest to his countertenor timbre and have contributed to the unproven but persistent rumor that he might have been castrated as a child.

David Levering Lewis brilliantly analyzes Du Bois's long and prolific life. The first volume of his acclaimed biography *W. E. B. Du Bois: Biography of a Race, 1868–1919* (New York: Henry Holt, 1993) is most pertinent here. During my childhood, I recall family visits with W. E. B. Du Bois ("Dr. Dubious"), who was a friend of the Logans. Arnold Rampersad's *The Art and Imagination of W. E. B. Du Bois* (Cambridge, MA: Harvard University Press, 1976) and Kwame Anthony Appiah's *Lines of Descent: W. E. B. Du Bois and the Emergence of Identity* (Cambridge, MA: Harvard University Press, 2014) are among other works of insight and scholarship.

In part, I base my account of Adella Hunt Logan's first meeting with Dr. Du Bois on a story shared in 1986 by another African American scholar: Charles H. Wesley. Dr. Wesley told me that in 1912 Adella invited him for tea at her home in Tuskegee when he was visiting the institute as a recent Fisk graduate. He raved about how brilliant and attractive she was. When I protested that "compared to you, she was pretty old at the time," he chuckled and said, "Not all that old! We later exchanged photographs and letters. I'll never forget that afternoon!"

All of Atlanta University's presidents were Caucasian until the trustees appointed John Hope to that position in 1929—and he looked white.

Adella Hunt Logan definitely attended the second, third, and fourth Atlanta University Conferences on the Condition of the Negro, and I base my reading of her concerns about the conflicts between "nurture" or "nature" exclusively determining the human condition on the paper she delivered there in 1897, titled "Prenatal and Hereditary Influences." The presence of Alexander Walker's book on racial "hybridity" in her grandfather's estate suggests that it may have been one source of her interest. For Charles Darwin's inquiry to Dr. Walker about the (in)advisability of endogamous marriage, see Frederick Burkhardt and Sydney Smith, eds., *The Correspondence of Charles Darwin,* vol. 2 (Cambridge: Cambridge University Press, 1986).

Adella attended several summer Chautauquas to earn higher-education credits, at least once on Martha's Vineyard. I cannot confirm the exact years when she did so. The definitive (but very early) account of that important American educational movement is Jesse Lyman Hurlbut, *The Story of Chautauqua* (New York: G. P. Putnam, 1921).

The public librarians in Weston, Massachusetts, found references in their town directories to Thomas Francis Hunt's employment there and in nearby Wayland and his residence at the home of police chief O'Hara. Tom graduated from the University of Massachusetts's agricultural program in 1905. His obituary compiled by the University of California at Berkeley describes him as "born in Georgia of old American stock" and credits his longtime academic, financial, and moral support by his unnamed sister (Adella).

On Ida B. Wells-Barnett and lynching, see Wells-Barnett, *A Red Record: Tabulated Statistics and Alleged Causes of Lynching in the United States 1892-3-4* (1895), in *Selected Works of Ida B. Wells-Barnett,* ed. Trudier Harris (New York: Oxford University Press, 1991). The 1895 incident in which the white John Alexander was wounded by a stray bullet in Macon County, Alabama, is widely documented, but the death of the black man who bore the same name is far less so. Despite Booker T. Washington's accumulation of data on lynching throughout the country, he was loath to protest one in his own "backyard," since he prioritized maintaining cordial relations with whites who reluctantly tolerated the institute's students and faculty as their neighbors.

In addition to my relatives' vivid accounts, several others whom I talked with at Tuskegee Institute confirmed Adella Hunt Logan's and Margaret Murray Washington's very testy relationship. One repeated story was that Margaret was jealous because Adella and Booker T. had a romance when she was still single and he was a widower—but it's only a rumor.

10. *Up from Slavery,* Off to the White House

For an excellent examination of the conflicts inherent in African Americans' responses to their country's empire building, see Willard B. Gatewood Jr., *Black Americans and the White Man's Burden* (Urbana: University of Illinois Press, 1975). One of Adella's letters to Emily Howland (Patty Winston) reveals her dismay over the federal government's imperialism.

Adella and her youngest brother, Tom, stayed in close touch after he moved west. She mentioned to Emily Howland that he'd recently written her. I haven't found any of Tom's letters, but in this chapter and elsewhere, I include facts about his life in California from his obituary and through his acknowledged but unfound correspondence with his sister.

I don't know for sure that Margaret Washington wheedled a gift of one of the Logans' heirloom rugs for The Oaks, but photographs of the two homes show virtually identical ones.

I've paraphrased the exchange between Susan B. Anthony, Emily Howland (my Patty Winston), and Howland's niece Isabel about Adella's possible participation in the 1900 N-AWSA convention. Those letters appear among the published Anthony-Stanton Papers. Kathleen Barry, Susan B. Anthony's biographer, downplays Miss Anthony's racist impulses and suggests that Adella wasn't even aware of the debate concerning her possible presentation at the eightieth birthday event. Perhaps not, but that doesn't negate Anthony's insensitivity at least and racism at worst.

I don't know that Adella received a personal invitation to that White House reception, but such a bid almost certainly would have come to her as a Lifetime Member of the organization. Several Tuskegeeites told me that while Booker T. Washington's brother oversaw the institute's post office, faculty and student mail was always monitored, often opened, and sometimes even withheld from the intended recipients.

Concerning birth certificates for African Americans in Alabama, my mother, born in that state (to Adella's friend Georgia Stewart Bond) in 1906, told me that she did not have such a document on record, but her brother, born three years later, did.

I've imagined Adella's preparation and submission of her master's thesis and her correspondence and interactions with Dr. W. E. B. Du Bois concerning it, but she almost certainly purchased that black taffeta gown at Rich's department store and definitely had her photograph taken at the neighboring Edwards studio when she went to Atlanta to attend the 1902 graduation ceremony at which she was awarded an honorary master's degree. To receive service at those establishments, Adella would have had to pass for white. She looks weary and intense in that photo, which shows the fabulous dress and pansy brooch, and reveals her torn earlobe. My observant grandsons, Solomon and Simon Ghebreyesus, surmised that a "wild child" had ripped out an ear stud. David Levering Lewis suggests that when the opportunity arose, "the Doctor" tried to seduce most of the intelligent, attractive women with whom he interacted.

Booker T. Washington's best-known book is *Up from Slavery* (New York: Doubleday, 1901). Despite its general obsequiousness, that memoir did use the capital *N* throughout.

Deborah Davis's *Guest of Honor: Booker T. Washington, Theodore Roosevelt, and the Dinner That Shocked a Nation* (New York: Atria Books, 2012) fully details that controversial incident. Linda Kenney Miller's excellent novel *Beacon on the Hill* (Dallas: Harper House, 2008) documents the life of her grandfather Dr. John Kenney, Tuskegee Institute's physician and the Logans' close friend, whom I remember visiting with my family in the 1940s.

The Emma Willard girls' school in Troy only admitted its first known African American students in the 1950s. The Vassar student mentioned in "Patty Winston's" imagined note was Anita Florence Hemmings, who was probably a peripheral descendant of Sally Hemings. See Jillian A. Sim, "Fading to White," *American Heritage 50*, no. 1 (1999). Similar stories of "racial deceit" were reported at many of the country's "elite" educational institutions.

11. Minds, Bodies, and *Souls*

I've based "Della Winston's" story on the recorded experiences of a number of light-skinned African American women who led comparably convoluted and stressful double lives.

Robert Curtis Ogden, the chairman of Tuskegee Institute's board of trustees, for whom Walter Ogden Logan was named, amassed a substantial fortune through his collaboration with the merchant prince John Wanamaker, but Ogden dedicated much of his later life to advancing educational opportunities for African Americans.

Christine Vella discusses Carver's probable homosexuality but also claims he adored Adella and considered her sister Sarah a "pale substitute." I've re-created this scenario and his letter by culling through Carver's correspondence. His "romance" with Sarah ended shortly before her abrupt departure for New Jersey and probably prompted it. Letters recruiting a director for the Newark settlement house appear in both the Booker T. Washington and W. E. B. Du Bois papers.

The incident when Frances Benjamin Johnston and George Washington

Carver were attacked in Ramer, Alabama, often has been retold, but no additional travel companion has been mentioned. It seems impossible, however, to think that Booker T. Washington would have sent off the interracial "couple" without a chaperone. If he'd done so, Miss Johnston would have had to travel by herself in an all-white rail car and stay alone in a hostile town. Mr. Washington was far too savvy to make such a mistake. Who else but Adella? The "escort" had to be an intrepid, mature woman who looked white. As indicated by Miss Johnston's photos of the Logan children and her correspondence with Adella's husband, she and the Logans developed something of a personal relationship. The best work on Johnston is Pete Daniel and Raymond Smock's *A Talent for Detail: The Photographs of Miss Frances Benjamin Johnston, 1889–1910* (New York: Harmony Books, 1974). My own articles about her appeared in both *Ms.* and *Washingtonian* magazines. A reader of my piece in *Ms.* protested that I refused to acknowledge her as a lesbian, while a reader of the one in *Washingtonian* complained that because I mentioned that Johnston sometimes wore men's clothing, I was "maligning" her by questioning her femininity.

For more about Georgia Stewart, her fiancé and future husband J. Percy Bond (I've changed his given name here to J. *Harris* Bond to avoid duplicate Percys), and their family, see my *Homelands and Waterways.* My maternal grandmother Georgia's stories, written in a "Negro dialect," which appeared in the *Colored American Magazine* in 1901, are truly egregious. I believe that Georgia's flirtation (as clearly indicated by her letters) with Booker T. Washington persuaded him to facilitate their publication and to promise her a "respectable" job at the institute. Rumors swirled at Tuskegee about the absence of passion in Margaret and Booker T. Washington's conjugal life and why they had no children, since he very much wanted more.

My mother told me that both of my light-skinned grandmothers passed for white to attend suffrage conferences together in the South. In "The Pink Hat," *Opportunity,* December 1926, Georgia's older daughter, Caroline Bond Day, fictionalized her own experiences when she was mistaken for a white woman. One of Adella's letters to Emily Howland (Patty Winston) described her discussions with the N-AWSA's leaders in New Orleans. Terborg-Penn quotes Sylvanie Williams's "tribute" to Anthony in *African American Women in the Struggle for the Vote.* Nicolle Muller Dunnaway shared with me her fine 2011 Southeastern Louisiana State University dissertation: "Flowers in Their Beauty: The Phillis Wheatley Club of New Orleans."

There's little question that white leaders of the woman suffrage movement became more overtly racist after 1900, reflecting both the overall temper of the times and the aging of the former idealists who'd begun their political activism in the antebellum abolitionist movement.

The earliest of Arthur P. Bedou's many photos at Tuskegee that I've seen is one that I have of my aunt Ruth Logan dated 1904, perhaps taken on her thirteenth birthday that November.

From the 1880s through 1929, Andrew Carnegie donated millions of dollars to construct an estimated twenty-five hundred libraries in the United States and abroad. Those in the South at schools for African Americans such as Tuskegee Institute were always segregated.

W. E. B. Du Bois's first tirade against Booker T. Washington in *The Souls of Black Folk* was deserved but also somewhat unfair. Mr. Washington was clearly an accommodationist, but he always exhorted the institute's male faculty to register and vote in their segregated town. I have a copy of my grandfather Warren Logan's 1903 receipt for payment of his poll tax. Unfortunately, his papers at Tuskegee have not been catalogued.

For Adella's brother Henry, see Frank Horne, "Henry A. Hunt, Sixteenth Spingarn Medalist," *Crisis*, August 1930; Donnie Bellamy, "Henry A. Hunt and Black Agricultural Leadership in the New South," *Journal of Negro History*, Summer 1975; and Dr. Du Bois's eulogy for him, which is further discussed in the notes for chapter 19. Fort Valley State University is now a flourishing branch of the University of Georgia's higher-education system. Thanks to Henry Hunt's decades-long, acquisitive leadership, Fort Valley's campus includes more acres than any other branch, save the flagship one in Athens, and houses most of the state's agricultural programs. Some tensions, however, have arisen about its identity as an HBCU (a historically black college and university) since many of its longtime African American academic and administrative leaders have been replaced by whites, but the university is addressing that issue.

Mamie McLendon Thomas, Adella's niece, shared this account of the Hunt sisters' (her three aunts') encounter with New York City policemen who accused them of "consorting and cavorting with Negroes." In my childhood, I remember hearing about Rector's restaurant as one of my uncle-by-marriage Dr. Roberts's favorites. For more on E. P. Roberts, see Dennis C. Dickerson, "Eugene Percy Roberts: Black Physician and Leader," *New York State Journal of Medicine*, April 1985.

Here and in ensuing chapters, I've combined, excerpted, and edited Adella's letters and published writings but taken care to maintain their essence, style, vocabulary, and meaning.

12. Recalled to Life

My daughter has the silver bonbon dish that my mother told me Adella Hunt Logan (my paternal grandmother) gave Georgia Stewart Bond (my maternal grandmother) as a wedding gift.

I've paraphrased President Roosevelt's October 1905 speech at Tuskegee Institute, for which the most accessible source is the chronological online "Almanac of Theodore Roosevelt."

I researched how, when, and where physicians sectioned and removed kidneys in the early 1900s. Dr. William Stokes Goldsmith was a respected surgeon from Grady Hospital who also consulted at Spelman's MacVicar Clinic. He almost certainly performed Adella's dangerous and rare nephrectomy in 1905. The *Transactions of the Southern Surgical Association,* available online, document some of his operations. For Grady itself, see Martin Moran, *Atlanta's Living Legacy: A History of Grady Memorial Hospital and Its People* (Atlanta: Kimbark, 2012). I appreciate Dr. Moran's insights and patience with my many questions. He agreed with my assumption that Dr. Goldsmith only would have performed that surgery at the well-equipped, "modern" Grady Memorial, but his account virtually ignores the ugly realities of segregation and its deleterious impact on medical care for African Americans. Adella's correspondence with Emily Howland (Patty Winston) details the tests and preparatory procedures she went through, her frustration with needing her husband's permission to undergo the operation, and her profound sorrow on learning of Susan B. Anthony's death during her rehabilitation at MacVicar.

The phrases included here from Alice Moore Dunbar's "In Unconsciousness," in *Violets,* can be found in *The Works of Alice Dunbar-Nelson,* ed. Gloria T. Hull, vol. 1 (New York: Oxford University Press, 1988). Eleanor Alexander's *Lyrics of Sunshine and Shadow: The Tragic Courtship and Marriage of Paul Laurence Dunbar and Alice Ruth Moore* (New York: NYU Press, 2001) details the Moore-Dunbars' turbulent personal history.

I scoured writings by and about Dr. Du Bois for clues concerning his friendship with Henry Hunt and concluded that they almost certainly met when Adella was hospitalized in 1905.

In a letter to Emily Howland, Adella mentioned that her brother Tom wrote her that he'd survived the 1906 San Francisco earthquake. Passing as a white man, Thomas *Francis* Hunt taught agricultural sciences at the University of California, Berkeley, for decades. His "boss," the school of agriculture's dean, was Thomas *Forsyth* Hunt. Berkeley only knew that it hired any African American faculty in the 1960s, half a century after Tom Hunt went there.

This account of the race riots quotes Dr. Du Bois's "A Litany of Atlanta," which first was published in the *Independent* magazine, October 1906.

13. Live Not on Evil

Booker T. Washington's oft-told story "The Pig Is My Favorite Animal" appears in his *My Larger Education* (Garden City, NY: Doubleday, Page, 1911) and elsewhere.

For more detailed notes on "Cherie Rideaux," see my "Susannah and the Elders or Potiphar's Wife: Allegations of Sexual Misconduct at Booker T. Washington's Tuskegee Institute," in Farnham, *Women of the American South.* To protect the family's privacy and "Cherie's" memory, I've changed her name, but I appreciate the snapshot shared by her granddaughter Beth Thomas. Beth also shared with me what she'd heard of "Cherie's" later life, including her civil court petition that established her status as an emancipated minor.

Louis Harlan's biography of Washington details this incident involving Edgar Penney and his subsequent forced departure from Tuskegee. I like to think of Adella as "Cherie's" savior and situate her in that role but cannot be certain. I do believe that Rev. Penney molested the girl. Others do not, but there's little question that the Washingtons, in their own interests, ruthlessly quashed the personal and legal rights of both their student and the reverend.

For timeless insights on menstruation, I rely on Janice Delaney, Mary Jane Lupton, and Emily Toth, *The Curse: A Cultural History of Menstruation* (New York: E. P. Dutton, 1976).

I don't remember hearing anyone call my aunt Myra Logan My 'Del but recently came across that pet name in an old letter from her father.

14. Reckless and Insubordinate

As indicated in Adella Hunt Logan's correspondence, she clearly wanted to end her ninth pregnancy—at least the ninth, because she may have had previous miscarriages or stillbirths in addition to her prior eight live births. How rigorously she tried to stimulate a miscarriage or get an abortion I don't know. I believe she'd had enough of childbearing and thought it should be her choice and not forced on her. Adella's daughters supported a woman's "right to choose" before it became a "respectable" stance or certainly the law of the land, and although they adored children, none of them had any of their own. I have to think that their mother's experiences and tragic death influenced them in that respect, among many others.

I don't know for sure that Dr. Samuel Courtney performed a tubal ligation for Adella following Arthur's birth, but I think he did. Such procedures were in their infancy then, and certainly, that was her last pregnancy. I do know she went to Boston that September to enroll Ruth at Sargent College. Something also changed at that point in her relationship with Dr. Courtney. He became more important to her: worthier of her appreciation and recognition. She'd known him well for twenty-five years, but my father, Arthur, was the one on whom she finally bestowed Courtney as a middle name. Holly Robbins graciously shared her research about Samuel Courtney and shares my belief that his children passed over into the white world.

I can't absolutely confirm that Adella and her friend Patty Winston (Emily Howland) heard Dr. Sigmund Freud's lectures at Clark University (Carl Jung also delivered several talks at that same gathering), but the coincidence of her presence in Boston the previous week and her children's later intense interest in Freudian analysis convince me that she probably did. Those famous discourses in their entirety are accessible online, as is ample information about the event itself. I have no evidence that Dr. Freud mentioned Charlotte Perkins Gilman's *The Yellow Wallpaper* at that time or any other, but its subject certainly coincided with his psychological concerns. There is considerable online discussion comparing Gilman's book with Sigmund Freud's theories and case studies.

The first American gathering on women's rights took place in Seneca Falls, New York, in 1848, but the Worcester event two years later is considered the first actual, national convention.

Henry Ford's dictum that customers could get his Model Ts in any color "as long as it's black," is well known, but in 1909, in fact, they were forest green.

Booker T. Washington was rumored to be in line for a cabinet position even before 1900, but not until 1966 did President Lyndon Baines Johnson actually appoint Robert Weaver as the first African American to hold such a position: in the new Department of Housing and Urban Development (HUD). Franklin Delano Roosevelt named Frances Perkins as the country's first female cabinet secretary at the Department of Labor in 1933, and finally in 1977, Jimmy Carter appointed an African American woman, Patricia Roberts Harris, also to lead HUD.

15. The Princess and the Pen

In *You Need a Schoolhouse: Booker T. Washington, Julius Rosenwald, and the Building of Schools for a Segregated South* (Chicago: Northwestern University Press, 2013), Stephanie Deutsch deftly reports and analyzes this important alliance. Stephanie told me about Theodore Roosevelt's adventures in South America described in *Through the Brazilian Wilderness* (New York: Scribner, 1914). Regarding Augusta Rosenwald, her first known interest in woman suffrage seems to have been in 1913, when Illinois granted her sex the right (often dependent on not their own but their husbands' citizenship status) to vote in federal but not most local elections.

One must ask, concerning Theodore Roosevelt's breakaway political party in 1912, what nomenclature could be more sexist, even misogynistic, than "Bull Moose"? Woodrow Wilson's racism has been largely papered over, but he dismissed or harshly segregated African Americans in the federal workforce and celebrated the incendiary motion picture *The Birth of a Nation*.

My essay "Adella Hunt Logan, the Tuskegee Woman's Club, and African Americans in the Suffrage Movement" discusses the 1913 National Medical Association gathering in Tuskegee. The NMA journal is available online and provided me with information about Drs. John Kenney, Eugene Percy Roberts, and Samuel Courtney, as well as the organization's early history. I found the program with Adella's reconfigured lyrics to "Comin' thro the Rye" in the Booker T. Washington Papers at the Library of Congress. On the American Medical Association's institutional bigotry, see especially Robert B. Baker, "The American Medical Association and Race in the AMA's *Journal of Ethics*," *Virtual Mentor*, June 2014. A group of black physicians petitioned for membership in 1870, but the national organization accredited its first official African American delegate, Dr. Peter Marshall Murray, only in 1950. I remember my elders discussing that important "breakthrough." In 2008, the AMA issued a public apology for its historical racial discrimination.

Myriad online sites discuss the March 1913 suffrage march in the nation's capital. Press coverage at the time included scant mention of the attempted segregation and exclusion of African American women, but recent analyses address that aspect of the event in great detail. The *Woman's Journal* reported both that event and Emily Wilding Davison's ensuing, fatal protest at the English derby. As to the use of *suffragist* versus *suffragette,* for the most part (though not exclusively), in the United States, the *-ist* suffix was the preferred suffix, while in England, *-ette* was more common.

I've long believed that Tuskegee Institute, Booker T. Washington, and Adella Hunt Logan inspired W. E. B. Du Bois's "Princess of the Hither Isles," which appeared in *Crisis* in October 1913. She may not have written Dr. Du Bois following its publication, but it seems likely that she did. At some point around that time, she definitely sent him Frances Benjamin Johnston's photograph of her children, because he published it (although both the subjects and the photographer are unidentified) in the September's 1914 Children's Issue. Caroline Bond Day also included that image in *A Study of Some Negro-White Families in the United States,* but I didn't know that Johnston had taken it until I stumbled across the same one, along with several others of the Logans, in the Frances Benjamin Johnston collection at the Library of Congress's photographic division, among those she took at Tuskegee Institute in 1902 and 1906.

In 1913, African American faculty at the small college in Talladega, Alabama, formed the state's first, small branch of the NAACP.

George Washington Carver's voluminous papers, including some issues of *The Negro Farmer,* are available through Tuskegee University's archives and at the Library of Congress.

16. Firestorm

Warren Hunt Logan's (Junior's) tuberculosis went into remission, then recurred several times for another decade, during which he married and had a child. He passed away in 1924.

For Coden, Alabama, see Sylviane A. Diouf, *Dreams of Africa in America: The Slave Ship Clotilda and the Story of the Last Africans Brought to America* (New York: Oxford University Press, 2007).

In 1988, shortly before she died at age 101, I interviewed Bess Bolden Walcott, a firecracker feminist who'd gone, eighty years before, from her studies at Oberlin College to Tuskegee Institute as a science teacher. She told me about her friend Adella's physical and emotional breakdown. Driving her phaeton as she returned from town, where she'd challenged "town-gown" racial protocols by trying to get Arthur's hair cut at the "white" barber shop and using the main road instead of the Jim Crow bypass, Adella, her barefoot son, and the Logans' Dalmatian actually visited not Alfreda Kenney but Mrs. Walcott that rainy September afternoon. Bess Walcott also described the second Mrs. Logan as a "good kindergarten teacher" who played bid whist ("card games almost bored your grandmother to death") with Warren.

In *The New Woman in Alabama: Social Reform and Suffrage, 1890–1920* (Tuscaloosa: University of Alabama Press, 1992), Mary Martha Thomas expounds on the struggle for suffrage in that state, including its segregated and profoundly racist aspects. Alabama's legislature didn't ratify the Nineteenth Amendment giving women the right to vote until 1953.

By 1915, Tuskegee Institute had a number of office and institutional telephones, but only a few of its top officials had them in their private homes.

The *Tuskegee Student* reported both the mysterious fire in Warren Logan's office that September and the subsequent "emergency" visits to Tuskegee by Adella's sisters and her brother Henry. I assume that in contemporary times, she would have been diagnosed as suffering from a bipolar disorder. She obviously experienced periods of intense activity and functionality, not just the lassitude and depression usually associated with "neurasthenia."

For more about Nella Larsen, Adella's nurse at Tuskegee in 1915, see Thadious M. Davis, *Nella Larsen, Novelist of the Harlem Renaissance: A Woman's Life Unveiled* (New York: Oxford University Press, 1994); and especially George Hutchinson, *In Search of Nella Larsen: A Biography of the Color Line* (Cambridge, MA: Harvard University Press, 2006).

B. T. Washington's letter about Adella to Dr. Kellogg at the Battle Creek Sanitarium, which I paraphrase here, appears in volume 13 of Harlan and Smock, *Booker T. Washington Papers* (1984).

Dr. Du Bois's flirtation with the eugenics movement probably stemmed from the same elitist impulses that led him to advocate the empowerment of a "Talented Tenth," but he clearly never espoused the tenets of scientific racism, which touted the supremacy of a "master race."

17. Exile

Miles of Smiles, Years of Struggle, a 1982 documentary film by Mark Santino and Paul Wagner, effectively portrays the personal and organizational lives of the Pullman car porters, whose members comprised a significant portion of the African American middle class from Reconstruction throughout the Jim Crow Era.

I have Ruth Mackie Logan's gold locket. The intertwined initials (RML) indicate that E. P. Roberts gave it to her prior to their 1917 marriage. In 1912, the New York Police Department hired Samuel Battle, a patient and protégé of Dr. Roberts, as its first African American officer.

In the early twentieth century, the Battle Creek Sanitarium, commanded for years by Dr. John Kellogg, was the country's most renowned establishment of its ilk. Myriad materials about it are available online, including photographs of the glassed-in, jungle-like Palm Court and its various treatment facilities and devices, classes, recreational facilities, even menu cards. But T. Coraghassen Boyle's sardonic novel *The Road to Wellville* (New York: Viking, 1993) and the subsequent movie should not be missed. In 1996, I visited "the San," which is now a regional federal office building but retains much of the original architecture, and its historian dug out information from its archives for me and identified Mary Hunter Newlove as Adella's personal physician.

I've read everything I could find about early electrical shock treatments. They were rare, painful, dangerous, and terrifying but used, mostly to treat severe depression, in Battle Creek at the time. Boyle includes histrionic (and grotesquely hilarious) descriptions of such "remedies."

18. Flight

Ann Dibble Jordan and Clarice Dibble Walker told me that their mother, who was with Louise Logan in their sixth-grade classroom on the day of her death, remembered seeing Adella Hunt Logan, with her long skirt billowing around, "fly" past their window. My interviews with members of the institute's classes of 1915–1919 include accounts of one student who was taking Ruth Logan's gym class in the basement that morning and another who was on the quadrangle rehearsing with the band when he saw Mrs. Logan fall. A group of typescript interviews housed at

Tuskegee University's archives includes additional details about her hospitalization and death.

19. After the Fall

For the conspiracy theories (which I understand but do not buy into) on Booker T. Washington's death, see Paulette Davis-Horton, *Death in 60 Days: Who Silenced Booker T. Washington?* (Bloomington, IN: AuthorHouse, 2008). Black Americans suffered widespread abuse in the Jim Crow South, often exemplified by malpractice, mistreatment, even the denial of medical care, so such suppositions are hardly without foundation. For one pertinent, later example from the 1930s and '40s, see Susan M. Reverby, *Examining Tuskegee: The Infamous Syphilis Study and Its Legacy* (Chapel Hill: University of North Carolina Press, 2004).

Many descriptions and photographs of Booker T. Washington's funeral are available online, especially the Booker T. Washington Society's detailed report by Washington's protégé Isaac Fisher. In the Ella Barksdale Brown Papers at Yale University's Beinecke Library, Jeffrey Gonda located Sarah Hunt's letter to her friend Mrs. Brown, in which Sarah detailed both her sister Adella's decline and Mr. Washington's funeral. A May 13, 1965, profile of my father, Arthur Courtney Logan, in the *New York Times* includes his memories of George Washington Carver inviting him to conduct "science experiments" in his laboratory.

After I stumbled across the eulogy by Dr. Du Bois that I've portrayed Adella reading at Booker T. Washington's gravesite, I discovered that others already had cited it as representative of his often-overlooked religiosity and spirituality. See especially Edward J. Blum and Jason R. Young, eds., *The Souls of W. E. B. Du Bois: New Essays and Reflections* (Macon, GA: Mercer University Press, 2009).

I don't know whether during Adella's hospitalization at Battle Creek, Warren Logan actually had an affair that prompted her suicide, and I believe that her self-inflicted death was the result of many mutually exacerbating factors. Her niece Rowena Hunt Bracken told me how irrational she became during her final year and how profoundly her son Warren Jr.'s tuberculosis distressed her. Daria Willis-Joseph thinks that the fatal act was a manifestation of Adella's attempt to take control of her life, rather than one that reflected only abject despair.

Respecting the privacy of the woman's descendants, I don't use the real name of Warren's presumptive paramour, but three years after Adella died, he married her and raised her child, who assumed the Logan name. My hunch is that the young teacher comforted him in his wife's absence at Dr. Kellogg's Sanitarium, but they didn't actually have intercourse at that early juncture. Some Tuskegeeites swore to me that it was definitely a consummated relationship, while others deemed an affair "impossible," because, they insisted, Warren Logan was "such a gentleman." The story that my father, Arthur, threatened to split open her son's head with a toy hatchet, however, was retold in my family. Soon after Warren's remarriage, Arthur was sent off to New York City to live with his older sister Ruth Logan Roberts.

The documents that accompany Adella Hunt Logan's will archived at the Macon County, Alabama, courthouse, reveal sixteen-year-old Paul Howland Logan's surprising and angry but understandably futile attempt to be named, in lieu of his father, as executor of that will.

In October 1915, Augusta Rosenwald wrote her husband a note (in the Julius Rosenwald Papers at the University of Chicago Archives) saying that she'd sent Adella a check to help cover the expenses of her treatment at "the San," but I don't know that Mrs. Rosenwald also informed Adella about Margaret Washington's scheming machinations that followed Booker T.'s death. Mrs. Washington certainly wanted no one but Hampton's Robert Russa Moton to succeed her husband as Tuskegee Institute's principal, and he proved to be a good choice.

Another Tuskegeeite, Emmett J. Scott (B. T. Washington's secretary, whom I omitted from this account in my efforts to simplify the story), was also considered a possible heir apparent to the principalship. But when Scott was tapped and stepped in to replace Warren Logan as Tuskegee Institute's designated speaker at Booker T. Washington's memorial service after Adella's death, he flaunted his own candidacy so blatantly, instead of just eulogizing Mr. Washington, that he inadvertently sabotaged his ambitions to lead the school. Scott soon left the institute, while Logan maintained his position as treasurer and vice principal until his retirement in the 1920s, and he, his second wife, and her son resided next door to the Washingtons' home until Warren's death in late 1943. The Motons didn't move into the principal's official residence, The Oaks, until after the formidable Margaret Murray Washington died in 1925.

Lena Horne actually was born two years after Adella died, but her grandmother definitely sent her to live with her uncle Frank Horne and with the Henry Hunts at Fort Valley, reportedly to provide a safe haven for her young beauty. W. E. B. Du Bois's essay "The Significance of Henry Hunt" was published in the *Fort Valley State College Bulletin: Founders and Annual Report,* October 1940, and the original typewritten transcript is in the W. E. B. Du Bois Papers at the Library of Congress.

A Tuskegee Institute graduate whom I interviewed told me that in his campus quarters, George Washington Carver painted a postmortem mural honoring Adella and Mr. Washington.

One of the "dirty little secrets" that Portia Washington Pittman's biographer Roy Hill shared with me was that Portia believed that the woman I call Angela Kurtz

Johnson had an affair with her father several years earlier, after they'd first met at Howard University, that the boy whom I call "Harland" was Booker T.'s "love child," and that on his death bed, Mr. Washington begged Warren Logan to care for the boy—as he did. It puzzles me that "Angela" not only reassumed her "maiden" name herself but also imposed it on her son. It seems as if she was attempting to totally erase her ex-husband's brief presence from their lives. Perhaps "Mr. Johnson" wasn't "Harland's" biological father at all. Also, the boy did resemble Booker T. "He looks more like Daddy than my own brothers do," Portia informed Mr. Hill, adding that she'd told "Harland," "You and I are family!" I don't, however, know if Portia Washington Pittman's hunch is true.

Do the assemblage of visitors and the behavior and conversations I've imagined in Adella's hospital room seem unlikely? Yes they do, but consider this: several decades ago, Tuskegee archivists, designated as its "keepers of the eternal flame," deliberately (and wrongly!) destroyed John Andrew Hospital's medical records. Thus, no alcoholism, terminated pregnancies, spousal or child abuse, sexual misconduct, mental illness, suicides, or other possible embarrassments from the Washington era, and for some time thereafter, can be fully documented.

Afterword

My portrait of Adella Hunt Logan by the African American painter William Edouard Scott, which appears on this book's cover, is dated 1918. She sat for him during his residency at Tuskegee Institute early in 1915, as did both G. W. Carver and Booker T. Washington. At Ruth Logan Roberts's request, Scott finished the portrait several years after Adella's death, fleshing out his original sketches by using a photographic image from 1913 by Arthur P. Bedou: one of the same set that Bedou took of the Logan family on Adella and Warren's twenty-fifth wedding anniversary. For more about Scott, see William E. Taylor and Harriet G. Warkley, *A Shared Heritage: Art by Four African Americans* (Indianapolis: Indianapolis Museum of Art, 1996).

Nella Larsen's novel *Passing* (New York: Knopf, 1929) was published fourteen years after Adella had been Larsen's patient at Tuskegee Institute. Given the obvious physical resemblance of Larsen's tragic protagonist, Clare Landry, to Adella Hunt Logan and their almost identical deaths, I find it hard to think that Larsen didn't, to some extent, model Clare on Adella.

The brief biographical introduction to Adella's essay "What Are the Causes of the Great Mortality among the Negroes in the Cities of the South and How Is That Mortality to Be Lessened?," in *Twentieth Century Negro Literature; or, A Cyclopedia of Thought on the Vital Topics Relating to the American Negro,* ed.

D. W. Culp (Atlanta: J. L. Nichols, 1902), mentions her "education of a private nature" and reveals her concerns with health issues.

My daughter Elizabeth's poem "Race" first appeared in her *Antebellum
Dreambook.*

Paul Howland Logan's godmother, Emily Howland (whom I've called Patty
Winston), encouraged him to attend Cornell University, near her home in Shel-
burne, New York, for his graduate studies in forestry. For more on Paul's career, see
James G. Lewis, *The Forest Service and the Greatest Good: A Centennial History*
(Durham, NC: Forest History Society, 2005). The U.S. Forest Service didn't hire
any "visible" African Americans until the 1960s.

Oregon's venal nineteenth-century "Black Exclusion Laws," which decreed
that African Americans could be summarily arrested and banished from the state,
weren't repealed until 1926, around the time when Paul Logan moved there.

My cousin Cynthia Hunt Easley, a superb and generous genealogist, not only
identified "Angela Kurtz Johnson's" elusive first spouse but shared much more,
including the photographs she found of Thomas F. Hunt's sons in the 1941 Berkeley University, Kappa Delta Rho fraternity yearbook. Later that year, they enlisted
in the egregiously segregated U.S. Navy (as white men), and both of them died
during World War II in the service of their country.

Acknowledgments

My unending gratitude goes to the family members with whom I grew up, who shared their many stories, gave me strength and unequivocal love, as well as Adella Hunt Logan's name and spirit. They are my mother, Wenonah Bond Logan; my father, Arthur Courtney Logan; and his sisters Myra Adele (and her spouse, my dear godfather and uncle, Charles "Spinky" Alston), Louise Thrasher Logan, and Ruth Mackie Logan (and her husband, Dr. Eugene Percy Roberts). Also, my maternal grandmother, Georgia Fagain Stewart Bond, and her older daughter, Caroline Bond Day, helped to guide me. I love, remember, and miss them all.

I still recall my grandfather Warren Logan's annual visits to New York in my early childhood, those of my uncle Paul, and one from Sarah Hunt Rogers, my father's beloved "Aunt Sarah." I saw my "Tuskegee uncle" Harold Koontz Logan (my father's and aunts' younger stepbrother) only rarely, but he also deserves thanks, as do his daughters, Carol Logan Smith and Valerie Logan Burston. Until the 1980s, I had little contact with my Hunt relatives, but since then, Lorin and Charity Hunt, Charity's siblings, their mother, Kate, and many others, especially Billy Gilchrist, Cynthia Hunt Easley, Wanda Hunt McLean, Arthur Silvers, Rowena Hunt Bracken, and Mamie McLendon Thomas, in various ways have contributed to this narrative. I know that Warren Arthur Logan and our mutual father loved each other, so to that extent, he too bears a portion of the family legacy.

The institutions that have provided help and documentation include Hampton University (especially Fritz Malval), Howard University and its Moorland-Spingarn Research Center (Dorothy Porter Wesley, from the really old days, and then Janet Sims-Wood and Jo Ellen El-Bashir), Harvard University's Peabody Museum, the Presbyterian Historical Center, Donnie Bellamy at Fort Valley State University, Tuskegee University (Daniel Williams and Dana Chandler), Atlanta University and its Woodruff Library, the Georgia Department of Archives and History, the University of Virginia Archives, Duke University Divinity School, the Peabody Museum at Harvard, the Greensboro North Carolina Historical Society, the Library of Congress, especially its manuscript, photographic, and rare books divisions, the archivists at the Anthony-Stanton Papers, and those at the awesome Battle Creek Sanitarium.

The cadre of friends and colleagues who've read portions of the manuscript and offered wisdom, insights, advice, and encouragement as I struggled over the years include Elizabeth Alexander, Tracy Alexander, Hilton Als, Arica Coleman, Janice Delaney, Stephanie Deutsch, Nancy Eppler-Wolff, Virginia Gould, Michael Kaplan, Leslie Nelson, Colleen O'Brien, Lonnae O'Neal, Dan and Jean Rather, Rosalyn Terborg-Penn, and Tamara Tunie.

Louis Harlan first told me how singularly bold he thought Adella's letters to Booker T. Washington were, then Ray Smock, Pete Daniel, and Maceo Dailey continued the Tuskegee conversations, as did Charlotte Moton Hubbard, Linda Kenney Miller, Helen Dibble Cannaday, Anne Dibble Jordan, and Clarice Dibble Walker. David Levering Lewis and I speculated about the relationship between Adella and W. E. B. Du Bois. Ruth Ann Stewart and Roy Hill both talked with me about Portia Washington Pittman; Paula Giddings and the Dusters discussed Ida B. Wells-Barnett; and Linda McMurry, Peter Burchard, Christina Vella, and Vanessa Northington Gamble shared their insights into George Washington Carver. Phillip Stern shared incidents he remembered about his forebears' (the Rosenwalds') long relationship with Tuskegee Institute, Holly Robbins about Samuel Courtney, and Allison Porter concerning "elite" black women, depression, and early electric shock treatments. Decades ago and several times since, Gail Jones Buckley and I speculated about our antecedents' (Cora Calhoun and Adella Hunt's) friendship at Atlanta University and the close relationship of Gail's mother, Lena Horne, with the Henry Hunts at Fort Valley, Georgia. My preceding "Rationale, Methods, Sources, and Notes" cites a number of others.

Jim Basker, Justine Ahlstrom, and Nicole Seary at the Gilder-Lehrman Institute of American History have my heartfelt appreciation for publishing the excerpted Frederick Douglass incident from the book in their magazine, *History Now*.

My longtime friend and agent Ron Goldfarb said he'd been awed by Adella's portrait when he first saw it in my house half a century ago, and then forty years later, he frankly (but gently) told me when he found the manuscript nearly unreadable. But he believed deeply in the project and in my ability to tell the story and finally found its proper "home." He and his incomparable colleague Gerrie Sturman sustained me as the negotiations ground along.

A'Lelia Bundles, Lucy T. Cromwell, Janet Davila, the "exercise ladies" under the aegis of Justice Sandra Day O'Connor and Dega Schembri, my "Fieldston posse," Henry Louis Gates Jr., Glenda Gilmore, Kate Lemay, Chris McKay, Linda Betsy Miller, Alondra Nelson, Mitchell Nelson, Tim O'Brien, Geidy Palacios, Steven Peitzman, Yamaris Rivera, Edward Rodriguez, Betty Sams, Elizabeth D. Taylor, the Thompson sisters, Angela Vallot, Bob Washington, Daria Willis-Joseph, and Cris Wittenberg all, in various ways, helped to keep me going.

Adina Berk at Yale University Press loved Adella's story and provided that "home" for her, as well as an editor's discerning eye and guiding hand. The manuscript's anonymous readers deserve my sincere thanks as well. I greatly value the efforts of the whole team associated with the press, Eva Skewes, Mary Pasti, Elizabeth Pelton, and Andrew Katz, for their dedication, skills, and hard work on my behalf. I also thank the wonderful photographers of both me (Joss'yan Musumeci) and my cherished old photos and my portrait of Adella (Mark Gulezian).

I think back fondly on those who've recently left us: Juanita Gilchrist, Jim Horton and Jim Miller, Rosemary Reed, Ruth Ann Stewart, Mary Martha Thomas. I especially think of dear Rosalyn Terborg-Penn, who first alerted me to Adella's importance as a suffragist, and Beckie McGowan and Eve Tyler Wilkins, whose enduring friendship I cherish every day. Willard Gatewood read every draft of every book I wrote several times and offered his priceless support and advice. I greatly miss our long phone chats and his peerless guidance. He remains "the godfather" to everything I write.

And I still credit my dissertation team, Joseph Reidy, Eileen Boris, Edna Medford, and Asunçion Lavrin, at Howard University, who held me to their lofty standards and oversaw the research and completion of that tome. Even decades later, this book still owes a great deal to them.

Several years ago, my husband and I relocated from Washington, D.C., to New York City, with papers and photographs sadly lost in transition. A subsequent "computer incident" gobbled up precious names, email addresses, and phone numbers, so I offer my sincere apologies and beg the indulgence of anyone whom I may have missed mentioning here but absolutely haven't forgotten.

Last but hardly least is my family who surround me now with their sustenance and love. My beloved grandchildren are Jonah, Maya, and Calvin Alexander, Solomon and Simon (also my favorite techies) Ghebreyesus, and Maggie and Lola Weidenborner. My brilliant daughter, Elizabeth, my perfect son, Mark, and his lovely, kind Tracy can't be improved upon. And how I miss Ficre Ghebreyesus, who taught me the importance of evoking the ancestors from seven generations back.

As for Clifford, my dearest, you sat patiently day after day (sometimes peacefully snoozing), as I read the entire weighty manuscript to you, but more important, six decades together have brought me joys and blessings I can't begin to count. In addition to our incredible descendants, in all truth, I wrote this book for myself but also for you and for those who've preceded us, who always fought the good fight, and always voted.

Index

Photos are indicated by italicized page references.